THE MUSEUM FORMS BOOK

third edition

Texas Association of Museums

TAM

Published by the Texas Association of Museums

Texas Association of Museums
3939 Bee Caves Road
Bldg. A, Suite 1 B
Austin, Texas   78746

Library of Congress Cataloging-in-Publication Data

The Museum Forms Book/edited by Kenneth D. Perry
        p.   cm.
        ISBN 0-935260-05-6   (pbk.)

                        Library of Congress Catalog Card Number: 98-83233

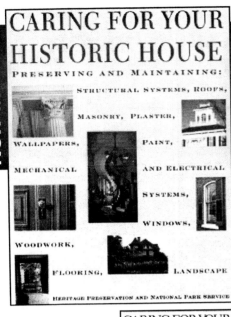

Lance Brown's Tribute to Will Rogers

THE PERFORMANCE

Lance Brown's Tribute to Will Rogers

"Your one-man show on my father was excellent!...It was an audience holding experience."

—*Will Rogers, Jr.*

For booking information, contact:

 Artists of Note, Inc.
(630) 557-2742

or visit Lance Brown's web page at
www.mcs.com/~jmurdock/lance/brown.html

THE BOOK

On the Road With Will Rogers

"As an actor, humorist, singer, writer, and humanitarian himself, Lance has a unique connection to, and understanding of, Will Rogers... Reading Lance Brown is as great as seeing and hearing him."

—*Jim Rogers*

This book can be ordered through your local bookstore, barnesandnoble.com, amazon.com, or directly from:

Biddle Publishing Co.
Toll Free at (888) 315-0582
M–F 9:00 A.M. – 5:00 P.M. EST

TAM MEMBERSHIP APPLICATION

PLEASE ENTER MY MEMBERSHIP IN THE TEXAS ASSOCIATION OF MUSEUMS.

Check whether ❑ INDIVIDUAL ❑ INSTITUTIONAL ❑ BUSINESS ❑ TRUSTEE

YOUR NAME _____

MUSEUM AFFILIATION _____

TITLE _____

MAILING ADDRESS _____

_____ ❑ WORK ❑ HOME

CITY _____ STATE _____ ZIP _____

TELEPHONE _____ ❑ WORK ❑ HOME

E-MAIL _____ ❑ WORK ❑ HOME

The Texas Association of Museums is a nonprofit 501 (c) (3) organization established for educational purposes, to provide a network among museums, to improve the level of professionalism within the museum community, to encourage the use and enjoyment of museums by all Texans, to serve as an information clearinghouse for and about museums, and to serve as a liaison between museums and museum-related agencies and organizations.

To order additional copies of The Museum Forms Book, call the Texas Association of Museums at 888/842-7491 or 512/328-6812 or e-mail at tam@io.com.

TAM ANNUAL DUES
(Check applicable category)

INDIVIDUAL
❑ $1000 Benefactor ❑ $500 Patron
❑ $250 Supporting ❑ $100 Sustaining
❑ $75 Friend ❑ $50 Trustee
❑ $50 Contributing ❑ $40 Individual
❑ $25 Student *(With copy of current student I.D.)*

INSTITUTIONAL
❑ .0005 x Budget *(If budget is over $100,000. Maximum $1,000)*
❑ $50 *(If budget is below $100,000)*

BUSINESSS
❑ $500 Level 4 ❑ $250 Level 3
❑ $150 Level 2 ❑ $100 Level 1

CREDIT CARD
Card Type:
❑ Visa ❑ MasterCard
❑ AmExpress ❑ Discover

Card Number:

_____

Card Exp(m/d/y):

_____

Contents

FOREWORD

The Texas Association of Museums is pleased to publish the Third Edition of *The Museum Forms Book*. It was first published by TAM in 1980. TAM, in partnership with the Mountain-Plains Museum Association, published as revised edition in 1990. Both editions were popular with museums throughout the nation and around the world. In fact, we sold out of two reprints of the revised edition. The *Forms Book* has become a standard reference for the museum community.

When it became apparent that TAM could not keep the revised edition in stock, we began considering a new edition. Rapid advances in the area of information technology and intellectual property has given rise to a number of new museum forms over the past decade. In addition, continuing requests for personnel-related forms prompted us to consider adding "personnel" as a new category for the Third Edition.

Kenneth D. Perry, editor of the first two volumes and Director of the Museum of the Big Bend in Alpine, agreed to once again serve as editor. He was assisted by the TAM Publications Committee, chaired by Susan Sternberg, Curator of Education, Blanton Museum of Art. With the capable advice of the Editorial Committee, Ken reviewed and screened over three thousand forms from all kinds of museums from around the world. The end result is a completely new compilation of up-to-date forms covering a wide variety of museum-related topics.

TAM is grateful to all who volunteered their time and expertise to produce this useful reference book. Members of the Editorial Committee included: Ruth Ann Rugg, Public Relations Manager, Amon Carter Museum; Oliver Franklin, Director, Texas Historical Foundation; 2 from ft. worth; Wesley Hathaway, Assistant Curator of Science, Fort Worth Museum of Science and History; Sue Ellen Jeffers, Blanton Museum of Art, Austin; Anne Jones, Librarian, McNay Art Museum, San Antonio; Ann Johnson, Development Associate, Museum of Fine Arts, Houston; Terry Prather, Vice-President for Operations, Witte Museum, San Antonio; Lisa Rebori, Manager of Collections, Houston Museum of Natural Science; Ali Turley, Curator of the Capitol, State Preservation Board, Austin;

I commend Susan Sternberg, Chair of the Publications Committee, for assembling such an outstanding Editorial Committee and overseeing the project from its inception. Acknowledgment of efforts of the TAM staff in production of the book is also in order. Joy Barnett, Administrative Assistant, spent many long hours numbering and preparing the forms for publication. Gena Hooper, Program Associate for Public Information, and Jack Nokes, Executive Director, both served on the Editorial Committee and helped guide the project to completion.

The museum community all owes a debt of gratitude to Ken Perry for conceiving of the book, editing all three versions, and providing the vision and leadership to make this project a reality. In addition, we are especially grateful to the many institutions which contributed forms to this edition. The museum field is especially generous in the sharing of information, thus making important resources such as this available to the entire museum profession.

One cautionary note: while the forms in this edition have proven useful to the museums which created them, they are presented solely as examples for use in designing forms appropriate for the unique circumstances of the user. Forms are offered only as a reference to help identify relevant issues and procedures. Users are encouraged to create original forms to address their specific needs and to consult legal counsel when necessary.

Wesley Hathaway, President
Texas Association of Museums

INTRODUCTION

In 1979 when the first edition of *The Museum Forms Book* assembled, it seemed a remote impossibility that twenty years later that same process would once again occur. The revised edition published in 1990 expanded the book's scope to include the international museum community. After two printings, the Texas Association of Museums decided to publish the book once more as demand continued. It appears that a simple idea has withstood the test of time. As editor, once again, I find myself evaluating and comparing some 3,000 museum forms from 183 institutions located around the world. Reflecting the changes in the museum field that have taken place since the last edition, these initial 3000 forms provided a more than ample basis for a completely new, fully revised third edition.

Having reviewed close to 10,000 museum forms over the last twenty years one can see great change, yet in many ways things have stayed the same. The computer revolution changed the way many records are kept and produced, but it does not appear to this editor to be a panacea to museum record keeping. Without doubt more museum information is stored in computers, and access to this information has broadened. However, this computerized process does not replace a steady, knowledgeable museum professional diligently recording accurate information about objects, collections, and other museum processes. It is satisfying to know that, although computerized record keeping is accelerating into the new millennium, a Clean Restroom Log still has a place in museums.

As museums design and adopt new forms and revise others, a few recommendations may be useful: 1.) The institutional name and date of adoption should appear on all forms both external and internal. 2.) Revision dates should appear when changes are made. 3.) Each institution should establish a form bank to hold blank copies of all the forms it uses. Explanations of use should be included. 4.) Each museum should establish an archive to house past records. 5.) Legally sensitive forms such as gift contracts, accession records, and others should be held in hard copy on acid free paper. Good forms and record management will be extremely beneficial to future administrators, registrars, and curators.

This edition is the largest and most comprehensive to date. It includes some fourteen categories of museum records. Forms were selected based upon clarity and usefulness to a broad audience. Also, this addition includes a comparative sample of record keeping from an international perspective. I would like to thank the many individuals that sent sample forms. This work essentially mirrors your effort. Also thanks go out to Jack Nokes for his encouragement, guidance, and patience along with TAM staff Joy Barnett and Gena Hooper who prepared the final manuscript. Finally, a big thanks to Susan Sternberg and all members of the Publications Committee for not only assisting in sorting forms, but also for allowing me the freedom to make the hard editorial decisions necessary in a project of this type.

Since beginning this project for a third time, I have received encouragement from many colleagues throughout the museum community. The most universal comment is that this book is useful to the museum profession. Many, with no forms to send, sent letters and e-mail applauding the effort and requesting copies when completed. Certainly these remarks provided succor during the many long hours of reviewing, sorting, and selecting forms for publication. It should be noted that this edition does not replace the previous two, it only expands upon them. All three editions, hopefully, will serve their purpose in museum libraries. As a final note I am requesting your feedback on the use of *The Museum Forms Book*. In order to create an interactive file for future reference, please send comments to perry@overland.net.

Kenneth D. Perry, Editor
Museum of the Big Bend
Sul Ross State University
Alpine, Texas
December 15, 1998

ACCESSIONS

The Sixth Floor Museum

411 Elm Street, Suite 120
Dallas, Texas 75202-3301
214/653-6659   Fax 214/653-6657
http:/www.jfk.org

ACCESSION RECORD

Accession/Collection Number: **Accession Date:**

Received From:
        Address:

How Acquired: ❐Gift   ❐ Purchase   ❐ Loan   ❐ Other (please describe):

Number of items:

Accepted by:

Brief Description of Collection:

Collector:

Condition:

Significance:

Provenance:

References:

Action Checklist:

❐ Temporary Receipt issued   ❐ Items numbered
❐ Added to current acquisitions list   ❐ Preliminary Cataloging
❐ Sent to Interpretation Committee: ❐ In-Depth Cataloging
        ❐ Accepted   or   ❐ Denied   ❐ Entry on database
❐ Gift Agreement completed and returned   ❐ Photographed
❐ Collection number assigned   ❐ Stored - Location in museum:_____
❐ Accession file prepared   ❐ Donor/Source address forwarded to Museum
❐ Registered in Accession log   Advancement Coordinator
❐ Collection record entered on database

THIS FORM SHOULD BE FILED IN NUMERICAL ORDER IN THE ACCESSION LOG BOOK

The Sixth Floor Museum is a non-profit organization, operated under the auspices of the Dallas County Historical Foundation.

AQUISITION CHECKLIST

Object(s)_____ Source_____

Curator_____ Date Assigned_____

Date   **Initials**   **Task**

_____ _____ Entry receipt filled out and sent to Collections Management (CM).

_____ _____ Object picked up or received.

_____ _____ Temporary (acq. consdr) # assigned by CM: #_____

_____ _____ Curator interview of Donor. Fill out interview form or equivalent.

_____ _____ Curatorial review (If declined, check here_____ and go to reject checklist below.)

_____ _____ Fill out catalog worksheet (Curator).

_____ _____ Collection Manager change status to Acquisition Candidate.

_____ _____ Catalog data entered into computer.

_____ _____ Computer record authorized by curator.

_____ _____ Consideration by CollRevComm. (If declined, check here_____ & go to reject checklist below.)

_____ _____ Consideration by Museum Board (If declined, check here_____ & go to reject checklist below.)

_____ _____ Assign Acc. # (Perm. #_____)

_____ _____ Log accession.

_____ _____ Create accession file.

_____ _____ Gift Agreement sent.

_____ _____ Signed and dated Gift Agreement returned.

_____ _____ Update legal fields in computer.

_____ _____ Place # on object(s).

_____ _____ Photograph object(s).

_____ _____ Store object(s).

_____ _____ Update location field in computer.

_____ _____ Cur. sends acc. file material (photos, donor interview form, etc.) to recordkeeping.

_____ _____ Accession file complete and filed.

REJECT CHECKLIST

_____ _____ Curator contact donor to explain reason for rejection.

_____ _____ Disposition

    _____Physical return

    _____Destruction

    _____Donation/Transfer

_____ _____ Computer status updated.

2

ART MUSEUM OF SOUTHEAST TEXAS
GIFT REPORTING FORM

ART MUSEUM
OF SOUTHEAST TEXAS

1. This form is to be completed by any department head, employee or volunteer who solicits successfully or receives a gift for any purpose for any department at AMSET.
2. Forward one copy to the Executive Director, Assistant to Director, Development Office and Public Relations Office with a copy of cash, check or securities attached. Retain a copy for your files.
3. Person accepting the gift should acknowledge donor; the Development Office will prepare an official AMSET acknowledgement.
4. Attach a copy of acknowledgement and any other pertinent information.

I. **DONOR**
Name_____
Home Address_____Home Phone_____
City_____State_____Zip_____
Company or Organization_____Title_____
Business Address_____Business Phone_____
City_____State_____Zip_____
Acknowledgement Specifications for Credit in Printed Materials_____
_____

II. **DONOR CLASSIFICATION** (check one)
____Foundation____Organization____Individual____Corporation

III. **GIFT**
Date Received_____Amount/Value $_____Check #_____
Type of Gift (check one)
____Cash____Letter of Intent____Securities____Pledge (describe terms below)____Service (describe below)____Gift in Kind (describe below)
_____

IV. **PURPOSE OF GIFT** (check one)
____Unrestricted (Operating)____Restricted(describe)_____
____Program (name & date)_____
____Other (describe)_____

V. **GIFT RECEIVED BY** (your name)_____

VI. **ACKNOWLEDGEMENT**
Please attach, or forward later, a copy of your acknowledgement correspondence. Check those whom you feel should also send an acknowledgement:
____Board President____ Executive Director____Dev. Director
____Approp. Dept. Head____Volunteer Chairman____Other_____

VII. **CHECKLIST AFTER CONFIRMATION**
____(date)Contact sent____(date)Rtnd. ____(date)Resent____(date)Rtnd.
____(date)Invoiced____(date)Reinvoiced____(date)Reinvoiced
____(date)Thank you for payments
____(date)Invitation to use facility (if level of gift is high enough)
5/91   ____(date)Final Report with Thank you

3

ANNISTON MUSEUM OF NATURAL HISTORY

SALVAGED MATERIALS RECORD

Please use this form to record receipts of all natural history materials deposited by visitors to the Museum, including non-commercial animals, eggs, nests, artifacts and other materials for which legal documantation is required by State and Federal authorities. When complete, the form should be routed to the Registrar for inventory purposes. Commercially obtained materials should be processed using a Notice-to-Registrar so that Gift Agreements can be completed.

Object/Common Name		Scientific Name	
Type of Materials	Current Location		Date Received
Description: (age, sex, biological characteristics)			
Measurements:		Weight:	

Collector: (name, address, phone number)

Date Collected: _____

Where Collected: State_____   County_____

    Nearest Town_____   Nearest Road_____

    Topographic Quadrangle_____   Township____ Range____ Sec.____

                                         ____Quarter of the ____ Quarter

Special History/Cause of Death:

MANY TYPES OF NATURAL HISTORY MATERIALS ARE PROTECTED BY STATE AND FEDERAL LAWS. THE MUSEUM IS AUTHORIZED TO ACCEPT, SALVAGE, POSSESS, TRANSPORT, MOUNT AND/OR COLLECT NONGAME WILDLIFE, INCLUDING ANIMAL PARTS, NESTS, AND EGGS, BY THE U.S. FISH AND WILDLIFE SERVICE. THE MUSEUM ALSO SALVAGES ARCHAEOLOGICAL MATERIALS OF QUESTIONABLE PROVE-NIENCE FOR TRANSFER TO AN APPROPRIATE REPOSITORY OR FOR EDUCATIONAL USE AS REQUIRED BY STATE AND FEDERAL LAWS.

In accordance with the above statement, I hereby deposit this specimen at the Anniston Museum of Natural History.

Signed: _____   Date: _____

Received by: _____   Title: _____

FINAL DISPOSITION:

CMN COLLECTION ACQUISITION SUBMISSION FORM

Acquisition #: _____

Source: _____

Institution: _____

_____

Address: _____

_____

City: _____ **Prov./State:** _____

Country: _____ **Postal Code:** _____

Telephone: _____ **Fax:** _____ **E-Mail:** _____

Material Rec'd by: _____ **Date received:** _____

COLLECTION: _____ **No. of objects:** _____ **Category:** _____

(Additional collections and numbers attached ☐) (Indicate additional categories
on detailed object list ☐)

General description: _____

Collector(s): _____

Date(s) collected: _____ **Country:** _____

Mode of Acquisition: Donation ☐ Exchange ☐ Staff field trip ☐ Transfer ☐

Purchase ☐ Other ☐ (specify: _____)

Ownership: _____ **Clear title:** ☐ **Doubtful:** ☐

RATIONALE FOR ACCEPTANCE: (attachment ☐)

a) Importance for National Collection:

b) Research:

c) Exhibition:

RECOMMENDATIONS:

Coll. Manager: Accept ☐ Decline ☐ Signature: _____

(Comments attached: ☐) Date: _____

Research: Accept ☐ Decline ☐ Signature: _____

(Comments attached: ☐) Date: _____

APPROVAL: _____ **Date:** _____

› **Declined - reason:** _____

5

Preservative: _____

Inspected by: _____ **Date:** _____

Condition:

Treatment: required ☐ not required ☐ done ☐ (Date: _____)

(Attach treatment report)

COSTS: **Processing (hrs):** _____ **By Staff (Name):** _____

Shipping: $_____ **Brokerage fees:** $_____

Shelving/cabinets/etc.: $_____

Other (specify): $_____

Resources accompanying collection: _____

_____

PRICE: **Price asked:** $(Cdn)_____ **GST No.:** _____

PST: $(Cdn)_____

GST: $(Cdn)_____

Total: $(Cdn)_____

Appraisals and cost of evaluation:

a) $(Cdn)_____ by:_____ Cost:_____

b) $(Cdn)_____ by:_____ Cost:_____

c) $(Cdn)_____ by:_____ Cost:_____

Recommended price: $(Cdn)_____ **Foreign:**_____

Estimate of total cost to the CMN to acquire this material: $_____

ATTACHMENTS: **OTHER MATERIALS RECEIVED:**

(Originals to accompany submission)

☐ Detailed Object List ☐ Field notes/books

☐ Additional Collections ☐ Labels

☐ Deed of Gift/Purchase Agreement/Invoice ☐ Drawings

☐ Permits (Import/Export, Collecting) ☐ Maps

☐ Correspondence ☐ Photographs (slides / prints)

☐ Condition report

☐ Treatment report ☐ Other (please list)

☐ Additional remarks

Date entered into computer: _____	Date of Accession: _____
Staff Initials: _____	Staff Initials: _____

Accession Worksheet
UIHC Medical Museum

Your Name _____   Today's Date _____

Catalog # _____   Accession # _____

Object Name _____   Classification _____

Category _____

Collection (circle one): Permanent   Education   College of Medicine

Date of Acquisition _____   Type of Accession _____

Source _____

_____

_____

_____

Credit Line _____

_____

Object Description: (materials, color, inscriptions - give location, function/purpose, etc.)

Dimensions (inches): _____

Condition: _____

Old Numbers (include location of #): _____

Reference for id: _____

_____

Accompanying Materials: _____

Object History:

Date/loc. collected by donor _____

_____

Previous Owner(s) _____

_____

_____

Manufacturer _____

_____

      date of manufacture _____

      patent date _____

Miscellaneous Information (info. re. donor's family, comments from donor, etc.)

_____

_____

_____

_____

_____

Appraisal:

Accession value $_____

Insurance value $_____ date effective _____

    Reference _____

_____

    Appraiser _____

_____

Actions Taken

☐ Gift Receipt   date sent _____   ☐ Photo Taken   date _____

☐ Gift Agreement   date rec'd _____   ☐ Object Numbered date _____

☐ Request for Info. date rec'd _____   ☐ Condition Report date _____

☐ Gift Acknowledgment date sent _____

☐ Foundation Letter date sent _____

Permanent Storage Location _____

NATIONAL MUSEUM OF AMERICAN JEWISH HISTORY

Independence Mall East • 55 N. 5th St. • Philadelphia, Pennsylvania 19106 • (215) 923-3811

DONOR QUESTIONNAIRE

Please answer any questions that you are able to. This information is very important in helping us to fully document artifacts in our collection and to use them in our interpretive programs and exhibitions.

Name _____ Object _____

How long have you owned this object? _____

How did you acquire it?　　Purchase _____ Inheritance _____ Gift _____ Found _____

　　　　　　　　　　　　Other _____

From whom did you acquire it?　Name _____ Relationship _____

　　　　　　　　　　　　Place _____

When did you acquire it? _____

Were there any previous owners? _____　Relationship _____

　　　　Name _____

　　　　Birthdate _____ Place of Birth _____

　　　　Marriage Date _____ Spouse _____

　　　　Children _____

　　　　Death Date _____

　　　　Where Lived _____

　　　　Occupation _____

Who made it? _____ Where Made/Purchased? _____

When Made/Purchased? _____

What materials is it made of? _____

Did you perform any repairs or make any changes to it while it was in your care?　(Y) _____ (N) _____

If yes, explain: _____

How was it used? _____

Who used it? _____

Where was it used? _____

When was it used? _____

Additional comments: _____

_____

_____

_____

_____

If you run out of room, please use back of sheet or attach additional pages. Thank you for your time and effort in completing this form.

ARKANSAS STATE UNIVERSITY MUSEUM
DONOR QUESTIONNAIRE

Please answer any questions that you are able to. This information is very important in helping us to fully document artifacts in our collections and to use them in our interpretive programs and exhibitions.

Name _____

Object _____

How long have you owned the object? _____

How did you acquire it? Purchase _____ Inheritance _____ Gift _____ Found _____

                      Other _____

From whom did you acquire it? _____

Were there any previous owners? _____

Relationship? _____

        Name _____

        Birthdate _____ Place of Birth _____

        Marriage Date _____ Spouse _____

        Children _____

        Death: Date _____ Lived Where _____

              Occupation _____

Maker _____ When Made/Purchased _____

Where Made/Purchased _____

Of what materials is it made? _____

Did you perform any repairs or make any changes to it while it was in your care?

        Yes _____ No _____

        If yes, please explain: _____

        _____

        _____

        _____

How was it used? _____

_____

Who used it? _____

Where was it used? _____

When was it used? _____

Additional comments: _____

_____

_____

_____

_____

If you run out of room, please use the back of this sheet or attach additional pages. Thank you for your time and effort in completing this form.

Mint
Museum
of Art

ARTIST REPORT

The following information is necessary to complete the file on your recently acquired work of art. Please be as accurate and detailed as possible when completing this form.

Name_____

Address_____

_____

Birthyear and place_____

Title of artwork acquired by the Mint Museum of Art

_____

Date(s) artwork was created_____

Where artwork was created (In the studio, in the field, on a trip, etc.)

_____

List all materials used_____

_____

_____

Other comments regarding this work_____

_____

_____

Please include any personal history, resume, news clippings, or other information that would provide further data relating to your work.

Celebrating Our 60th Year!

Museum Accession Number _____

DONOR DOCUMENTATION WORKSHEET

The information you provide aids the museum's understanding and documentation of its collection.
Please take a few moments to tell us about your donated object. We appreciate your time and effort.
The museum may (or may not) use this information for exhibition, programming, or research purposes.

Donor Name _____ Telephone _____

Donor Address _____

Please describe the object _____

_____

Where or from whom did you obtain the object? When? Why? Or did you make it? _____

_____

_____

How did you use the object? Where did you keep it? Do you know how other people used it? _____

_____

_____

_____

Are there any documents (such as photographs, letters, bill of sale, maker's notes, newspaper articles)
related to the object that you would like to include with the donation, or allow the museum to copy? _____

_____

_____

If you have donated a photograph, please describe the event or the people it depicts and/or the place and
date it was taken. _____

_____

_____

Was the object ever altered, broken, and/or repaired? If so, do you know when or where any restoration
or conservation was done? Do you know who did it? Do you know what materials were used to repair it?

_____

_____

Do you have any personal memories or stories about the object that you would like the museum to know?

_____

_____

_____

_____

_____

If any of the above information is used in exhibition labels or publications created by the museum, would
you like to: be named_____ remain anonymous _____ be otherwise acknowledged _____
Please write EXACTLY how you would like to be acknowledged: _____

_____

Donor Signature _____ Date _____

Form Completed by _____ (Title_____) Date _____
Please use the back of this form if you need room to write additional information.

Museum Accession Number_____

DONOR DOCUMENTATION INTERVIEW CHECKLIST

The information the donor provides aids the museum's understanding and documentation of its collection. Please take a few minutes to ask the donor about their object.
The museum may (or may not) use this information for exhibition, programming, or research purposes.

Donor Name _____ Telephone _____

Donor Address _____

Object description _____
_____

Where/from whom the donor obtained/made the object. When and why it was obtained/made. _____
_____

Uses of the object by the donor and other people, including where it was used. _____
_____
_____
_____

Documents (photographs, letters, bill of sale, artist's notes, newspaper articles) related to the object that the donor is willing to include with the donation, or allow the museum to copy. _____
_____
_____

If a photograph is donated, description of the event or the people it depicts and/or the place and date it was taken. _____
_____
_____

Object alterations, breaks and/or repairs. When/where restoration or conservation took place. Materials used to repair the object. _____
_____
_____

Personal memories or stories about the object that the donor would like the museum to know. _____
_____
_____
_____
_____

If any of the above information is used in exhibition labels or publications created by the museum, the donor wants to: be named _____ remain anonymous _____ be otherwise acknowledged _____
This is EXACTLY how the donor wants to be acknowledged: _____
_____

Donor Signature _____ Date _____

Form Completed by _____ Title _____ Date _____
Use the back of this checklist to write additional comments/information.

SOUTH
DAKOTA STATE
HISTORICAL SOCIETY
CULTURAL HERITAGE CENTER
900 Governors Drive
Pierre, SD 57501-2217
(605) 773-3458   Fax (605) 773-6041

Object history

Please take a few minutes to answer the questions you can on this form.
The more information we have about an object, the more useful it is to us.

Object:_____

     Donor's name: _____

     Donor's address: _____
                           _____
                           _____

     When did you acquire this object?_____
                                (date if possible, or time period)

     How did you acquire this object?   ____purchase
                                     ____gift (from whom?_____ __)
                                     ____inheritance (from whom?_____)
                                     ____found it
                                     ____excavated it
                                     ____other (describe) _____
                                                     _____

     In what geographical location did you acquire the object? (state, county, city, or specific site)
     _____

     List the previous owners of the object if you know who they were: _____

     Name the person who made the object, if you know, and how you know this information.

     Do you know where the object was made? If so, how do you know? _____
     _____

     Do you know any unusual details about the manufacture of this object?

     Can you identify the materials from which this object was made?_____
     _____

     Do you know why the object was made? (personal use by maker; gift; resale or trade, etc.) _____
     _____

     How has this object been stored or used? _____

     Are you aware of any good sources of information about this object? (Publications, photographs, individuals,
     etc.) _____
     _____
     _____

Thank you. Your answers to this form helps us record vital information about the object you donated.
It may be of help to us in the future, and we can make better use of your donated object.

RECORD OF
INCOMING MATERIAL

Received from _____ Date _____

Address _____

_____ Phone _____

PURPOSE: _____ potential acquisition   _____ request identification

I understand that if I do not claim the object(s) listed on this form within TWO MONTHS, then it (they) will be considered abandoned property, and I will forfeit ownership. In such cases, VMNH will handle the object(s) in accordance with its Collections Policies.   (signature) _____ (date) _____

DESCRIPTION:

(WHAT is it?)   (WHERE was it collected/found?)   (WHEN was it found?)

Number of items _____   Photographs?   ___ YES ___ NO
Location of material within Museum: _____   Field Notes?   ___ YES ___ NO
DATE specimens were received at Museum: _____   Permits?   ___ YES ___ NO
                                                   Correspondence? ___ YES ___ NO
METHOD ACQUIRED: Other data?   ___ YES ___ NO

___ GIFT
___ INTERAGENCY TRANSFER
___ EXCHANGE
___ PURCHASE: Price_____ Funds Used _____
___ SALVAGED MATERIAL
___ FIELD WORK   General dates of field trip:
                   Locality:
                   Field numbers:
                   Collectors(s):

Identifications

made by _____
date _____
date owner notified (1) _____
             (2) _____
             (3) _____
date material returned: _____
date material abandoned:_____

RECORDED BY_____

DATE _____

Potential acquisitions

Department review: date _____
   Under acquisition plan? ___ YES ___ NO
   Recommend to   ___ ACCEPT ___ NOT ACCEPT
   BY _____

ACCESSION NUMBER _____
       date _____ by _____
VMNH Catalog numbers: _____
_____

15

rev. 8/94

LYMAN HOUSE MEMORIAL MUSEUM

276 HAILI STREET • HILO, HAWAII 96720
PHONE (808) 935-5021 • FAX (808) 969-7685
EMAIL: lymanwks@interpac.net

PRE-ACQUISITION FORM

The following items received for examination at the Lyman Museum.
Items offered as a: GIFT___ LOAN___ DONATION OF MATERIALS___   OTHER___
Formal notification of disposition will come after a meeting of the Museum Plant &
Function Committee.

Date in:_____

Received from:_____

Address:_____

_____Phone_____

Item:_____

_____

_____

Origin & Date of item:_____

Made by: _____

Remarks: _____

_____

_____

Condition: _____

_____

_____

Received from_____ Date_____
                          Signature

Received by_____ Date_____
                  Museum Staff Signature

Accredited by the
American Association
of Museums

16

ACQUISITION DATA SHEET AND QUESTIONNAIRE

DESCRIPTION OF ACQUISITION: Date Received: _____

    Number/nature of Items _____

    _____

    _____

    _____

    _____

    Donor: _____   Received from: _____

    Address: _____   Address: _____

    _____   _____

    Phone: _____   Phone: _____

    Provenience (Origin, time, source): _____ _____

    _____

    _____

    Collector: _____

    Type of acquisition: gift ___; collecting ___; purchase ___; deposited vouchers ___; transfer ___;

    other ____ (explain _____)

    Value: Aesthetic ___; Historical ___; Scientific ___; Social ___; Utility ___; Commercial ___ (if

    so, what is estimated value _____);.

PROPOSED COLLECTION(S):

    Library __; Archaeology __; Ethnography __; History __; Minerals and Rocks __; Fossils __;

    Plants __; General Invertebrates __; Mollusks __; Arthropods __; Echinoderms __; Fish __;

    Amphibians __; Reptiles __; Birds __; Mammals __; Other __ (Explain _____)

PROPOSED TYPE OF COLLECTION(S):

    Public Use Collection ____; Educational Reference Collection ____; Research Collection ____

PROPOSED BY _____ DATE _____

    Accept ___; Accept with contingency ____; Reject ___; Postpone decision ___; Recommend

    different recipient ; Dispose or destroy ____; Other ____ (Explain _____

    _____)

Acc. No. _____

EVALUATION

Yes	Maybe	No	???	
___	___	___	___	Does the acquisition specifically apply to SMC collections?
___	___	___	___	Does the SMC already possess similar items?
___	___	___	___	Is the acquisition needed by the SMC?
___	___	___	___	Will the acquisition be used in the next 5 years?
___	___	___	___	Is documentation available providing full and clear title to the acquisition?
___	___	___	___	Are all objects of the acquisition currently under SMC possession?
___	___	___	___	Are all data and associated parts of all possessed objects under SMC possession?
___	___	___	___	Does the acquisition serve the mission and goals of SMC?
___	___	___	___	Is it likely that objects and associated data would be used for research?
___	___	___	___	Is it likely that the objects would be used for teaching?
___	___	___	___	It is likely that the objects would be used for exhibition?
___	___	___	___	Does the SMC want all parts of the acquisition?
___	___	___	___	Is the SMC possession of the acquisition totally legal?
___	___	___	___	Is the SMC possession of the acquisition totally ethical?
___	___	___	___	Are resources available for management and care of the acquisition?
___	___	___	___	Does the acquisition have any special preservation requirements?
___	___	___	___	Is the acquisition free from extenuating circumstances that may influence decision-making?
___	___	___	___	Does acquisition serve mission, development plans, and priorities of the collections (discipline <u>and</u> type) in question?

COMMITTEE RECOMMENDATION

Accept ___; Accept with contingency ____; Reject ___; Postpone decision ___; Alternative recipient ___; Dispose of or destroy ____; Other ____ (Explain _____
_____)

Public Use Collection ____; Educational Reference Collection ____; Research Collection ____

Archaeology ___; Ethnography ___; History ___; Minerals and Rocks ___; Fossils ___; Plants ___; General Invertebrates ___; Mollusks ___; Arthropods ___; Echinoderms ___; Fish ___; Amphibians ___; Reptiles ___; Birds ___; Mammals ___; Other ___ (Explain _____)

DIRECTOR'S DECISION:

__ Accept committee recommendation   ___ Reject committee recommendation

SIGNATURE _____ DATE _____

18

BBHC ACQUISITION PROPOSAL FORM

[Buffalo Bill Historical Center]

MUSEUM _____ DATE _____

OBJECT _____

_____

_____

ARTIST/MAKER (IF KNOWN) _____

DATE OF MANUFACTURE (IF KNOWN) _____

PHYSICAL DESCRIPTION _____

_____

_____

CONDITION _____

CONSERVATION NECESSARY? _____ IF YES, COST ESTIMATE $ _____

OFFER OF (CHECK ONE):   GIFT _____ BEQUEST _____ EXCHANGE _____ PURCHASE _____

DONOR'S NAME AND ADDRESS   VENDOR'S NAME AND ADDRESS

_____   _____

_____   _____

_____   _____

CONTACT, IF DIFFERENT: OWNER, IF DIFFERENT:

CURATOR'S APPRAISAL $ _____   ASKING PRICE $ _____

TERMS, CONDITIONS, AND/OR RESTRICTIONS _____

_____

_____

CREDIT LINE FOR PUBLICATION _____

RECOMMEND _____   _____
            CURATOR   DATE

APPROVED   _____   _____
            DIRECTOR   DATE

IF BY PURCHASE OR TRADE, DATE ADVISORY BOARD APPROVAL WAS RECEIVED _____

    DATE EXECUTIVE COMMITTEE OF THE BOARD APPROVAL WAS RECEIVED _____

PROPOSED FUND SOURCE _____

SEE REVERSE FOR PHOTOGRAPH AND ADDITIONAL REMARKS (IF NEEDED)

PRESENT LOCATION _____

19

LAFAYETTE NATURAL HISTORY MUSEUM
Ethnographic Collection • Artifact Inventory

CULTURE _____ DATE _____ RECORDER _____

ACCESSION #	ARTIFACT	DESCRIPTION	MAKER	SOURCE	LOCATION • POSTAL SQUARE 1 •
					BOX #
					BOX #
					BOX #
					BOX #
					BOX #
					BOX #
					BOX #

20

ACCESSIONS LOG SHEET

# Assigned	Donor	Object(s)	Enter Date				
			Rec'd	Cata-loged	Computer Entry	Form Sent	Form Rec'd

THE UNIVERSITY MUSEUM
UNIVERSITY OF ARKANSAS
ACCESSION LOG

Acc. No.	Item	Date Rec'v.	Donor Form Signed	Acc. Record Sheet	Name File Card	Header Card	Items No.'d	Cat. Cards	Comp. Donor/ Cat. Record	Photograph	
										Date	Neg.

Rev. 1/1997

ADMINISTRATION

Check requests
Contracts
General
Gift shop
Personnel
Application
Evaluation
Exit interview
General
Publications
- Digital
- Print
Travel

CHECK REQUEST FORM

! Please use one form per check

! Only for urgent payment or staff reimbursement

▲▲▲▲▲▲▲
The
Children's
Museum
◆◆◆◆◆◆◆

5210	Contract Labor
5220	Consultants
5230	Contract Services
5240	Legal Fees
5290	Other Contracts
5310	Publicist
5320	Printing
5330	Other Production
5340	Advertising Space
5350	Distribution
5390	Other Promotion
5410	Telephone
5420	Postage
5430	Duplicating, Printing
5440	Travel
5450	Professional Fees
5490	Other Communications
5510	Materials, Supplies-Exh. Ctr.
5520	Equipment, Furnishings
5530	Books, Films, Periodicals
5540	Collections
5590	Other Program Materials
5610	Materials, Supplies-Support
5620	Equipment, Furnishings
5630	Insurance
5640	Interest
5650	Bank Service Fees
5690	Other Support Materials
5910	Courtesies
5990	Other Non-Budgeted Expense

Payable to:_____

Address:_____

_____

_____

Purpose:_____

Please charge check amounts to projects and accounts listed below

Acct#	Project #	Amount
		$.
		$.
		$.
		$.
		$.

Total Amount: $ _____ .

Authorized:_____

Not the payee

Date Submitted:___/___/___

Date Needed: _____

Return to Requestor ☐

Mail Directly ☐

Other Instructions:

Please attach supporting documents on reverse side ☞

Request for Check

Walker Art Center

To   Administrative Office

From _____

Approved By _____

Date of Request _____

Date Needed _____

(Please allow 5 business days)

Check payable to _____

Address _____

_____

City _____ State _____ Zip _____

For _____

_____

_____

DESCRIPTION	OBJECT	FUND	DEPT	PROG	ACTIVITY	GRANT	AMOUNT

Amount of check

_____ Please mail check

_____ Please hold check and

notify _____ @ ext. _____

_____ Please place in weekend safe

_____ CASH needed (travel, artist fee, etc.)

_____ 1099 (honorarium, artist fee, etc.)

Social Sec. # _____

_____ Foreign Draft or Wire (circle one)

Currency _____ Amt. _____

_____ 8233 (payments to nonresident aliens)

Administrative Office use:

Date Received _____

Admin. Approval _____

Reference # _____

Notified _____ Picked Up _____

Remember to attach backup for all expenditures

(copy of contract, order form, invoice, etc.)

CONTRACT

The Children's Museum

PLEASE NOTE:
This is NOT a payment request !
Use check request for payment !

Has the contracted party ever worked for TCM?
☐ Yes. ☺ Please continue
☐ No. ☹ Please attach a finished W-9 Form, then continue

Contracted Party

Name: _____

Address: _____
Number and Street

_____
City

_____
State   _Zip Code_

Phone #: _____

FIN or SSN: _____

The Children's Museum

Period of Contract: _____

Services/Responsibilities: _____

_____

_____

_____

Payment Amount and Schedule: _____

_____

_____

Immediate Supervisor: _____

AUTHORIZED: _____   **Date:** _____

Other Signatures*

_____   **Date:** _____
President/Vice President, CFO, The Children's Museum

_____   **Date:** _____
Contracted Party

* If the total payment is in excess of $500.00 the signature of president or CFO is necessary

CONTRACTUAL SERVICES FORM

SPENCER MUSEUM OF ART
_____
(Department/Unit Name)

SPENCER MUSEUM OF ART
_____
(Department/Unit Mailing Address)

864-4710
_____
(Department/Unit Phone #)

This form is to be used to obtain the signature of an individual who is to be paid a fee for a lecture, consultation, participation or other contractual service that qualifies for payment by APO/Payment voucher, when no invoice is available for submission. Contractual Services payments are to be paid as a single sum directly to the contractor. This payment includes all agreed upon amounts for fees, and reimbursement of travel, lodging, meals, and other related expenses. Direct payment to travel agencies and lodging establishments on the contractors behalf are allowed. **Please complete the back of this form first. Only complete the front if results indicate you are to treat the service provider as an Independent Contractor.** After completion, please attach to a completed APO/Payment voucher and submit to Accounts Payable for processing.

CONTRACTOR CERTIFICATION

Name_____

Taxpayer Identification Number (if a business) _____

   Or Social Security Number (if an individual) _____

Home Address _____

Amount of fee to be paid $_____ Date(s) service provided _____

Location service will be provided (i.e. Lawrence campus) _____

Description of service _____

_____

_____

_____

_____

Contractor's Signature _____ Date _____

DEPARTMENT/UNIT CERTIFICATION

Department/Unit Number and Name ___#2136--Spencer Museum of Art_____

Certification: The services described above have been received and payment is to be made from the account shown above.

Department/Unit Signature _____ Date _____

26

********************TO BE COMPLETED BY DEPARTMENTAL PERSONNEL ONLY*********************

EMPLOYEE/INDEPENDENT CONTRACTOR CLASSIFICATION CHECKLIST

This questionnaire is to be used to determine whether an individual performing services should be classified for federal, state and FICA tax purposes as an employee of the University or as an Independent Contractor. If determined to be an employee, please process an Employee Information Form.

PART I - SERVICE PROVIDER INFORMATION

1. Does the individual currently work for the University as an employee providing the same or similar services?

	Yes - Treat as employee	No - See following note

NOTE: If services provided by the individual are that of a teacher, lecturer, or instructor, go to Part II now, otherwise complete Part I.

	YES	NO
2. a) Will the department provide the individual with specific instruction regarding performance of the required work rather than rely on the individual's expertise?		
b) Will the department provide tools, supplies, additional labor and space to perform the work?		

If the answer to both questions 2a and 2b is 'Yes', then treat as an employee. Otherwise, go to question #3.

	Treat as employee	Go to #4
3. Will the individual perform the services on a continuing basis as part of the department's ongoing operations?		
4. Does the individual provide the same or similar services to other entities or to the general public as part of a trade or business?	Treat as Independent Contractor Complete Part III	Treat as employee

PART II - TEACHERS/LECTURERS/INSTRUCTORS

	YES	NO
1. Is the individual a "guest lecturer" (e.g. an individual who lectures at only a few class sessions)?	Treat as Independent Contractor Complete Part III	Go to #2
2. a) Is the individual teaching a course for which students will not receive credit toward a University degree?		
b) Does the individual provide the same or similar services to other entities or to the general public as part of a trade or business?		

*If the answer to both questions 2a and 2b is 'Yes', then treat as an independent contractor and **complete Part III**, otherwise, go to question #3.*

	Treat as Independent Contractor Complete Part III	Treat as employee
3. In performing instructional duties, will the individual primarily use course materials that are created or selected by the individual?		

PART III - MUST BE COMPLETED FOR ALL INDEPENDENT CONTRACTORS

1. Is the individual a Foreign National? ____ Yes ____ No   If yes, please provide:

	Visa Type	Country of Residence

   If no, return to front of form and continue.

2. Does the individual have an alien registration card (green card)? **Please circle one:**   YES   NO

   If yes, please attach copy. If no, **taxes may be withheld from payment at the rate of 30%,** unless Form 8233-*Exemption From Withholding on Compensation for Independent Personal Services of a Nonresident Alien Individual* is completed and attached.

TEXAS TECH
U N I V E R S I T Y

MUSEUM OF TEXAS TECH UNIVERSITY

Fourth and Indiana Avenue
Box 43191
Lubbock, TX 79409-3191
(806) 742-2442
FAX (806) 742-1136

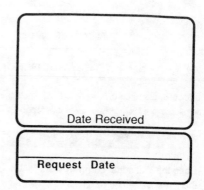

Date Received

Request Date

Purchase Approval

The following items have been approved for purchase from:

Vendor Name

Address

| City | State | Zip |

Vendor Phone #   Fax #

Vendor Contact

Item	Quantity	Unit Cost	Total Amount
1		$	$
2		$	$
3		$	$
4		$	$
5		$	$
6		$	$
7		$	$
8		$	$
Order Total			$

Requested By: Intended Use

Date Goods/Services Needed   Supervisor Approval

Approval: Gary Edson, Executive Director   Date Approved

Account Type: (Check one box)

☐ P.O.   ☐ R.I.   ☐ Departmental Transfer

☐ Petty Cash   ☐ Blue Slip   ☐ Other_____

Account Name   Account Number

An EEO/Affirmative Action Institution   28

PROJECT PROPOSAL WORKSHEET

Proposed Title: Your proposed working title.

Project Description: What do you plan to do and how?

Objectives: What are you trying to achieve?

Rationale: How does this project address Glenbow's Goals and Strategies?

Market: Who are the potential audience/clients for this project?
How do you know? (survey and evaluation data)
What are their characteristics? (knowledgeable, tourist, seniors?)
How many do you expect to attend?

Content: What is the content of the project?
How does it relate to the collection and research of Glenbow?
How does it relate to the program aims and criteria of the programs Master Plan?

Project Specifics: What will the project consist of? (exhibit, lectures, school program, etc.)

Timeline: When do you propose is the best time for this project?
How long will it take to develop it?
When are the critical starts?

Labour: Who will need to work on the project?
How may hours will each person need to commit?
Will contract assistance be required? Specify.
Will volunteers be required? How many?
Who will coordinate and train them?

Budget: An outline of all costs needed to complete the project.
(A sample budget worksheet is attached)

Source of Funds: Grants, corporate support, ticket sales, etc.

Income generating
potential: Ticketed special events, shop merchandise, donations.

Evaluation: How will we judge the success of the project?
How will we learn what to improve?

Date_____

N. C. MUSEUM OF HISTORY DIVISION
MEDIA CONTACT

MUSEUM: ___MGM ___MCF ___MOA ___MOH ___MOHD ___NCMHA

TYPE:

_____RADIO _____TELEVISION _____MAGAZINE _____NEWSPAPER

_____NEWSLETTER _____OTHER

CONTACT:

_____NAME _____ORGANIZATION
NAME

_____TELEPHONE NUMBER _____FAX NUMBER

_____ADDRESS

DISCUSSION:

_____
_____
_____
_____
_____
_____

MATERIALS SENT:

_____WRITTEN _____PHOTOGRAPH _____SLIDE

RESULTS (TO BE COMPLETED LATER BY JANICE)

_____
_____
_____
_____

_____**NAME OF STAFF MEMBER**

RETURN TO JANICE WILLIAMS BY END OF WORK DAY!

Marketing Services Requests

Your Name _____

Extension _____

Charge to _____

Today's Date _____

Due Date _____

Originating Department _____

What Is It?

❑ Press Kit   ❑ Media Advisory   ❑ Press Release

❑ Program/Direct Mailer   ❑ Advertisement   ❑ Flyer

❑ Brochure/Pamphlet   ❑ Postcard   ❑ Poster

❑ Sign   ❑ Table Tent   ❑ Kiosk

❑ Drawing   ❑ Video Taping   ❑ Video Duplicate

❑ Cassette Taping   ❑ Cassette Duplicate   ❑ Other

❑ Photography   Color   Black/White   Slide

❑ Photography Dup.   Color   Black/White   Slide

What's The Scoop?

Date_____ Time _____ Cost_____

Reservation Necessary _____ Deadline _____

Presenters_____ Sponsors_____

_____

Target Audience_____

_____

Topics for Discussion _____

_____

SUL ROSS STATE UNIVERSITY
MUSEUM GIFT SHOP REVENUE
DEPOSIT COVER SHEET
$1429-38701-00

Date_____

Cash Turned In

     Cash---$_____

     Checks---$_____

     Visa/MC---$_____

       Total--$_____

Register Sales

       Total Sales---$_____

Sales Tax---$_____

Register Total--$_____

Void--$_____

Cash Over/Short--$_____

     Actual Sales (div. Total cash by 108.25%) $_____

     Actual Tax (mult. Actual sales by 8.25%) $_____

                                   $_____

Amount of tax exempt sales included in sales $_____

Cash Refunds $_____

_____
Secretary (Initial)

_____
Received: Cashier

_____
Director (Initial)

_____
Receipt Number

Revised 6/26/96

32

CASH COUNT SHEET

CASHIER:	DATE:

PAYMENT		Admission	Misc Sales*
$	0.01		
$	0.05		
$	0.10		
$	0.25		
$	0.50		
$	1.00		
$	5.00		
$	10.00		
$	20.00		
$	50.00		
$	100.00		
TOTALS CASH (a)			

	Admission	Misc Sales
CHECKS		
T.CHECKS		
MC		
VISA		
AMEX		
TOTALS CK/CC (b)		

BRACK		
CONTRACT		
PREPAID		
TOTALS OTHER (c)		

TOTAL FUNDS (a+b+c)		*
LESS CHANGE	$ (200.00)	N/A
LESS CHECK REQUESTS		N/A
NET FUNDS	1.	2.
TTL Funds (1+2)		
TTL SALES		

OVER/SHORT

MISC SALES

TYPE	QTY	AMOUNT
MEMBERSHIPS -INDIVIDUAL		
MEMBERSHIPS - FAMILY		
Memberships -		
Memberships -		
TOTAL MEMBERSHIP SALES (X)		

TYPE	QTY	AMOUNT
Gift Certificates Adult		
Gift Certificates Senior		
Gift Certificates Child		
TOTAL CERTIFICATE SALES (Y)		

TOTAL MISC SALES (X + Y)   ★

	QTY	TTL AMOUNT
VOIDS		

Manual Admissions   Y   N
IF Y = REINPUT   Y   N   If N - send to BC

BUSINESS OFFICE USE:

ADMISSION	
MEMBERSHIP:	GIFT CERT:
CASH OVER/SHORT:	
BANK	
VISA/MC	AMEX
A/R	PREPAID
AUDITED BY	DATE
VOUCHER#	

Anniston Museum of Natural History
Museum Store
Consignment Agreement

Lender: _____

Address: _____
_____

Telephone: _____

     In accordance with the conditions printed below, the objects on the reverse Consignment Inventory are placed on consignment with the Museum Store of the Anniston Museum of Natural History.

Conditions:

1.   The lender will be responsible for any incoming and outgoing shipping arrangements and costs unless specifically agreed otherwise in writing.

2.   The lender will be responsible for insuring his own works while in the Museum. The Museum Store (and/or the Museum) assumes no responsibility for loss or damage to the objects but will exercise such precautions for the safekeeping of the same as are now in force, or may hereafter be put in force, for the safekeeping and preservation of the property of the Museum itself, unless otherwise specifically agreed.

3.   The Museum Store will retain 40% of the sale price of any object sold while displayed on the premises. The Museum Store will remit to the lender of the object the sum of 60% of the sale price in a timely manner.

4.   The Museum Store reserves the right to request retrieval of unsold merchandise after a period of 90 days.

     I have read and agree to the above conditions and I am authorized to agree thereto:

_____   _____
Lender   Date

_____   _____
Museum Representative   Date

1997 Consignment Inventory
Anniston Museum of Natural History
Museum Store

Item No.	Description	Selling Price	Artist 60%	Store 40%	Date Sold	Date Paid

We consider applicants for all positions without regard to race, color, religion, sex, national origin, age, marital or veteran status, the presence of a non-job-related medical condition or handicap, or any other legally protected status.

(PLEASE PRINT)

Position(s) Applied For	Date of Application

How Did You Learn About Us?
☐ Advertisement   ☐ Friend   ☐ Walk-In
☐ Employment Agency   ☐ Relative   ☐ Other_____

Last Name	First Name	Middle Name
Address *Number* *Street* *City* *State* *Zip Code*		
Telephone Number(s)	Social Security No.	

If you are under 18 years of age, can you provide required proof of your
eligibility to work?   ☐ Yes ☐ No

Have you ever filed an application with us before?   ☐ Yes ☐ No
If Yes, give date _____

Have you every been employed with us before?   ☐ Yes ☐ No
If Yes, give date _____

Are you currently employed?   ☐ Yes ☐ No

May we contact your present employer?   ☐ Yes ☐ No

Are you prevented from lawfully becoming employed in this country because of Visa or Immigration Status?   ☐ Yes ☐ No
Proof of citizenship or immigration status will be required upon employment.

On what date would you be available for work?   _____

Are you available to work: ☐ Full Time   ☐ Part Time

Are you currently on "lay-off" status and subject to recall?   ☐ Yes ☐ No

Can you travel if a job requires it?   ☐ Yes ☐ No

Have you been convicted of a felony within the last 7 years?   ☐ Yes ☐ No
Conviction will not necessarily disqualify an applicant from employment.

If Yes, please explain_____

WE ARE AN EQUAL OPPORTUNITY EMPLOYER

Education

	Elementary School					High School				Undergraduate College/University				Graduate/ Professional			
School Name and Location																		
Years Completed	4	5	6	7	8	9	10	11	12	1	2	3	4	1	2	3	4
Diploma/Degree																		
Describe Course of Study																		

Describe any specialized training, apprenticeship, skills and extra-curricular activities	
Describe any honors you have received	
State any additional information you feel may be helpful to us in considering your application	

Indicate any foreign languages you can speak, read and/or write			
	Fluent	Good	Fair
Speak			
Read			
Write			

List professional, trade, business or civic activities and offices held.
You may exclude memberships which would reveal sex, race, religion, national origin, age, ancestry, or handicap or other protected status:

_____

_____

_____

References

Give name, address and telephone number of six references who are not related to you, including a current or former supervisor, colleague and subordinate, and thru personal references.

1._____   4._____

2._____   5._____

3._____   6._____

Have you ever had any job-related training in the United State military?   ☐ Yes ☐ No

If yes, please describe_____

Driver's license number (if job related)_____ State_____

BACKGROUND VERIFICATION DISCLOSURE WITH CREDIT

As part of the employment process, The Kansas City Museum may obtain a Consumer Report and/or an Investigative Consumer Report. The Fair Credit Reporting Act as amended by the Consumer Reporting Reform Act of 1996 requires that we advise you that for purposes of employment only, a Consumer Report may be made which may include information about your credit standing, credit capacity, character, general reputation, personal characteristics, or mode of living. Upon written request, additional information as to the nature and scope of the report, if one is made, will be provided, in the event the Report contains information regarding your character, general reputation, personal characteristics, or mode of living.

AUTHORIZATION AND RELEASE

During the application process and at any time during any subsequent employment, I hereby authorize Pinkerton, on behalf of the Kansas City Museum, to procure a Consumer Report which I understand may include information regarding my credit worthiness, credit standing, credit capacity, character, general reputation, personal characteristics, or mode of living. This report may be complied with information from credit bureaus, courts record repositories, departments of motor vehicles, past or present employers and educational institutions, governmental occupational licensing or registration entities, business or personal references, and any other source required to verify information that I have voluntarily supplied. I understand that I may request a complete and accurate disclosure of the nature and scope of the background verification, to the extent such investigation includes information bearing on my character, general reputation, personal characteristics or mode of living.

_____   _____

Applicant/Employee Name and Signature   Date

_____-____-_____   _____

Social Security Number*   Date of Birth*

* Optional

Employment Data Record

VOLUNTARY SURVEY

(Please Print)   Date _____

Government agencies at times require periodic reports on the sex, ethnicity, handicap, veteran and other protected status of employees. This data is for statistical analysis with respect to the success of the Affirmative Action program. SUBMISSION OF THIS INFORMATION IS VOLUNTARY.

Name	
Address	
City State Zip	
Social Security No.	

Complete Only The Sections Below That Have Been Checked	
	Current Job:
X	Check One: Male Female | Age
X	Check One of the Following: (Ethnic Origin) ☐ White ☐ Hispanic ☐ American Indian/Alaskan Native ☐ Black ☐ Other ☐ Asian/Pacific Islander
X	Check If Any Of The Following Are Applicable ☐ Vietnam Era Veteran ☐ Disabled Veteran ☐ Individual with Disability

Employment Experience

Start with your present or last job. Include any job-related military service assignments and volunteer activities. You may exclude organizations which indicate race, color, religion, gender, national origin, handicap or other protected status.

1.

Employer		Dates Employed		Work Performed
		From	**To**	
Address				
Telephone Number(s)		Hourly Rate/Salary		
		Starting	**Final**	
Job Title	Supervisor			
Reason for Leaving				

2.

Employer		Dates Employed		Work Performed
		From	**To**	
Address				
Telephone Number(s)		Hourly Rate/Salary		
		Starting	**Final**	
Job Title	Supervisor			
Reason for Leaving				

3.

Employer		Dates Employed		Work Performed
		From	**To**	
Address				
Telephone Number(s)		Hourly Rate/Salary		
		Starting	**Final**	
Job Title	Supervisor			
Reason for Leaving				

4.

Employer		Dates Employed		Work Performed
		From	**To**	
Address				
Telephone Number(s)		Hourly Rate/Salary		
		Starting	**Final**	
Job Title	Supervisor			
Reason for Leaving				

If you need more space, please continue on a separate sheet of paper. If you have a resume, you may attach it to this application; however, submission of a resume is not in lieu of a completed application.

<u>Special Skills and Qualifications:</u> Summarize special job-related skills and qualifications acquired from employment or other experience. _____

_____

_____

Applicant's Statement

I certify that answers given herein are true and complete to the best of my knowledge.

I authorize investigation of all statements contained in this application for employment as may be necessary in arriving at an employment decision.

This application for employment shall be considered active for a period of time not to exceed 45 days. Any applicant wishing to be considered for employment beyond this time period should inquire as to whether or not applications are being accepted at that time.

I hereby acknowledge that any employment relationship with this Company is of an "at will" nature, which means that the Employee may may resign at any time and the Employer may discharge employee at any time with or without cause. It is further understood this "at will" employment relationship may not be changed by any written document or by conduct unless such change is specifically acknowledged in writing by an authorized executive of the Company.

In the event of employment, I understand that false or misleading information given in my application or interview(s) may result in discharge. I understand, also, that I am required to abide by all rules and regulations of the employer.

_____   _____
Signature of Applicant   Date

FOR PERSONNEL DEPARTMENT USE ONLY

Arrange Interview   ☐ Yes   ☐ No

Remarks   _____

              _____   _____
              Interviewer   Date

Employed   ☐ Yes ☐ No   Date of Employment_____

Job Title   _____   Hourly Rate/Salary _____

Department   _____

By   _____   _____
         Name and Title   Date

41

The Museum of Fine Arts, Houston
Performance Appraisal Form for Nonexempt Employees

Employee's Name	
Title:	
Reviewed By:	
Date of Review Meeting:	

Instructions:
1. Review the job description prior to the meeting and update it if the job has changed. This can be done by the employee or the supervisor as long as both agree on the changes.
2. If you would like to have input from the employee, ask him or her to complete the Individual's Worksheet (Page 5, Optional).
3. Complete the Appraisal Form (Pages 1-4). Keep the following guidelines in mind (for more suggestions, see Page 8):
   - Review the employee's performance for the entire period; try to refrain from basing your judgments on recent or isolated events only. Disregard your general impression of the employee and concentrate on rating one factor at time.
   - Take into consideration the amount of time the employee has held the job. Rate the employee's performance based on what you would expect from a person performing the job for that amount of time.
   - Place a checkmark next to the rating that best summarizes the employee's performance in each factor since the last appraisal (or since the date of hire or transfer if this is your first review of the employee's performance).
   - The relative importance of each factor will vary depending on the position you are reviewing; some factors may not be relevant to a particular position. In such cases, write "N/A" or explain why the factor is not significant.
4. Meet with the employee and discuss what you wrote. Allow the employee time to look at the review and write a response (if he or she desires to respond in writing).
5. Sign the forms and forward them to personnel. If the employee's job description was updated, attach a copy to the review.

In the space below, summarize and list the most important job responsibilities, tasks, and/or special projects performed by the employee during the past year.

PERFORMANCE FACTORS: Rate the employee's performance by placing a checkmark next to the appropriate rating and enter your comments to support your rating directly below. Be as specific as possible; include examples from the responsibilities, tasks, and projects listed above, where applicable. If improvements are desirable or required, refer to Pages 6 and 7.

Exceptional	Performance that far exceeds the requirements of the job.
Excellent	Performance that frequently exceeds the requirements of the job.
Very Good	Performance that meets all job requirements.
Needs Work	Performance that meets most of the job requirements; some improvement is desirable.
Unsatisfactory	Performance that falls well below the requirements of the job; improvement is required.

JOB KNOWLEDGE	Exceptional	Excellent	Very Good	Needs Work	Unsatisfactory
How well the employee gets to the root of problems. The adequacy of the employee's skills. Employee's understanding of normal job requirements. Employee's understanding of related functions. Employee's efforts to keep skills current.					

QUALITY OF WORK	Exceptional	Excellent	Very Good	Needs Work	Unsatisfactory
Consider neatness, thoroughness, and accuracy of the work the employee produces.					

QUANTITY OF WORK	Exceptional	Excellent	Very Good	Needs Work	Unsatisfactory
How well does the employee maintain his output of work. Volume of work employee performs under normal conditions.					

INITIATIVE	Exceptional	Excellent	Very Good	Needs Work	Unsatisfactory
How well does the employee grasp instructions without close follow-up. How well does the employee perform in the face of obstacles. How alert is the employee in the absence supervision.					

DEPENDABILITY/RELIABILITY	Exceptional	Excellent	Very Good	Needs Work	Unsatisfactory
How well the employee can be relied on to accept responsibility and complete work assignments. How well does the employee meet deadlines.					

DEALINGS WITH PEOPLE	Exceptional	Excellent	Very Good	Needs Work	Unsatisfactory
The mutual cooperativeness that exists with others. The confidence others have in the employee. Employee's tactfulness and diplomacy.					

ATTITUDE	Exceptional	Excellent	Very Good	Needs Work	Unsatisfactory
The interest and enthusiasm employee shows to job and organization. Employee's sustained efforts to achieve organization and departmental objectives. Employee's respect for confidences.					

RESOURCEFULNESS	Exceptional		Excellent		Very Good		Needs Work		Unsatisfactory
Employee's resourcefulness in solving unusual problems. The frequency and value of employee's suggestions to simplify, modify, or improve the job.									

ATTENDANCE/PUNCTUALITY	Exceptional		Excellent		Very Good		Needs Work		Unsatisfactory
How conscientious is the employee about attendance, punctuality, lunch periods, completing time sheets, etc. Consider time spent away from work area in idle conversation, etc. Consider number of absences and number of times late since last review: (A report of the employee's absences is available from personnel if you would like to include it in your review).									

OTHER	Exceptional		Excellent		Very Good		Needs Work		Unsatisfactory
List and comment on any other significant performance factors relevant to this position:									

	Assess the employee's strengths and areas needing improvement. Be specific and provide examples as you answer the following questions.
In which job responsibility, task, or special project does the employee show the strongest results? What skills, knowledge, or abilities contributed most to the achievement of these strong results? What can be done to build on these strengths? (Special assignments, promotions, education, training, new responsibilities?)	
In which responsibility, task, or special project does the employee most need improvement? What can be done to help the employee improve his or her performance? What can the individual do, what can you do, what can the museum do? If you would like to develop an Improvement Plan with the employee, see Pages 6 and 7.	

SUPERVISOR'S COMMENTS: Use the space below to make any additional comments:

APPRAISER: I have discussed all items reviewed on this form with the employee.

Appraiser's Signature: Date:

CHECK ONE BOX: ☐ Job Description has not changed.   ☐ Job description has changed. A revised copy Job Description is attached.

EMPLOYEE'S COMMENTS: Employee is encouraged to use the space below to describe any reaction to ratings, thoughts about current position, future plans, steps being taken to reach goals. Use additional paper if you wish.

EMPLOYEE: I have seen and reviewed the appraisal. All items covered have been discussed fully with me. I have been encouraged to make comments. I realize that my signature does not necessarily imply that I am in full agreement with the appraisal.

Employee's Signature   Date:

Department/Division
Head's Signature: Date:

INDIVIDUAL'S PERFORMANCE APPRAISAL WORKSHEET (Optional)

Employee's Name:	
Reviewer's Name:	
Date:	

These questions will help you prepare for your performance review meeting with your supervisor.
Be as specific as possible; use examples, if possible. Use more paper if you wish.

What do you consider to be your major accomplishment at work since your last review?	
How well do you know what you need to know in order to do your work? What additional information do you need?	
Are there any changes that could be made to improve your effectiveness?	
What skills or new knowledge would you like to develop in order to improve your performance?	
What can you, your supervisor, or the museum do to improve your performance and increase your job satisfaction?	
What are your long range career objectives and what are your plans to accomplish these objectives? (For example: job rotations, promotions, additional responsibilities, education, training).	
Are there any goals you would like to work toward between now and your next performance evaluation? How will progress toward the goal or goals be measured?	

IMPROVEMENT PLAN WORKSHEET (Optional)

Employee's Name:	
Reviewer's Name:	
Date:	

Diagnosing Employee Performance Problems: In order to understand the reasons for performance problems, the supervisor and employee must work together to determine the causes of poor performance. Once the cause of a performance problem is understood, strategies can be developed to improve the performance. The following questions can help pinpoint the causes of poor performance.

- Does the person have the skills to do the job as expected?
- Has the person performed as expected before?
- Does the person have the interest to perform as expected?
- Does the person clearly perceive what is actually involved in performing as expected?
- Does the person have a chance to grow and use valued skills and abilities?
- Does the organization offer career paths to the individual?
- Are there established goals? Are the goals clear, specific, and with some degree of difficulty?
- Is the person certain about what to do, what others expect, about job responsibilities, or about levels of authority?
- Does the person receive on-going feedback about what is right and wrong with performance?
- Does this feedback tell the person how to improve?
- Does the person get information frequently? Is there a delay between the time the employee performs and receives feedback on performance?
- Can the information be easily interpreted by the person?
- What are the consequences of doing what is expected? Is it punishing to do as expected immediately or long term?
- Are there no apparent consequences of failing to perform as desired?
- Are there no positive consequences of performing as desired?
- Can the person mobilize resources to get the job done? Does the person have the information, equipment, or other resources needed to do the job?
- Can the person influence others to get them to do what is needed?

Instructions: Use the following checklist to analyze the employee's improvement needs.
Enter comments next to any areas where improvement is needed. Be specific. Provide examples.

Employee Skills, Knowledge, and Abilities

Planning and organizing to meeting deadlines, objectives	
Generating or implementing new ideas	
Decision making: willingness and/or ability to make timely, quality decisions	
Job knowledge	
Acceptance of constructive criticism, new ideas, change	
Oral and/or written communication	
Keeping supervisor informed	
Resolving conflicts, getting along with others	
Cooperativeness	
Attendance, punctuality	
Compliance with policies, procedures, rules, instructions	

Other (explain)	
Supervisory/Managerial Skills, Knowledge, and Abilities	
Delegation of tasks, authority, responsibilities	
Establishing performance goals for subordinates, evaluating performance, monitoring progress	
Establishing policies, procedures	
Training and developing employees	
Controlling costs, operating within budget	
Selecting, hiring, motivating, coaching, counseling subordinates	
Other (Explain)	

Use the space below to outline a plan for improvement. What will you do? What will the employee do? Include expected completion dates in your plan and schedule an appointment or appointments to review progress.

Suggestions for Effective Performance Appraisals

Ask your supervisor if he or she would like to look at and discuss the reviews you have prepared before you meet with employees. This gives your supervisor the opportunity to make suggestions which you may want to include in your meeting with employees.

Establish a climate of confidence and respect; reassure employees that the annual review is a routine procedure required by the museum's personnel policies. Encourage employees to participate in the discussion to increase their satisfaction and acceptance of the review.

Remember--this is a review of past performance. Don't save up problems to discuss for the first time in the review. There should be no surprises for the employee.

Allow sufficient preparation time to show the employee that you put some thought into the evaluation. Set the meeting in advance and allow the employee time to prepare. You may want the employee to give you his worksheet before the meeting. Avoid rescheduling, delaying, putting off, or interrupting the meeting; otherwise, you send the message that this is unimportant to you.

Remember that an important purpose of the meeting is to achieve agreement and mutual understanding about job responsibilities, roles, problem areas, priorities, and objectives. Encourage open, two-way discussion to explore performance problems and to discuss alternatives for solving problems. Remember that people who participate in solving problems are more willing to make changes.

Be realistic and specific, and establish some goals for the future. Even though a positive review can be gratifying, research shows that a flattering review is not as effective as one that uses realistic feedback given in a supportive way along with the establishment of goals for the future.

Don't discuss raises during a performance review meeting. Let the employee know that you will discuss raises later in a separate meeting and that your decision about raises will be based on your evaluation of the employee's performance. If the employee is waiting to hear about his raise during the review meeting, he may not pay attention to the discussion about performance. And if the raise isn't what he hoped for, the discussion may get side-tracked. Remember, the main purpose of this meeting is to discuss performance.

Give the employee effective feedback rather than criticism to strengthen your working relationship and improve performance. Effective feedback has the following characteristics:

- Specific rather than general. Use specific examples to illustrate your points. It is more helpful to say, "you were late for work more than thirty minutes five times in the last month" than it is to say, "you are always late."
- Focuses on behavior rather than on the person. Discuss what a person does rather than who he is. For example, it is better to say "you talked more than anyone else at the meeting" than to say "you are a loudmouth." Talking about behavior makes change possible; labeling a person implies a fixed personality trait.
- Takes into account the needs of the person receiving it. Feedback given out of a desire to cut someone down to size is destructive; feedback should be given to help, not to hurt.
- Shares information rather than gives advice. By sharing information, you allow the person to decide what changes need to be made.
- Is well-timed. In general, immediate feedback is most useful, depending on the person's readiness to hear it. Performance appraisal should be an on-going process, not a once a year meeting.
- Provides the amount of information a person can use. Overloading the person decreases the probability that he or she will be able to use the information effectively.
- Concerns what is said or done and how -- not why. Don't speculate about motives, intentions, or attitudes or you will wind up in a debate. These things are intangible and arguable. Stick to behavior you have personally observed.
- Checked to assure clear communication. Ask the employee to rephrase your comments to see if he understood what you said. As in any communication, feedback about the employee's performance is subject to miscommunication.

End the meeting by reviewing the discussion, confirming understandings, getting commitments for change, reviewing goals, and assigning deadlines for specific improvement plans, if applicable.

BISHOP MUSEUM
ANNUAL PERFORMANCE EVALUATION
Management Evaluation Form

Employee Name_____   Position_____

Unit and/or Department_____   Evaluation Date: _____

Appraiser_____   Annual Evaluation Period: _____

Performance Ratings (PARTS 1 through 3)

1 Significantly exceeds performance expectations.
2 Capable and qualified; delivers competent performance in meeting key objectives and/or operational expectations.
3 Some improvements needed to meet performance expectations. Identify key actions recommended in Part 6 (Summary of Performance Development Plan) of this form.
4 Performance which is unacceptable

PART 1. Operating Plan Results - 30%

In the interest of preserving space, please group similar objectives together

Weight	OP #	Operating Plan Objectives	1	2	3	4	Score: rating x % x100
%							
%							
%							
%							
%							
30%	=	Weight of factors by significance, not allocation of time **Subtotal**					

PART 2. Management of Unit - 30%

Include key responsibilities not covered in Operating Plan objectives here.

Weight	Major Unit Responsibilities	1	2	3	4	Score: rating x % x100
%						
%						
%						
15 %	Budget Planning and Control (ability to manage & control bottom line)					
30%	= Weight of factors by significance, not allocation of time **Subtotal**					

PART 3.   Other Performance Factors - 19 %

A. *Job Knowledge: Knowledge of job gained through experience, education, and/or specialized training. Degree of knowledge to effectively carry out job. (Select rating that best describes employee's job knowledge)*

_____1   Excellent technical knowledge of profession; understands job and has good perspective of its relationship to institutional issues; excellent understanding of museum operations, policies, & manager's role.
_____2   Good technical knowledge of position and general museum operations; knowledge of managerial role good & meets expectations.
_____3   Job knowledge generally acceptable with few technical & managerial deficiencies.
_____4   Unsatisfactory knowledge of job.

Comments:_____
_____

B. *Planning & Organizing: Level of effectiveness in determining strategies to achieve objectives. (Select rating that best describes employee's planning and organizing skills.)*

_____1   Unusual capacity to anticipate future needs and to plan, organize & execute strategies to obtain highly desirable results. Highly organized and efficient in establishing and organizing priorities to meet deadlines regardless of numerous ongoing projects.
_____2   Effective in coordinating activities, organizing & establishing priorities and achieves most objectives.
_____3   Occasionally has difficulty organizing work flow to comply with priorities.
_____4   Ineffective in establishing priorities & coordinating activities.

Comments:_____
_____

C. *Judgment & Decision Making: Ability to arrive at sound decisions with positive results. (Select rating that best describes employee's judgement & decision making skills.)*

_____1   Exceptional ability to weigh available information and make very sound decisions while considering final impact. Shows timeliness & conviction in making recommendations that withstand critical examination. Formulates realistic solutions valued by upper management.
_____2   Achieves good results through sound decisions and recommendations.
_____3   On occasion reluctant to make decisions. Decisions not always sound.
_____4   Ineffective in making decisions and recommendations.

Comments:_____
_____

D. *Initiative: Ingenuity, self-reliance and resourcefulness, assertiveness, ambition and ability to know what needs to be done. Ability to take needed action without direct instructions. (Select the rating that best describes employee's use of initiative.)*
_____1   A self-starter, resourceful in situations with excellent follow through. Recognizes and often recommends creative solutions that achieves highly significant results.
_____2   Generally resourceful and takes initiative most of the time. Good follow through and results generally valued.
_____3   Follows established pattern of doing job without innovation.
_____4   Resists change. Slow in getting started. Allows projects to lag after starting, requires direct supervision.

Comments:_____
_____

E.   *Communication: Ability to clearly exchange both written/verbal information. (Consider listening and interpersonal skills as well as ability to effectively communicate ideas.) (Select the rating that best describes employee's communication skills.)*

_____1   Very effective communicator. Strong writing skills and ability to speak and relate to all levels of personnel to influence and/or persuade to accomplish highly desirable results.
_____2   Good communicator with speaking , writing and interpersonal skills consistently satisfying job requirements and expectations.
_____3   Communication skills generally acceptable; improvements to oral, written and/or interpersonal skills would contribute to greater managerial effectiveness.
_____4   Written communication is often ineffective (due to poor grammar, sentence structure and/or writing style); ineffective oral communication may often be a result of interpersonal problems.

Comments:_____
_____

***F.** Directing & Leadership Skills: Effective in causing people to take effective & efficient action to accomplish desired results through understanding & cooperation. (Select the rating that best describes employee's directing & leadership skills.)*

_____1   Consistently effective in motivating others and directing activities to obtain desired results. Is respected by others as an effective leader.

_____2   Generally obtains cooperation from others & usually gets the job done on time. Delegates/directs others in acceptable manner to obtain desired results.

_____3   Occasionally has difficulty in getting job done through others due to inadequate directions or inability to obtain cooperation.

_____4   Ineffective in directing & leading others or supervising subordinates.

Comments:_____

_____

Part 3 - Subtotal

A_____ + B_____ + C_____ + D_____ + E_____ + F_____ = _____ X 19% X 10 = _____

PART 4. Demonstration of Corporate Shared Values (staff feedback) - 21%

Summarize employee's overall performance in his/her demonstration of corporate values based on staff feedback.

Ratings	1	Exemplifies the value; a true role model.
	2	Meets expectations.
	3	Needs to improve behavior.
	4	Ignores the value; sets a negative example.

Weight	Corporate Shared Values	1	2	3	4	Score: rating x % x100
3%	Teamwork					
3%	Mutual Respect					
3%	Integrity					
3%	Customer-Oriented					
3%	Rooted in Hawai'i					
3%	Innovative					
3%	Fiscally Responsible					
21 %	Subtotal					

COMMENTS:_____

_____

_____

_____

PART 5. OVERALL PERFORMANCE

		SCORES		RATINGS	
Part 1	Operating Plan Results (30%)	_____		1	100-125
Part 2	Management of Unit (30%)	_____		2	126-220
Part 3	Other Performance Factors (19%)	_____		3	221-320
Part 4	Corporate Values (21%)	_____		4	321-400
	TOTAL	_____ = _____ (Overall Rating)			

Use the following space to write a narrative specifying results and accomplishments this review period. Difficulty factors associated with this person's assignment should be identified. Performance trends should be outlined.

_____

_____

_____

_____

_____

_____

Section 5 (continued)

_____
_____
_____
_____
_____
_____

PART 6. SUMMARY OF PERFORMANCE DEVELOPMENT PLANS

Outline developmental plan. Identify key actions to build strengths and improve performance in needed areas.

_____
_____
_____
_____
_____
_____
_____
_____
_____
_____
_____
_____
_____

PART 7. MAJOR GOALS & OBJECTIVES FOR NEXT REVIEW PERIOD

_____
_____
_____
_____
_____
_____
_____
_____
_____
_____
_____
_____
_____

Evaluator's Signature	Date	Evaluator's Supervisor's Signature	Date
Employee's Signature	Date	HR Reviewer's Signature	Date

(   ) Check here if you disagree with this evaluation. Comment below or, file statement with Personnel Manager within 10 working days.

_____
_____
_____
_____

ANNUAL PERFORMANCE EVALUATION
Management Evaluation Form

A. PERFORMANCE EVALUATION OBJECTIVE

The objective of the annual performance evaluation is to conduct a thorough appraisal of all aspects of the employee's performance based on mutually understood performance expectations and to effectively communicate and document the process. The evaluation serves the purpose of 1) identifying areas needing improvements to assist employees in realizing and using their full potential in carrying out the Museum's mission, goals and objectives; and, 2) providing information to employees and managers for use in making work-related decisions.

B. ELEMENTS OF EFFECTIVE PERFORMANCE APPRAISAL

The major elements of an effective performance appraisal program are:
- All employees should know the responsibilities and results for which they are accountable.
- Employees should know and understand how their performance affects the department's performance and the overall performance of Bishop Museum.
- Employees should know how their personal performance will be measured (based on results and behavior, not on personality).
- Evaluations should be based on mutually understood performance expectations.
- Performance appraisals should be part of a continuous process achieved through regular communication; this allows employee's room for improvement.
- A formal appraisal discussion between supervisor and employee should be held at least annually. For management (corporate executives, unit managers and selected others) staff, the appraisal should be tied to Fiscal Year results.
- Performance appraisals should not make reference to age, sex, sexual orientation, race, impending retirement, or any other subjects in conflict with government regulations on discrimination in employment.

C. PERFORMANCE APPRAISAL PROCESS

The Performance Appraisal should be conducted within 30 days after the Fiscal Year ends.

- During the course of the Fiscal Year, review the manager's operating plan objectives and major unit responsibilities, and summarize and weight the accountabilities in Parts 1 and 2. Provide copy of this page to manager so he/she may report the results of operating plan objectives and accomplishments of major unit responsibilities shortly after the Fiscal Year ends.

- Solicit feedback from selected staff (see Bishop Museum shared values feedback form instructions).

- Evaluate manager's performance in operating plan results (Part 1), major unit responsibilities (Part 2); provide assessment of manager's skill level in area of management performance dimensions (Part 3).

- Review feedback forms; summarize information and provide overall rating for each shared value in Part 4.

- Calculate scores for each section and complete Part 5.

- Summarize performance development plans (Part 6). Outline major goals and objectives for next review period (based on next FY Operating Plan Objectives and Major Unit Responsibilities).

- Conduct performance appraisal: discuss your ratings, discuss strengths and weaknesses, recommend areas for improvement, possible plans for museum-sponsored training, self-initiated training, employee's personal goals. Get employee's signature at close of interview; provide copy to employee if requested. Obtain appropriate supervisor's signature, discuss merit recommendation with appropriate authorized individual (i.e., unit manager, corporate vice-presidents), submit evaluation and signed Personnel Action Form to the Personnel Department for processing.

Buffalo Society of Natural Sciences
Buffalo Museum of Science - Tifft Nature Preserve

Intern Evaluation Form

Name of Intern: _____

Department in which intern served: _____

Date internship began: _____ Date internship ended: _____

Approximate number of hours per week worked: _____

Name of department member supervising work of intern: _____

- - - - - - - - - - - - - - - - - - -

1. Did the intern complete the goals set out in the job description? If no, why not?

2. Please comment on the following performance factors. What was the degree of effectiveness which the intern applied her/him self in achieving the results expected? Use the following rating scale:

       4 Strength - consistently exceeded expectations
       3 Satisfactory - consistently met expectations
       2 Needs Improvement - did not consistently meet expectations
       1 Unsatisfactory - failed to meet expectations

PERFORMANCE FACTORS	RATING	COMMENTS AND/OR EXAMPLES
A. **Production** (produces the expected amount of work)		
B. **Thoroughness/Accuracy** (gets the job done right)		
C. **Independent Action** (uses initiative, does not require close supervision)		
D. **Work Methods** (works efficiently, organized)		
E. **Problem Solving** (analyzes relevant facts, makes sound recommendations)		

F. Interpersonal Skills (clear, well organized, grammatically correct, efficient)		
G. Written Communication (clear, well organized, grammatically correct, efficient)		
H. Job Knowledge (proficient in methods or skills required; acquired knowledge)		
I. Work Habits (good attendance; personal calls or discussions did not interfere or disrupt)		
J. Attitude (situationally appropriate; matched to task)		
K. Suitability for Museum work (understands what a Museum is and what one does?)		
L. Other		

3. Summary of the overall performance (include intern strengths and areas which need improvement).

4. Was the internship mutually beneficial?

5. If given the opportunity, would you have the intern return? ___ yes ___ no. If yes, in what capacity?

Supervisor's Signature: _____ Date :_____

EXIT INTERVIEW

Conducted by_____Date_____

Employee _____SS#_____

What positions have you held at the San Antonio Museum of Art?
_____

What did you like *most* about working for the Museum?
_____

What did you like *least*?_____

Please rate the Museum on the following: "E" (excellent) "A"(average) "B" (below average)

Training_____   Supervision_____
Wages _____   Working Conditions_____
Holidays/Vacations_____   Health Care Benefits_____

What suggestion(s) would you make to improve the company.
_____

Why are you leaving the San Antonio Museum of Art?
_____

Do you have another job? If yes, where? _____

Why have you selected this new job? _____

Other comments by employee_____
_____

COMMENTS BY IMMEDIATE SUPERVISOR

Why is this employee leaving?_____

What are employee's strengths?_____

Weaknesses?_____

Would you rehire this employee?_____

_____   _____
Employee Signature   Date

_____   _____
Supervisor   Date

Prepared by the San Antonio Museum of Art

57

GLENBOW
MUSEUM · ART GALLERY · LIBRARY · ARCHIVES

EXIT INTERVIEW FORM

We are always striving to improve the performance of our volunteer managed system. As one of our volunteers, we would appreciate your help in identifying areas in which we might do better. Please be as complete and honest as you can in answering the following questions - all of the information collected will be kept strictly confidential, but it will be utilized to ensure others who volunteer will receive the best possible treatment.

Name: _____ Date:_____

How long did you volunteer with us? _____

Types of volunteer positions held:

1._____

2._____

3. _____

Why are you leaving (check all that apply):

____Job accomplished   ____Moving to a new location   ____Need a change
____Returning to School   ____Didn't feel well utilized   ____Other time commitments
____Didn't like job(s) given

                          Other:_____

What did you like best about volunteering with us?

_____

_____

_____

What suggestions would you make for changes/improvements in our volunteer effort?

_____

_____

Overall, how would you rate your experiences with us?

NOT SATISFACTORY   AVERAGE   GREAT
1   2   3   4   5   6   7

Please return this form to: *Glenbow Museum*
                                    c/o Valerie Cooper, Manager: Volunteer Resources
                                    130 - 9 Ave. S.E.
                                    Calgary, Alberta   T2G 0P3

                                                            ref: exit.frm

KANSAS CITY MUSEUM
PERSONNEL REQUISITION FORM

1. Complete requisition for replacement personnel in full with approvals before routing to Human Resources Management.
2. Please attach current job description.
3. If requisition is for a new position, please consult with Human Resources Management prior to completing form.
4. Replacement positions may take approximately 4-6 weeks to fill.
5. Positions requiring evaluation may take approximately 3 months to fill.

DATE_____ JOB TITLE _____ DATE NEEDED _____

REQUISITION #_____ REPORTS TO _____ DEPARTMENT _____

☐ Regular Full Time   ☐ Regular Part Time   ☐ Temporary Full Time   ☐ Temporary Part Time

SCHEDULE _____ IF TEMP., THROUGH _____

REASON FOR HIRE

☐ New Position   ☐ Replacement For _____   Date Vacated _____

_____ (name)

QUALIFICATIONS

REQUIRED

Education _____   Experience _____   Other _____

_____   _____   _____

_____   _____   _____

DESIRED

Education _____   Experience _____   Other _____

_____   _____   _____

_____   _____   _____

PRIMARY DUTIES/RESPONSIBILITIES

_____

_____

_____

_____

_____

SALARY BUDGETED AS OF _____

(date)

SUGGESTED RECRUITMENT SOURCES _____

_____

_____

DATES AVAILABLE FOR INTERVIEW _____

APPROVALS

SUBMITTED BY _____ TITLE _____ DATE_____

REVIEWED BY _____ TITLE _____ DATE_____
Human Resources Management

APPROVED BY _____ TITLE _____ DATE_____
Department Head

APPROVED BY _____ TITLE _____ DATE_____
President

REVIEWED BY _____ TITLE _____ DATE_____
Director of Finance

59

PAYROLL AUTHORIZATION

▲▲▲▲▲▲▲
The
Children's
Museum
◆◆◆◆◆◆◆

Employee Name: _____   ❑   New Employee

Home Base: _____   ❑   Termination

Effective date: _____   ❑   Leave of Absence

Job Title: _____   ❑   Pay Rate Change

Salary (100%): _____   ❑   Change in Hours

Percentage: _____   ❑   Temporary Position

Salary Distribution: _____

Hourly Rate: _____   ❑   Other:_____

Payroll & Business Office Use:

File Number: _____
Pro-Rated Salary: _____
Salary Per Pay Period: _____
Cafe Benefit: _____
Pension: _____   Date of Birth:_____

Remarks:

_____

_____

Supervisor: _____   Date: _____
Division Director: _____   Date: _____
HR Director: _____   Date: _____
Vice President F & A: _____   Date: _____

Initiating Supervisor Please Forward To:

HR Manager: _____   Payroll Coordinator: _____   Controller: _____

9/12/96

60

WITTE
MUSEUM

VERBAL WARNING DOCUMENTATION

Employee: _____ Date: _____

Title: _____ Department: _____

Describe in detail examples of the employee's unsatisfactory/satisfactory performance or behavior.

Describe the solutions or agreements discussed by you and the employee. Make sure the employee knows the consequences if this type of behavior occurs again.

Employee Comments:

Employee Signature: _____

Supervisor's Signature: _____

WITTE
MUSEUM

<u>WRITTEN WARNING DOCUMENTATION</u>

Employee Name: _____   Date: _____

Title: _____   Department: _____

Please check: [ ]   First Written Warning and 30 day probation
                [ ]   First Written Warning, Verbal Warning has not been given, but
                         situation is serious enough to warrant a written warning.
                [ ]   Second Written Warning
                [ ]   Reassignment or Suspension
                [ ]   Dismissal

Check the performance problems that have led to this warning:

[ ] Falsification of Museum documents including
     timeclock/timecard violations
[ ] Violation of Company's drug and alcohol policy
[ ] Failure to notify supervisor of absence
[ ] Rudeness
[ ] Failure to follow Museum rules, procedures &
     policies
[ ] Failure to get along with fellow employees
[ ] Personal phone calls on work time
[ ] Substandard job performance, including failure to
     follow directions and careless errors

[ ] Discount abuse
[ ] Violation of dress/personal appearance
     standard
[ ] Disclosure of confidential information
[ ] Intentional or negligent damage to Museum
     Property
[ ] Insubordinate behavior, including failure or refusal
     to perform job assignments
[ ] Excessive absenteeism/tardiness
[ ] Other

With specific examples, describe the unsatisfactory performance/behavior, and what performance/behavior you expect from the employee. (Attach additional pages if necessary.)

Has this employee been warned about this or a similar problem?   [ ] Yes   [ ] No
If yes, How?   [ ] Verbal Date _____ [ ] Written Date(s)_____

Employee Comments (attach additional pages if necessary):

The above performance/behavior has been discussed with me. I understand that either failure to improve my performance/behavior or the occurrence of additional incidence(s) of unsatisfactory performance/behavior will result in further corrective action up to and including termination.

_____   _____
Employee   Date   Supervisor   Date

HOMESTEAD MUSEUM   WEB PAGE REQUEST

Title:
Installation date: ☐ no later than _____   ☐ no earlier than _____
Removal date: ☐ no later than _____   ☐ no earlier than _____

Requested by: Date:

Authorized by: Date:

Purpose/Description:

Keywords:

Internal Links: ☐ Home [index]   ☐ La Casa Nueva   ☐ Workman House
                       ☐ El Campo Santo   ☐ Events   ☐ shown on attached
                       ☐ Other:

External Links: ☐ none   ☐ http://www.
                       ☐ shown on attached   ☐ http://www.

Content: ☐ on disk   ☐ attached   ☐ to be determined/developed
Images: ☐ on disk   ☐ attached   ☐ to be determined/developed
Design ideas:

File name: www.homesteadmuseum.org/
Subdirectory: ☐ none   ☐ name:
Subpages: ☐ none   ☐ quantity: _____

Conceptual design: ☐ completed   ☐ review design with:
External links: ☐ all current   ☐ need updating:
Page colors: ☐ standard   ☐ special:
Images prep: ☐ scanned   ☐ resized   ☐ retouch   ☐ other:
Images stored: ☐ with page   ☐ in images file
Special: ☐ Java   ☐ video   ☐ mapping   ☐ frames   ☐ other:
Copyright: ☐ completed   ☐ need permissions:
Spellcheck: ☐ completed
Final review: ☐ approved
                   ☐ approved with modifications
                   ☐ not approved
                   By: Date:
Installation: ☐ completed on:
Submit update: ☐ Yahoo   ☐ Excite   ☐ Alta Vista   ☐ Lycos   ☐ Other

Web Site Proposal for New Material

From: _____ Ext. _____

Desired date online: _____ Is this a deadline? ____ Yes ____ No

To use this form:
1. Fill out the purpose and permissions section.
2. Get initials from review group.
3. Present to Web Task Force Committee. They will review and return proposal with their decision and further questions about organization.

Review

(   )   Info has been reviewed by my Program Director.

_____   _____
Initials   Date

(   )   Info has been reviewed by my Division Head.

_____   _____
Initials   Date

(   )   Info has been reviewed by the Marketing Department.

_____   _____
Initials   Date

Hard copy of proposed web material attached. _____ Yes _____ No

Disc with text attached. ____ Yes ____ No
(Preferred disk format is ASCII. Please talk to MIS Director if you need assistance with converting files.)

Purpose

Please describe your new material.

What audience do you wish to target?

How do you hope your audience will use this information?

How will this benefit the Society?

Is this content currently being distributed in other ways? Please list.

Permissions

Does the Oregon Historical Society hold the rights to all the material your entry be using? If not, who holds the rights and is there a cost?

Organization

What other Web Sites have you visited which you see as possible models for your entry? Please provide URLs and explanations of what you like about them.

Where do you think your new content should fit into the existing OHS Site? Please list the buttons.

What links would you suggest to other OHS information? To or from other sites?

Formatting

If your proposal is accepted, there will be a technical advice meeting to assist in answering the questions below.

● **Text**

Disc is submitted in: ___ ASCII　　　____WordPerfect 5.1, 6.0, 7.0 (circle one)

● **Graphics**

My proposed material includes graphics.

_____ Yes _____ No

Ready to:

_____ FTP _____ Pass on to Imaging Technician

I have my graphic material ready to pass on to the Imaging Technician for scanning in the following format:

_____ Photo _____ Slide _____ CD _____ Included on Disk

I have included a list of 8-character file names.

_____ Yes _____ No

I have included information about whether the image should be full size, mid-size, or thumbnail.

_____ Yes _____ No

Will this image be a link to a full size image or another page?

_____ Yes _____ No

If yes, give page name or image file name.

I have attached hard copy intended to show layout ideas.

_____ Yes _____ No

Walker Art Center   **WEB SITE DESIGN REQUEST FORM**

PROJECT TITLE:

Submitted by: Date:

Department:

Who will approve?

Description:

Audience:

Related Programs:

Has the text been published? (include printed version)

If yes, name of print designer:

Are there ☐ related images   ☐ audio   ☐ video   ☐ other

Where should information be linked from/to
    on Walker Web site:

    to other sites?

Is there a specific email contact that you want included on the Web?

Who owns the information?

Who owns the images?

Who owns the audio files?

Who owns the video files?

If not WAC, do we have permission to use text and related materials on the Web? (include copies of permission correspondence)

Author(s):

Deadline for Event: Web Posting Date (if different):

Project Expiration Date (content valid until):

How often will a new version be provided?

Funding Source:

Credit Line(s) Required:

version 1 10/22/97

We can add a link from one part of the Walker Web site to another part – or to a different Web site entirely. Complete this form to have a hyperlink added.

Where would you like to *link from*:
Section: ☐ Closed Mondays ☐ Artist Programs ☐ Education + Community Programs
☐ Collection + Resources ☐ Gallery 9 ☐ Other

Subsection:

Page Name:

Identify the specific phrase to link from or provide the wording that should be added (e.g. "For further information see ___"):

Link To (WALKER):
Section: ☐ Closed Mondays ☐ Artist Programs ☐ Education + Community Programs
☐ Collection + Resources ☐ Gallery 9 ☐ Other

Subsection:

Page Name:

Word(s):

Link To (NON WALKER SITE):
url:

_____

Thank you for your help. Please provide your name and email address in case we have questions.
Name:

Email:

We regret if you have come across an error or problem on the Walker Art Center Web site. Please let us know.

Where did you find the error?
Section: ☐ Closed Mondays ☐ Artist Programs ☐ Education + Community Programs
☐ Collection + Resources ☐ Gallery 9 ☐ Other

Subsection (e.g. Current Exhibitions, Artists in Focus, Archives):

Page Name (look in the "location" line of your browser – or guess):

What is the nature of the problem? ☐ bad link ☐ broken image ☐ factual inaccuracy
☐ interface design issue ☐ slow to load ☐ typo ☐ other

Describe the problem:

Often problems are specific to your hardware and software configuration. Providing the following information can help us track down the problem.

Platform: ☐ Apple/Macintosh ☐ PC ☐ Unix

Operating System: ☐ PowerPc (Macintosh) ☐ 68xx (Macintosh) ☐ Windows 95 ☐ Windows 3.1
☐ Windows NT ☐ Linux ☐ Other

Browser: ☐ AOL 2.x ☐ AOL 3.x
☐ Internet Explorer 2.x ☐ Internet Explorer 3.x ☐ Internet Explorer 4.x
☐ Netscape 1.x ☐ Netscape 2.x ☐ Netscape 3.x ☐ Netscape 4.x
☐ Other

Internet Connection: ☐ 14.4 modem or slower ☐ 28.8 modem ☐ 35.5 modem ☐ 56 modem
☐ ISDN ☐ T1 ☐ Other

Thank you for your help. Would you like to be contacted about this problem and its resolution?
Name:

Email:

Job Request Form

Graphics and Publications

Please complete this form and send it to Diane Lovejoy, Publications Director.

Job Name: _____

Description

_____

Department: _____

Contact Person: _____

Telephone Ext.: _____

This job is:
- ❑ for design only
- ❑ for design and printing

This job is:
- ❑ a reorder, no changes
(attach sample of last order)
approximate date last ordered: _____

- ❑ a reorder, new information
(attach sample of last order with changes marked)
approximate date last ordered: _____

- ❑ a new project

Please list any restrictions or requests for the following items:

Size: _____ Fold(s): _____

Paper color, weight: _____ Ink (# of colors): _____

Check if relevant:
- ❑ Please submit color mock-up for my approval
- ❑ Please submit paper samples for my approval
- ❑ Please submit ink samples for my approval

Other: Specify desired "look" or target audience, if relevant:

_____

Budget: $ _____ Department: _____

Account #: _____

Please remember to include:
- Corresponding, double-spaced, hard copy.
- File saved as MS Word for Windows 6.0 on a 3-1/2" IBM diskette OR, Montrose building departments only, indicate directory and file name.
- Illustrative material with appropriate identification.
- Signed P.O. (unless job is budgeted in publications department).

Check all items and provide quantities to be ordered. In the case of packages with multiple items, please note any different delivery dates that apply.

- ❑ Letterhead — Qty.:
- ❑ Invitation — Qty.:
- ❑ Outer envelope — Qty.:
- ❑ Response card — Qty.:
- ❑ Response envelope — Qty.:
- ❑ Other: — Qty.:

Delivery Date(s):

Delivery Location(s):

1) _____ Qty.: _____

Attn: _____

2) _____ Qty.: _____

Attn.: _____

3) _____ Qty.: _____

Attn.: _____

4) _____ Qty.: _____

Attn.: _____

5) Department samples Qty.: 25
MFA Publications Dept. Attn.:
5100 Montrose Blvd., Houston, TX 77006

6) Staff Distribution Qty.:
MFA Office Services Dept. Attn.: Tony Domingo
5100 Montrose Blvd., Houston, TX 77006

FOR GRAPHICS AND PUBLICATIONS DEPARTMENT USE ONLY:

DATE:

JOB NUMBER:

EDITOR:

DESIGNER:

70

Graphics and Publications

Label Request Form

Please complete this form and send it to Diane Lovejoy, publications director.

Today's date: _____   Date needed: _____   Installation date: _____

Curator: _____   Curatorial Assistant: _____

Gallery: _____   Requested by: _____

☐ Standard label size: Specify size and/or type below.

A Wall and Case Label   **B Deck and Platform**   **C Horizontal Chat Label**   **D Didactic Label**

6.5 inches / 4 inches   8.5 inches / 5.25 inches   11.5 inches / 4 inches   11 inches / 17 inches

☐ Nonstandard label size: Specify size and orientation below.

1) Size: _____   Orientation: __ [Horizontal] __ [Vertical]

Label color: _____

Other installation elements: ☐ Vinyl: _____

☐ Silkscreened panels
(For silkscreened panels, complete a Graphics and Publications Job Request Form and send to Diane Lovejoy.)

☐ Other: _____

Please attach corresponding, double-spaced, printed hard copy and file saved as MS Word for Windows 6.0 on 3-1/2" IBM diskette.

Use a separate Label Request Form for each group of different-sized labels.

Return this completed form and your materials to Diane Lovejoy, publications director.

This completed form must accompany label requests in order for production to proceed and for materials to be delivered according to deadline specified.

Production Time Guidelines Use this outline for planning production time for your request.

If you are requesting...		count back...		from delivery date, for final copy-due date.
	Banners		8 weeks	
	Silkscreened panels		7 weeks	
	Photomurals		7 weeks	
	Labels		6 weeks	
	Title walls		6 weeks	
	Signage		4 weeks	

71

PRINTING AND PRE-PRESS INFORMATION

Buffalo Bill Historical Center
Publications Department
720 Sheridan Ave., Cody Wyoming 82414

Renee Tafoya or Jan Woods
phone: (307) 578-4054 fax: 578-4003

PROJECT:
DESCRIPTION:

QUANTITY:

STOCK:

SIZE:

DATE DUE & DELIVERY:

PRE-PRESS INFORMATION
FILE NAME:

QUARKXPRESS 3.32 FOR MACINTOSH

FONT INFORMATION
List All Fonts Used:

_____
_____
_____
_____

LINKED FILES
List All Linked Art Files by Name and File Type:

_____
_____
_____
_____

OUTPUT MEDIA
__ Film Negative with Dylux Proof (blueline)
__ Color Proof (Matchprint prefered)

RESOLUTION / DPI
__ 1200/1270   __ 2400/2540   __ 3000+

SCREEN RULING / LPI
__ 85   __ 120   __ 133   __ 150

COLOR SEPARATION PLATES
__ Black only
__ 4-Color Process (CMYK)
__ Black plus:

SCANNING INFORMATION
List All Art/Photos To Be Scanned
by Page Number, Name, and Final Size:

_____
_____
_____
_____
_____
_____

for additonal space use back of page

COPYRIGHT INFORMATION
All that appears on the enclosed medium (including, but not limited to, floppy disk and removable media) is unencumbered by copyrights. We ave full rights to reproduce the supplied content. All supplied artwork and photography is the property of the Buffalo Bill Historical Center and may not be reproduced except as requested here. All artwork and photography must be returned within 10 days.
Signature:
Date:

OTHER INFORMATION
List information about the job here:

_____
_____
_____
_____
_____
_____
_____
_____

REQUEST FOR SIGNS

by Roeyer   or other staff/dept._____   today's date _____

date needed:
process: give to Sally to clarify, schedule
Sally gives to Valerie
Valerie creates, prints out, returns to Sally for proofing
Sally gives to requester if no corrections needed

Exhibition: _____

Sign A: horizontal   or   vertical

# of copies _____ Paper: white label___   yellow label____   other_____

Size: 8.5x11___   8.5x14___   other_____

Text exactly as you want it to appear on sign: _____

_____

Arrow: none straight left   left with bend   straight right   right with bend

Sign B: horizontal or vertical

# of copies _____ Paper: white label___   yellow label____   other_____

Size: 8.5x11___   8.5x14___   other_____

Text exactly as you want it to appear on sign: _____

_____

Arrow: none straight left   left with bend   straight right   right with bend

Sign C: horizontal or vertical

# of copies _____ Paper: white label___   yellow label____   other_____

Size: 8.5x11___   8.5x14___   other_____

Text exactly as you want it to appear on sign: _____

_____

Arrow: none straight left   left with bend   straight right   right with bend

Additional info or special instructions: _____

_____

Sally has ____verified information / ____proofed and returned to Valerie for final draft

SOUTH DAKOTA TRAVEL REQUEST
BOA FLEET & TRAVEL MANAGEMENT
SFN 01239-0002

Bureau or Department	Program
Division	Circle One: In-State Out-of-State

Billing Center Code   (Last Two Digits Optional)   Method of Travel

Est. Miles (Personal Vehicle)

Traveler's Name (Last, First, MI)	Office Phone	Home Phone
Purpose of Travel		License Number

JOURNEY INFORMATION

Journey Number	Origin	Odometer Reading	Departure Date	Departure Time	Circle One:
Segment	Destination				AM/PM
1.					AM / PM
2.					AM / PM
3.					AM / PM
4.					AM / PM
5.					AM / PM
6.					AM / PM
7.					AM / PM
8.					AM / PM
REQUIRED: Return to Origin	Final Odometer Reading	Return Date and Time			AM / PM

Comments/Vehicle Problems/Repairs

White - Fleet and Travel Management;   Yellow - Agency

COST ESTIMATES FOR OUT OF STATE TRAVEL

Transportation $	Meals $	Lodging $	Misc. Fees $	Total $
General Funds $	Federal Funds $	Other Funds $	Non-State Funds $	

SIGNATURES   NOTE: Driver MUST sign to certify he/she holds a valid driver license

Traveler Signature	Date	Driver License Number	Expiration Date
Approving Officer	Date	Approving Officer	Date

AGENCY TRAVEL COORDINATOR USE

Coordinator Name	Date of Entry	Mode
Comments		
Ride Share Contact	Office Phone	Home Phone

FLEET AND TRAVEL MANAGEMENT USE - FOR HIGH MILEAGE REQUEST ONLY

Approval Signatures	Date	Comments
Authorization Number		

WITTE MUSEUM
EXPENSE REPORT

Name _____   **DATE SUBMITTED** _____

	Sun	Mon	Tue	Wed	Thu	Fri	Sat	Totals
Airfare								
Auto Rental								
Miles Driven								
Parking and Tolls								
Taxi / Bus								
Other								
Transportation Total								
Lodging								
Other								
Breakfast								
Lunch								
Dinner								
Lodging & Meals Total								
Supplies / Equipment								
Phone, Fax								
Other								
Other								
Other								
Entertainment								
Total Per Day								

DETAILED ENTERTAINMENT RECORD

Date	Item	Persons Entertained Business Relationship	Place Name & Location	Business Purpose	Amount

PURPOSE OF TRIP	**SUMMARY**	
	TOTAL EXPENSES	
	LESS CASH ADVANCE	
	LESS COMPANY CHARGES	
	AMOUNT DUE EMPLOYEE	
	AMOUNT DUE COMPANY	

PREPARED BY _____   DATE _____   75   APPROVED BY _____   DATE _____

FORM 13.20.20
Effective 1/1/93

Dept.   Serial

TRAVEL AUTHORIZATION

CHECK ALL APPLICABLE TRAVEL ITEMS REQUESTED HEREIN:

IN-STATE _____ OUT-OF-STATE _____ OUT-OF-COUNTRY _____ TRAVEL ADVANCE _____
(See backside for instructions)

EMP.
NAME _____

EMP.
TITLE _____

EMP.
SS# _____

AGENCY _____ DIVISION/BUDGET UNIT _____

DATE(S) OF MEETING/TRIP _____ DESTINATION(S) _____

TITLE OF MEETING _____

PURPOSE/BENEFITS OF TRIP/MEETING _____

_____

_____

TTL.EST.COST: _____ FUND # _____ GEN/SPEC. (circle one)

TRAVEL ADVANCE AMOUNT REQUESTED WITH THIS FORM: _____

TTL ACTUAL COST _____ DIF. IN EST. AND ACTUAL COST _____

TO BE COMPLETED BY AGENCY/INSTITUTION
(To the extent required by individual Agency/Institution)

FUNDS CERTIFICATION _____ TITLE _____

DIVISION HEAD APPROVAL _____ TITLE _____

AGENCY HEAD APPROVAL _____ TITLE _____

TO BE COMPLETED BY DEPT OF FINANCE & ADMIN
IF TRAVEL IS OUTSIDE CONTINENTAL U.S.

BUDGET ANALYST FUND CERTIFICATION _____ DATE _____

DFA EXECUTIVE DIRECTOR APPROVED _____ DATE _____

TO BE COMPLETED BY DEPT OF FINANCE & ADMIN
IF SUPPLEMENTAL APPROVAL FOR EXCESS EXPENDITURE
ON INTERNATIONAL TRAVEL IS REQUESTED

BUDGET ANALYST FUND CERTIFICATION _____ DATE _____

DFA EXECUTIVE DIRECTOR APPROVED _____ DATE _____

EMPLOYEE'S SIGNATURE

INSTRUCTIONS FOR TRAVEL AUTHORIZATION

1. Complete all applicable items and obtain approval PRIOR to commencing travel. Prior approval is required by statute for travel outside the continental United States.

2. A separate form must be completed for each traveler.

3. Be specific as to purpose/benefits of the trip or meeting.

4. Be as accurate as possible in estimating costs, including air, lodging, meals, gratuities, taxis, rental cars, or any other applicable travel requirement.

5. The travel advance requested, if any, should include a total of only those items not prepaid (airline ticket, registration, etc.), and must be cleared on return. Advances outstanding for 60 days or more may result in your paycheck being held until the advance is cleared. You may only have one advance outstanding at one time. Travel advances are available only for travel outside the State.

6. An approved copy of this form with supporting documentation (receipts, air itinerary form) must be submitted with the travel expense voucher in order to receive reimbursement.

7. Be sure that all out-of-state travel arrangements (air, hotel, rental car) are made by the State contract travel agency if airline/train/bus transportation is involved.

WORKSHEET

	EST. COST	ACTUAL COST
AIR	$_____	$_____
MEALS (____DAYS @ $____/DAY)	$_____	$_____
LODGING (____DAYS @ $____/DAY)	$_____	$_____
REGISTRATION FEE	$_____	$_____
RENTAL CAR (____DAYS @ $____/DAY)	$_____	$_____
OTHER_____	$_____	$_____
_____	$_____	$_____
_____	$_____	$_____
TOTAL	$_____	$_____

DEACCESSIONS

Recommendation
Record
Worksheet

The Sixth Floor Museum

411 Elm Street, Suite 120
Dallas, Texas 75202-3301
214/653-6659   Fax 214/653-6657
http:/www.jfk.org

DEACCESSION RECOMMENDATION

Accession Number   **Accession Date**   **Description**

Reason for recommended deaccession (documentation and detailed explanation attached)**:**

ACTION TAKEN ON RECOMMENDATION

Interpretation Committee:

✕ Approved for deaccessioning and referred to Board of Directors
✕ Not approved for deaccessioning
      Reason for non-approval:

Executive Director, The Sixth Floor Museum   **Date**

Board of Directors:

✕ Approved for deaccessioning
      Approved method of disposal: ✕ exchange   ✕ donation
                                   ✕ auction/sale   ✕ return to donor
✕ Not approved for deaccessioning
      Reason for non-approval:

President, Board of Directors   **Date**

FINAL DISPOSITION OF DEACCESSIONED ITEM

✕ Exchange with another non-profit/educational institution
      Name of institution:
      Items received in exchange:
✕ Donation to another non-profit/educational institution
      Name of institution:
✕ Public auction
      Monies received:
✕ Return to donor
      Name of donor:

The Sixth Floor Museum is a non-profit organization, operated under the auspices of the Dallas County Historical Foundation.

BOOT HILL MUSEUM

DEACCESSION RECOMMENDATION & DISPOSAL WORKSHEET

RECOMMENDED FOR DEACCESSIONING:

Accession Number: Date of Acquisition:

Category: Name of Donor:

Description:

Documentation of Artifact:
- ❑ Donor Agreement   ❑ Photograph   ❑ Condition Report
- ❑ Catalogue Sheet & Card ❑ Recent Appraisal   ❑ Other, explain: _____

Reason for Deaccessioning:

THE MUSEUM IS FREE TO DEACCESSION AND DISPOSE OF THE ARCHIVAL MATERIAL(S), HISTORIC PHOTOGRAPH(S) OR MUSEUM OBJECT(S) IF ALL OF THE FOLLOWING ARE ANSWERED YES:

1. The Curator and Assistant Curator jointly apply the criteria (listed on the following page) and deem that the criteria for deaccessioning has been met.   ❑ Yes ❑ No

   _____   _____
   Curator's Signature   *Date*

   _____   _____
   Assistant Curator's Signature   *Date*

2. Executive Director's Approval of recommendation for deaccessioning: ❑ Yes ❑ No

   _____   _____
   President's Signature   *Date*

3. Museum Team approve recommendation for deaccessioning: ❑ Yes ❑ No

   _____   _____
   Museum Team Chairman's Signature   *Date*

4. Board of Directors approve recommendation for deaccessioning: ❑ Yes ❑ No

   _____   _____
   Board of Directors Chairman's Signature   *Date*

5. The Curator or Assistant Curator shall maintain all records documenting all deaccessions. ❑ Yes ❑ No

RECOMMENDATION FOR MEANS OF DISPOSAL:

The board of directors approve of the means of disposal: ❑ Yes ❑ No
   If no, explain:

   _____   _____
   Board of Directors Chairman's Signature   *Date*

The Curator or Assistant Curator has carried out the means of disposal upon the Board of Directors approval.   ❑ Yes ❑ No

   _____   _____
   Curator's or Assistant Curator's Signature   *Date*

BOOT HILL MUSEUM
DEACCESSIONING CRITERIA:

To initiate the deaccession and disposal process the archival material(s), historic photographs(s), and/or museum objects(s) must meet the following criteria:

1. **Free from donor imposed restrictions.** ❏ Yes ❏ No

2. **The Museum fully and legally owns the archival material(s), historic photograph(s), or museum object(s).** ❏ Yes ❏ No

3. **The archival material(s), historic photograph(s), or museum object(s) has been accessioned into the Museum's collection for at least two years** (hazardous and actively decomposing materials excepted). ❏ Yes ❏ No

4. **Meet at least one of the following:**
   A. The archival material(s), historic photograph(s), or museum object(s) is outside the scope of the statement of purpose of the Museum and its acquisition policy ❏ Yes ❏ No
   B. The archival material(s), historic photograph(s), or museum object(s) is a duplicate. Duplicates not otherwise needed for exhibit purposes of for the circulation of educational traveling exhibits and which are in fact duplicates, may be disposed. Reproductions or other artificial duplications may be replaced by the original of such artifact. ❏ Yes ❏ No
   C. The archival material(s), historic photograph(s), or museum object(s) has deteriorated beyond usefulness, or has failed to retain its identity or authenticity. ❏ Yes ❏ No
   D. The archival material(s), historic photograph(s), or museum object(s) poses a physical hazard or is dangerous to the health of museum personnel. ❏ Yes ❏ No
   E. The archival material(s), historic photograph(s), or museum object(s) which are the subject of irreversible deterioration or infestation, particularly when they may imperil the condition of other artifacts in collections and on exhibit. ❏ Yes ❏ No
   F. The archival material(s), historic photograph(s), or museum object(s) which are determined to be frauds or fakes or not proper representatives of their class of artifacts. ❏ Yes ❏ No
   G. The museum is unable to preserve the archival material(s), historic photograph(s) or museum object(s). ❏ Yes ❏ No
   H. Artifacts acquired in 'block' acquisitions may be 'pruned' where in the judgment of the Curator and Assistant Curator portions of such 'block' acquisition are not consistent with the exhibit or the intended educational purpose to be served by such collections, and in compliance with the Museum's statement of purpose. ❏ Yes ❏ No
   I. The archival material(s), historic photograph(s), or museum object(s) are acquired contrary to this Collections Policy after the effective date of such Policies or amendments, shall be returned to the original owner, provided that return to the owner shall not perpetuate the artifacts having been obtained illegally. ❏ Yes ❏ No

5. **All recommendations for deaccessioning shall be taken to the Executive Director, Museum Team, and Board of Directors for approval. All recommendations shall include:** ❏ Yes ❏ No
   A. Fullest documentation of the item(s)
   B. Reason for Deaccessioning
   C. Copy of recent appraisal, if available
   D. Recommended Means of disposal

RECOMMENDED MEANS OF DISPOSAL

1. SALE - In utilizing the sale procedure, the order or preference as to the method of sales is as follows:
   A. Public Auction
   B. Private Auction
   C. Private Sale

2. EXCHANGE - The criteria for exchange is as follows:
   A. The value of the archival material(s), historic photograph(s) or museum object(s) to be received shall be reasonably commensurate with the value of the artifact to be disposed of.
   B. The item(s) received fulfills a particular need in the Museum's exhibits or education programs.

3. Donation - Archival material(s), historic photograph(s) or museum object(s) may be donated to another library, historical society or museum when the item(s) would benefit the collection of the other institution. The library, historical society or museum selected must collect the type of item(s) offered and must be able to properly care for the donated item(s).

4. Destruction - Archival material(s), historic photograph(s) or museum object(s) which are worn, infested with deleterious chemical substances or varmint or are hazardous and dangerous to the health of museum personnel may be destroyed in an appropriate manner.

Canadian Musée
Museum of canadien de la
NATURE

PERMISSION TO DEACCESSION

All requests for permission to deaccession objects from the collections of the Canadian Museum of Nature must be accompanied by this form.

CMN Collection: _____

Deaccession request initiated by: _____ Date: _____

List material to be deaccessioned, including catalogue numbers (if applicable), name or description and the reason they should be deaccessioned.

Catalogue number	Categ. no.	Name / Description	Reason for deaccession

☐ Additional objects listed on _____ attached pages.
   Proposed disposition:

_____

_____

_____ (If objects are to be sold, enter total price: _____)

Research Evaluation: Deaccession request has been evaluated by Research Division.

☐ Comments attached.
Researcher's signature: _____ Date: _____

Conservation Evaluation: Deaccessions requested because of deterioration must be evaluated by Conservation Section.

☐ Comments attached.
Conservator's signature: _____ Date: _____

☐ Recommended ☐ Not Recommended	Signature of Chief, Collection Section	Date
☐ Recommended ☐ Not Recommended	Signature of Chair, Collection Development Committee	Date
☐ Recommended / Approved ☐ Not Recommended / Not Approved	Signature of Manager, Collection Division	Date
For material in Categories 1 - 4:		
☐ Recommended ☐ Not Recommended	Signature of Chair, Collection Advisory Committee	Date
☐ Recommended ☐ Not Recommended	Signature of the President	Date
☐ Approved ☐ Not Approved	Signature of Chair, Board of Trustees	Date

RETURN COMPLETED FORM TO REGISTRAR

(1996.03.11)

PANHANDLE-PLAINS HISTORICAL MUSEUM

DEACCESSIONING PROPOSAL

Accession Number: _____

Object Description: _____

_____

Date Acquired: _____ **Acquired From**: _____

Type of Transaction: (gift, purchase, transfer, exchange, deposit) _____

Reason for Deaccession Proposal (check all that apply)

No longer relevant to mission statement   _____
Not museum quality   _____
Redundant   _____
Deteriorated beyond repair   _____
Other   _____

Explain: _____

_____

_____

Exhibit History: _____

_____

If object was a gift:

Is donor still alive? _____ (yes/no/unknown)

Is the donor likely to make a further gift or bequest? _____

Have donor or heirs been contacted and what were results? _____

_____

_____

If object was purchased:

Purchase price: _____ Fund(s) used: _____

82

DEACCESSIONING PROPOSAL

CURATOR	*Page 2 of 4*

Value:

Value at acquisition: _____   Current market value: _____

How was current value determined? _____

_____

1. _____   _____
   <small>Name of Appraiser</small>   <small>Value</small>

2. _____   _____
   <small>Name of Appraiser</small>   <small>Value</small>

Reason appraisal not necessary: _____

If artist is still living, describe results of efforts to contact him/her: _____

_____

_____

Disposition Recommendation:

Public Auction: _____

Exchange for/from: _____

Transfer to: _____

Destroy (must justify): _____

Other: _____

Elaboration/Justification: _____

_____

Attach: *Condition Report*
Photograph, if appropriate
Appraisals, if obtained

Curator Name (print): _____ *Signature:* _____ *Date:* _____

Rev. 36

DEACCESSIONING PROPOSAL

REGISTRAR	*Page 3 of 4*

Does the Panhandle-Plains Historical Society hold clear title to this object and how is ownership documented? _____

_____

List any restrictions on the original transaction that would affect deaccessioning or disposal: _____

_____

√	Notifications Required		
	Who	**Reason**	**Date Notified in Writing**
	Donor		
	IRS		
	Tribe (name):		
	Attorney General		
	Artist		

Other Notes/Recommendations: _____

_____

_____

Registrar Name (print): _____ *Signature:* _____ *Date:* _____

Staff Collections Committee Recommendation

Date Presented to Staff Collections Committee: _____ **Approved / Not Approved**

Attach minutes of Staff Collections Committee meeting.

84

DEACCESSIONING PROPOSAL

| *Director and Board of Trustees* | *Page 4 of 4* |

Date Presented to Museum Director: _____ Approved / Not Approved

Reason for non-approval: _____

_____

Date Presented to Board Collections Committee: _____ Approved / Not Approved

Reason for non-approval: _____

Attach pertinent pages of minutes from Board Collections Committee meeting.

Date Presented to Society's Board of Trustees: _____ Approved / Not Approved

Reason for non-approval: _____

Attach pertinent pages of minutes from Society Board of Trustees meeting.

Director Name (print or type): _____

Signature: _____ *Date:* _____

Collection Committee Chair Name (print or type): _____

Signature: _____ *Date:* _____

Board President Name (print or type): _____

Signature: _____ *Date:* _____

RETURN ENTIRE FORM WITH ALL ATTACHMENTS TO REGISTRAR.

US Department of the Interior
National Park Service

Deaccession Number

Deaccession Form

Park Name

DEACCESSION TYPE:
☐ Return to Rightful Owner
☐ Loss, Theft, or Involuntary Destruction
☐ Voluntary Destruction/ Abandonment
☐ Outside Scope of Collection
☐ Destructive Analysis
☐ NAGPRA Compliance

DISPOSITION FOR OBJECTS OUTSIDE SOC:
☐ Transfer to NPS unit
☐ Transfer to other federal entity
☐ Exchange with federal entity
☐ Exchange with non-federal institution
☐ Exchange with individual
☐ Conveyance (Donation) to private institution
☐ Conveyance (Donation) to non-federal governmental entity
☐ Voluntary Destruction/Abandonment

OBJECTS IN DEACCESSION: List Attached   Number of Objects: _____   Value _____
(Attach List of Objects, or for a few objects, list required information here)

DISPOSITION DOCUMENT (attached):
☐ Receipt for Property
☐ Report of Survey
☐ Witness statement for Destruction
   or Abandonment

☐ Memorandum (for Destructive Analysis)
☐ Repatriation Agreement
☐ Transfer of Property
☐ Exchange Agreement
☐ Conveyance Agreement

ATTACHMENTS:
☐ Justification
☐ Copies of Catalog Records
☐ Photographs
☐ Appraisals
☐ Solicitor's Opinion/Court Order
☐ Justification for Disposition Out of the
   Order of Preference

☐ Correspondence
☐ Comments from Reviewers
☐ NAGPRA Consultation Notes
☐ NAGPRA Cultural Affiliation Documentation
☐ Notice of Intent to Convey (Donate)
☐ Documentation of Advertising throughout NPS and Response
☐ Other:

NOTES ON DEACCESSION:

CURATORIAL REVIEW AND RECOMMENDATION:

Deaccession Recommended: Yes: ___ No: ___ (if no, attach explanation)
Disposition Recommended: Yes: ___ No: ___ (if no, attach explanation)

Curator:_____   _____
                    Print Name   Signature   Date

COLLECTIONS ADVISORY COMMITTEE MEMBER REVIEW AND RECOMMENDATION

See attached Collections Advisory Committee Member Review (required for non-DOI transfers, conveyances, non-DOI exchanges, voluntary destruction)

APPROVAL:
Deaccession Approved: Yes: ___ No: ___
Disposition Approved: Yes: ___ No: ___

Attach explanation if decision is contrary to one or more committee member recommendations. Attach written approval from non-accountable reviewing official for abandonment.

Superintendent: _____   _____
                           Print Name   Signature   Date

NPS Form 10-643 Rev.
February 1998

Kalamazoo Valley Museum
OBJECT DEACCESSION RECORD

ACCN # _____   CAT #(s) _____

OBJECT(s) _____

_____

SOURCE _____

METHOD OF ACQUISITION _____ DATE _____

OBJECT LOCATION _____

DOES MUSEUM HOLD LEGAL TITLE? ____ Yes   ____ No

If No, please explain _____

DEACCESSION CRITERIA (check all that apply)
    ____ no longer relevant or useful
    ____ deteriorated beyond repair or consumed in use
    ____ beyond capability of museum to properly preserve
    ____ object is duplicate or redundant
    ____ more appropriately placed at another institution
    ____ inappropriately accessioned or accessioned twice
    ____ other _____

RECOMMENDED METHOD OF DISPOSAL
    ____ transfer to museum's Teaching Collection ____ Object Document File ____ Collection Research Files ____
    ____ transfer to another museum or cultural institution _____
    ____ exchange or trade with another museum or cultural institution _____
    ____ private sale
    ____ public auction
    ____ other _____

DEACCESSIONING RECOMMENDED AND APPROVED BY:

Yes ____   No ____   Collections Committee _____ DATE _____
                                      (signature of authorized committee member)

Yes ____   No ____   Museum Director _____ DATE _____

Comments: _____

NOTIFICATION TO KVCC BOARD OF TRUSTEES: Yes ____   Response Received _____

Comments: _____

KVCC Board Approval: Yes ____   No ____   _____ _____
(if valued at or > $10,000)   (signature of Board Chairman)   (date)

Comments: _____

FINAL DISPOSITION OF OBJECT(s):
(attach photographs if applicable)

revised 5/96

RECORD OF DEACCESSION

The Deaccession section of the Homestead Museum Collections Management Policy should be consulted when recommending that an object be deaccessioned.

The following item(s) are recommended for deaccession:

DESCRIPTION:

REASON FOR DEACCESSION:

DEACCESSION APPROVED BY: _____ DATE: _____
(Director)

DEACCESSION APPROVED BY: _____ DATE: _____
(Curator)

DEACCESSION APPROVED BY: _____ DATE: _____
(City of Industry Representative)

COMPLETE BOTH SIDES OF FORM: CONDITION REPORT AND TERMS AND CONDITIONS ON REVERSE.

FINAL DISPOSITION OF OBJECTS:

15415 East Don Julian Road ☂ City of Industry, California 91745-1029 ☂ Telephone (818) 968-8492 Fax (818) 968-2048

TERMS AND CONDITIONS:

A. Deaccession is a term used by the Homestead Museum (hereinafter referred to as the HM) to indicate that after museum staff evaluation or after having consulted with outside consultants, an object is being removed from the collections pending disposal by sale, transfer, exchange, or donation to another non-profit organization with similar purposes. Collection items which have been stolen or irreparably damaged should be deaccessioned for recordkeeping purposes.

1) In the case of loans to the HM, objects will be returned to the lender.

2) As a general rule, objects will be deaccessioned unless there are special restrictions to the contrary.

B. Objects in the HM collections will be retained permanently if they continue to be relevant and useful to the purposes and activities of the HM and if they can be properly stored, preserved and used. The deaccession of objects may be considered when these conditions no longer prevail or when deaccessioning will improve the collections for the HM's purposes and activities. Additional criteria for elimination of objects from the HM collections include the following:

1) Object is outside the HM's defined scope.

2) Object is not significant and cannot be used for research, exhibition or loan.

3) Object is so badly damaged or deteriorated that it is of little or no use.

4) Object would be better utilized in another institution.

5) Object is duplicated many times in the HM collections.

C. Objects in the collections may be deaccessioned only upon the recommendation of the HM Director and Curator and with the approval of the City of Industry.

D. The following considerations apply to the disposition of deaccessioned objects:

1) The manner of disposition is in the best interests of the institution, the public it serves, and the scholarly or cultural communities the HM represents.

2) Consideration is given to retaining city, county, state, national or international material that is pertinent to the HM's historical or cultural heritage.

3) Consideration is given to placing the objects through gift, exchange, loan, or sale in another public or private non-profit institution wherein they may serve the purpose for which they were originally acquired by the City of Industry for the HM.

4) In the event that the deaccessioned object cannot be placed in another public or private non-profit institution, such object may be disposed of at an advertised public sale.

   a) No object may be given to or exchanged with an individual.

   b) No object may be sold to an individual except at an advertised public sale.

   c) Objects may not be given or sold privately to City of Industry, HM or HRI employees and officials. Such individuals, however, may purchase HM objects at an advertised public sale.

   d) Proceeds from the sale of objects may be used only to obtain additional objects and will not be used to subsidize the operation of the HM.

E. Before disposing of objects from the collections, appropriate efforts will be made to ascertain that the HM staff is free to do so. Where restrictions as to use or dispostion of the objects under question are found to apply, the HM staff will act as follows:

1) Mandatory restrictions will be observed strictly unless deviations from their terms are permitted by law.

2) If there is any question as to the intent or effect of restrictions, the HM will seek the advice of legal counsel.

F. An adequate record of the conditions and circumstances under which objects are deaccessioned and disposed of will be made and retained as part of the HM's permanent collection's records.

Initials of Homestead Museum Representative _____

MUSEUM OF THE SDSHS
DEACCESSION RECORD

SOUTH
DAKOTA STATE
HISTORICAL SOCIETY

900 Governors Drive
Pierre, SD 57501-2217
Phone (605)773-3458
Fax (605)773-6041

The following object(s) have been deaccessioned from the collection of the Museum of the South Dakota State Historical Society in accordance with the Administrative Rules of South Dakota (ARSD 24:52:02 Museum Deaccession).

Catalog Number:	Description of Object(s)/Condition

Reason for Deaccession:

❑ Notice of *Intent to Deaccession* sent to donor on _____
                                                                                                (date)

❑ Not applicable

DISPOSITION	COPY OF DEACCESSION RECORD TO:
❑ Transfer _____	❑ Deaccession File
❑ Sell _____	❑ Donor or Reference File
❑ Exchange _____	❑ Recipient
❑ Return to Lender _____	❑ Donor if applicable
❑ Destroy	❑ Other _____
❑ Other _____	

Authorization Signatures:

_____
Museum Director/date

_____
Director of the SDSHS/date

_____
Chairperson of the Collections Committee/date

_____
President of the SDSHS Board of Trustees/date

Cooper-Hewitt National Design Museum Smithonian Institution
DEACCESSION WORKSHEET

OBJECT NAME:	ACCESSION NO.:
DONOR/VENDOR:	FUND NAME:

RECOMMENDATION BY DEPARTMENT OF:	VALUE: $
REASON FOR DEACCESSION:	
SIGNATURE OF CURATOR:	DATE:

AUTHORIZATIONS

Legal restrictions:

Moral restrictions:

Signature of Registrar:	Date:
Acquisitions Committee Decision: yes ☐ no ☐ defer ☐ Comments:	
Signature:	Date:

Two **appraisals** *must be obtained if appraised at more than $1000 or recommended for disposal from any Cooper-Hewitt, National Design Museum Collection by exchange or sale:*

Appraised Value: $	Appraiser:	Date:
Appraised Value: $	Appraiser:	Date:

The following **approvals** *must be obtained if appraised at more than $10,000 or recommended for disposal from any Cooper-Hewitt, National Design Museum Collection by exchange or sale:*
Cooper-Hewitt, NDM Board of Trustees Collections Committee Decision: yes ☐   no ☐   defer ☐
            Signature: Date:

SI Office of General Counsel Decision: yes ☐   no ☐   defer ☐
            Signature: Date:

SI Provost Decision: yes ☐   no ☐   defer ☐
            Signature: Date:

SI Secretary Decision: yes ☐   no ☐   defer ☐
            Signature: Date:

The following **approval** *must be obtained if appraised at more than $50,000:*
SI Board of Regents Decision: yes ☐   no ☐   defer ☐   Date:
            Signature:

ACTIONS

METHOD OF DISPOSAL:	
FUNDS OBTAINED: $	OBJECT(S) PURCHASED:

REGISTRAR RECORDS AMENDED:	DATE:
REGISTRAR REPORT TO ACQUISITION COMMITTEE:	DATE:

rev.02/18/97 JVI
wksheet.dea

DEACCESSIONING WORKSHEET

Accession number: _____

Donor's name: _____

Number removed from object by: _____ Date: _____

All signature and date lines on Deaccessioning Proposal checked by _____ Date _____

Notifications complete as per Deaccessioning Proposal by _____ Date _____

Disposition:

_____ Exchange/Transfer Agreement completed
_____ Appropriate documentation attached
_____ Destroyed by: _____ Date: _____
_____ Method: _____
_____ Copy of receipt of sale/exchange/transfer form to Accession file
_____ Original receipt of sale/exchange/transfer form to Deaccession file
_____ Legal title transfer completed

Current photo on file _____ yes _____ no

_____ Pull slide/photo of object write DEACCESSIONED [date] on back; file in Deaccession folder
_____ If there is a photo on file in the Research Center, pull and mark back of photo DEACCESSIONED [date] and file in Deaccession folder
_____ Check all Curators areas for photographs
_____ If no photo, photo made date _____ and filed with this form

DEACCESSIONED [date] stamped on the following records in indelible red ink:

_____ Accession book } If partial, write PARTIAL DEACCESSION [date] beside high level
_____ Donor file card } accession number or DEACCESSIONED [date] if complete
_____ Accession card
_____ Catalog form
_____ Gift Agreement by item
_____ Archeology cards
_____ Archive cards
_____ Curator records stamped and copied or transferred to Registrar

Microfilming: All deaccession records microfilmed Roll _____ Frames _____
All stamped records microfilmed Roll _____ Frames _____

Database Updated: _____ Date _____ by

Deaccessioning Proposal:

_____ Original to deaccession file
_____ Copy to accession file
_____ Copy to appropriate curator

This form filed: Original: Deaccession file
Copy: Accession file

Deaccession Number _____

Park Name _____

DEACCESSION FOLDER COVER SHEET

INSTRUCTIONS: This Deaccession Folder cover sheet may be used whenever a park deaccessions museum collections. Insert this in the deaccession folder.

A.   DEACCESSION INFORMATION IN FOLDER

☐ Deaccession Form
☐ List of Objects
☐ Justifications
☐ Museum Collection Committee Comments
☐ Superintendent Comments
☐ System Support Office Curator Comments
☐ Field Area Director Comments

B.   DEACCESSION TYPE

☐ Return to Rightful Owner
☐ Loss, Theft, or Involuntary Destruction
☐ Abandonment or Destruction
☐ Outside Scope of Collection
☐ Destructive Analysis
☐ NAGPRA Compliance

C.   DISPOSITION DOCUMENT

☐ Receipt for Property
☐ Report of Survey
☐ Witness Statement for Destruction or Abandonment
☐ Exchange Agreement
☐ Transfer of Property
☐ Memorandum (for Destructive Analysis)
☐ Repatriation Agreement

INDICATE LOCATION OF THE FOLLOWING:

	Accession Folder	Catalog Folder	Deaccession Folder
1. Correspondence relating to deaccession			
2. Case Incident Record			
3. Research Notes			
4. Appraisals			
5. Photographs			
6. Shipping Documents			
7. Documentation of abandonment or destruction			
8. NAGPRA Consultation Notes			
9. NAGPRA Cultural Affiliation Documentation			
10. Solicitor's Opinion/Court Order			
11. Other			

OBJECT DEACCESSION CHECKLIST

Accession# _____

Description _____

_____

Acquisition Date _____

☐ Photo in File
☐ Conservation needed

Value _____

Date _____

Authority _____

Reason for Deaccession:

☐ No longer relevant to Mission Statement
☐ Not Museum Quality
☐ Redundant
☐ Deteriorated Beyond Repair
☐ Other

Recommended for Deaccession by:

Director
_____
               Signature   *Date*

Assoc. Director
_____
               Signature   *Date*
Curator
_____
               Signature   *Date*
Registrar
_____
               Signature   *Date*

Deaccession Committee

_____
               Signature   *Date*

Records Searched for Restrictions:

☐ Deed of Gift   ☐ Bill of Sale
☐ Acc. Record   ☐ Other
☐ Clear Title Verified

Restrictions:

Source:

Gift

Donor: _____

Address: _____

Phone: _____

Credit Line: _____

Date Notified: (Deceased_____)

Purchase

Vendor: _____

Address: _____

Fund: _____

Source Unknown

_____

Recommended Disposition:

☐ Public Auction   ☐ Transfer   ☐ Trade

94

☐ Destruction *(reason)*

NOTES:

Approved for Deaccession by:

Director
                    Signature   *Date*

Curator
                    Signature   *Date*

Board of Trustees
                    Signature   *Date*

(Attach minutes of Board meeting)

Deaccession Commission
                    Signature   *Date*

Not Approved:

Reason:

Signature   *Date*

DISPOSITIO N:

☐ *Sale*

Auction House:

Date   *Sale Price*

☐ *Transfer*

Institution:

                              Date

☐ *Exchange*

Dealer/Institution:

Date

☐ *Destruction*

Means:

Changes Noted in:

☐ Object File
☐ Museum Labels Removed
☐ Computer Record
☐ Acc# removed from Object
☐ Location Recorded
☐ Photography in archives moved to Deaccession File

Net Funds Actualized

Deposited in Account #

Sale Records Files:

Credit Line for funds when used:

95

Conservation

ARTIFACT REPORT: ❏ DAMAGE ❏ MISSING ❏ THEFT

Public Museum of Grand Rapids
272 Pearl Street NW • Grand Rapids MI 49504
616/456-3977; fax 616/456-3873

The Public Museum is supported by

 michigan council for
arts and cultural affairs

Date: _____ Time: _____ Prepared by: _____

Object Name: _____ Accession No.:_____

Location of Object: Building: _____

Room/Gallery: _____

Section/Case/Box: _____

if reporting DAMAGE, complete the following:

Summary of Condition After Damage:
❏ generally unsound ❏ generally sound ❏ insecure ❏ disfigured
❏ incomplete ❏ stable ❏ secure

Damage Estimated To Be:
❏ structural ❏ requires further examination ❏ surface
❏ requires minor treatment ❏ requires major treatment
❏ irreparable

Damage Due To:
❏ accident ❏ vandalism ❏ deterioration ❏ improper handling
❏ water ❏ vermin ❏ fire/smoke ❏ heat ❏ mold ❏ chemical

Remarks/Comments:

if reporting a MISSING or STOLEN artifact, complete the following:

Last known location of object:

Circumstances of discovery of loss:

FOR COLLECTION MANAGEMENT DIVISION USE:
__Condition Report __Curatorial Notification __Photo Documentation __Treatment Proposal

Were all pieces/parts recovered? __yes __no
Current location of object: _____ /_____ /_____ /_____
　　　　　　　　　　　　　bldg　　　　room　　　sec/case/shelf/box

ARTIFACT CONDITION REPORT
IDAHO STATE HISTORICAL MUSEUM

Object_____   Person reporting_____
Accession number_____   Date of report_____
Inventory location_____   Photographs: B/W_____ Neg#_____
Site_____   Color_____Slide #_____
Physical description of object(color; construction; materials; size--LxWxH inches/cm):_____
_____
_____

Structure: glass   ____   Surface decoration/attachments_____
            ceramic   ____   _____
            metal   ____
            wood   ____   Structural damage_____
            textile   ____
            basket   ____   _____
            paper   ____   Areas of insecurity/weakness_____
            leather   ____   _____

Surface: unfinished ____   Areas of loss_____
            varnished ____   _____
            painted   ____   _____
            patina   ____   _____
            veneer   ____   Previous repairs/restorations_____
            glazed   ____   _____
            unglazed   ____
            oiled   ____   Previous alterations/additions/modifications_____
            other   ____   _____
                                _____

Condition: Degree of damage (slight, moderate, major, extreme)_____
____dirt/grime
____worn
____abrasions   ┌───┐
____stained   │ Location of damage (draw sketch or diagram)   │
____corrosion   │   │
____tarnish   │   │
____warping   │   │
____shrinking   │   │
____flaking   │   │
____powdering   │   │
____holes   │   │
____tears   │   │
____scratches   │   │
____bulges   │   │
____cracked   │   │
____rotted   │   │
____insects/rodents   │   │
____mold/mildew   │   │
____moisture damage   │   │
____embrittlement   │   │
____accretions   │   │
____delamination   │   │
____deformations   │   │
____other   └───┘

General condition summary

Present treatment needs

excellent _____
good _____
poor _____
stable _____
insecure _____
(add this information to the catalog card)

dust with brush/cloth_____
vacuum with screen_____
damp wipe_____
damp wipe with detergent_____
minor mending/repairs_____
reinforce/support_____
other_____

Condition noted (date/initial)

Action taken (date/initial)

_____   _____
_____   _____
_____   _____

Restrictions and special handling instructions (add this information to catalog card)

_____
_____
_____

Recommendations--notify conservator

____requires further examination
____requires stabilization/support
____requires treatment
        ____fumigation
        ____grime removed
        ____minor local treatment
        ____major treatment
        ____repairs/consolidation
        ____other

Storage recommendations

____rolled on tube
____hung on padded hanger
____special padded form
____flat on shelf
____flat in drawer
____interleaved with acid-free tissue
____interleaved with ethafoam
____wrap with acid-free tissue
____wrap with jeweler's tissue or cloth

____dust cover
____acid-free envelope/folder
____hanging/suspended on peg rack
____needs crate or special box
____needs special support/cradle
____stuff with acid-free tissue
____needs display support, mount, or fastening
____other_____
_____
_____
_____

Comments_____
_____
_____
_____
_____
_____

GENERAL CONDITION REPORT
MUSEUM OF TEXAS TECH UNIVERSITY

Artifact/Type: _____

Photodocumentation (B&W/Color): _____

PROVENIENCE

Continent & Country: _____

State/Province: _____

Site: _____   Feature: _____

Level/Strat: _____   Date/Time Period: _____

Purpose of Report:

__ accession (dept. _____)

__ loan (from _____)

__ inventory (dept. _____)

__ other _____

Previous Assigned #: _____

DIMENSIONS

Height(cm): _____

Length/Depth(cm): _____

Width/Diameter(cm): _____

MATERIALS

Warp & Weft: _____

Pile: _____

Additional Elements: _____

INDIVIDUAL COMPONENTS - General (Ceramic, Stone, Etc.)

1. _____   5. _____   9. _____
2. _____   6. _____   10. _____
3. _____   7. _____   11. _____
4. _____   8. _____   12. _____

Description:

_____

_____

_____

_____

_____

_____

_____

_____

_____

_____

_____

_____

_____

_____

__ More information on reverse side

Rough Sketch:

General Condition:
__ Excellent
__ Good
__ Fair
__ Poor

Stability:
__ Stable
__ Unstable

Priority:
__ 1 (low)
__ 2
__ 3
__ 4 (high)

Recommendation:
__ Inhouse
__ Conservator
__ Monitor
__ Other _____

OVER »»»»»»»»

Report By: _____   Date/Date Updated: _____

SPECIFIC CONDITIONS

Evidence of:
__ 1. Prehistoric Deposits
__ 2. Ethnographic Deposits
__ 3. Previous Repairs
    __ 4. Indigenous
    __ 5. Subsequent
    __ 6. Unknown
       __ 7. Major
       __ 8. Minor
__ 9. Other _____

Biological:
__ 10. Dry Rot
__ 11. Insect Damage
__ 12. Vermin Damage
__ 13. Mold
__ 14. Other _____

Chemical:
__ 15. Corrosion Products
__ 16. Crystalline Deposits
__ 17. Faded
__ 18. Odorous
__ 19. Oxidized/Tarnished
__ 20. Red Rot
__ 21. Stained
__ 22. Other _____

Physical:
__ 23. Abraded
__ 24. Scratched
__ 25. Brittle
__ 26. Distorted-Warped,
      Bent, Crushed, Etc.
__ 27. Hole(s)

Physical (continued):
__ 28. Cracked
__ 29. Dry
__ 30. Foreign Deposits
    __ 31. Dirty
    __ 32. Dusty
    __ 33. Greasy
    __ 34. Unknown
__ 35. Paint Flaking
__ 36. Parts Missing
__ 37. Spalling
__ 38. Torn
__ 39. Wet
__ 40. Smoke Damage
__ 41. Water Damage
__ 42. Shipping Damage
__ 43. Other _____

NUMBER   REMARKS

ADDITIONAL COMMENTS

MUSEUM AND ART GALLERY OF THE NORTHERN TERRITORY

MARITIME VESSEL - EXHIBITION MAINTENANCE REPORT

Accession Number: _____

Name of Boat: _____

General Condition: □ good □ fair □ unstable

□ presence of dust/dirt

□ presence of mould

□ visible insect activity [past or present]
   (identify the location(s) on diagram)
        □ sample of frass/insect obtained
        □ insect identified _____

Additional problems:

□ major damage to wood _____

□ corrosion of metal _____

□ loose components _____

□ inadequate support system/cradle _____

□ other _____

_____

Treatment carried out:

□ Dry cleaning-   □ brush/vacuuming

                 □ other _____

□ Wet cleaning -   □ 30 water:70 ethanol + Terric N9 detergent

                 □ other _____

□ Fumigation -   □ MeBr   □ Freezing   □ Other

Completed by: **Date:**

ARIZONA STATE MUSEUM
CONDITION REPORT

Cat. # _____   Object: _____   Recorder: _____   Date: _____

Materials (General): _____

Damage (If Known) Due to-
____ Fire/Smoke/Water*
____ Display/Interpretive Programs*
____ Handling/Shipping*
____ Storage
____ Other _____

Evidence of-
____ Prehistoric/Ethnographic Deposits*
____ Prehistoric/Ethnographic Usewear*
____ Prehistoric/Ethnographic Repairs*
____ Minor/Major Restoration *
____ Minor/Major Repair*
____ Other _____
____ Modern Use _____

Parts are-
____ Detached
____ Missing
____ Moving
____ Loose

Deposits
____ Corrosion/Tarnish *
____ Crystalline
____ Encrustations
____ Marks
____ Dusty
____ Greasy/Waxy*
____ Soiled
____ Finger Marks
____ Other Deposits _____

Physical-
____ Abraded/Worn*
____ Brittle/Dry*
____ Broken
____ Burned/Charred*
____ Cracked
____ Cut/Split/Tear*
____ Folded/Creased*
____ Hole
____ Discolored
____ Darkened
____ Dye Bleeding
____ Faded
____ Stained
____ Distorted
____ Bent
____ Crushed
____ Warped
____ Frayed/Shredded*
____ Shedding
____ Weave Breakage/Loss *
____ Selvage Breakage/Loss*
____ Warp Breakage /Loss*
____ Weft Breakage/Loss*
____ Wrinkled
____ Surface Damaged
____ Buckled/Lifted Areas*
____ Chipped/Flaked*
____ Crackled/Crazed*
____ Powdered
____ Scratched
____ Spalled
____ Other _____

Biological-
____ Past/Present Insect Damage or Infestation*
____ Past/Present Mold*
____ Other _____
____ Pesticide Use

Smell
____ Chemical
____ Moldy
____ Other _____
____ Drawing on back

Stability-
____ Stable
____ Unstable
____ Uncertain

General Condition-
____ Excellent (Perfect)
____ Good (Minimal, minor defects)
____ Fair (Many defects, but stable)
____ Poor (Might need stabilization)

Actions Completed-Date
____ Frozen
____ Vacuumed

Action Recommendation-
____ None
____ Monitor
____ To Conservation _____

Comments: _____

Check conditions if they apply, use space at end of condition to clarify "where" and "what." *If used, cross out term that does not apply.

11/20/96
REH

University of Iowa Hospitals and Clinics Medical Museum

CONDITION REPORT

Object Number: _____   Report Date _____

Object Name: _____   Value _____

Borrower: _____

Report completed by: _____

Summary of Condition:

☐ Unsuitable for exhibition or loan   ☐ Requires Conservation Treatment[*]
☐ Minor treatment/cleaning required before loan
☐ Stable - suitable for exhibition or loan

General Description:

Dimensions: (l x w x h) _____

Structure compromised:
☐ losses   ☐ crack(s)/split(s)   ☐ other _____
☐ chipping/dent(s)   ☐ loose element(s)   _____
☐ distortion(s)   ☐ embrittlement   _____
☐ fragmentary   ☐ tear(s)   _____
☐ restoration(s)/repair   _____

Surface damage:
☐ accretion (incrustation)   ☐ foxing   ☐ restorations/overpainting/old adhesive
☐ bleeding   ☐ mold, mildew   ☐ other _____
☐ soiled   ☐ lifting paint/coating   _____
☐ stained/discolored   ☐ insect/pest damage   _____
☐ crumbly   ☐ abrasions/minor damage _____

Other:
☐ auxiliary attachments
☐ insect infestation (active)
☐ former treatment: _____
☐ other damage: _____
_____
_____

[*] Conservation Treatment should be performed only by a professional conservator. Unless you are absolutely certain that treatment or cleaning can be performed with no damage to the artifact, always let a conservator do the work. See Collections Management Handbook for guidelines.

4/97

2130 South Race St. • Denver, CO 80208 • (303) 871-4384 • FAX (303) 871-2736

Condition Report

Incoming Loan Tracking Number: _____

Object: _____ Owner: _____

Other Information: _____

Examiner: _____ Date: _____

Height: _____ cm Width: _____ cm Depth: _____ cm Diameter: _____ cm

Description/ Materials:

__ Inorganics   __ Organics   __ Composite   __ Non-Composite

Structure:

__ glass	__ ceramic	__ stone	__ wood	__ plastic
__ metal	__ paper	__ textile	__ leather	__ skin/hide/fur
__ ivory	__ horn	__ shell	__ feather	__ bone/antler/teeth

__ other: _____

Surface:

__ paint	__ glaze	__ veneer	__ enamel	__ varnish

__ other: _____

Condition:

Structure:

__ insecurities	__ breaks	__ cracks/splits	__ tears	__ losses
__ missing pieces	__ warps	__ loose elements	__ distortions	__ buckling
__ checking	__ creases	__ adhesive failure	__ restorations (fills, overpainting)	

__ other: _____

Surface:

__ insecurities	__ soil	__ abrasions/scratches	__ accretions	__ spalling
__ delamination	__ cleavage	__ friable surface	__ flaking paint/coating/glaze	

__ stained	__ discolored	__ faded	__ tide line	__ bloom
__ verdigris	__ spew	__ leaching plastisizers		

__ efflorescence	__ corrosion	__ devitrification	__ weeping/crizzling glass

__ mold/mildew	__ vermin	__ insects

__ other: _____

Notes/ Drawings:

Possible Conditions

CERAMICS: chips, cracks, breaks, scratches, abrasions, crumbling, wear, losses, crazing (craquelure), kiln faults (cracks, bubbles, impurities), stains, soiling, restorations/ repairs, salt incrustations, salt efflorescence, spalling, flaking glaze, localized loss of surface decoration

FEATHERS: stains, soiling, breaks (quill), losses, deformations, misalignment, insect damage (surface grazing & loss)

GLASS (glass, beads, mirrors): chips, cracks, breaks, scratches, abrasions, wear, losses, stains, soiling, restorations/repairs, salt incrustations, salt efflorescence, sweating or weeping glass/ crazing, iridescence, devitrification

HORN/BONE/ANTLER/IVORY/TEETH chips, cracks/ splits, breaks, scratches, abrasions, wear, losses, checks, warps, buckles, distortions, stains, soiling, restorations/ repairs, fading, discolorations

LACQUER, PAINT, VENEER, GLAZE, ENAMEL GILDING chips, cracks/ splits, breaks, scratches, abrasions, wear, losses, accretions, checks, warps, buckles, distortions, friable, flaking, cleaving, delaminating, stains, soiling, restorations/ repairs, fading, discolorations, tide lines, bloom

Possible Conditions (continued)

METAL:

chips, cracks, breaks, scratches, abrasions, wear, losses, deformations (twisted, bent, dented...), soiling, restorations/ repairs, corrosion:

    silver - dark gray, black

    copper alloys - light green, dark

      green, blue, red, brown, black

    iron or steel - rust red, blue, brown,

      black

    lead, nickel, or tin - gray, white

PLANT MATERIAL:

chips, cracks/ splits, breaks, scratches, abrasions, wear, losses, brittle, friable, checks, warps, buckles, distortions, join failure, loose elements, mold/mildew, insect damage (wood borer), stains, soiling, restorations/repairs, fading, discolorations

PLASTICS:

chips, cracks/ splits, breaks, scratches, abrasions, wear, losses, checks, warps, buckles, distortions, stains, soiling, restorations/ repairs, fading, discolorations, flammable, leaching plasticizers

SHELL:

chips, cracks/ splits, breaks, scratches, abrasions, wear, losses, checks, warps, buckles, distortions, powdery stains, soiling, restorations/ repairs, fading, discolorations

Possible Conditions (continued)

SKIN/ LEATHER/ FUR:
brittle, creases, tears, holes, cracks,/splits, shrinkage, distortions, weak, powdery (red rot), verdigris (contact with copper alloy), spew, mold/ mildew, pest damage (moth, beetle, vermin), hair slippage, stains, soiling, restorations/ repairs, fading, tide lines

STONE:
chips, cracks, breaks, scratches, abrasions, crumbling, wear, losses, salt incrustations, salt efflorescence, spalling, stains, soiling, restorations/ repairs

TEXTILES:
holes, tears, shrinkage, frayed sections, broken threads, pest damage (moth, beetle, vermin), stains, soiling, tide lines, fading, color shift, corrosion (metallic threads)

WOOD:
chips, cracks/ splits, breaks, scratches, abrasions, wear, losses, shrinkage (checks, warps, buckles, distortions), join failure, loose elements, mold/ mildew, insect damage (termite, wood borer), stains, soiling, restorations/ repairs, fading

Definitions

Corrosion: A chemical alteration (texture, color) of the surface of metals.

Deformations: Dents, twists, warps, or bent surface, or structure.

Devitrification: Loss of transparency caused by crystallization or deposition.

Efflorescence: Surface debris, usually white in color, resulting from salts.

Iridescence: A multicolored surface phenomenon resulting from the structural breakdown of glass, enamel, or ceramic glazes.

Spalling: Loss of surface, usually in conchoidal sections, resulting from freeze thaw cycles or salts

Tide Line: A line formed by the movement of water or liquid through a material

Weeping/ Crazing Weeping is an early stage of glass deterioration in which components of the glass have leached out leaving the glass feeling oily or wet. Weeping is associated with humid conditions. Crazing is an interior craquelure pattern which is a result of weeping glass. Crazing is associated with dry conditions.

THE SCIENCE CENTRE & MANAWATU MUSEUM
Te Whare Pupuri Taonga o Manawatu

396 Main Street   Private Bag 11 055   Palmerston North   New Zealand   Phone +64 6 355 5000   Fax +64 6 358 3552

Exhibition Title

INITIAL CONDITION REPORT

EXHIBIT: _____

ACCESSION NO: Sc /   /

EXHIBIT STAND:

Structure:	OK ☐	Damaged ☐	Not applicable ☐
Paintwork / Surface:	OK ☐	Damaged ☐	Not applicable ☐
_____	OK ☐	Damaged ☐	Not applicable ☐

Specify damage:

_____

_____

_____

_____

_____

_____

ACTIVITY PARTS:

Loose exhibit components:	OK ☐	Damaged ☐	Not applicable ☐
Electrics:	OK ☐	Damaged ☐	Not applicable ☐
_____	OK ☐	Damaged ☐	Not applicable ☐
_____	OK ☐	Damaged ☐	Not applicable ☐

Specify damage:

_____

_____

_____

_____

_____

_____

_____

_____

SIGNAGE PANEL:

Structure / Surface:	OK ☐	Damaged ☐	Not applicable ☐
Lettering / Label:	OK ☐	Damaged ☐	Not applicable ☐
Perspex:	OK ☐	Damaged ☐	Not applicable ☐

Specify damage:

_____

_____

_____

_____

_____

Signed: _____   Date: _____

CONDITION REPORT

University Museum
Southern Illinois University at Carbondale
(618) 453-5388

Any item that is in the possesion of the University Museum must have a condition report made for it. This includes loans (to and from the museum) and all items in our permanent collection. Exhibition loans may all be entered on one condition report form with additional pages added if necessary. Fill in all information when applicable; enter N/A when not applicable.

1. Accession/Loan # _____ Report Date _____

2. Lending/Borrowing Institution: _____

   _____

   Date loan received _____ Returned _____

   Number of pieces _____

See Loan Agreement form for further information.

3. This item is:

   ___ on loan to the museum
   ___ on loan from the museum
   ___ a loan to gift status (Date became part of collection _____)
   ___ an extended loan
   ___ a permanent collection item

4. Where will/is item stored?

   ___ Main storage - downstairs   ___ Main storage - upstairs
   ___ Melanesian Storage   ___ Art Storage
   ___ Print Storage   ___ On Loan Campus
   ___ Historic Clothing Room   Location:_____
   ___ Textile Room   ___ On loan to another Person/Institution
   ___ Ethnographic Textile Room   Who:_____

CONDITION REPORT
Page Two

5. Insurance:
   All items on loan must be insured with University Risk Management unless specified otherwise with the borrowing/lending institution.

   Is this item insured? ___ yes   ___ no

   By _____ Date _____

   Value _____

6. Dimensions (inches/centimeters)*:

Height	_____ in.	_____ cm.
Width	_____ in.	_____ cm.
Depth	_____ in.	_____ cm.
Diam/Circum.	_____ in.	_____ cm.

   * Specify if measurements are with or without frame.

7. Descriptive information

   Media: Describe, if possible, materials used in fabrication of the piece.

   Colors:

   Other Descriptive Information: (For example: matted, framed, etc.)

8. Describe the condition of the item. Please look at the piece very thoroughly and denote on which side, top or bottom, front or back, problems occur. Describe the item in terms of the viewer's right and left.

9. Number of crates: _____

   Describe condition of crates:

10. Is any repair needed on an item or crate? If so, be explicit.

    Have any repairs been made on this object? If so, when? _____
    By whom? _____
    Was permission given by the lending institution/person?   ___ yes   ___ no
    Date _____

Examined by _____ Date _____

111

HONOLULU ACADEMY OF ARTS

Accession No.: _____ Exhibit No.: _____ Artist Name: _____

Condition upon un-packing at

__ Condition unchanged

__ Condition changed

_____

_____

_____

_____

_____

Examined by: _____ Date: _____
　　　　　　　Honolulu Academy of Arts Representative

Examined by: _____ Date: _____
　　　　　　　Borrower Representative

Condition upon packing at

__ Condition unchanged

__ Condition changed

_____

_____

_____

_____

_____

Examined by: _____ Date: _____
　　　　　　　Honolulu Academy of Arts Representative

Examined by: _____ Date: _____
　　　　　　　Borrower Representative

112

Buffalo Bill Historical Center • 720 Sheridan Ave. • Cody, Wyoming 82414

CONDITION REPORT

EXHIBITION/LOAN: Date Examined:

TITLE: Accession No.

ARTIST:

SUPPORT:

		CONDITION OF SUPPORT:			
canvas	paper board	draws	cradled	lined	stained
wood	presdwood	sagging	hole	brittle	foxed
paper	panel	patched	torn	creased	mounted
masonite					

MEDIUM:

oil watercolor tempera collage mixt crayon pencil charcoal ink
casein etching lithograph engraving woodcut gouache acrylic

GROUND, PAINT, SURFACE:

cleavage buckling powdered-off flaking blistering abraded scratched
smudged grimy blooming stained finger-printed crackle

FRAME: **BACKING:**
scratched gilt loss nicked dirty rotted solid open wire hooks

---

COMMENTS:

GRAPH OF SHAPE & CONDITION:
glassed
plexiglass

By: _____

ART CARE, INC.
OBJECT/ ARTIFACT FIELD CONDITION REPORT
PRIORITY: 1 2 3 4 5 6

MUSEUM: _____
DESCRIPTION: _____
MANUFACTURER: _____
SIZE: _____

CATALOG #: _____
ARTIST: _____
DATE: _____
EXAMINER: M. Frederickson

MATERIALS:
  Primary: _____
  Secondary: _____

SUPPORT:
___ Insect damage
___ Insect infestation
___ Mold
___ Mildew
___ Scratches
___ Cracked
___ Rotten

___ Splitting/cracked members
___ Loose joints
___ Missing parts
___ Lifting or split veneer
___ Sagging door(s)/drawer(s)
___ Warping
___ Lifting or missing marquetry

___ Worn gilding
___ Worn glaze/enamel
___ Spalling
___ Kiln faults
___ Crizzeling
___ Iridescence
___ Sweating/weeping

___ Worn silver plating
___ Worn engraving
___ Tarnish
___ Rust/corrosion
___ Dents
___ Bronze disease
___ Patina loss

SURFACE TREATMENTS:
___ Varnished
___ Waxed
___ Oiled
___ Painted

___ Flaking
___ Powdering
___ Cracking
___ Scratches

___ Cupping
___ Natural wood
___ Stained
___ Abrasions

___ Water damage
___ Bloom
___ Faded
___ Efflorescence

ATTACHMENTS: _____

PREVIOUS TREATMENTS: _____

STORAGE AND EXHIBIT COMMENTS:
  HOUSING: ___ Stable ___ Biological problem ___ Physical problem ___ Chemical problem

  SUPPORT/MOUNT: ___ Stable ___ Biological problem ___ Physical problem ___ Chemical problem

  ENVIRONMENT: ___ Stable ___ Biological problem ___ Physical problem ___ Chemical problem

AC 106a HP

114

CATALOG #: _____

RECOMMENDED TREATMENT:

___ Written documentation noting the procedures and processes used in the conservation of the object.
___ Photographs provided that document the actual condition of the object before, during, and after treatment.
___ X-ray examination.
___ Fumigation/ infestation control.
___ Test and identify surface coating(s) and solubilities.
___ Removal of surface coatings.
___ Cleaning to reduce the surface dirt and grime.
___ Overpaint removal.
___ Varnish removal.
___ Lining.
___ Tarnish/oxidation removal.
___ Protective coating.
___ Removal of non-original additions _____
___ Replacement of missing elements
___ Reattachment of loose or separated elements _____
___ Reconstruction of missing elements _____
___ Tighten loose joints.
___ Consolidation.
___ Fill voids.
___ Abrasion or scratch removal.
___ Refinish
___ Inpainting of losses only.
___ Construction of protective housing _____
___ Construction of a support _____
___ _____
___ _____
___ _____
___ _____
___ _____
___ _____
___ _____
___ _____
___ _____

ESTIMATED HOURS FOR TREATMENT: _____
ESTIMATED COST OF TREATMENT: _____

115

AC 106b HP

ART CARE, INC.
PHOTOGRAPHIC FIELD CONDITION REPORT
PRIORITY: 1 2 3 4 5 6

MUSEUM: _____
TITLE: _____
SIGNATURE: _____
SIZE: _____

ACCESS. #: _____
ARTIST: _____
DATE: _____
EXAMINER: M. Frederickson

FRAMING: ___ Framed ___ Unframed
— Sound frame
— Weak frame
— Loose miters
— loose/missing ornaments
— Flaking/loss of finish
— Inadequate hanging hardware
— Insect infestation
— Cracked
— Rotten
— Contact with glass
— No dust cover
— Weak/loose rabbet
— Plexiglass

MATTING:
— Acid
— Acid-free
— Dirty
— Slipping
— Abraded
— Other _____
— Yellowed
— Brittle

IMAGE LAYER/PRIMARY SUPPORT:
— Colored
— Toned
— Retouched
— Painted
— Stuck to glass
— Previous treatment _____
— Surface dirt
— Stains
— Cracking
— Losses
— Fogged
— Accretions
— Adhesive residues
— Adhesive staining
— Ink/pencil on surface
— Adhesive tapes on surface
— Tears
— Folds
— Creases
— Collage
— Insect damage/mold
— In fragments

SECONDARY SUPPORT:
— Intact
— Layers peeling
— Light weight
— Medium weight
— Heavy weight
— Losses
— Tears
— Stains
— Weak
— Mold
— Attached to strainer
— Foxing
— Mildew
— Tapes _____
— Concave
— Insect damage
— Abrasions
— Glues _____
— Convex

NOTES:
— Negative on file
— Prints already made
— In adequate housing
— In adequate storage

STORAGE AND EXHIBIT COMMENTS:
_____
_____
_____

116

AC 104a HP

ACCESS. # _____

RECOMMENDED TREATMENT:

| | Written documentation noting the procedures and processes used in the conservation of the object.
| | Unframe.
| | Test for cellulose nitrate.
| | Copy nitrate film.
| | Make copy negative.
| | Make ___ print(s) for display/public usage.
| | Provide storage housing for nitrate film until it can be copied.
| | Photographs to document the actual condition of the object before, during, and after treatment.
| | Photograph written data on front/back.
| | Fumigation/infestation control.
| | Test solubilities.
| | Superficial cleaning where necessary to reduce the surface dirt and grime.
| | Removal of tapes and adhesives.
| | Support removal.
| | Save removed support/matting materials for curator.
| | Stain removal and or reduction to extent safely possible.
| | Wash.
| | Solvent cleaning.
| | Mend tears and breaks.
| | Line.
| | Fill voids.
| | Attach to a supporting backing material.
| | Reduction of creasing and flattening.
| | Removal of previous additions.
| | Stain reduction only carried out to the extent deemed safely possible.
| | Inpainting of losses only.
| | Matting using acid free, non-buffered mat boards and materials to a standard size.
| | Provide protective polyester cover for matted item.
| | Framing.
| | The frame is to be provided by the owner.
| | Ultraviolet filtering plexiglass (UF3) to be utilized in the framing of the object.

ESTIMATED HOURS FOR TREATMENT: _____
ESTIMATED COST OF TREATMENT: _____

AC 104b HP

117

CONDITION REPORT

Two Dimentional: Paintings, Prints, Drawings, Photographs

I.D. # _____   REPORTED BY: _____ DATE: _____

ARTIST: _____

TITLE: _____

OVERALL CONDITION (check one): Excellent ____ Good ____ Fair ____ Poor ____

FRAME:

Losses: _____

Abrasions/Scratches: _____

Soiled/Stained: _____

Miters: _____

Other: _____

IMAGE:

Abrasions/Rubs: _____

Accretions: _____

Cracking: _____

Folds: _____

Tears/Rips: _____

Losses: _____

Repairs: _____

Foxing: _____

Scratches: _____

Soiled/Stained: _____

Surface Distortions (i.e. buckling): _____

Other: _____

CONDITION SURVEY
DEPARTMENT OF CONSERVATION
The Nelson-Atkins Museum of Art
4525 Oak Street, Kansas City, Missouri 64111-1873

TITLE: ACCESSION #:

ARTIST/PROVENANCE: EXAMINED BY:

SIGNATURE/DATE: DATE:

SECTION III: GILT MOULDING/FRAME

DIMENSIONS:

HEIGHT	WIDTH	DEPTH

ORIGINAL:		SURFACE LAYER:	
REPLACEMENT:		SURFACE ABRASION:	
LABELS/ LEGENDS		SPLITS:	
FLAKING GESSO:		WARPING:	
LOSS:		CORNER JOINTS:	
PREVIOUS RESTORATIONS:		RABBET:	
ALTERATIONS:		LOSSES IN SUBSTRATE:	

CONDITION SUMMARY / COMMENTS:

B/W PHOTOS	35MM SLIDES	RADIOGRAPHS	SEM SAMPLE	DENDROCHRONOLOGY

PAINT ANALYSIS	WOOD ANALYSIS	CROSS SECTIONS	INFRARED VIDICON	UV LIGHT EXAM.

CONDITION SURVEY
DEPARTMENT OF CONSERVATION
The Nelson-Atkins Museum of Art
4525 Oak Street, Kansas City, Missouri 64111-1873

TITLE: ACCESSION #:

ARTIST/PROVENANCE: EXAMINED BY:

SIGNATURE/DATE: DATE:

SECTION II: PAINTED SURFACE

TAPE/LABELS:		TENTING / GESSO:	
GRIME:		FLAKING / GESSO:	
DUST:		TENTING / GOLD GROUND:	
ACCRETIONS:		FLAKING / GOLD GROUND:	
DISCOLORATION:		TENTING / PAINT FILM	
ABRASION:		FLAKING / PAINT FILM:	
LOSS:		SURFACE FILM:	
SURFACE ALTERATIONS:			

PREVIOUS RESTORATIONS:

SURFACE COATINGS:		OVER PAINT	
FILLS		INSERTS:	
CONSOLIDATION:			

CONDITION SUMMARY / COMMENTS:

B/W PHOTOS	35MM SLIDES	RADIOGRAPHS	SEM SAMPLE	DENDROCHRONOLOGY
PAINT ANALYSIS	WOOD ANALYSIS	CROSS SECTIONS	INFRARED VIDICON	UV LIGHT EXAM.

CONDITION REPORT - MOUNTED SPECIMENS

Reported by: _____ date: _____

CATALOG NO. _____   COMMON NAME_____

PREPARATOR _____   GENUS/SPECIES _____

PREP. NO. _____   FAMILY _____

NATURE OF SPECIMEN: ____ full mount   __ head & shoulders   __ cast   __ other: _____

NATURE OF BASE / SUPPORT: _____

CONDITION of specimen   __ Excellent   __ Good   __ Fair   __ Poor

Condition of base   __ Excellent   __ Good   __ Fair   __ Poor   __ steady   __ wobbles

IDENTIFYING MARKS/LABELS (list initials, numbers, sketch; note location on specimen)
_____ tag
_____ tatoo
_____ other
_____ none

PREPARATION REPORTS:
_____ prior to mounting
_____ mounting/taxidermy records
date: _____
source: _____

EVIDENCE OF PREVIOUS REPAIRS/TREATMENTS
___ none
___ re-attached parts
___ other _____

BIOLOGICAL DAMAGE
__ none
__ mold / mildew
__ insects   __ active   __ inactive
type insects _____

CHEMICAL DAMAGE
__ none   __ powdery deposits
__ stains   __ crystalline deposits
__ faded (foxed) __ odorous
__ other_____

PHYSICAL DAMAGE

	Broken / Torn	Cracked	Loose	Detached	Grease	Dirty / Dusty	Dry	Holes	Water Damage	Worn spots	Dis-colored	Other
Ears	___	___	___	___	___	___	___	___	___	___	___	___
Antlers/horns	___	___	___	___	___	___	___	___	___	___	___	___
Eye openings	___	___	___	___	___	___	___	___	___	___	___	___
Beaks / bills	___	___	___	___	___	___	___	___	___	___	___	___
Nose region	___	___	___	___	___	___	___	___	___	___	___	___
Mouth	___	___	___	___	___	___	___	___	___	___	___	___
Wings	___	___	___	___	___	___	___	___	___	___	___	___
Legs	___	___	___	___	___	___	___	___	___	___	___	___
Fins	___	___	___	___	___	___	___	___	___	___	___	___
Feet	___	___	___	___	___	___	___	___	___	___	___	___
Tail	___	___	___	___	___	___	___	___	___	___	___	___
Body	___	___	___	___	___	___	___	___	___	___	___	___
Feathers	___	___	___	___	___	___	___	___	___	___	___	___
Hair	___	___	___	___	___	___	___	___	___	___	___	___
Base / Support	___	___	___	___	___	___	___	___	___	___	___	___

COMMENTS:

LOCATION OF SPECIMEN_____

Museum and Art Gallery of the Northern Territory

CONDITION REPORT
PAPER

ACC/REF NO: .... CATALOGUE NO: ....

ARTIST: ....

TITLE: ....

DATE: ....

MEDIA: ....

DIMENSIONS: ....

GENERAL CONDITION...

SUPPORT...

1 Planar distortion:...

2 Physical damage: ....

....

....

....

3 Accretions/discolourations:...

MEDIUM...

4 Adherence:...

5 Losses:...

6 Abrasions:...

MOUNT/MAT...

7 Physical damage: ....

8 Accretions/discolourations:...

FRAME:...

10 Condition:...

GLAZING...

11 Condition:...

OTHER

SPECIAL RECOMMENDATIONS:
Wear clean cotton gloves when handling works.
Environmental parameters -   Relative humidity at 50%±5%, Temperature 20°C±2.5°C
                                    Light levels on paper must not exceed 60 lux.
                                    Ultra violet light must not exceed 75microwatts/lumen.

NAME: DATE:

ROYAL ONTARIO MUSEUM
Registration Department

<u>REQUEST FOR CONSERVATION APPROVAL</u>

PLEASE EXAMINE THE PROPOSED LOAN MATERIAL (see attachments), COMPLETE
COMMENTS AS NEEDED, ENSURE THAT ALL SIGNATURES ARE COMPLETE, AND
RETURN ALL DOCUMENTS TO THE LOANS COORDINATOR, REGISTRATION.

TYPE OF LOAN: DATE:

LENDER: BORROWER:

TITLE OR PURPOSE OF LOAN:

TYPE OF MATERIAL:

LOAN PERIOD (shipping dates):   (out)   (in)

ATTACHMENTS: LISTS: FACILITIES REPORT:
        REQUEST FORM: ITINERARY:
        WORK REQUEST: CONDITION REPORT:

REGISTRATION COMMENTS:

CONSERVATION COMMENTS:

RELATIVE HUMIDITY: TEMPERATURE:

LIGHT LEVELS:

DISPLAY:

OTHER:

TIME REQUIRED FOR CONSERVATION TREATMENT:_____
TIME REQUIRED FOR CONDITION REPORTS: _____
INTERIM CONDITION REPORTS REQUIRED/FREQUENCY: _____
       ( ) APPROVAL RECOMMENDED FOR ALL ITEMS
       ( ) APPROVAL RECOMMENDED WITH RESERVATIONS (see Comments)
       ( ) APPROVAL DENIED (see Comments)

Conservator(s):_____Date:_____

Head of Conservation:_____Date:_____

123

UNITED STATES DEPARTMENT OF INTERIOR
NATIONAL PARK SERVICE

OBJECT TREATMENT REQUEST

BRANCH OF CONSERVATION LABORATORIES
DIVISION OF MUSEUM SERVICES
HARPERS FERRY CENTER

To be completed by Park

PARK	DATE OF REQUEST
OBJECT	CATALOG NO.

Is object owned by NPS?   Yes ☐ No ☐

If no, who authorizes preservation treatment?

Purpose of treatment request (Check boxes below)

PREPARE FOR EXHIBIT ☐	*RESTORE MISSING PARTS* ☐	*CLEAN* ☐	*STABILIZE* ☐
PREPARE FOR STORAGE ☐	*APPLY BARRIER* ☐	*FUMIGATE* ☐	*TREATMENT BY* ☐ *CONTRACTOR*
OTHER: ☐ _____			

Requested date of completion: (State reason for this date: new exhibit, dedication, etc.)

Statement of special importance of object
(e.g.: provenience, association with historic person, importance to collection)

Person to contact should questions concerning treatment arise.

Name:	Title:	Phone No.

NOTE: COPIES OF THE OBJECT'S CATALOG CARD AND PHOTOS (etc.) MUST ACCOMPANY THIS REQUEST.
OBJECTS SHOULD NOT BE SENT UNTIL NOTIFIED BY REGISTRAR, DIVISION OF MUSEUM SERVICES.

Regional use only

APPROVAL ☐ Yes ☐ No	Name:	Title:	Date:
REMARKS			

Laboratory use only

DATE RECEIVED:	CONSERVATOR:	Date object received:
Location:	Total lab hours authorized:	Required completion date:
Photographed: ☐ Yes ☐ No	Total lab hours required:	Date treatment completed:
Date:	Photographer's Name:	Date report completed:
OBJECT RETURNED: Signature:	Title:	Date:

Form 10-252 (5/79) Test

Penobscot Marine Museum
Frame Examination & Rehousing Form

<u>Object:</u> _____   Acq. # _____

Dimensions of Support   (L) _____   (H) _____

<u>Existing Framing & Matting</u>

- Frame Size (L) _____   (H) _____   (W) _____

- Shape: _____   Marks: _____

- Glazing   ☐ No   ☐ Yes   Type: _____

- Window Mat   Type: _____

   (L) _____   (H) _____   Margins: _____

- Back Mat   Type: _____

   Size: _____   Mount: ☐ Yes   ☐ No

- Hinging   Type: _____   Adhesive: _____

Notes: _____

<u>Backing Materials</u>

☐ Cardboard   ☐ Foamcore   ☐ Matboard   ☐ Acid-free

☐ Wooden shakes   ☐ Board   ☐ Dust jacket

   Condition: _____

   Notes: _____

<u>Retaining Hardware</u>

☐ Nails (wire)   ☐ Nails (cut)   ☐ Glazer's points   ☐ Other   ☐ Screw eyes

   Condition: _____

   Notes: _____

<u>Examined by:</u> _____   Date: _____

<u>Rehousing Actions</u>	Date:	By:	Materials Used:
☐ Unframing	_____	_____	_____
☐ Unmatting	_____	_____	_____
☐ Foldering	_____	_____	_____
☐ New Matting	_____	_____	_____
☐ Dimensions:	_____		
☐ New Hinge	_____	_____	_____
☐ Rehoused	_____	_____	_____
☐ Reframed	_____	_____	_____

Notes: _____

Object Worksheet

Use for logging in objects; noting basic cleaning & condition

Entered on database (date):_____

Object: _____   Acc #: _____

Current location: CSC.121   CSC.123   Other: _____   date: _____

Location notes:

Dimensions: H:_____   W:_____   D:_____   Diam:_____
Framed Dimensions: H:_____   W:_____   D:_____   Diam:_____

Basic Description: _____

_____

_____

Marks/Inscriptions: _____

_____

Materials: _____

_____

● ●

Cleaning/Condition

What cleaning methods did you use?

Vacuum cleaner	mineral spirits	water/ethanol	steel wool & WD40
Calcium carbonate	Never-Dull	wire brush	stove polish
Renaissance Wax	Butcher's wax	Photo-Flo	hanging hardware

Does object need further attention: yes   no

What?   More in-house cleaning   re-mounting   conservation

Condition Notes:

Your name: _____   date: _____

DAMAGE REPORT

Date of Report_____

Object #_____   Person Reporting_____

Description_____

Location_____   Photographs: B/W_____   Neg._____

                                                   Color_____   Slide_____

Date of Damage_____   Curator Notified____   Date/Time_____

List Physical Changes that have Occurred to the Object as a Result of the Damage:

_____

_____

_____

_____

Summary of Condition After Damage: **Damage Estimated to Be:**____ structural
_____ generally unsound   ____ surface
_____ generally sound   _____ requires further examination
_____ insecure   _____ requires minor treatment
_____ disfigured   _____ requires major treatment
_____ incomplete   _____ irreparable
_____ stable

                                                 Suggested Treatment:_____
                                                 _____
                                                 _____

Damage Due To: **Artifact Location When Damaged:**
_____ accident   _____ museum exhibit
_____ vandalism   _____ collections storage
_____ deterioration   _____ offsite exhibit
_____ improper handling   _____ offsite storage
_____ water   _____ staging room
_____ insect/rodent   _____ traveling
_____ fire/smoke/heat   _____ other_____
_____ mold/mildew   _____
_____ chemical
_____ other:_____

Were All Pieces/Parts Recovered? _____ Yes _____ No

List Pieces/Parts Missing:_____

Location of Broken Pieces/Parts of Object:_____

Recommendations to Avoid this Type of Damage in the Future:_____

Comments/Clarification:_____

_____

_____

_____

_____

THE RICHARD NIXON ✦ LIBRARY & BIRTHPLACE

DAMAGE REPORT

Date of occurrence: _____

Accession number: _____ Location: _____

Object description and materials of manufacture: _____

_____

Damage due to:

_____ Accident
_____ Vandalism
_____ Deterioration
_____ Water/Heat/Smoke/Mold

Specific cause/events leading to damage: _____

_____

List the physical changes that have occurred to the object as a result of above damage: _____

_____

Were all the pieces of the object recovered? _____

What is missing? _____

_____

Damage estimated to be:

_____ Irreparable

_____ Reparable by the following treatment:

_____

_____

Curator notified _____

_____ Owner/lending institution notified

_____ Photograph taken and attached

Recommendations/Comments: _____

_____

Prepared by: _____ Date: _____

Distribution
Copies to:
○ Director
○ Security
○ Building Engineer
○ File

128

PUBLIC MUSEUM OF GRAND RAPIDS
DAMAGE CHECKLIST

ACCESSION No._____ OBJECT NAME_____

DATE DAMAGE NOTED_____/_____/_____ NOTED BY:_____

DATE   **INITIALS**   **TASK**

_____   _____   ARTIFACT DAMAGE REPORT FILLED OUT AND SENT
TO COLLECTION MANAGER.

_____   _____   DAMAGED OBJECT SECURED AND/OR MOVED.

_____   _____   ATR (ARTIFACT TRACKING RECORD) COMPLETED TO
RECORD NEW LOCATION AND DATE OF MOVEMENT.

_____   _____   CURATOR RECEIVES COPY OF DAMAGE REPORT.

_____   _____   CURATOR INSPECTS DAMAGED OBJECT.

_____   _____   CURATOR RECOMMENDS ACTION:
[] TREATMENT, IN-HOUSE
[] TREATMENT, CONTRACTED
[] NO TREATMENT, STORAGE AS IS
[] OBLITERATION/DISPOSAL

IF RECOMMENDED TREATMENT:

_____   _____   CURATOR COMPLETES TREATMENT PROPOSAL
AND FORWARDS TO COLLECTION MANAGER FOR
COLLECTION COMMITTEE REVIEW

_____   _____   COLLECTION COMMITTEE REVIEWS TREATMENT PROPOSAL
[] APPROVE   []DISAPPROVE

_____   _____   CURATOR PREPARES WORK ORDER FOR MOVEMENT/
SHIPMENT OF OBJECT FOR TREATMENT

_____   _____   TREATMENT COMPLETED & TREATMENT LOG SENT TO CM
RECORDS OFFICE.

_____   _____   OBJECT STORED AND/OR RETURNED TO EXHIBIT AND
TRACKED ON ATR THAT IS SENT TO CM RECORDS
OFFICE.

IF RECOMMENDED NO TREATMENT, STORAGE:

_____   _____   CURATOR COMPLETES WORK ORDER REQUESTING
STORAGE OF OBJECT

_____   _____   OBJECT STORED AND TRACKED ON ATR WHICH IS
FORWARDED TO THE CM RECORDS OFFICE

IF RECOMMENDED OBLITERATION/DISPOSAL:

_____   _____   CURATOR COMPLETES DEACCESSION RECOMMENDATION
*** CONTINUE WITH "DEACCESSION CHECKLIST" ***

Anthropology Division
University of Nebraska State Museum

PEST INFESTATION CONTROL

Catalogue # _____   Object name _____

Object materials: _____

Basic construction: _____

_____

Observed pest problem (use codes below): _____
(e.g., A/1=dermestid frass, D/4 & 6=wood-boring beetle tunnels & carcasses)

type of pest		evidence of infestation
A. dermestid	G. fly/wasp	1. frass
B. clothes moth	H. rodent	2. specks
C. silverfish/firebrat	I. cockroach	3. droppings
D. wood-boring (powder post) beetle	J. spider	4. tunnels/holes
E. cigarette/drugstore beetle	K. termites	5. cast skins
F. other _____	L. undetermined	6. carcass
		7. webbing
LIVE PEST _____		8. egg casings
		9. casings
Comments: _____		10. other _____

_____

Control Measures Undertaken

_____ 1a. Object cleaned of pest debris   _____ 1b. Object sealed in bag for life-cycle observation

_____ 2. Pesticide   date: _____   pesticide: _____
                   description of treatment process (include amount and duration):

_____ 3. Freezing   date: _____   temperature: _____   duration: _____

_____ 4. Oxygen deprivation date: _____   description of process:

name & date _____

Infestation Report - Collections/Divisions
The Museum of Texas Tech University • P.O. Box 4499, Lubbock, Texas 79409

1. Date of Report: _____

2. Date of Infestation Detection: _____

3. Person Investigating: _____

4. Collection/Division involved: _____

5. Specific location of infestation: _____

6. Identification of Infesting Organism:_____
     Life stage(s): _____
     Measurements:_____

7. Target material:_____

8. General description of infestation and extent of damage:_____
_____
_____
_____

9. Action(s) indicated: 1) _____
                             _____

                             2) _____
                             _____

                             3) _____
                             _____

10. Chemical/Physical agent(s) used:
     Repellant:_____
     Fumigant:_____
     Freeze Chamber: ☐   Temp:_____ Duration:_____

11. Recommended follow-up procedures :
     1) _____
                   _____

     2) _____
                   _____

     3) _____
                   _____

     4) _____
                   _____

Report filed by: _____
                     name   title

Copies to: Director   Curator(s) of collection(s)
              Assistant Director for Operations   Registrar
              Collection Manager, Humanities   Collection Manager, NSRL

Pest Management Log

Nelson-Atkins Museum of Art (6/97)

Accessibility

☐ tool ☐ key ☐ alarm

Materials of Concern

☐ wood ☐ textile ☐ organic
☐ ivory ☐ paper ☐ other
☐ panel painting ☐ canvas ptg.

Trap Type

☐ Bell
☐ Woodstream

Trap location notes:

☐ see reverse

Environment Monitored

☐ open display

Closed Display

☐ wall case
☐ free standing case

Room Type

☐ gallery ☐ storage
☐ Inside Object

Monitored By

☐ visual inspection
☐ single trap
☐ multi trap

trap #_____ of _____

Object Location

Gallery #_____

Gallery Name_____

Case _____

Department_____

Object #(s)_____

_____

_____

Title/Name_____

_____

date	party	trap active	condition inactive	specimen live	dead	sample #	trap new	replaced	visual inspection	vacuumed	probation	fumigation	Observations

CURATORIAL

MUSEUM of
WESTERN
COLORADO

Accredited By The American Association of Museums
Museum of Western Colorado
Sites: History Museum, Cross Orchards Living History Farm, Dinosaur Valley
P.O. Box 20000-5020, Grand Junction, CO 81502-5020
(970) 242-0971 X 211

APPLICATION FOR ACCESS TO MUSEUM COLLECTIONS

INSTRUCTIONS: Complete all applicable areas and submit a current resume and research design (if requested) for review. Read all conditions on back of form before signing.

1. NAME OF APPLICANT: _____

2. ORGANIZATION: _____

3. DATE OF APPLICATION: _____   4. PHONE: _____

5. COLLECTIONS TO BE USED:

_____ BLM-CRM Collection

_____ MWC Anthropology Collection

_____ History Collection

_____ Other (specify): _____

6. SPECIFY MATERIAL TO BE USED (collection name, site number, accession number, material(s), etc.):

7. NATURE OF PROPOSED USE AND IMPACT ON COLLECTIONS:

8. DATES OF USE (PREFERRED): From _____   To _____

                  (ALTERNATE): From _____   To _____

9. APPLICANT'S SIGNATURE: _____

DO NOT WRITE BELOW THIS LINE - FOR MUSEUM USE ONLY
_____

DATE OF ACTION: _____

_____ APPROVED _____ DENIED

_____   _____
Authorized Museum Representative Signature   Title

Collections Access

Collections and records may be made available for examination and study to qualified individuals after approval by the Curator of the collection. Appropriate forms will be sent on request and must be completed and returned to the Registrar. (See **Application for Access to Museum Collections** form.) All Museum security and handling requirements must be met. The Museum of Western Colorado does not allow open, unmonitored access to the Museum's storage areas or collections.

Requests for Access

Requests for access should be made at least one week in advance. A written description of the proposed project and a list of the objects to be accessed should accompany the request. Researchers may be required to submit a resume and research design. Verbal requests for short term access by previously approved individuals will be granted if time and personnel allow. Access to CRM Collections will also be governed by the owning agencies guidelines and policies.

Conditions Governing Access to Collections

1.   If granted access, applicant agrees to abide by the Museum's guidelines for handling and using Museum collections as found in its Collections Management Plan.

2.   Applicant agrees to provide full acknowledgement of the Museum in any publication, report, film, photograph, etc., which utilizes material or information derived from any use of the Museum's collections. In the case of CRM collections, the Bureau of Land Management will also be acknowledged.

3.   Applicant agrees to provide the Museum with a copy of any report or publication that results from, describes, or refers to the proposed study. If no reports or papers are available within two years, a letter describing the results of the study should be sent to the Registrar.

4.   Applicant agrees that the Museum may, without special permission, utilize any findings, interpretations or conclusions resulting from the proposed study in interpretive exhibits or programs, understanding that the Museum agrees to acknowledge/credit any work and findings.

5.   All catalog, accession, and archival records that are the property of the Museum shall be treated as public information unless the data are excluded 1) under state and federal freedom of information acts, 2) under state and federal antiquities laws, or 3) are covered by copyright laws.

   a)   Site locations and other sensitive or restricted information are not available for open or casual use by the public.
   b)   Sensitive information may be open wholly or in part to qualified individuals with approved research projects. Prior permission for access to sensitive information will need to be obtained from owners of CRM collections.
   c)   Data may be studied on site only and may not be duplicated.
   d)   No original document from the CRM collections will be loaned.

6.   Human remains will be made available only to serious and qualified researchers with approved projects and research designs.

7.   No researcher may do anything which will alter the appearance of an object or document without written permission of the Museum of Western Colorado. This includes conservation, cleaning, casting, or sampling for testing.

8.   Restrictions may be placed on fragile materials. These may include:

   a)   handling restricted to collections staff
   b)   handling is not permitted
   c)   access may be denied, in which case photographs or drawings may be supplied at cost

9.   Prior written permission from the Museum of Western Colorado is required before photographs are taken of collections artifacts. Commercial use of such photographs require payment of a fee to the Museum.

10. Commercial use of the collections is subject to a fee. Individual or academic research projects may be considered commercial if a saleable product results.

11. Behind the scenes tours may be given for specific purposes. Prior approval and scheduling is required. Group sizes will be limited.

P.O. Box 2087
Santa Fe, New Mexico
87504-2087

505 827-6344
FAX 827-6497

Museum of
Indian Arts & Culture
Laboratory of Anthropology

REQUEST FOR ACCESS TO COLLECTIONS

The MIAC/Lab Collections are held in public trust and use of the collections is encouraged. Please fill out pertinent information below and read and sign the procedures on the back of this form. Please return to the appropriate curator before visiting the collections.

Name(s):_____ Date:_____
Title, Institution, and Address:_____
_____

Describe as explicitly as possible the collections you wish to see:
_____
_____

Type of access requested (check all that apply):
_____Examine specimens   _____Photograph/draw specimens yourself
_____Have Museum photograph specimens   _____General tour
_____Other:_____

Examination of collections is for following purpose (check all that apply):
_____Publication of these specimens   _____Independent research
_____Class project   _____Identification/comparison
_____Exhibit or other loan   _____General interest
_____Other:_____

Describe as explicitly as possible the project on which you are working:
_____
_____

Date(s) you wish access:_____ Time required:_____

Professional references or instructor/project
supervisor:_____

****
FOR COLLECTIONS DIVISION USE ONLY
Date received_____ Approved
by:_____
Type of access granted (check all that apply):
_____accompanied by curator   _____removal of specimens from storage
_____unaccompanied by curator   _____photography/illustration
_____one-time access   _____general tour
_____continuing access   _____no access granted
Other forms needed: _____Photo Request _____Scientific Testing _____Loan Request
Notes/Special Conditions:_____
Curator(s):_____
Staff time required:_____

New Mexico
Office of Cultural Affairs

VISITOR GUIDELINES FOR WORKING WITH MIAC/LAB COLLECTIONS

The following procedures apply to everyone to ensure the preservation and safe handling of collections:

- **Visitors should notify the Curator by filling out this form at least two weeks in advance.**

- **Visitors are advised that access to collections for contract-supported or for-profit research purposes is subject to the assessment of fees for curatorial staff time at $25.00/hour. (See Photo Services Fee Schedule for fees connected with photography of collection items.)**

BEFORE ENTERING COLLECTIONS:
- Backpacks, purses, coats, etc. are not permitted in collection storage areas. Pencils, notebooks, and other paraphernalia necessary for research are permitted, however, pens, markers, and sharp implements are not permitted.
- Food, drinks, smoking, and chewing gum are not permitted in storage areas.
- Visitors should not touch or handle objects unless allowed by the accompanying Curator. All visitors must wash hands before handling collections.
- Rings, necklaces, large jewelry, belt buckles, hanging glasses, and other protruding paraphernalia can damage artifacts. These items must be removed before working with collections.

WORKING WITH COLLECTIONS:
- Minimal handling of collections is optimal. Before handling, inspect the object for surface damage or structural weakness. Curators may refuse to allow handling of artifacts if doing so would be unduly hazardous to the object.
- Sampling is not permitted. Requirements for sampling/scientific testing must be approved by the Collections Committee.
- Certain objects will require handling with gloves. Many organic objects have been treated with chemicals or pesticides. Dust masks and respirators are available upon request.
- Handle one object at a time with both hands supporting the base. Never handle objects by appendages such as rims, handles, straps, spouts, etc. Do not place objects in a precarious position and use padding if necessary.
- If an object is housed in a container, handle the container and not the object. If an object is wrapped or in a closed box, put the container on a surface, then unwrap or open carefully checking the wrappings for fragments.
- Save any object fragments, labels, tags, or information and keep them with the artifact. Notify the Curator of such instances.
- Never remove or undo repairs, tape, glue, stitching, etc. from an artifact.
- If any type of accidental damage does occur, do not attempt any remedial action by collecting fragments or putting them together. Notify the Curator immediately.
- Any evidence of insect infestation or other uncharacteristic activity should be reported to the Curator immediately. Do not move the affected artifact.

PHOTOGRAPHY OF COLLECTION ITEMS:
- **Photography of collection objects is subject to reproduction, photo services, and publication fees. These fees must be negotiated with the Curator before photography occurs (see Photo Services Fee Schedule).**
- Photographers must provide all their equipment. We encourage the use of flash or strobes to minimize the effects of light and heat on artifacts. The MIAC/Lab is not responsible for non-museum photographic equipment and will not store it.
- Artifacts should be photographed with minimal handling and will not be arranged in any manner detrimental to them. No alterations, repairs, or cleaning can be attempted.
- Artifacts may not be taken from the area specified for photography without permission.
- Photography of certain objects may be subject to restrictions.
- **Permission to photograph artifacts does not imply permission to publish/reproduce such materials. Requests for permission to publish/reproduce must be submitted in writing and approved by the Curator.**

I HAVE READ AND WILL COMPLY WITH THE TERMS OF THE PROCEDURES AND CONDITIONS SET FORTH AND OUTLINED HEREIN.

Signature_____**Date**_____

rev. 11/96

University of Denver Museum of Anthropology

2130 South Race St. • Denver, CO 80208 • (303) 871-4384 • FAX (303) 871-2736

Request For Collections Access

Name of Person Requesting Access: _____

Title: _____

Affiliation: _____

Address: _____

City: _____ State: _____ Zip: _____ e-mail: _____

Telephone: _____ FAX: _____ Local Telephone: _____

Local Address: _____

City: _____ State: _____ Zip: _____

Requested Appointment Date: _____ Time: _____

Requested Appointment Date: _____ Time: _____

Reason for Request: _____

Title of Project/Paper: _____

Final Product(s): _____

Estimated Date of Publication/Presentation: _____

Artifacts Required for Research:	1.	6.
	2.	7.
	3.	8.
	4.	9.
	5.	10.

Documentation Required for Research:	1.	6.
	2.	7.
	3.	8.
	4.	9.
	5.	10.

Geographic Region(s): _____ Cultures: _____

Granting or Funding Source: _____

Proposed Activities:
_____ Examine artifacts
_____ Examine documentation
_____ Take photographs for research purposes only
_____ Make photocopies of documentation
_____ Obtain photographs for purposes other than research
_____ Other: _____

NATURAL SCIENCES CATALOGUE SHEET

Page
of

P1

specimen/lot number R	specimen/lot ? R	accession number R	collection type R
department	museum collection	previous numbers	A.O.U. number
catalogue number	quantity R	number of elements R	element number

element name	element name modifier
general identification R	lithology
common name	
taxonomic group	former taxonomic group
type status	

overall measurements: R dimension/unit measure remarks	part measurements: dimension/unit/part/measure remarks

C

description

C

specimen location R date R	move purpose date out date in

C

source R	acquisition mode R acquisition date R

collector	collection date	collection method

collection remarks

locality

cataloguer R catalogue date R	specimen/lot numbered R YES/NO	Transfer of Ownership completed R YES/NO	specimen restrictions YES/NO

P2

identifier R	identification date R

identifier remarks

sex	sexing method	age/stage of development	fat class

condition R	examiner name R examination date R

condition remarks

C

R = REQUIRED FIELDS   CDM 20

conservation future R	R follow-up date

conservation treatment	treatment date	conservator

conservation file number	conservation remarks

breeding data	diet data	skeleton/skull

preparator	date prepared	preparation technique

preparation remarks	record restrictions YES/NO

P3

tax receipt requested YES/NO	tax receipt date

appraisal purpose	appraisal date	appraised value $	appraiser

purchase price $	purchase remarks

C

cataloguers remarks	cataloguer's references	cataloguers sources

loan history	sketch or photo
exhibition history	
publications	

C

photo required YES/NO	photographer	photo date

negative number	microfiche/film number	other media

disposition mode	date	recipient

disposition remarks

VMNH Paleo Catalog Sheet - individual specimens

DATE: _____

CATALOG NO.: _____

FIELD NO. (collector/s no. for individ. specimen): _____

OTHER NO. (field no. for locality, etc.) : _____

VMNH LOCALITY NO.: _____   VMNH LOT NO.: _____

ORDER: _____   FAMILY: _____

GENUS: _____   SPECIES: _____

AUTHORITY: _____

IDENTIFIED BY: _____   DATE id.: _____

LOCALITY NAME: _____

GEOLOGICAL/LOCALITY REMARKS: _____

_____

SQUARE: _____   LEVEL NO.: _____(from _____ to _____)   DEPTH: _____

QUAD: _____   COORDINATES: _____   MESH SIZE: _____

COLLECTOR: _____

DATE COLLECTED: _____

TYPE OF SPECIMEN (circle all that apply):   FOSSIL   CAST / MOLD   MODEL / REPRODUCTION   TRACKWAY

TOTAL QUANTITY OF ELEMENTS: _____

TYPE OF ELEMENTS: _____

_____

_____

_____

CONDITION /PREPARATION RECORD?   YES   NO

CONDITION REMARKS: _____

_____   ANCILLARY MATERIALS
(circle all that apply):

_____   Field Notes
Maps
Negatives
Prints
PHOTO NO.: _____   SLIDE NO.: _____   Photo Slides
SEM Samples

TYPE: _____

FIGURED: YES   NO

CITATION: _____

_____

ASSOCIATED SPECIMENS: _____

_____

STORAGE LOCATION: _____

RESTRICTIONS: _____

REMARKS: _____

_____

23 Oct 91

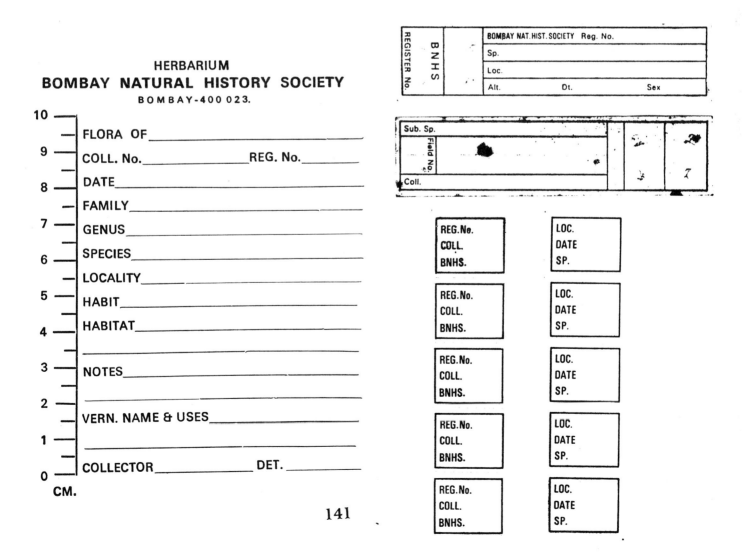

Durban Natural Science Museum, P.O.Box 4085   **BIRDS**

DM No _____ Date _____ Sex _____
Name _____
Locality _____
_____
Collector _____ Skinner _____

NOTES:

_____ ° _____ 'S; _____ ° _____ E

HABITAT: _____
_____
_____

HERBARIUM
BOMBAY NATURAL HISTORY SOCIETY
BOMBAY-400 023.

FLORA OF_____

COLL. No._____ REG. No._____

DATE_____

FAMILY_____

GENUS_____

SPECIES_____

LOCALITY_____

HABIT_____

HABITAT_____

_____

NOTES_____

_____

VERN. NAME & USES_____

_____

COLLECTOR_____ DET. _____

10
9
8
7
6
5
4
3
2
1
0
CM.

REGISTER No.   **B N H S**

BOMBAY NAT. HIST. SOCIETY Reg. No.
Sp.
Loc.
Alt.   Dt.   Sex

Sub. Sp.
Field No.
Coll.

REG.No. COLL. BNHS.	LOC. DATE SP.
REG.No. COLL. BNHS.	LOC. DATE SP.
REG.No. COLL. BNHS.	LOC. DATE SP.
REG.No. COLL. BNHS.	LOC. DATE SP.
REG.No. COLL. BNHS.	LOC. DATE SP.

141

MINERAL CATALOG SHEET

Catalog #: _____   Accession #: _____

Registration #: _____   Other #'s: _____

Class: _____

Common Name: _____

Locality: _____

Date Collected: _____

Geologic Formation: _____   Geologic Date: _____

Collector: _____

Preparator: _____

Physical Properties

Color: _____   Luster: _____

Hardness: _____   Cleavage: _____

Measurements: _____   Weight: _____

Chemical Makeup: _____

Matrix: _____

Crystal Formation: _____

Fluorescent: _____ Yes _____ No   Color: _____

Other Description: _____

Permanent Location: _____   Location Date: _____

Loan Location: _____   Loan Dates: _____

Inventory Status: _____   Inventory Date: _____

Subjects/Themes: _____

Condition Note: _____

Restrictions: _____

Conservation Activity: _____

How Acquired: _____   Acquisition Date: _____

Value: _____   Value Date: _____

Appraiser: _____

Source: _____

Designation: _____ (A=Fine specimen   B=Study/Research specimen, Exhibit material   C=Educational specimen)

Photo: _____ Yes _____ No   Note: _____

Notes: _____

_____

_____

_____

_____

_____

Cataloger: _____   Cataloging Date: _____

GENERAL HISTORY/ART CATALOGUE SHEET

record number	object number R	object term R

department	collection type	museum collection	theme	previous numbers

quantity   1

component I.D.

no. of components _____

component name

alternate name

title/variation		subject/image

| overall measurement:

dimension/unit/measurement R	part:	dimension/unit/measurement R	remarks

C

material R	technique R	medium	support

C

producer role R	producer name R

date of production R	place of production R	notes on production

serial number / model number	brand name / model name R

marks / labels / inscriptions / signature	edition number or patent or © nos / dates / country

C

brief description   R

C

condition R	date / examiner name R	functional state

condition remarks

C

conservation future R	follow-up date R

C

location R	date R

| source name   R | acquisition mode   R   acquisition date | object numbered

YES / NO | object restrictions

YES / NO |
|---|---|---|---|

| cataloguer   R | catalogue date | transfer of ownership completed

YES / NO | acknowledgement sent

YES / NO |
|---|---|---|---|

.to Catalogue Binder

move	date out	date in

culture 1 (nationality) R	culture 2	

place of use R	place of origin R	cultural tradition

current owner	original owner	other previous owner(s)

associated with	nature of association date	notes on association

history of use R	R	historical context

conservation treatment	treatment date	file number
conservation remarks		conservator
photo required R YES / NO	record restrictions YES / NO	

batch number R	tax receipt requested YES / NO	tax receipt date
appraisal purpose appraisal date	appraised value $	appraiser
purchase price $ purchase remarks		
catalogue number cataloguer's remarks		
cataloguer's references	cataloguer's sources	

inscription translation		
copyright restrictions copyrighter YES / NO	credit / acknowledgement to?	
military unit	school / style	merchant
photo date negative number photographer	microfiche/film number	other media

loan history	sketch or photo
exhibition history	
publications	
	disposition mode date recipient

MASTER INFORMATION CARD OF THE GOVERNMENT MUSEUM AND ART GALLERY (MIC-GOMAG), CHANDIGARH, INDIA
(A computer based documentation system of works of art in multimedia)

ACADEMIC	ADMINISTRATIVE
1. Category of object:	1. Unit no.:
2. Title:	2. Entry register no.:
3. Medium/material/technique:	3. Accession register no.:
4. Provenance:	4. Source:
5. Date/period:	5. Mode of acquisition:
6. Style/school:	6. Price/value :
7. Tribe/dynasty/community/patron:	7. Photo-negative/slide no.:
8. Artist:	8. Photograph/video/audio cassette no.:
9. Dimention/ weight/denomination(coin):	9. Location:
10. Brief Description:	10. Condition of the object:
	11. Restoration done, if any:
11. Inscription:	12. Last update:
12. Original source information:	
13. Published source references:	Photograph
14. Remarks/comments:	

Catalouged by: Condition report by: Photographed by: Supervised by:

COSTUME HISTORY

Mint

Museum

of Art

Costume Accession Number: _____

Costume Title/Description : _____

_____

Circa Date: _____

Donor Name: _____

Original Owner of Costume: _____

Relation to Donor: _____

Birth place/date: _____

Death place/date: _____

Wedding place/date: _____

Residence while Costume was Worn: _____

Photograph: **Y N**   Photograph of Owner in Costume: **Y N**   Available for Copy: **Y N**

Biographical Information: _____

_____

_____

_____

Costume History (where worn, occasion, season, misc.): _____

_____

_____

_____

Accessories Included: _____

Manufacturer/Maker/Retailer: _____

_____

Alterations/Repairs: _____

Family History: _____

_____

Celebrating Our 60th Year!

Date: _____

2730 Randolph Road   Charlotte, NC 28207-2031   704-337-2000   Fax 704-337-2101

146

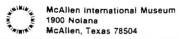

McAllen International Museum
1900 Nolana
McAllen, Texas 78504

CATALOGUE RECORD, TEXTILE

OBJECT NUMBER	LOC CODE	CATALOGUE NUMBER

OBJECT NAME

ALT NAMES	PIECES

TITLE

TITLE TRANS

MAKER NAME	CATEGORY

SUBCAT	SECTION	SUBSECT	TYPE

DESCRIPTION

DIMENSION 1	DIM 2	DIM 3	OTHER DIM

SUB/IMAGE	AGE ASSOC	GENDER ASSOC

FUNCTION

DECORATIVE MOTIF

FIBER TYPE

THREAD DIAMETER

THREAD COUNT

COLORS

COLOR REF	DYES

TECHNIQUE

MATERIAL

COMPONENT PARTS

COMPLETION DATE	SIGNATURE LOC

MARKS/LABELS

CONT	COUNTRY	STATE/PROV

COUNTY	REGION

SPECIFIC LOC

SITE PHOTOS

CULT CONTEXT	SCHOOL/STYLE

HIST PERIOD	DATING TECHNIQUE

COLLECTOR	COLL DATE	FIELD NO

PREV COLL NO	PREPARATOR	PREP DATE

PREPARATION

ID BY	CATALOGUER	DEACC DATE

REF

SPECIAL INSTR

ACKNOWLEDGEMENT

REMARKS

PUBLICATIONS

CATALOGUE RECORD, FOLK/DECORATIVE ART

OBJECT NUMBER		LOC CODE		CATALOGUE NUMBER	

OBJECT NAME

ALT NAMES		PIECES

TITLE

TITLE TRANS

MAKER NAME		CATEGORY	

SUBCAT	SECTION	SUBSEC	TYPE

DESCRIPTION

DIMENSION 1	DIM 2	DIM 3	OTHER DIM

SUB/IMAGE		AGE ASSOC		GENDER ASSOC

FUNCTION

DECORATIVE MOTIF

COLORS

COLOR REF	MEDIUM

TECHNIQUE

MATERIAL

COMPONENT PARTS

COMPLETION DATE	SIGNATURE LOC

MARKS/LABELS

	© DATE

© HOLDER		© PLACE	

© AGREEMENT	CONTINENT	COUNTRY

STATE/PROVINCE	REGION

COUNTY	SPECIFIC LOCALITY

CULT CONTEXT

SCHOOL/STYLE	HIST PERIOD

SITE PHOTOS

DATING TECHNIQUE		COLLECTOR

COLLECTION DATE	FIELD NUMBER	PREVIOUS COLL NO

PREPARATION

PREPARATOR	PREP DATE	ID BY

CATALOGUER	DEACC DATE

REF

SPECIAL INSTR

ACKNOWLEDGEMENT

REMARKS

PUBLICATIONS

QUILT CATALOG FORM
PANHANDLE-PLAINS HISTORICAL MUSEUM

Accession no. _____ Size (l x w) _____ Location _____

Donor _____

Provenance/Background Information _____

_____

Name of maker _____ Date made _____

Pattern _____

Description _____

_____

_____

Techniques:

    Fabrics used _____

    Pieced _____

    Applique _____

    Reverse-applique _____

    Printed whole-cloth top _____

    All-white top _____

    Backing _____

    Decorative quilting or tying _____

    Embroidery _____

    Stuffing _____

    Binding _____

    Hand-sewn or machine sewn _____

Unusual characteristics _____

_____

Condition: ___Excellent ___Good ___Fair ___Poor ___Stable ___Unstable

Comments _____

_____

Cataloguer _____ Date catalogued _____

149

GENERAL RECORD SHEET

Registration number	

Object name: _____

Object donation no: _____   Office file no: _____   Registration photograph no: _____

Donor/vendor: _____

Acknowledgment condition (as appropriate): _____

Purchase price: _____   Donation/purchase date: _____

Date of manufacture: _____   Manufacturer's name: _____   Place of manufacture: _____

Dimensions: _____

Materials: _____

_____

Condition: _____

_____

Description: _____

_____

_____

_____

Provenance: _____

_____

_____

References: _____

_____

Subject areas: _____

Associated name/s: _____

Associated locality: _____

Classification:			

Previous registration number:	
Current location:	

Number	
Register	
Thank you letter	

Accessioned by:

GENERAL RECORD SHEET DATA FIELDS

Object name
Use Australian/History Trust of South Australia museum thesaurus to describe an object.

Use simple terms such as book, boots, dress, anchor, candleholder. Avoid descriptive terms. For example when referring to a dress avoid terms like yellow, day or floral.   Such descriptions are recorded elsewhere on the sheet.

Registration photograph number
Enter the object's registration photograph number here.

Office file number
Enter all relevant museum official office yellow file numbers here.

Object donation number
Enter the number from the object donation form here.

Donor/vendor
Enter the donor's/vendor's full name and address.

Acknowledgment condition.
Note any special display, publication or other conditions on the public use of donor's name.

Purchase price
Enter the purchase price in Australian dollars as relevant.

Date of manufacture
Enter the date of manufacture. Research will be required to verify donor/vendor information or to ascertain approximations.

Manufacturer's name
Enter the full name of the object's manufacturer/s.

Place of manufacture
Enter the primary location where the object was made, assembled or created.

Dimensions
Accurate measurements of objects dimensions and other important characteristics such as mass, power, displacement are to be made before this data is recorded.

Australian standard SI metric units are to be used.

The recording of non-metric units may be relevant in the case of historic specifications such as engine power, ship displacements or lighthouse brightness. The dual recording of accurate metric conversions is desirable.

Obviously, actual calculations of such things as ship displacements or piston bore sizes may be too difficult or unnecessary. Manufacturer's specifications may be recorded if appropriate but should be clearly identified as such.

In general, use a prefix to unambiguously record a measurement:

h	height
l	length
b	breadth
w	width
d	depth
diam	diameter

Dimensions are recorded in standard *length x breadth x height* order.

Millimetres (mm) should be used to measure length. Metres (m) would be appropriate for large objects such as ships and aircraft. The extreme ends of an object should be measured for length.

Grams (g) should be used to measure mass. Kilograms (kg) would be appropriate for large objects such as cars. Tonnes (t) would be appropriate for larger objects such as ships.

The emphasis must be on *accurate* measurements. This is vital for a range of reasons including:

- object monitoring for change in dimensions
- identification of damage
- organisation of appropriate storage
- construction of display and storage supports and cases without handling the object
- aiding repairs and treatments
- detection of fakes

Materials
Use simple terms such as cotton, oak, ivory, electro-plated silver, cast iron. Always list materials in order of dominance. For example, a pair of boots with rubber soles and brass eyelets will be described as leather, rubber and brass. Indicate on the record sheet any uncertainty regarding materials. Do not be descriptive, eg green silk, red painted metal.

Condition
List defects, stain, breakage, crack, mould growth, area of rust etc. It is important to note where the affected areas are. Do not use terms such as good, bad, poor, sound or excellent without qualification.

Detailed information will assist identification of changes in object condition which may occur while in storage, on display or on loan to another institution.

Description
Describe the object's physical attributes, its shape, texture, colours, finish, decoration or brief specification of machinery and equipment.

State whether it was naturally created, handmade or machine made. Particular details need to be recorded which distinguish the object from similar ones eg brands, trademarks and serial numbers.

Include descriptions of modifications which could indicate the period of the object. Its purpose should also be included if it is not obvious.

Provenance
Enter detailed history of the object. Include aspects of manufacture, use, association with people, events and places.

References
List the references and sources of information used in compiling the entries for this form/database.

Subject areas
Use the divisional/History Trust authority list.

For example, a dress worn in Burra by a Cornish woman who decorated the bodice front with traditional embroidery could have the following subject areas from its authority list:

    South Australia/copper
    Mining history/copper
    Cornish/handcrafts
    Handcrafts/embroidery   (Note according to the appropriate terms on the form).

Associated name
Complete if the object was associated with a person, company or institution of prominence or historical interest.
Person, name, institution.

Associated locality
Complete if the object was connected to the history of a particular town, region or country.
Big to small.

Classification
Classification is a means of sorting the collection into sections. The History Trust of South Australia uses the West Australian Museum Summerfield classification system with divisional variations according to need. Classify objects by what they are, not by their use. For example a woman's dress worn at the goldfields should be classified from the general to the specific as COSTUME, female, dress, and not as MINING HISTORY, Gold, Ballarat. This information is important to list under subject areas or associated name or associated locality.

Previous registration number
Enter previous registration numbers of the object if it has been transferred or donated from an institution other than the History Trust.

Current location
Indicate where the object is stored by entering the storage code.

Number
Indicate with a tick that the object has been physically numbered.

Register
Indicate with a tick that details have been completed in the divisional register. At this point indicate in the divisional register that the object has been accessioned.

Thank you letter
If donated indicate with a tick that an acknowledgement letter and certificate, if one is used by the division, has been sent to the donor. These should be sent when records are transferred onto card or computer.

Accessioned by
Curator's name.

ACCESSION NUMBER: _____ **CATALOGUE NUMBER:** _____

PREVIOUS NUMBER(S): _____ , _____ ,

NAME OF OBJECT: _____

MATERIAL:

PREVIOUSLY BOXED WITH:

ASSOC. NOTES OR TAGS: (don't forget to record the catalogue number on the old tag!)

HISTORY OF OWNERSHIP:

GEOGRAPHICAL INFORMATION

CONTINENT: _____	**SURFACE FIND?** _____	**EXCAVATION?** _____
COUNTRY: _____	**SMITHSONIAN:** _____
STATE/PROV. _____	**QUADRANGLE:** _____
COUNTY/CITY: _____	**SITE NAME:** _____
OTHER: _____	**T/R/S:** _____
FEDERAL LAND? YES NO UNKNOWN	**UTM GRID:** _____
DATE OF EXCAVATION:	**PROJECT PARTICIPANTS:**

NATIVE AMERICAN GRAVE PROTECTION AND REPATRIATION ACT

☐ **HUMAN REMAINS;** ☐ **ASSOCIATED FUNERARY OBJECT;**

☐ **SACRED/ CEREMONIAL/ CULTURAL PATRIMONY;** ☐ **UNASSOCIATED FUNERARY OBJECT**

WHO MADE IT?: _____ **WHO USED IT?** _____

CULTURAL PERIOD: _____

TIME PERIOD OF MANUFACTURE: _____ **TIME PERIOD OF USE:** _____

DESCRIPTION (nature of material(s); markings; manufacture; use):

DIMENSIONS: H: ___ **cm. L:** ___ **cm. Depth/Diameter:** ___ **cm. Weight:** ___ **gm.**

CONDITION REPORT

  EXCELLENT..............GOOD....................FAIR....................POOR (circle one)

CONSERVATION REQUIREMENTS

HIGH PRIORITY.....MODERATE PRIORITY.....LOW PRIORITY.....NONE REQUIRED

PHOTOGRAPHY

_____ **B & W CONTACT PRINT;** _____ **35 mm SLIDE;** _____ **COLOR PRINT;**

B & W PRINT; **OTHER:** _____

CATALOGUER'S NAME: _____ **DATE:** _____

PERMANENT STORAGE LOCATION

BUILDING: PH **ROOM:** ____ **UNIT TYPE:** _____ **UNIT:** _____ **LEVEL:** _____

DATE STORED: _____ **STORED BY:** _____

Museum of
New Mexico

P.O. Box 2087
Santa Fe, New Mexico
87504-2087

505 827-6344
FAX 827-6497

Museum of
Indian Arts & Culture
Laboratory of Anthropology

INFORMATION AND REQUEST FORM
FOR APPLICANTS OF SCIENTIFIC TESTING

It is the policy of the MIAC/Lab to encourage research and publication, however this must be balanced by the Museum's responsibility to preserve objects for education, exhibition, and future research purposes.

All Scientific Testing Request forms must be submitted to the Collections Committee six weeks prior to the date the material is needed. The researcher will be informed of whether or not the request has been approved.

All scientific testing proposals will be reviewed by the MIAC/Lab Collections Committee and MNM Senior Conservator and, if circumstances warrant, will also be submitted to appropriate scientists for review. Decisions will be based on soundness of analytic technique, competence of researcher, potential knowledge gained from analysis, extent of loss weighed against the uniqueness of the specimen, and possible cultural sensitivity of material requested. In approving requests the Museum and requestor both acknowledge responsibility for the least possible damage or loss to the specimen(s), that research is likely to conclude in positive results, and that results are fully documented and disseminated.

The reseacher will meet the Museum's requirements for out-loans (separate requirements and form). Any individual signing these agreements must be fully authorized to act on behalf of his/her institution. If an object in the custody of the Museum is the property of another party, the Museum will negotiate with the other party, if necessary.

The researcher will be held financially responsible for any damage to objects beyond the approved test area. No restoration may be done except by MNM Conservators. Cost of conservation will be borne by the researcher.

A copy of all research, test results, and publications must be received by the MIAC/Lab Curator of Collections within one year of the return of all tested material.

Please answer the questions on the back and next page.

ATTACH REFERENCES, CURRICULUM VITAE, PERTINENT BIBLIOGRAPHY, AND DETAILED DESCRIPTION OF RESEARCH PROPOSAL TO THIS REQUEST FORM.

New Mexico
Office of Cultural Affairs

I agree to abide by all of the policies and conditions on the other side of this form.

Signature_____ Date_____

Name   _____

Position   _____

Institution _____

Address   _____

            _____

Telephone   _____

What type of analysis is to be performed?_____
_____
_____

What kind of information will the analysis provide?_____
_____

If the test is destructive, is there a non-destructive test that would acheive the same results? Explain_____
_____
_____

What kind of object/material is requested? _____
_____

What sample size (measurements/weight) is necessary?_____
How many samples are required from each object?_____
Will the analysis involve visible or non-visible damage to objects?
_____

Where will testing be done? _____
_____

Who will select the objects (applicant or staff)?_____
If a loan, what is the period of the loan?_____
Who will do the sampling and how experienced is this person?
_____
_____

Will the sample be completely destroyed?_____
If not, can the sample be reused?_____
Will the analyzed sample require special storage?_____
If yes, please specify _____

Is similar material for testing being requested from other institutions?_____
Please list institutions _____
_____
_____

PEABODY MUSEUM OF NATURAL HISTORY
YALE UNIVERSITY
170 WHITNEY AVENUE
P.O. BOX 208118
NEW HAVEN, CT USA O6520-8118

TECHNICAL ANALYSIS/DESTRUCTIVE SAMPLING AGREEMENT

The sample of _____ from the collections of the Peabody Museum of Natural History is provided for technical analysis/destructive sampling with the following conditions:

1. Usable samples and unused portions of specimens will be returned to the Peabody Museum so they can be retained for future use.

2. Resulting analytical data pertaining to the listed specimens, as specified below, will be provided to the Peabody Museum with a short summary report to become part of the specimen's permanent record. Such data, except published reports, shall remain confidential for a period of three years following the close of the original loan due date unless indicated otherwise in writing by the researcher. Data to be supplied: _____

3. Sampling methods and extent are thoroughly documented for each specimen according to guidelines provided by the appropriate division of the Peabody Museum.

4. Costs of the analysis are the responsibility of the researcher unless otherwise indicated in writing.

5. A copy of any publication that includes information resulting from the analysis of the specimens will be provided to the Peabody Museum.

RESEARCHER   PEABODY MUSEUM OF NATURAL HISTORY

_____   _____
Researcher's signature   Curator or curatorial designee

_____   _____
Researcher's institution   Date

_____
Address

_____

_____   I waive the right to hold confidential the results
                      Telephone   of these analyses.

_____   _____
Date   Researcher's signature

PEABODY MUSEUM OF NATURAL HISTORY
YALE UNIVERSITY
170 WHITNEY AVENUE, P.O. BOX 208118
NEW HAVEN, CT USA O6520-8118

Date _____

TECHNICAL ANALYSIS/DESTRUCTIVE SAMPLING REQUEST

Name _____

Position _____

Institution _____

Address _____

_____

_____

Telephone   *Fax*   *Email*

1. Description of proposed sampling and testing procedure: _____

_____

_____

2. Purpose of this analysis: _____

_____

3. If the analysis involves damage to the specimens, could other, non-destructive analyses provide comparable information?   Yes _____   No _____

   If yes, specify: _____

_____

4. List the specific specimens requested from the Peabody Museum, including catalogue or other identification number, provenance, and location of sample for each specimen. *(Attach a separate sheet if needed.)*

   <u>Cat/ID No.</u>   <u>Specimen/Provenance/Sample Location</u>

5. Dates specimens are needed: _____ to _____

6. Will any previous treatment affect the success of the proposed analysis? Yes _____ No _____
   If yes, explain on attached sheet.

7. Will the analysis involve visible damage to the specimens? Yes _____ No _____

   Will the analysis result in chemical or other changes to the specimens? Yes _____ No _____

   Will the sampling or analysis alter the specimens in such a way as to affect the outcome of future analyses? Yes _____ No _____

   If yes, how? _____

   _____

   _____

8. Will the specimens be sampled? Yes _____ No _____

   If yes, provide justification and details: _____

   _____

   _____

   Who will take the sample? _____

   How many samples are required from each specimen? _____

   What is the size/weight of the samples requested? _____

   Will the sampling be done at the Peabody Museum? Yes _____ No _____

   If no, where will the sampling be done? _____

9. Where will the analysis be performed?

   Institution _____

   Address _____

   _____

   _____

   Contact _____ Telephone _____

10. Will the samples be completely destroyed? Yes _____ No _____

    Can the samples be reused? Yes _____ No _____

    Will the returned samples require special storage? Yes _____ No _____

    If yes, specify: _____

11. Is material being requested from other institutions? Yes _____ No _____

    If so, from which? _____

    _____

12. Place and date of publication of results and testing, if known, or plans for publication: _____

    _____

    _____

159

Approved, Board of Curators, September 12, 1994

MUSEUM of WESTERN COLORADO

Accredited By The American Association of Museums

Museum of Western Colorado

Sites: History Museum, Cross Orchards Living History Farm, Dinosaur Valley
P.O. Box 20000-5020, Grand Junction, CO 81502-5020
(970) 242-0971 X 211

CRM PROJECT CURATION SUMMARY FORM

(This form must accompany any archaeological material submitted to MWC and must be filled out as completely as possible.)

1. Name of Permittee or Firm/Donor: _____

2. Principal Investigator: _____

3. Address: _____

4. Phone w/area code: _____

5. Permit #: _____   6. Type of Permit: _____

7. Name of Project: _____

8. Date of Project: From: _____   To: _____

9. Site #s (state assigned): _____

10. Landowner: (state, private, federal agency): _____

11. Name of Contracting Organization: _____

12. Contract #: _____

13. How material was collected: Survey _____; Test: _____

    Excavation _____   Other: _____

14. Material being turned over to the Museum: # of boxes: _____   # of notebooks: _____

    whole/reconstructed ceramics: _____   large groundstone: _____   other: _____

15. Special storage requirements exist for parts of this collection.   YES   NO   Box #: _____

    Explain: _____

    _____

    _____

16. Items needing conservation are present in this collection.   YES   NO   Box #: _____

    Explain: _____

    _____

    _____

nch 5/1997 crm.doc

17. Reconstructible items are present in this collection. YES   NO   Box #(s): _____

    Explain: _____

    _____

    _____

18. Other remarks: _____

    _____

    _____

CHECKLIST OF MATERIALS BEING TURNED OVER TO MWC

Note: All paper documentation must be submitted on acid-free paper.

19. <u>Documentation</u> (please check all applicable items): _____ Computer files

    _____ Contract or Grant Proposal / Permit   _____ Field Notes

    _____ Maps   _____ Photos

    _____ Survey Site Forms   _____ Negatives

    _____ Inventory Record(s)   _____ Slides

    _____ Forms — please provide a complete listing by form title. Include all form types (e.g., field, lab, analysis, coding, etc...) and continue on separate page if necessary.

    1. _____   6. _____

    2. _____   7. _____

    3. _____   8. _____

    4. _____   9. _____

    5. _____   10. _____

20. <u>Documentation of Project Procedures.</u> Please provide complete list by title (e.g., field or lab manuals, research design, coding formats, etc.) and continue on separate page if necessary.

    1. _____   6. _____

    2. _____   7. _____

    3. _____   8. _____

    4. _____   9. _____

    5. _____   10. _____

25. **Prehistoric Materials**

_____ Ceramics

_____ Flaked Lithics

_____ Non-flaked Lithics

_____ Nonhuman Skeletal material, worked

_____ Nonhuman Skeletal material, non-worked

_____ Human Skeletal Material, worked

_____ Human Skeletal Material, non-worked

_____ Vegatal/Botanical Remains, worked

_____ Vegatal/Botanical Remains, non-worked

_____ Shell, worked

_____ Shell, non-worked

_____ Other (list)

26. **Historic Materials**

_____ Ceramics

_____ Glass

_____ Textiles

_____ Metal

_____ Paper

_____ Synthetics

_____ Organic

_____ Leather

_____ Skeletal material, nonhuman

_____ Skeletal Material, human

_____ Photographs

_____ Other (list)

27. Are all archaeological materials and associated documentation for this project/collection being turned over to the Museum at this time (circle appropriate): YES   NO (explain)

THE MUSEUM OF WESTERN COLORADO

_____
Signature of Staff Accepting Collection

_____
Printed Name

_____
Title

_____
Date

_____
Company

_____
Signature of Authorized Representative

_____
Printed Name

_____
Title

_____
Date

21. Reports: Please provide a complete reference list for all reports, manuscripts, or articles involving project data (include title, author, date, publisher, or periodical title and series #). Continue on separate page if necessary.

   1. _____

   2. _____

   3. _____

   4. _____

22. Final Project Report (2 copies):

   Title: _____

   _____

   Author(s): _____

   Date: _____

23. Other documentation: _____

   _____

   _____

   _____

   _____

Material Checklist

24. **Samples**

   _____ Dendrochronological   _____ Sediment

   _____ Flotation (micro-recovery) _____ Botanical

   _____ Coprolites   _____ Pollen

   _____ Radiocarbon   _____ Pollen Cores

   _____ Other (list)   _____ Stratigraphic Columns

   _____

   _____

Accepted Abbreviations

Material Types

Prehistoric

Ceramics	CER
Flaked Lithics	FL
Non-flaked Lithics	NFL
Human Bone	HB
Non-human Bone	NHB
Other Inorganic	INORG
Other Organic	ORG
Vegetal	VEG
Historic	HIST
Other	OTHER
Indeterminate	INDET

Historic

Ceramic	HCER
Non-human bone	HNHB
Human bone	HHB
Synthetic	HSYN
Leather	HLEA
Metal	HMET
Glass	HGLA
Plastic	HPLA
Shell	HSHE
Composite	HCOM
Other	HOTH
Indeterminate	HIND
Organic	HORG
Inorganic	HING

Samples and Special Items

Archaeomagnetic samples	AM
Radiocarbon samples	CF
Dendrochronological samples	DD
Material source samples	MS
Pollen cores	PC
Pollen samples	PS
Stratigraphic columns	SC
Sediment samples	SS
Bulk soil samples	BS
Botanical specimens	BT
Latex peels	LP
Plaster positive	PT
Monolith	ML
Soil peel	SP
Ethnobotanical sample	EB
Film/Prints	FM
Experimental archaeomagnetic samples	EA
Reconstructible ceramics	RC
Reconstructible flaked lithics	RL
Reconstructible non-flaked lithics	RN
Reconstructible human bone	RH
Reconstructible non-human bone	RB
Reconstructible vegetal and/or other organic matter	RV
Coprolites	CP
Isolated finds	IF
Video material	VM
Laser disks	LD
Floppies	FD

U.S. Department of the Interior
National Park Service
COLLECTIONS MANAGEMENT REPORT

Fiscal Year: _____

Park: _____

Center: _____

I. TOTAL COLLECTION SUMMARY FROM PREVIOUS YEAR ( )

	Archeology	Ethnology	History	Archives	Biology	Paleontology	Geology	TOTAL
A. Objects Cataloged								
B. Catalog Backlog								
C. Total Collection								

II. COLLECTION SUMMARY FOR FISCAL YEAR

A. ACCESSIONS

	Gifts	Exchanges	Purchases	Field Collections	Transfers	Incoming Loans	TOTAL
1. Obj Accessioned							

	Archeology	Ethnology	History	Archives	Biology	Paleontology	Geology	TOTAL
2. Obj Accessioned		.						

B. DEACCESSIONS

	Exchanges	Transfers	Losses	Thefts	Loan Return	NAGPRA	Other	TOTAL
1. Obj Deaccessioned								

	Archeology	Ethnology	History	Archives	Biology	Paleontology	Geology	TOTAL
2. Obj Deaccessioned								

C. CATALOGING

	Archeology	Ethnology	History	Archives	Biology	Paleontology	Geology	TOTAL
1. Objects Cataloged								

D. USE OF COLLECTION

1. Total Number of Outgoing Loans	2. Total Number of Objects in Outgoing Loans	3. Total Objects in Exhibits	4. Total Number of Research Requests within Park	5. Total Number of Research Requests from Outside Park

III. TOTAL COLLECTION SUMMARY FOR ALL YEARS

	Archeology	Ethnology	History	Archives	Biology	Paleontology	Geology	TOTAL
A. Objects Cataloged								
B. Catalog Backlog								
C. Total Collection								

IV. NOTEWORTHY ACCESSIONS, DEACCESSIONS, & OTHER (Attach a separate sheet if necessary)

V. FORM COMPLETION INFORMATION

Form Completed By:

(Name)	(Title)	(Phone)	(Date)

Approval: _____

(Superintendent for Park Reports; Manager for Center or Repository Reports)

Form 10-94 (Rev. 3/96)

The Morton Arboretum
Plant Clinic

PLANT PROBLEM DIAGNOSIS CHECKLIST

NAME _____ PHONE _____ DATE _____

ADDRESS _____

CITY _____ STATE _____ ZIP _____

BACKGROUND INFORMATION *(check or add appropriate information)*

What type of plant is it?
species _____
☐ Tree   ☐ Shrub
☐ Vine   ☐ Ground cover
Other _____

Who planted it?
☐ Yourself
☐ Previous Owner
☐ Nursery
Year _____ *(approx)*

How tall is it?
Feet _____ Inches _____
Diameter of trunk _____ in.

SITE AND MAINTENANCE

Sun Exposure
☐ north   ☐ south
☐ east   ☐ west
☐ full sun   ☐ part shade
☐ full shade

Soil and Drainage
☐ clay   ☐ loam   ☐ sand
☐ high area   ☐ low area
(relative to surroundings)

Surrounded by or near
☐ lawn   ☐ mulch
☐ ground cover
☐ near building ___ft.___in.
☐ near pavement ___ft.___in.

Your watering program is:
☐ never   ☐ dry periods
☐ once/day   ☐ once/week
☐ once/month

Do you use a lawn service?
☐ yes   ☐ no
Do you fertilize?
☐ spring   ☐ summer   ☐ fall
☐ all   ☐ never

Has the property been sprayed for:
☐ insects   ☐ diseases
☐ weeds   ☐ other
chemical used _____

SYMPTOMS

Leaf Color
☐ yellow   ☐ light green
☐ brown   ☐ other

% of leaves affected _____

Flowers
☐ fail to bloom
☐ undersized
☐ abnormal
other _____

Fruit/Seed
☐ distorted
☐ damaged
☐ reduced size
other _____

Branches Showing Symptoms
☐ all   ☐ top
☐ middle   ☐ bottom
☐ one side   ☐ scattered
dead branches # _____

Trunk Wounds
☐ yes   ☐ no   ☐ unknown
Small Holes Present?
☐ yes   ☐ no
☐ irregular   ☐ patterned
Sap Dripping   ☐ yes   ☐ no

Number of Plants Affected
☐ single plant
☐ multiple
☐ entire group

SYMPTOMS

Other Comments:

COLLECTING AND TRANSPORTING SPECIMENS FOR DIAGNOSIS

To Bring in a specimen:

- Select samples from the plant that show various stages of the problem.
- If insects are present, include them with the sample.
- Branch samples should be approximately ½ inch diameter and 6-8 inches long.
- Collect the sample on the same day you are going to bring it in, if possible.
- Place it in a plastic bag to preserve the moisture. **Do not add water.**
- Keep in a cool place. If it will be in a closed, hot car for any length of time, place the sample in an insulated cooler with ice.

To mail in a specimen:

Fresh Sample

- Place sample in a perforated plastic bag.
- Do not add water as moisture in the sample is adequate to keep the specimen fresh.
- Place bag in a strong cardboard box and press between two sheets of cardboard.

Dry Sample

- Place sample between 6-12 sheets of newspaper.
- Place under several large books for 4 to 5 days.
- When dry, slip it between a folded sheet of newspaper and cover with two sheets of cardboard.

Mail To:

The Morton Arboretum
Plant Clinic
4100 Illinois Route 53
Lisle, IL 60532-1293

Mark Shipping Label:

"PLANT SPECIMEN"

You will receive a response by mail or phone within 7 - 10 business days.

Plant problems can be caused by a combination of factors.
We will need the above information in order to help you.
So please fill out this form as thoroughly as possible.

The
Morton
Arboretum

4100 Illinois Route 53
Lisle, IL 60532-1293

500/6/97/COP © 1997 The Morton Arboretum

PLANT IDENTIFICATION CHECKLIST

The Morton Arboretum Plant Clinic

Plant Information

NAME _____ PHONE _____ DATE _____

ADDRESS _____

CITY _____ STATE _____ ZIP _____

TYPE & SOURCE OF SPECIMEN *(check or add appropriate information)*

What type of plant is it?
- ❏ indoor plant
- ❏ outdoor plant
- ❏ cultivated   ❏ wild
- ❏ Tree   ❏ Shrub
- ❏ Vine   ❏ Ground cover

Other _____

Where is it from – habitat?
- ❏ cultivated landscape
- ❏ woodland
- ❏ open field
- ❏ roadside
- ❏ near stream

Other _____

When was it collected?

Date _____

Location collected from

City/State _____

_____

DETAILED DESCRIPTION *(include a sample if possible or sketches may be useful)*

Leaf Description:

Flower Description:

Fruit Description:

Growth Habit
- ❏ upright
- ❏ prostrate
- ❏ climbing

Other _____

Sun Exposure
- ❏ north   ❏ south
- ❏ east   ❏ west
- ❏ full sun   ❏ part shade
- ❏ full shade

Other Observations:
(over for additional space)

IDENTIFICATION *(staff use only)*

Identification:

Staff member: _____ Date _____

COLLECTING AND TRANSPORTING SPECIMENS FOR DIAGNOSIS

To Bring in a specimen:
- Select a generous sample from the plant, 6 to 12 inches long — twigs, or branches with leaves — include fruits, and/or flower, when present.
- Collect the sample on the same day you are going to bring it in, if possible.
- Place it in a plastic bag to preserve the moisture. Do not add water – moisture in the sample is adequate to keep the specimen fresh.
- Keep in a cool place. If it will be in a closed, hot car for any length of time, place the sample in an insulated cooler with ice.

To mail in a specimen:

Fresh Sample
- Place sample in a perforated plastic bag.
- Do not add water – moisture in the sample is adequate to keep the specimen fresh.
- Place bag in a strong cardboard box and press between two sheets of cardboard.

Dry Sample
- Place sample between 6-12 sheets of newspaper.
- Place under several large books for 4 to 5 days.
- When dry, slip it between a folded sheet of newspaper and cover with two sheets of cardboard.

Mail To:
The Morton Arboretum
Plant Clinic
4100 Illinois Route 53
Lisle, IL 60532-1293

Mark Shipping Label:
"PLANT SPECIMEN"

You will receive a response by mail or phone within 7 - 10 business days.

ADDITIONAL COMMENTS:

The
Morton
Arboretum

4100 Illinois Route 53
Lisle, IL 60532-1293

500/8/97/COP © 1997 The Morton Arboretum

Plant Information

Insect and Arachnid identification request form

Please print the following information and leave this form and specimen(s) with the security guard.

Your name _____

Phone number _____

    best time to call _____

Today's date _____

Do you want the specimen back?
_____ yes - alive
_____ yes - dead
_____ no (Suitable specimens will be incorporated into CU's collections.)

Date specimen was collected _____

Location (i.e. basement of house) _____

City _____

Additional notes _____

_____

_____

_____

_____

_____

We try to identify material as quickly as possible, however some specimens, particularly small insects, spiders, and specimens brought in during the busy season may require a week for identification. If you have not heard from us, and it has been at least a week since the specimen was brought in, please call (303) 492-6270.

IDENTIFICATION: _____

_____

ANNISTON MUSEUM OF NATURAL HISTORY

LIVE ANIMAL RECORD

Common Name _____Scientific Name_____

SOURCE:

1.   Collector/Donor: (Name, Address and Phone No.)

    _____ Phone No. _____

    _____

    _____

2.   Date Collected: _____ Date Presented: _____

3.   Where Collected:

    A. State _____ B. County _____ C. Nearest Town _____

    D. Habitat _____

4.   Complete the applicable section below:

    A.   ❑ I present this personally owned animal at the Anniston Museum of
              Natural History as a gift.

    B.   ❑ I present this personally owned animal to the Anniston
              Museum of Natural History as a loan.

    C.   ❑ I transport this wild animal to the L.A.B. on behalf and under the
              permits of the Anniston Museum of Natural History.

SIGNED: _____ DATE: _____

DESCRIPTION OF ANIMAL:

1. Age (approx.) _____ 2. Sex _____ 3. Weight _____

4. Measurements: _____

5. Comments: _____

_____

Received by: _____ Title: _____

(CONTINUED ON BACK)

Basic Information: _____

_____

_____

_____

_____

_____

_____

_____

_____

Data: _____

_____

_____

_____

_____

_____

_____

_____

_____

_____

_____

Final Outcome: _____

_____

_____

ANTIQUITIES AUTHENTICATION CERTIFICATE

MISSOURI DEPARTMENT OF NATURAL RESOURCES
Division of Parks & Historic Preservation

Acquisition Number _____

I, _____ , Seller, and I _____ ,
Furnisher, hereby certify that to the best of our knowledge the object herein described is an authentic antique (object) of the
_____ style, _____ period, _____ date and has _____
_____ historical and/or geographical origin. Said
object is described as follows:

1. Description of object _____

_____

_____

_____

_____

_____

2. Parts damaged _____

_____

3. Parts missing _____

_____

4. Parts not original _____

5. Surface finish . . . original _____

. . . partially refinished _____

. . . totally refinished _____

6. Seller's price of object $ _____ .

_____   _____   _____   _____
(Date)   (Signature of seller)   (Date)   (Witness of seller and furnisher signatures)

_____   _____
(Address)   (Address)

_____   _____   _____   _____
(Date)   (Signature of furnisher)   (Date)   (Witness of seller and furnisher signatures)

_____   _____
(Address)   (Address)

The antique (object) herein described is approved for purchase
by the Missouri Department of Natural Resources.

_____   _____
(Date)   (Signature of Missouri Department of Natural Resources Agent)

D.P.H.P. FORM 54
REV. 6/79

173

CERTIFICATE OF AUTHENTICATION

ARTIST

TITLE

SIZE (Height/Length or Width/Depth)

MEDIUM

EDITION/No./SIZE OF EDITION

Documentation on Sculpture: Signature   Date   Copyright symbol

AUTHORIZATION for CASTING Given by:

DATE of CASTING:

METHOD of CASTING:

METHOD of CASTING:

    Surmoulage ?

NAME of FOUNDRY:

    Founder:

    Chaser:

    Patinator:

SCULPTOR'S ORIGINAL WORK FROM WHICH THE ABOVE SCULPTURE IS CAST:

Material:

Size (Height/Length or Width/ Depth):

Date of Execution:

I/We certify that all of the above information is correct.

SIGNATURE of the SCULPTOR: date:

SIGNATURE of FACTORY REPRESENTATIVE: date:

1533

THE BUFFALO BILL MEMORIAL ASSOCIATION
P.O. BOX 1000
CODY, WYOMING 82414

REQUEST FOR AUTHENTICITY

The undersigned requests The Buffalo Bill Memorial Association provide a written opinion as to the probable date and attribution of the item described below and on the overleaf. The undersigned declares the undersigned is the owner of that item, seeks the opinion for personal information only and will not rely upon such opinion in conjunction with any sale or transfer of ownership.

The undersigned understands the opinion will represent the professional view of the examiner only and will be neither a guaranty nor warranty.

NO ESTIMATE OR OPINION CONCERNING MONETARY VALUE
WILL BE GIVEN

In consideration of the opinion requested, the undersigned agrees to indemnify The Buffalo Bill Memorial Association, its Trustees, and members of its staff, including the staff member who provides the opinion, and to save and hold harmless each of them from any and all liability arising out of the rendering of the requested opinion.

_____   _____

(Owner's Signature)   (Date)

NAME:

ADDRESS:

* * * * * * * *

ITEM SUBMITTED FOR EXAMINATION:

175

SUBJECT TO THE AUTHORIZATION AND CONDITIONS PRINTED IN OVERLEAF

Description of Item:

Comments:

In the professional opinion of the undersigned

_____   _____

(Examiner's Signature)   (Date)

PROCEDURAL GUIDELINES FOR AUTHENTICATION

1. Only members of the professional staff of The Buffalo Bill Memorial Association authorized in writing by the Director may render an opinion regarding the authenticity of works of art, historical material, memorabilia, and other objects and items (herein "Item") submitted for examination.

2. No opinion may be given as to the monetary value of the Item.

3. Opinions are to be given only in writing and only at the written request of the owner or a duly appointed agent.

4. No opinion is to be given without the Item being physically present and available to the staff member authorized to give the opinion.

5. Any Item submitted for examination is to be accompanied by a photograph of archival quality and of sufficient clarity to provide positive identification. The photograph is to become the property of The Buffalo Bill Memorial Association and will be permanently affixed to the examination file. If the owner does not supply such a photograph, The Buffalo Bill Memorial Association may take the necessary photograph, which will be at owner's expense.

6. All costs of transportation of the Item to and from the Museum shall be at the expense of the owner and all risk of loss during such transportation and while the Item is at the Museum shall be borne by owner. In an appropriate case the owner may be required to deposit funds to defray such costs in advance of authentication.

7. No opinion is to be given without the owner or a duly appointed agent first completing a written request in a form approved by the Director.

8. Opinions shall only be given to Patrons of The Buffalo Bill Memorial Association and to educational or charitable institutions.

9. Any member of the professional staff may refuse to render an opinion, with or without explanation, even though authorized by the Director to provide the same.

The Nelson-Atkins Museum of Art

Art Movement Form

DATE OF REQUEST_____

PART I: PRE-MOVEMENT—TO BE COMPLETED BY PERSON REQUESTING MOVEMENT

Projected date of movement_____

IF ROUNDTRIP (MAX. TWO WORKING DAYS) Projected date of return_____

Accession Number_____

Artist/Culture_____

Title/Type_____

Present location_____

Requested location_____

Reason for movement_____

Signature of person requesting movement_____

Registrar's signature_____

PART II: INTERIM MOVEMENT—TO BE COMPLETED BY PERSON MOVING OBJECT(S)

Interim location_____Date moved_____

Signature of person moving object(s)_____

PART III: POST-MOVEMENT—TO BE COMPLETED BY PERSON MOVING OBJECTS(S)

Final location_____Date moved_____

Object(s) numbered/labeled?   ☐ YES   ☐ NO

Signature of person moving object(s)_____

ADDITIONAL INSTRUCTIONS

Part I should be filled out prior to the movement of the object and signed by a registrar. Part II should be filled out if there is an interim location, and the interim copy should be given to the Registration Department. Part III should be filled out when the object has been moved to its final location. Return the completed form to the Registration Department.

178

3/97

The Nelson-Atkins Museum of Art

Art Movement Form Attachment

To be completed by person requesting movement

Accession Number	Artist/Culture	Title/Type of Object	Present Location	Requested Location

To be completed by persons moving objects

Interim Location	Date Moved	Final Location	Date Moved

REGISTRATION'S POST-MOVEMENT COPY

3/97

Louisiana State Museum
OBJECT TEMPORARILY REMOVED
FROM EXHIBIT

OBJECT_____

PURPOSE_____

CURATOR_____

DATE_____

Form 16 (Rev. 7/97)

Louisiana State Museum
OBJECT TEMPORARILY REMOVED
FROM EXHIBIT

OBJECT_____

PURPOSE_____

CURATOR_____

DATE_____

Form 16 (Rev. 7/97)

Louisiana State Museum
OBJECT TEMPORARILY REMOVED
FROM EXHIBIT

OBJECT_____

PURPOSE_____

CURATOR_____

DATE_____

Form 16 (Rev. 7/97)

Louisiana State Museum
OBJECT TEMPORARILY REMOVED
FROM EXHIBIT

OBJECT_____

PURPOSE_____

CURATOR_____

DATE_____

Form 16 (Rev. 7/97)

Historic Deerfield, Inc.

Object Move - temporary

Accession #:

Object:

From location:

To location:

Reason: cleaning   photo   class
loan - exhibit   loan - conservation   study
notes:

Date removed: **by:**

Date expected to return:

Date returned: **by:**

white - location   yellow - object   pink - office   5/95

180

ASUM Temporary Change of Location Shelf Slip

Date: _____
Object No: _____
Object Name: _____
New Location: _____
Duration of Move: _____
Moved by: _____
Reason for move: _____
_____
_____
_____

Change of Location Record Completed?

☐ No   ☐ Yes

Date: _____

Notes: _____
_____
_____
_____

ASUM Temporary Change of Location Shelf Slip

Date: _____
Object No: _____
Object Name: _____
New Location: _____
Duration of Move: _____
Moved by: _____
Reason for move: _____
_____
_____
_____

Change of Location Record Completed?

☐ No   ☐ Yes

Date: _____

Notes: _____
_____
_____
_____

LOCATION CARD

ART MUSEUM OF SOUTHEAST TEXAS

Accession # _____

Artist _____

Title _____

Medium _____

Dimensions _____

Nationality _____

Dates: Born _____ Died _____

Location	Date	Location	Date

Public Museum of Grand Rapids

ARTIFACT TRACKING RECORD (ATR)

Date Moved: _____ / _____ / _____ Moved By: _____

Purpose: _____

Accession Number	Object Name/Description	Classification	MOVED FROM:				MOVED TO:				Perm.	Temp.
			Bldg.	Room	Sec.	Box/Shelf	Bldg.	Room	Sec.	Box/Shelf		

EDUCATION

Agreement/Contract/Release
Docent
Evaluation
Field Trip
General
Resource loan/Order
Tour confirmation/Information/Registration

THE MARION KOOGLER MCNAY ART MUSEUM

6000 North New Braunfels
Post Office Box 6069
San Antonio, Texas 78209-0069
tel 210/824-5368
fax 210/805-1760
www.mcnayart.org

DIRECTOR
William J. Chiego

TEACHING AGREEMENT WITH:

This letter confirms the agreement of the above-named instructor/presenter to teach for the McNay Art Museum under the conditions specified below.

TITLE OF WORKSHOP, EVENT, OR CLASS:

DATE:
TIME:
LOCATION:
AGE LEVEL / AUDIENCE:
MAXIMUM ENROLLMENT:
RATE OF PAY:
This pay rate is based on both teaching and preparation time.

SUPPLIES:

_____ will be furnished by instructor
_____ will be furnished by McNay from instructor's supply list
_____ will be furnished by students from instructor's supply list, sent to the McNay
_____ other:

With this signed agreement, instructors must submit
    -a completed W-9 form (enclosed)
    -an outline for the workshop or presentation
    -a supply list if applicable

The McNay reserves the right to cancel any offering that does not meet its minimum enrollment. Please sign all copies of this agreement to indicate your approval of these conditions. Keep one copy for your files and return two copies in the enclosed envelope.

Curator of Education _____ Date _____

Instructor _____ Date _____

MUSEUM of
WESTERN
COLORADO

LECTURE CONTRACT

This contract, is made and entered into on this _____ day of _____, 199__, by and between the Museum of Western Colorado, 233 N. 5th Street, Grand Junction, Colorado, and _____, street address _____, city _____, state _____, zip code _____, home phone number ( ) _____, business phone number ( ) _____. It is entered into for the express purpose of providing lectures and appearances as described below, upon agreement of the following terms and conditions:

1. Schedule of talks and appearances:

DATE(s)	TIME A.M./P.M.	AUDIENCE	TITLE

2. Lecturer's honorarium, if any, for the sum of _____
    ($ _____), payable to _____ after the presentation(s).

3. Travel and lodging will be provided as follows: _____
    _____
    _____
    _____

4. Special conditions as follows: _____
    _____
    _____
    _____
    _____

If either the Museum, or the Lecturer, defaults without reasonable cause on the terms of this contract, that entity will reimburse the other for any non-recoverable costs incurred to produce the program. If this contract expressed our agreement in connection with this Program, please sign below.

Signature: _____ Date:_____
      Lecturer

Signature: _____ Date:_____
      Janice McLean, Ph.D., Executive Director
      Museum of Western Colorado

<u>Note</u>: *Return one copy to Jan McLean, Executive Director, The Museum of Western Colorado*
P.O. Box 20,000, Grand Junction, Colorado 81502-5020

JMcL 8/96

Chevron Open Minds School Program
Release Form

Your approval is required so that we may take writing samples, photographs, sound recordings and/or videotape of students who take part in the Chevron Open Minds School program. These activities assist us in evaluating the program and helps educators and other interested groups learn more about Open Minds.

If you agree, please complete the form below and return it to your child's teacher as soon as possible.

****

Name of School _____ Name of Teacher _____

I/We, the parent/s or legal guardian(s) of _____
                                                                    Full name of student

hereby give express permission and consent for all writing samples, photographs and video and audio recordings of her/him participating in the Chevron Open Minds School program. This data will be used for education and public information purposes only.

_____
Parent or legal guardian

_____   _____
Parent or legal guardian   **Date**

GLENBOW
MUSEUM • ART GALLERY • LIBRARY • ARCHIVES

Chevron Glenbow Museum School

130 - 9th Avenue SE Calgary, Alberta T2G 0P3 403 268•4112 ph 403 262•4045 fx

SPENCER
MUSEUM
OF ART

DOCENT APPLICATION
1997

Name_____

Address_____

Telephone (Home) _____ (Work) _____

How long have you lived in the Lawrence area? _____

****

Docent experience:
- Name of museum(s): _____

- Dates of service: _____

Education:
- School(s): _____

- Degree(s): _____

   _____

Other relevant experience: _____

_____

_____

****

Please list all employment, community activities, and volunteer work in which you are
<u>currently</u> involved: _____

_____

_____

In what capacity have you worked with:

- Children _____

- Teenagers _____

- Senior citizens _____

- Persons with disabilities _____

- Others _____

****

In what languages are you fluent? _____

In what areas do you have artistic capabilities? (i.e., painting) _____

_____

How did you learn about the Spencer Museum of Art Docent Program?

_____

Why do you want to be a docent at the Spencer Museum of Art?

_____

_____

_____

_____

Return to: Betsy Weaver
            Docent Program Coordinator
            Spencer Museum of Art
            University of Kansas
            Lawrence, KS 66045-2136

            Phone: 785-864-4710
            FAX : 785-864-3112
            e-mail: bweaver@ukans.edu

SPENCER
MUSEUM
OF ART

DOCENT REQUIREMENTS

The docents at the Spencer Museum of Art serve as volunteer guides to the museum's collection and special exhibitions. The Docent Program is open to those who are eager to share their enthusiasm about art with others and who are willing to make a serious commitment of both time and study to the program.

To give docents the opportunity to do their best in the program, the museum expects the docents to follow the requirements listed below.

REQUIREMENTS FOR DOCENTS IN TRAINING
- A two year commitment to the docent program
- Attendance at all docent meetings and practice sessions
- Observe two school presentations (Third-grade Program only) and museum tours during both semesters.
- Give four school tours in the spring semester
- Audit an introductory art history course during the first year
- Join the Friends of the Art Museum

REQUIREMENTS FOR SECOND-YEAR DOCENTS
- Attend all docent meetings and practice sessions
- Give a minimum of two school presentations (Third-grade Program only) and four school tours each semester
- Observe and practice a minimum of two adult tours during the fall semester
- Give a minimum of **seven tours a year** in addition to the required school presentations and museum tours
- Membership in Friends of the Art Museum

REQUIREMENTS FOR EXPERIENCED DOCENTS
- Attend all docent meetings and required practice sessions
- Give a minimum of two school presentations (Third-grade Program only) and four school tours each semester
- Give a minimum of **seven tours a year** in addition to the required school presentations and museum tours
- Membership in Friends of the Art Museum

DOCENT ACCOUNTABILITY
- If a docent is unable to attend a docent meeting or practice session, she or he must call the Docent Program Coordinator (864-4710) in advance to receive an excused absence
- If a docent is unable to give a tour for which she or he has signed up, she or he must:
  1. Find a substitute docent
  2. Inform the Docent Program Coordinator of the change
- Second-year and experienced docents are allowed two excused absences from docent meetings each semester
- At the end of each semester, each docent's attendance record and tour record will be evaluated. Docents who are below the minimum number of tours or who have missed more than two docent meetings will be on probation. A second semester with below minimum participation will result in dismissal from the program.

BENEFITS OF BEING A SPENCER MUSEUM OF ART DOCENT
- Audit KU art history courses free of charge
- Lectures and gallery talks by art history faculty, museum curators, and graduate interns
- Work with Lawrence school children in the classroom and museum
- Camaraderie with others interested in learning and teaching about the museum's collection
- Trips to area museums to learn about their collections and special exhibitions
- As a museum volunteer, receive a 20% discount on most items in the Museum Book Shop

The Museum of Fine Arts, Houston
DOCENT INFORMATION FORM 1997-98

NAME:_____
(Please print name as you want it on your name tag)

Check here if you need a new name tag. _____

DOCENT CLASSIFICATION: ____Guild ____Senior ____Junior League
Please print your name below as you want it listed in Docent Directory:

NAME:_____

ADDRESS:_____(zip)_____

TELEPHONE: day ( ) _____evening( ) _____

In case of emergency, notify: Name_____

Telephone: _____ Relationship: _____

> DAY PREFERENCE: (Please mark from 1-4 in order of preference)
>
> Tuesday ___   Wednesday____   Thursday____   Friday____

I AM INTERESTED IN LEADING TOURS FOR THE FOLLOWING GROUPS:

Children __ Middle School __ High School __General Adult __Senior Citizens __

Special Needs Visitors __ Museum Special Events Functions __

PLEASE LIST TYPES/PERIODS OF ART IN WHICH YOU HAVE SPECIAL KNOWLEDGE OR INTEREST:

_____

_____

FOREIGN LANGUAGE SKILLS:
Do you speak another language fluently enough to lead a tour in that language? _____ If yes, which? _____

PLEASE GIVE ANY ADDITIONAL INFORMATION THAT MAY HELP TO SCHEDULE YOUR TOUR ASSIGNMENTS:

_____

_____

_____

Nelson-Atkins
DOCENT INQUIRY

Office Use

Docent Application Mailed On _____

Docent Application Returned On _____

Docent Information Packet Mailed On _____

Deadline for Application Jan. 15, 1999

3 Year Training Program

Next Class to begin
Spring 1999

Name _____

Address _____

Phone _____

Museum Membership (*must be a Museum member*) _____

Inquiry taken by _____   Date _____

Check for Related Experience:

_____   Experience working with children/students
_____   Studio art experience
_____   Art history background

--------------------------------✂--------------------------------

Please return the form to: Marti McLarney—Tour Office
                               Nelson-Atkins Museum
                               4525 Oak Street
                               Kansas City, Missouri 64111

DEADLINE FOR APPLICATION IS JAN. 15, 1999

GENERAL INFORMATION FOR ALL APPLICANTS

Feb. 10 10:30-12	Orientation Meeting All applicants must attend.
Feb. 23-26	All applicants must observe a 10 A.M., 11 A.M. or 1 P.M. School Tour and fill out observation form. This is followed by a 15 minute conference with Tour Coordinator, Kate Livers.
March 1 10-12:30 or 12:30-3:30	45 minute interview with docent pair.
March 8	Final selection of Class of 1999. All interviews and staff meet 10-12; 1:30-3:30
March 15	Applicants are notified by mail of the docent committees decision.
Fall 1999	Training begins—Sept.-Oct. Touring begins—Oct.-Dec.

DEADLINE FOR APPLICATION JAN. 15, 1999

Teacher Evaluation of Theatrical Presentation For
"Trading Post At Fort Williams"

Name _____

School _____

Grade _____

YOUR INPUT IS IMPORTANT TO US!! PLEASE COMPLETE AND RETURN TO THE SECURITY DESK UPON EXITING. THANK YOU!

1. Did you find presentation age appropriate for grade level or class?

     Y   N   Explain _____

2. Was information presented in a clear and interesting manner?

     Y   N   Explain _____

3. Do you think the class/theatre piece complimented the exhibition "Tribes of the Buffalo?

     Y   N   Explain _____

4. Would you like to see future exhibits/exhibitions with a theatrical interpretation?

     Y   N   Explain _____

Additional comments/suggestions _____

_____

_____

Thank You!
Museum Education Division
Buffalo Museum of Science
1020 Humboldt Parkway
Buffalo, New York 14211-1293

191

SCHOOL INFORMATION

Please complete the following information:

Date of visit to Buffalo Museum of Science or Tifft Nature Preserve _____

School Name _____

School District _____ County: ❑ Erie ❑ Niagara ❑ Ontario, Canada ❑ Other: _____

Type of School: ❑ Public ❑ Private ❑ Parochial ❑ Home School ❑ Other _____

Grade Level: ❑ Nursery/Daycare/Pre-K ❑ K - 2 ❑ 3/4 ❑ 5/6 ❑ 7/8 ❑ 9 - 12 ❑ College

Subject area: ❑ Elementary ❑ Science ❑ Social Studies ❑ Special Ed. ❑ Other _____

TEACHER PACKET

• Did you find the information in the teacher packet valuable? ❑ Yes ❑ No

If not, why? How could it be improved?

_____

_____

• Before your trip, did you use the activities in the teacher packet in your classroom? ❑ Yes ❑ No

If not, why? _____

_____

• After your trip, are you planning to use the activities? ❑ Yes ❑ No

If not, why? _____

_____

YOUR FIELD TRIP

• Did you preview the exhibit before visiting with your class? ❑ Yes ❑ No

If not, why?_____

Comments _____

_____

_____

• Who paid for the admission fee? ❑ School ❑ Students ❑ PTA/PTO ❑ Fundraiser ❑ Other _____

• How many field trips is your class taking this school year? _____

• What other locations are you visiting?

_____

_____

YOUR VISIT

• Why did your class come to the Museum or Tifft Nature Preserve?

_____

_____

• How does your visit relate to the curriculum?

_____

_____

• Was the educational content of your visit sufficient? ❑ Yes ❑ No

Comments _____

_____

• What can we do to improve your visit?

_____

_____

• What topics would you like to see us address?

_____

_____

• Do you feel your students had sufficient interaction with the staff?

❑ Yes ❑ No

Comments _____

_____

• Did you find parking, entering the Museum and interacting with staff easy to manage?

❑ Yes ❑ No

Comments _____

_____

MUSEUM OF INTERNATIONAL FOLK ART
FOLK ART TO GO
EVALUATION FORM

Teacher's Name _____   Grade Level _____

School _____   Date _____

Date of Museum Visit_____

Name of Museum Educator_____

PART I: INSTRUCTIONAL MATERIALS

Please rate the following by circling a number: **Excellent**   **Poor**

		1	2	3	4

1. **The written materials were overall**.....................1..........2............3.............4
    a. Appropriate to the grade level.....................1..........2..........3.............4
    b. Encouraged critical and creative thinking..........1..........2..........3.............4
    c. Maintained students' interest......................1..........2..........3.............4
    d. Helped students understand folk art................1..........2..........3.............4
    e. Helped prepare students for museum visits........1..........2..........3.............4
    f. Relevant to your curriculum.......................1..........2..........3.............4
    Which area(s)?_____

Comments_____

PART II: PRE MUSEUM VISIT

Date of Pre Museum Visit_____

Name of Museum Educator_____

1. **The pre-museum visit overall**............................1..........2..........3............4
    a. Appropriate to the grade level.....................1..........2..........3...........4
    b. Encouraged critical and creative thinking..........1..........2..........3...........4
    c. Maintained students' interest......................1..........2..........3...........4
    d. Helped students understand folk art................1..........2..........3...........4
    e. Helped prepare students for museum visits........1..........2..........3...........4
    f. Relevant to your curriculum.......................1..........2..........3...........4
    Which area(s)?_____

Comments_____

PART II: DOCENT TOUR

Name of Docent(s)_____

1. **The docent-led tour overall**.............................1.........2.........3.........4
    a. Appropriate to grade level.........................1.........2.........3.........4
    b. Encouraged critical and creative thinking........1.........2.........3.........4
    c. Communicated a theme and carried it
        throughout the tour...............................1.........2.........3.........4
    d. Engaged students in active discussion.............1.........2.........3.........4
    e. Used humor.......................................1.........2.........3.........4
    f. Managed the group................................1.........2.........3.........4
    g. Maintained students' interest....................1.........2.........3.........4

Comments_____

_____

PART III: ART PROJECT

1. **The art project overall**.............................1.........2.........3.........4
    a. Had the process clearly explained.................1.........2.........3.........4
    b. Helped students understand folk art..............1.........2.........3.........4
    c. Maintained students' interest....................1.........2.........3.........4
    d. Taught cultural history..........................1.........2.........3.........4
    e. Taught perceptual skills.........................1.........2.........3.........4
    f. Taught new vocabulary............................1.........2.........3.........4
    g. Taught art/craft techniques......................1.........2.........3.........4

Comments_____

_____

PART IV: SUMMARY

1. **Folk Art to Go overall**............................1.........2.........3.........4
    a. Maintained continuity throughout.................1.........2.........3.........4
    b. Enriched the school curriculum...................1.........2.........3.........4
    c. Was enjoyable....................................1.........2.........3.........4

2. Areas for improvement for Folk Art to Go_____

3. Strengths of Folk Art to Go_____

4. Other Comments_____

194

ANNISTON MUSEUM OF NATURAL HISTORY

EVALUATION SHEET FOR TRAVELING TRUNKS

_____
NAME OF TRAVELING TRUNK

Teacher_____   Pick-up Date_____

School _____   Date to be returned_____

Grade _____ Number of students using this trunk _____

PLEASE RANK THE FOLLOWING IN ORDER OF EFFECTIVENESS (with (1) being the lowest value and (5) being the highest value - circle one number for each category):

1. Objects
   - a. Educational Value   1   2   3   4   5
   - b. Student Enjoyment   1   2   3   4   5
   - c. Student Understanding   1   2   3   4   5
   - d. Teacher Usability   1   2   3   4   5
   - e. Instructions   1   2   3   4   5

2. Audio-visual materials
   - a. Educational Value   1   2   3   4   5
   - b. Student Enjoyment   1   2   3   4   5
   - c. Student Understanding   1   2   3   4   5
   - d. Teacher Usability   1   2   3   4   5
   - e. Instructions   1   2   3   4   5

3. Printed Material
   - a. Educational Value   1   2   3   4   5
   - b. Student Enjoyment   1   2   3   4   5
   - c. Student Understanding   1   2   3   4   5
   - d. Teacher Usability   1   2   3   4   5

4. What activities did students enjoy the least:_____

----

5. Suggestions for improving this trunk: _____

TRUNK RETURN: Tuesday-Friday 9:00AM-5:00PM ; Saturday 10:00AM-5:00PM; Sunday 1:00PM-5:00PM.

PLEASE GIVE THIS FORM TO THE RECEPTIONIST AT THE ADMISSIONS DESK WHEN RETURNING THE TRUNK.

<u>MONDAY</u> - FRONT DOORS TO THE MUSEUM ARE LOCKED (MUSEUM CLOSED TO PUBLIC). YOU MUST ENTER THE MUSEUM THROUGH THE COURTYARD ENTRANCE. PLEASE SEE PERSONNEL IN THE BUSINESS OFFICE DIRECTLY ACROSS LOBBY FROM COURTYARD ENTRANCE.

WICHITA ART MUSEUM
Student Group Evaluation Form -- Guided Visit

The information you provide will assist us in modifying and improving future museum programs. Your responses are very helpful. Please feel free to write additional comments on the back. Thank you!

Date of Tour_____

School/Group_____

✦ Was this your first visit to the Wichita Art Museum?   yes_____   no_____

  Did you visit because of a specific program or exhibit?   yes_____   no_____

    If yes, which one?_____

    If yes, how did you find out about it?_____

✦ What exhibition or collection was most enjoyable? Why?_____

  _____

  What exhibition or collection was least enjoyable? Why?_____

  _____

✦ What form of transportation did you use to get to the museum?   walk_____

    school bus_____   parent drivers_____   MTA_____   other_____

  If you used the sponsored bus transportation, how important was this to you?
    Couldn't come without it_____
    Very important_____
    Somewhat important_____
    Made little difference in decision to visit_____

✦ Was the tour age-appropriate for your group?   yes_____   no_____

✦ What mode(s) of teaching predominated? (Please check all appropriate responses)
    Lecture_____   Open-ended questions with time for response_____
    Time for self-directed learning_____   Perception games_____

Please return this form to the Education Office, Wichita Art Museum, 619 Stackman Drive, Wichita KS 67203.

Notes or drawings from students in response to their visit are welcomed. We will forward thank-you letters to docents or bus sponsors to the appropriate person.

#37041

School _____

Tour Date/Time _____ **Docent** _____

Pre-Tour Activities

1. **Which pre-tour materials did you use:**
    ___ Preparation and Logistics   ___ How to Look at Art

    ___ Student Letter/Name Tag   ___ MFA,H Parking Information
2. **Was the overall level appropriate for your class?** ___yes ___no

3. **In preparing for the tour, overall these materials were:**
    ____very useful ____fairly useful ____of no use

4. **Were the activities easily integrated into your classroom schedule? If no, why not?**

The Tour

1. **The docent was warm, friendly, and genuinely interested in my students.**
    ____always ____mostly ____somewhat ____not at all

2. **The docent kept the class interested in the art.**
    ____always ____mostly ____somewhat ____not at all

3. **The docent encouraged students' participation and worked from their comments.**
    ____always ____mostly ____somewhat ____not at all

4. **The information was at the right level for my students.**
    ____always ____mostly ____somewhat ____not at all

5. **Would you recommend any changes in the tour?**

Follow-Up Activities

1. **Which follow-up activities did you use?**
    ___ Writing and Art   ___ Creating Art

2. **Overall was the level of the activities appropriate for your class?** ___yes ___no

3. **Did the activities relate to and reinforce the tour experience?**___very much ____somewhat
    ____not at all

4. **Did you use Kaleidoscope?** ___yes ___no **Was it appropriate for your class?**___very much
    ____somewhat ____not at all

5. **How did your students respond to Kaleidoscope? Did they find it:**
    ___enjoyable ___interesting ___educational

Informal Tour Observation Form

DOCENT_____DATE_____

TOUR TOPIC_____

AUDIENCE/NUMBER IN GROUP_____

FIRST IMPRESSIONS
- Arrived in ample time
- Friendly and welcoming
- Enthusiastic

Comments:

PRESENTATION

TOUR STRUCTURE
- Introduction (Introduced self to the group, welcomed them to the museum and clearly stated the purpose of the tour)
- Clear transitions
- Effective Questions
- Conclusion

Comments:

TOUR CONTENT
- Clear organization of material
- Information and vocabulary appropriate for group
- Adaptable to group needs

Comments:

TECHNIQUE/AUDIENCE RELATIONSHIP
- Good audience rapport
- Oriented group in gallery before speaking
- Made eye contact with audience
- Projected voice well
- Correct pronunciation
- Encouraged audience participation
- Listened carefully and worked from audience input
- No unnecessary use of gestures or distracting mannerisms
- Able to adapt to unexpected events
- Able to identify and control minor discipline problems
- Moved group smoothly around the museum

Comments:

MUSEUM of WESTERN COLORADO

MEDICAL FACT SHEET
Field Trip Participant

DATE_____

NAME (Last) _____ (First) _____

Address_____ City _____ State _____ Zip _____

Home Phone _____

2. IN CASE OF EMERGENCY, NOTIFY:

Name _____ Relationship _____

Address _____ City _____ State _____ Zip _____

Phone (Day) _____ (Evening) _____

Alternative Name _____ Relationship _____

Phone (Day) _____ (Evening) _____

3. PHYSICIAN'S NAME _____

PHONE _____ PREFERRED HOSPITAL _____

4. DO YOU HAVE ANY MEDICAL CONDITION(s) ABOUT WHICH THE MUSEUM SHOULD BE AWARE? Please be specific. _____
_____

a. Special medication or treatment to be given _____
_____

b. Where is the medication located (i.e., purse, pocket etc.) _____
_____

c. How is the medication or treatment to be administered?
_____
_____

5. ARE YOU ALLERGIC TO ANY MEDICATION(s)? If yes, please specify _____
_____

6. ARE THERE ANY SPECIAL INSTRUCTIONS YOU WISH THE STAFF TO FOLLOW IN A MEDICAL EMERGENCY? _____
_____

_____
Signature

JMcL 9/96

TALLAHASSEE MUSEUM
FIELD TRIP CONFIRMATION & ADMISSION FORM
(Bring this form with you the day of your visit)

Date of visit:_____   Arrival Time:_____

#_____   Group:_____   State & County:_____

ADMISSION:

Total # of students:_____ · x Admission fee _____ = $_____

Total # of adults: _____ x Admission fee _____ = $_____

Total Entrance Fee: $_____

Total # of students _____ with: passes / membership cards / Leon County Public Schools

Total # of adults _____ with: passes / membership cards / Leon Co. Public Schools; or
No charge with appropriate number of students

PROGRAMS:

Program title: _____   **Program Fee: $_____**
(refer to "Program Payment" section on back)

Time of program: _____

Your program leader with meet you in front of the caboose. They will be wearing a khaki vest and nametag or be in period dress.

NOTE: To guarantee your program, the program fee must be paid at least ten (10) days prior to your visit. The Museum **does not** cancel programs because of rain.

PAYMENT METHODS: Check, purchase order, or cash.
Please have cash counted and in one lump sum before you arrive.

ADMISSION FEES:
General Rate: (when paying for less than 20 people)
$6.00/adult, $4.00/child, and $5.50/senior
Group Rate: (when paying for at least 20 people)
$3.50/child, one free adult per 10 students, additional adults $5.00 each
Educational Membership Rate:
$2.50/child, one free adult per 5 students, additional adults $5.00 each
Leon County Public Schools:
Covered by an annual contract, except for after-school programs

WELCOME TO THE TALLAHASSEE MUSEUM OF HISTORY AND NATURAL SCIENCE.
WE HOPE THAT YOU ENJOY YOUR VISIT!

PLEASE READ AND SIGN THE MUSEUM RULES ON THE BACK

In order to help insure that each visiting class has a safe, enjoyable, and informative experience, we ask that the following rules be strictly observed.

1. **All students must be under direct supervision of an adult leader at all times.** School groups that allow children to roam unattended will be asked to leave.

2. **Feeding Museum animals is prohibited**.

3. Food, drink, and smoking in exhibit spaces is prohibited.

4. Stay on identified trails. The Museum does not allow the collection of any plant or animal specimens.

5. Dispose of all trash in proper containers.

6. Treat the Museum resources and other visitors with respect.

I, the undersigned, do fully understand and agree to cooperate with the above stated rules.

_____   _____
Group leader   Date

PROGRAM PAYMENT INFORMATION

1. Program reservations are made on a first come, first served basis. If we can't serve your first request, we will attempt to find a time that will meet your needs.

2. To cancel a program without receiving a penalty, cancel **more than** 24 hours in advance of the scheduled program.

3. If cancellations are made **less than** 24 hours prior to the program, you will be billed $15.00.

4. Program fee is due 10 days prior to your scheduled visit. Call the Education Secretary if you have any questions.

5. The Museum reserves the right to cancel a program if a group is not prepared to begin their program on time. The Museum does not offer refunds for late arrivals. Please try to arrive at the Museum 30 minutes prior to your program.

6. The Museum does not cancel programs because of rain. Please have your students bring rain gear. If necessary, the Museum will substitute a program.

7. Make payment to: Tallahassee Museum of History and Natural Science
                                       Attn: Education Department
                                       3945 Museum Drive
                                       Tallahassee, FL 32310

Payment may be made with a company check, personal check, purchase order, or cash.

201

MUSEUM OF WESTERN COLORADO
LECTURE CHECK LIST
(To be filled out by sponsor)

SPONSORIONG INSTITUTION(S) _____
ADDRESS_____ CITY _____ STATE_____
ZIP_____

CONTACT PERSON_____ POSITION_____
ADDRESS_____ CITY_____ STATE_____ ZIP_____
PHONE ( )_____ HOME ( )_____
DATE_____ TIME_____ A.M./P.M.

LECTURE TITLE_____
_____
_____
_____
_____
_____
_____
_____

NAME OF AUDITORIUM_____ SEATING CAPACITY_____
LOCATION_____

SURROUNDING EVENTS (Please check one)

Breakfast____ Lunch____ Dinner____ Reception/Cocktail Party____ Media Coverage____
Book Signing: Before____ After____ Time(s)_____ A.M./P.M.
Location_____ Estimated Number of Persons Attending_____
Specifics:_____
_____
_____
_____

LECTURE FEES PAYABLE TO: _____
_____

TRAVEL ACCOMMODATIONS:

Air Fare Paid By:_____
Transport To/From Airport Name_____ Phone ( )_____
  Sponsor_____ Board Member _____ Colleague _____ Other _____
Meeting Location (be specific)_____

LODGING INFORMATION

Hotel/Motel/Other: Name_____ Room No. _____
Address _____ Phone ( )_____
Check-in Time:_____ A.M./P.M. Check-out Time:_____ A.M./P.M.

BOARD MEMBER/FRIEND/OTHER

Name:_____ Address:_____
_____ Phone (   )_____

Arrival Date:_____Time:_____A.M./P.M. Departure Date:_____Time:_____A.M./P.M.

EQUIPMENT NEEDED

35mm Slide Projector   Screen   Other_____
Slide Carousel w/ Remote Control   Podium   _____
Electric Pointer   Projectionist   _____
Microphone   Glass of Water   _____

Is flash photography permitted during the lecture? Yes_____ No_____. Is recording permitted during the lecture? Yes_____ No_____.

JMcL 8/96

SCHOLARSHIP APPLICATION
DEADLINE: MARCH 1, 1998
1998 Summer Institute in Western American Studies
Buffalo Bill Historical Center
Cody, Wyoming

Please print or type. Use additional sheets when necessary.

Name _____ Date _____

Address _____

City _____ State _____ Zip Code _____

Phone (home) _____ (office) _____

1. Indicate in which course(s) you wish to enroll.

_____   *"Indians Never Attack at Night": Creating the Indians' West through Popular Images - From Wild West Shows to Film*
                L. G. Moses   (June 1 - 12)

_____   *Picturing the West: Visual Art as Cultural History*
                Martha A. Sandweiss   (June 1 - 12)

_____   *Powwows: A Tradition of Cultural Persistence in Change*
                Patricia Albers and Beatrice Medicine   (June 15 - 26)

_____   *The Women of America's First Nations: A Legacy of Accomplishment and Pride*
                Patricia Albers and Beatrice Medicine   (June 15 - 26)

2. Indicate the type and number of scholarship(s) you are seeking (these cover tuition charged by the Center only, not that charged for academic credit by a university):

_____ half tuition scholarship(s)   _____ full tuition scholarship(s)

3. Have you received scholarships for previous Summer Institute courses?

_____ no   _____ yes   _____ what year(s)?

4. Scholarships are awarded on the basis of well-founded need. Use reverse side of this page or additional sheets to explain.

In addition to the scholarship applications, we ask that you submit a letter of recommendation from an individual who can attest to your financial need as well as to the extent to which you will personally benefit from and/or share with others what you have learned.

Letter of recommendation: _____ enclosed _____ under separate cover

Please return this form by appropriate deadline date to:
Lillian Turner
1998 Summer Institute
Buffalo Bill Historical Center
720 Sheridan Avenue
Cody, Wyoming 82414

204

Art is created in many different ways for different purposes. This results in variety and complexity in the art exhibited in an encyclopedic museum. Individuals are attracted to art for vastly different reasons and often have great curiosity about the unfamiliar works they see in a museum. The object of this activity is to help you develop a five step strategy that will help you understand a work of art.

Choose a gallery of MFA permanent collection art. Look carefully at the works of art in the gallery. Read object labels and wall text panels. Pick one work of art that makes you curious. Then read the list of viewing strategies below. Choose five that you think would help you make sense of the artwork, and rank the strategies in order you would use them by writing the numbers 1-5 in the spaces provided.

Make a diagram to show how the artist organized the main shapes. _____

Ask a question about the time in history when the work was made. _____

Look for clues about *how* the object was made. _____

Describe the mood of the work. _____

Tell what the work reminds you of. _____

Tell how the work makes you feel. _____

Relate the art to something in your own life. _____

Compare the work you chose to another one in the same room. _____

Describe your first reaction. _____

Tell what made you choose this work of art. _____

Make the same pose and facial expression you see in one figure. _____

Ask for more information about the artist. _____

Go to the library and find out more about the country it's from. _____

Imagine a story that fits what you see. _____

Write down a conversation between people in the artwork. _____

Find the focal point. _____

Make the sounds you could hear in this picture. _____

Talk about it with a friend. _____

Not enough strategies to choose from? Make up your own:

_____

_____

What questions would you like to ask about the work or the exhibition?

What will you remember most vividly about your chosen work?

CULTURAL HERITAGE CENTER
900 Governors Drive
Pierre, SD 57501-2217
(605) 773-3458 Fax (605) 773-6041

EDUCATION KIT LOAN AGREEMENT

Name and Address of borrowing institution:

«Company»
«Address1»
«City» «State» «PostalCode»
«WorkPhone»

Kit name and loan period: «Title»
                              «JobTitle»

The borrower agrees to accept the said loan subject to the following conditions.
The borrower agrees to pay a rental fee of $10.00 (plus $10.00 shipping, if applicable) per kit.
The rental fee is for a period of two weeks unless otherwise stated.

TERMS AND CONDITIONS

1. The borrower warrants that this educational kit will be kept in its entirety at the address specified herein during the loan period.
2. Unless otherwise specified herein, the borrower will transport or arrange for the transport of this educational kit to and from the borrower's premises.
3. The enclosed inventory of items in this educational kit will be considered to be a part of this agreement, but the Society may, without prior notice, substitute or omit items listed if such items are deemed by staff to be unfit for travel or display. **The kit return form must be filled out in its entirety**.
4. This agreement is not transferable.
5. The foregoing constitutes the entire agreement of the parties and neither this clause, nor this agreement, nor any subsequent modifications may be made except in writing signed by both parties hereto. Any changes herein of printed text or written addresses must bear the initials of the parties hereto.

_____   _____
authorized agent   date

_____   _____
for the South Dakota State Historical Society   date

Note: This agreement is sent to you in duplicate. One copy is for your records. Please sign and return one copy with the invoice and proper payment in the enclosed envelope.

Department of Education and Cultural Affairs
Office of History

KIT RETURN FORM

The checklist below is an easy way to make sure everything is back in the kit before it is returned. Feel free to check off the items as you pack them. Also, please note any damage that may have occurred to an object on the bottom of the form. Thank you!

1 bone flesher
1 spool of red ribbon
3 pieces of trade silver
1 hair pipe necklace
2 trade mirrors
2 silver conchos
1 porcupine tail brush
3 hanks of beads
1 horn comb
1 bag of sinew
6 leg bands with hawk bells
2 vials of porcupine quills
1 example of quillwork
1 string of trade beads
1 vial of pony beads
1 beaded toe piece
3 buffalo tooth bundles

1 bone awl
2 metal awls
1 silver bracelet
1 copper armband
1 stone maul head
1 Green River knife

2 stone arrow points
2 metal arrow points
1 tobacco twist
1 reed stem pipe
4 bags of dried plums
1 strand of wild turnips

2 pieces of Hudson's Bay blanket
1 strike-a-light with flint
1 lump of "vermillion"
1 powder horn
1 ermine pelt
1 otter fur hair tie
1 quill flattener

1 metal flesher
2 feathers
1 tomahawk with brass tacks
2 pieces of mink pelt
3 pieces of buffalo hide
1 piece of deerskin
1 beaver pelt
4 posters

3 pieces of unbleached muslin
3 pieces of blue & white gingham cloth
1 piece of red trade cloth
3 pieces of red calico cloth
3 pieces of blue calico cloth

Damage object? Tell us what happened

_____

_____

Did you use the news release? yes_____   no_____   If yes, where did you send it? _____

Number of students that used the kit_____

Teacher's signature:_____ Date_____

Thank you for completing this form

TEACHING AIDS ORDER FORM

Black Creek Pioneer Village
1000 Murray Ross Parkway
Downsview, ON M3J 2P3

Tel: (416) 736-1733
Fax: (416) 661-6610

TO: _____   SHIP TO: _____

_____   _____

_____   _____

_____   _____

Qty. Ordered	Description	Unit Price	Total
	GST #R-108-088-584	**Sub-Total**	
		G.S.T.	
		P.S.T.	
		TOTAL	

SHIP VIA: _____

_____

Payment: Purchase Order No.: _____

Credit Card (Type & No.): _____

Expiration Date: _____

metro region
conservation

208

MAPS:

All the maps included in this listing are copies of original maps with all the wording, spelling and misconceptions of the shape of the world at that time. The different packages were created to represent various themes such as the settlement of French-held Canada or the development of British North America.

Map Packages:

British North America	*$15.00*
New Found Land and St. Lawrence Bay	(1760's)
British Colonies in North America	(1780's)
A Map of the United States of America	1783
A New Map of Upper and Lower Canada	1807
British North America	1834
Canada West	1846
Canada East	1858
Canada West	1858

Canada 1690-1860's	*$15.00*
Nord America	1690
Partie de L'Amerique Septant	1755
British Colonies in North America	1785
A New Map of Upper and Lower Canada	1807
British North America	1834
Canada East	1858
Canada West	1858

French Canada	*$7.50*
Le Canada ou Nouvelle France	1656
America (Nord)	1690
Parti de L'Amerique septent qui comprent la Nouvelle France	1755
Canada Louisiane et Terres Anglaises	1755

Toronto and Area Pre-Confederation	*$11.00*
Tremaine's County of York	1860
Colton's Canada West	1858
City and Liberties Toronto	1842
Plan of York Harbour	(1815)
Upper Canada	1846

Single Maps (All reprinted on heavy white paper)

(Nord) America	1690	56cm x 46cm	**$2.60**
A New Map of Upper and Lower Canada	1807	56cm x 46cm	**$2.60**
Canada including New Brunswick and Nova Scotia	1830	56cm x 46cm	**$2.60**
Partie Occidentale de la Nouvelle France ou du Canada	1755	56cm x 46cm	**$2.60**
Le Canada ou Nouvelle France	1656	56cm x 46cm	**$2.60**
Upper Canada	1846	46cm x 36cm	**$1.75**
Colton's Canada West	1858	61cm x 41cm	**$3.45**
Colton's Canada East	1858	61cm x 41cm	**$3.45**
York County	1860	56cm x 46cm	**$3.45**
Toronto	1783	44cm x 40cm	**$2.60**
United States of America	1783	44cm x 40cm	**$2.60**

NEWSPAPERS:

These are printed full-size copies of 4 newspapers ranging from 1830 to 1859. They are prime examples of the newsprinting trade showing the development of weekly papers from one sheet of small type to elaborately illustrated four page copy. The two Toronto Weekly Message papers printed only two weeks apart are excellent examples of how the changing political scene in Europe, in 1859, was viewed here in Canada.

Newspapers	**$1.30** each or 4 for **$4.35**
The Colonial Advocate York	April 15, 1830
The Constitution by W.L. Mackenzie, Toronto	September 6, 1837
Toronto Weekly Message, W.L. Mackenzie	July 16, 1859
Toronto Weekly Message, W.L. Mackenzie	July 30, 1859

BOOKS:

Our Gift Shop has a number of valuable resource books on sale, only a few of which are listed here. Please feel free to visit the book corner of the Gift Shop on your visit.

The books listed below have proven to be great value to teachers year after year.

Black Creek Pioneer Village Guide Book
A must for unguided tours, it is an excellent overview of the village. It is also very useful for pre-tour preparations. 38 pages   **$2.80**

Black Creek Pioneer Village by Nick and Helma Mika
With 75 colour and 50 black and white illustrations, and a descriptive text, this book captures the daily activity of Black Creek Pioneer Village that we call "Life in the Past Lane".   **$18.95**

Charlie Needs a Cloak by Tomie de Poola
This is the children's story on which our most popular tour is based. Join "Charlie's" adventures from sheep to cloak, both in the book and at Black Creek Pioneer Village. Wonderfully illustrated.   **$7.98**

The Blacksmith of Fallbrook by Audrey Armstrong
The story tells of Walter Cameron, born in 1894, who was a blacksmith, woodcarver and storyteller. 96 pages   **$6.95**

Yesterday's Blacksmith by Charles W. Nolan
This the story of what the blacksmith did, how he did it, the tools he worked with and his role in community life at a time in our history when the world moved at a much slower pace. The author is a fifth generation blacksmith, a family trade, beginning prior to 1800. 79 photos and illustrations. 80 pages. Soft cover   **$11.98**

LEARNING THROUGH Art
at The Museum of Fine Arts, Houston

Innovative, multidisciplinary, art-centered **RESOURCE** curriculum kits *for* grades **one** through **six**

Learning Through Art at The Museum of Fine Arts, Houston, breaks new ground! This educational program uses outstanding works of art from the MFA's encyclopedic collection as the focus for instruction in art, language arts, social studies, science, and math. Each kit motivates students in every subject by teaching the importance of art in all areas of life and learning. Learning Through Art at The Museum of Fine Arts, Houston, pushes the limits of art education by helping teachers to integrate art successfully into school curricula.

Curriculum Kits

Two kits available, grades 1-3 and 4-6, each containing:
1. 24" x 36" color posters of works of art from the Museum of Fine Arts, Houston
2. Teachers' guide
   a. comprehensive lesson charts illustrated art-making lesson plans
   b. information on the works of art
3. Videotape introducing students to four Texas artists at work: Karin Broker, printmaker; photographer Keith Carter; Jesus Bautista Moroles, sculptor; Floyd Newsum, painter.

Prices

Curriculum kit for grades 1-3:

25 posters, teachers' guide, and videotape:
Schools $225
General public $375
Teachers' guide only $40
Shipping and handling 7% of sales total (minimum $3.50)

Curriculum kit for grades 4-6:

32 posters, teachers' guide, and videotape:
Schools $285
General public $480
Teacher's guide only $40
Shipping and handling 7% of sales total (minimum $3.50)

To order, complete and return the attached form. For further information, call (713) 639-7588, fax (713) 639-7707, or e-mail resource@mfah.org.

Learning Through Art at The Museum of Fine Arts, Houston, Order Form

Name: _____

School District: _____

School/Organization: _____

Mailing Address: _____

City: _____ State: _____

Zip: _____ Phone: (_____) _____

Item Code
A   Learning Through Art, grades 1-3
B   Teachers' Guide only, grades 1-3
C   Learning Through Art, grades 4-6
D   Teachers' Guide only, grades 4-6

Item	Quantity	Unit Price	Subtotal
A	_____	$ _____	$ _____
B	_____	$ _____	$ _____
C	_____	$ _____	$ _____
D	_____	$ _____	$ _____
		Shipping and handling:	$ _____
		TOTAL:	$ _____

❏ Check enclosed (payable to the Museum of Fine Arts, Houston)
❏ Please bill my institution: purchase order #_____

I will: ❏ receive the materials by mail.
       ❏ retrieve materials at 5100 Montrose, Houston, TX.
         (by appointment; please call (713) 639-7588)

Return form and payment to: Resource Center • The Museum of Fine Arts, Houston • P.O. Box 6826 • Houston, TX. 77265-6826

The Christmas Story in Art
40 slides, 40 min. audiocassette (NGA) H/A
Cat. #CS012
35 min. video (NGA) H/A
Cat. #CV012
35 min. video (NGA) H/A
Cat. #VC012

The Easter Story in Art
50 slides, 48 min. audiocassette (NGA) H/A
Cat. #CS013

Celebrating the Day of the Dead
20 min. video (EVN) M/H/A
Cat. #VC685

Ritual and El Día de los Muertos
study guide (SAMA) E/M/H/A
Cat. #SG600

Special Programs

Arts for Life:
Art Education in Schools
15 min. video (GCE) A
Cat. #VC624

Joseph Campbell:
The Message of the Myth
60 min. video (MF) A
Cat. #VC605

The Caravaggio Conspiracy
60 min. video (RMA) H/A
Cat. #VC784

National Gallery of Art:
Tour of the Collection
laser disc (NGA) H/A
Cat. #LD001

Protest and Patriotism:
A History of Dissent and Reform
study guide (SI) M/H
Cat. #SG607

They Risked Their Lives:
Rescuers of the Holocaust
23 min. video (GB) H/A
Cat. #VC669

Voices in Celebration:
Behind-the-Scenes at the NGA
45 min. video (NGA) H/A
Cat. #VC201

Art Across Time and Cultures
33 min. video (AIC) A
Cat. #VC747

Artists at Work
(Learning Through Art)
54 min. video (MFAH) E/M/H/A
Cat. #VC340

What Do You See?
20 min. video (AIC) A
Cat. #VC730

Teacher, Can We Go to the Art Museum?
13 min. video (UCSB) A
Cat. #VC729

Art-To-Go Poster Set

Twenty-four laminated posters of works of art from the collection of the Museum of Fine Arts, Houston. Includes labels, signs, art activities, a glossary, and information on each poster. Great for school festivals; hallway, library, and cafeteria displays; and classroom activities. Available for two weeks for single classroom or four weeks for library or cafeteria displays.
24 posters, text (MFAH) E/M/H
Cat. #SP312*

Poster Sets must be picked up and returned in person.

Learning Through Art at The Museum of Fine Arts, Houston Curriculum Kits

This multidisciplinary resource curriculum for grades 1-6 explores the permanent collection of the Museum of Fine Arts, Houston, through art, language arts, math, science, and social studies. This program was codeveloped, tested, and piloted by the museum and Clear Creek ISD.

The kit contains:
• manual with complete lesson charts, illustrated art-making lesson plans, and information on the works of art

• videotape of four Texas artists: Karin Broker, printmaker; Keith Carter, photographer; Jesus Bautista Moroles, sculptor; Floyd Newsum, painter

• 54 posters of works of art from the Museum of Fine Arts, Houston

Two kits are available:
Grades 1-3
25 posters, manual, and video (MFAH) E
Cat. #SP313*

Grades 4-6
32 posters, manual, and video (MFAH) E
Cat. #SP314*

This kit must be picked up and returned in person.

For the Hearing Impaired and Students with Special Needs

Closed-captioned videocassettes are available for many programs and are indicated by a "CV" in the catalogue number.

Beyond the Limits:
Creative Art Solutions for People with Special Needs
20 slides, postcards, text, art activities (MFAH) E/M/H/A
Cat #CS333
15 min. video (for those working with people with severe disablities) (MFAH) E/M/H/A
Cat. #VC333

How to Order

All materials are lent year-round, free of charge, to educators, community leaders, and docents, for up to two weeks. Request materials at least two weeks in advance.

You may check out materials

• by phoning the Resource Center at (713) 639-7588

• by e-mailing resource@mfah.org

• by faxing orders to (713) 639-7707

• by mailing a copy of this order form to:

> Art-To-Go Resource Center
> The Museum of Fine Arts, Houston
> P.O. Box 6826
> Houston, TX 77265-6826

You may return materials

• by mail to the Resource Center at the address listed above. You are responsible for the return shipping of materials, 4th-class library rate

• in person to 5100 Montrose, reception desk, Monday through Friday 8:00 a.m.–6:00 p.m., Saturday 9:00 a.m.-5:00 p.m.

The Resource Center charges $1 per day for late programs and the purchase price for all lost, damaged, or unreturned programs.

Note: All programs are provided as direct loans to groups and are for educational use only. Programs may not be broadcast, reproduced, or transferred to another medium or format without special license from the originating museum or producer.

Please do not remove this page. Photocopy this form to order.

ART-TO-GO RESOURCE CENTER ORDER FORM

BORROWER'S NAME

DATE   SCHOOL DISTRICT

SCHOOL/ORGANIZATION

MAILING ADDRESS

CITY   STATE   ZIP

DAYTIME PHONE #   EVENING PHONE #

FAX #   E-MAIL ADDRESS

Check one:

❏ Educator (list grade levels) _____ subject(s)_____

❏ Docent ❏ Community Leader ❏ Other_____

CATALOGUE NUMBER	TITLE	DATE NEEDED	ALTERNATE DATE

You will be notified if the materials are not available within the dates requested.

I would like to:

❏ receive the materials by mail

❏ pick up the materials at 5100 Montrose (Monday-Friday 8:00 a.m.-6:00 p.m., Saturday 9:00 a.m.-5:00 p.m.) Date: _____

HOMESTEAD MUSEUM

A City of Industry Historic-Cultural Landmark

Group Tour Confirmation

We are pleased to reserve a scheduled tour for your group of the Homestead Museum. Please review the following information to help make your group's visit to the site a more memorable and worthwhile experience.

Comfort	Please wear comfortable shoes and clothes and dress appropriately for the weather. Your group will spend about 40 minutes of the visit outdoors. On rainy days they will be outdoors for about 15 minutes. If some of the people in your group are sensitive to the sun, we suggest they bring hats for protection. Most of the site is accessible to wheelchair users, however, there is a maximum of 3 wheelchairs for every museum guide.
When you arrive	When you arrive, please meet your museum guide directly outside of the Pio Pico Gallery and divide into the number of groups indicated on the tour reservation confirmation. Please divide your group as equally as possible.
Cameras	In order not to detract from the continuity of the tour, the Homestead Museum asks that no one take photographs during the tour. Arrangements may be made to take photographs after the tour.
Picnics	The Homestead has a picnic area that can accommodate a maximum of 36 people. If your group would like to use this area during its visit, please call the Homestead office to make reservations.
What if. . .?	If you would like to add more people to your tour, please let us know a week in advance so that we can accommodate you. If your tour is postponed or cancelled, please call us as soon as possible at (818) 968-8492 so we can notify our volunteer museum guides.

**To confirm your reservation and the size of your group,
please call one week in advance at (818) 968-8492. Thank you!**

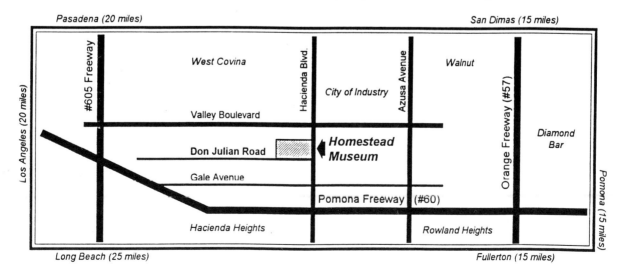

15415 East Don Julian Road ❦ City of Industry, California 91745-1029 ❦ Telephone (818) 968-8492 Fax (818) 968-2048

Invoice/Tour Confirmation Form

John Jay French Museum/ Beaumont Heritage Society

2985 French Road
Beaumont, Texas 77706
409-898-0348/FAX 409-898-8487

Read all Instructions Carefully!

1. Buses are to park in the front of the museum, cars can park in front of Museum Offices.
2. Report to the Museum offices as soon as you arrive.
3. Fees are paid prior to starting the tour.
4. The gift shop will be open during your tour. If your students wish to make purchases please advise them to bring money.
5. We do not have public restroom facilities, therefore arrangements for your group must be made prior to your arrival at the museum.
6. Please be aware that if you are 15 minutes late and *you have not called us to advise us that you will be late --your tour will be cancelled.*
7. Please sign the tour confirmation form and return it with payment to the John Jay French Museum. Keep a copy for your records. Receipt of the signed copy with payment confirms your reservations.

Date of Tour_____**Time of Tour**_____

Organization_____

Number of Guests_____**# of Chaperornes**_____**Grade (if students)**____

Contact Person_____

Mailing Address_____

City_____**State**_____**Zip**_____

Telephone (__)_____

Special Instructions_____

_____

_____

Admission	**Adults**		**$3.00**
	Seniors		**$2.00**
	Students (through college)		**$1.00**

School Groups

$30 per class (1 -3 classes)

$25 per class (4 or more classes)

(Adult to student ratio for school groups 1:5)

Amount Due $_____

Signature:_____**Date**_____

For office use only:
Doc:_____
Enclosed:_____

BB RW BM JH IW

11/97 Tourcon.WPS

INFORMATION FOR SCHOOL GROUPS

GETTING READY

SUPERVISION	- A minimum of one supervising adult for every five students/children is required
	- Supervisors and students are to remain with each other <u>at all times</u>
GUIDELINES	1. DO NOT RUN IN THE MUSEUM
	2. DO NOT TOUCH ANYTHING ON DISPLAY UNLESS THERE IS A PLEASE TOUCH SIGN
	3. DO NOT CHEW GUM IN THE MUSEUM
	4. DO NOT EAT OR DRINK IN THE MUSEUM
	5. DO NOT TALK LOUDLY, YELL OR SHOUT IN THE MUSEUM.
	- The above rules apply to students AND their adult supervisors!
	- These rules help make everybody's visit an enlightening, enjoyable experience, at the same time they help protect the artifacts for future visitors to study and admire
NAMETAGS	- Knowing your name helps us make your visit more personal

PARKING & PUBLIC TRANSIT

BUSSES	- Free bus parking is available on the north side of 10 Avenue SE (facing west) just past the traffic lights on 1 St. SE
CARS	- There are several paylots for cars located in areas surrounding Glenbow
PUBLIC TRANSIT	- The C-Train LRT stops a block north of the Glenbow...if you're coming from the northwest on a Brentwood train get off at the Centre Street station, if you're coming from the northeast on Whitehorn train or from the south on an Anderson train get off at the Olympic Plaza station
	- Several busses stop nearby - check with Calgary Transit for route information

YOU'VE ARRIVED

REVIEW	1. Review the five GUIDELINES listed above before going into the museum
ADMISSION	2. The group leader goes directly to the Admission desk to check the group in and pay the admission charge
COATS & BAGS	3. Then proceed to the Coat Check area where all Glenbow visitors are required to leave their coats, bags (other than purses), back packs, hats and lunches - please keep your school's items together (ie. on one rack if possible)

LUNCH

Although Glenbow doesn't have facilities for school groups to have lunch or snack breaks there are a couple of places nearby for that purpose... Olympic Plaza (outdoors - half a block east of the museum) or The Devonian Gardens in Eaton's Centre (indoors - three blocks west of the museum)

SOUTH
DAKOTA STATE
HISTORICAL SOCIETY

CULTURAL HERITAGE CENTER
900 Governors Drive
Pierre, SD 57501-2217
(605) 773-3458   Fax (605) 773-6041

Dear Teacher or Group Leader:

The South Dakota State Historical Society is very pleased that you are planning a tour of the Cultural Heritage Center. We have many exciting temporary and permanent exhibits that we invite all to see.

Prior to your arrival, please review with your group the following comments on museum etiquette. It is not our wish to quell any enthusiasm, but it may be helpful if everyone is aware of acceptable behavior in a museum atmosphere.

Thank you and best wishes for an enjoyable visit to the Cultural Heritage Center

MUSEUM MANNERS

The word "muse" means "to think." A museum is a place to think, to explore, to discover and to learn. This should be reflected in the way visitors conduct themselves while in a museum. Appropriate behavior makes it easier for all visitors to focus their attention on the displays and learn from their experience.

- If your tour is a guided one, please note that our guides have much information to impart. Please listen and feel free to ask questions.

- No food, drink, or gum are allowed in the gallery.

- Please be courteous, walking **behind** rather than in front of others who are looking at the exhibits. We encourage you to stop and look at the exhibits. Labels are posted for your information.

- The art and other objects at the Cultural Heritage Center are special for many reasons. You can help keep them in good condition by looking, **not touching,** unless there is a notation to the contrary.

- You should avoid touching or leaning against glass cases for your safety and to prevent breakage.

- For students -- a pencil or pen is only for writing on an activity sheet provided by your teacher or the Cultural Heritage Center. Using it as a pointer could ruin an artifact or hurt someone. Please be careful.

- Please use stairways so the elevator will be available for wheelchair users and others who have difficulty climbing stairs. Students are not allowed in the observation gallery without an adult supervisor.

- Please remind students that climbing, or running up the outside facade and grass area of the building can be hazardous due to the tall grass and terrain. We would not want them to encounter or startle any of the animals that may inhabit the area.

Finally, your guide is a valued volunteer. Please express your appreciation.

Department of Education and Cultural Affairs
Office of History

216

MUSEUM CUB SCOUT CAMP-INS

The intention and goal of the Camp-In Program at the Buffalo Museum of Science is to expose participants to hands-on science, aimed primarily at grade levels one through six.

It is a special program that inspires children to discover science in an entertaining and educational way. A unique relationship evolves between the children and the Museum, accentuated by the presence of informed staff.

The focus of this camp-in will correspond with the Museum's new exhibit, "Bats: Masters of The Night". Activities begin early Saturday evening after the Museum closes and resume again the following morning.

A typical camp-in includes activity stations, a film/video in the auditorium, science demos and workshops, snacks and breakfast.

What To Bring
Participants will need to bring a sleeping bag, comfortable clothing and shoes, and a minimum amount of personal items (comb, toothbrush, etc.) There are no shower facilities. You will probably be most comfortable sleeping in loose-fitting light clothing. **Do not bring any food or drinks.**

Camp-In Meals
The Museum provides an evening pizza snack and breakfast, so you should plan on eating dinner ahead of time.

Camp-In Safety
Security guards are on duty throughout the night. Additional fire and police protection are a short distance away.

How To Register
Cub Scout leaders may call the Museum Programs Department for registration information at 896-5200 ext: 203. Individual registrations cannot be accepted.

Camp-In Dates
October 7th & 8th and December 9th & 10th

Cost
The fee for 1995 Camp-Ins is $22 per camper; $11 per chaperone/leader

BUFFALO MUSEUM OF SCIENCE
1020 Humboldt Parkway
Buffalo, New York   14211-1293
(716) 896-5200

GROUP TOUR REQUEST FORM

Fill in areas in **bold** only (do not take other information, since this gets confused with confirming a reservation). Jean Perez schedules all tours (available Tuesday through Saturday). If short notice and Jean is not available, refer request to Sylvia Gutierrez.

Today's date: _____ ☐ Accept: forward to Admin. Assistant

Received by: _____ ☐ Reject: forward to Mary Roberts

Name of group: _____

Tour date: _____ Time: _____ Total number of persons: _____

Children (school/age level): _____ Teens: _____ Adult: _____ Senior: _____

Special considerations:

Comments to group: ☐ "Please have children wear nametags, first name only."
        (applies to pre-school to 6th grade only)

☐ "Picnic area reserved from _____ to _____."
        (maximum 36 adults or 48 children; suggest parks to larger groups)

☐ "Please divide your group into _____ upon arrival."
        (maximum of 15 persons per tour group)

Notes to staff: ☐ Interested in: _____
        "Are you interested in anything special? California history, architecture?"

☐ Special accommodations (specify): _____
        "Will anyone in your group require special accommodations?"
        (limit of three wheelchairs per tour; limit of 10 mentally challenged visitors per tour)

☐ Other language: ☐ *Spanish* ☐ *American Sign Language (3-5 days notice)*

☐ Include map to local picnic areas

☐ Include local restaurant guide

☐ We will provide refreshments upon arrival

☐ Other:

To confirm your reservation and the size of your group, please call one week in advance at (626) 968-8492. Thank you!

Contact: _____ **Title:** _____

☐ **home**

Address: _____ ☐ **business**

City: _____ **Zip:** _____

Phone: (_____)_____ **Best time to call:** _____

Reservation completed date: _____ By: ☐Jean Perez ☐Other: _____

Comments:

218

Forms\Tourreqt.doc 8/97

TOUR REQUEST FORM

Today's Date_____

TOUR INFORMATION

Date Requested _____

Time_____

People in Group_____Grade_____

Age Group:

Student	Adult
Pre-School	Adult
Elementary	Sr Citzn
MS	
HS	
College	

TOUR TYPE ☐ Docent-Led **TOUR TOPIC** 1.)_____
             ☐ Self-Guided
             ☐ Audio   2.)_____

☐ **SD**   ☐ **SSG**   ☐ **AD**   ☐ **ASG**   ☐ lunch in sculpture garden
                                             ☐ sketching

GROUP INFORMATION

Group/School Name_____ **DISTRICT**_____

Contact Person_____Title_____

Mailing Address_____

City_____ ST_____ **ZIP**_____

telephone - day # (   ) _____ evening # (   )_____
                                           fax # (   )_____

Notes:

TOUR CONFIRMATION

☐ Confirmed on book (date & time)_____
☐ Entered on database: (date)_____
☐ Notified Lobby & Security (attach copy of memo)
☐ Unable to schedule because: _____

TOUR SCHEDULING OFFICE / #18036

★ ★ ★ ★ ★ ★ ★ ★ ★ ★ **School Tour Scheduling Sheet** ★ ★ ★ ★ ★ ★ ★ ★ ★ ★ ★ ★

Agent _____   _____

School _____   Date of Tour

Address _____

_____   _____

_____   Date of Request

Teacher/Agent _____

Grade _____ **Telephone** (w) _____ (h) _____

Number of Students _____ **Teachers** _____

Total Tour Time _____

Tour Time	**Tour Size**	**Tour Type**
_____	_____	_____
_____	_____	_____
_____	_____	_____
_____	_____	_____
_____		

ADA needs _____ **Haversack** _____

Special requests _____

Group scheduled for other sites _____

Staff scheduled for tour _____

Admission _____ *(per student)* _____ *(per adult)* _____ *(adults free)*

Method of payment _____ *(upon arrival)* _____ *(bill)*

Confirmation sent _____ **On Calendar** _____

★ ★

Group Type _____

Group Size/Amount _____ *(students)* _____ *(adults)* _____ *(free)*

Total due _____ Tour completed _____ Paid _____

School Reservation
American Quarter Horse Heritage Center & Museum

Name of school _____

Contact person _____

Address _____

_____

Phone number _____

Day of visit _____

Arrival time _____   Grade level _____

Est departure time _____   No. of classes _____

No. of buses _____   No. of students _____

No. of bus drivers _____   No. of teachers _____

No. of other adults _____

_____Check if directions on bus parking provided.

_____Check if information given about "free time" under teacher supervision.

_____Check if the following rate information provided. Students ages 6-18, $1.50 each; teachers or official school employees and bus driver, free; all other adults, $3 each.

_____Check if information given about preferred method of group payment.

     _____Group plans to pay one lump cash amount.

     _____Group plans to pay with school check or purchase order.

     _____Group has special payment needs which need reviewed and approved <u>or</u> denied:_____

_____Yes, students will be able to shop.   _____No, students will not shop.

Program requested:

_____Special program request_____

_____4th grade which qualifies to receive ANB previsit packet

Special information _____

_____

_____

Date of inquiry_____   Reservationist_____

Date confirmed_____   Phone____   Mail____

Where can you... Make a tussy-mussy? Help build a wigwam? Visit a friend from Sweden? Eat an edible airplane? Go on a bear hunt? Why...

Time for Tots

at

The Children's **Museum** *of Houston*

1500 Binz, Houston, Texas 77004

Time for Tots is designed for **children two to three years of age** *and an adult*. Classes are offered on Friday and Saturday mornings throughout the year.

Each month's series introduces children to themes such as science, culture, cooking, movement and the arts. *An early childhood specialist facilitates activities, songs, stories and group time that support the theme. Accompanying adults work closely with the children and receive ideas, recipes and suggestions for at-home activities.*

Classes are small and **encourage creativity, provide young children with age-appropriate opportunities to enhance fine and gross motor skills, language development and, most importantly, provide parents and children with time to learn and grow together.**

Come join us as we explore, discover and just have lots of fun learning many wondrous, exciting new things parents and children can enjoy together!

For additional information or to register, call 713/522-8185.

Time for Tots Registration Form

❒ **Fridays— Month of** _____
9:30 - 10:30 a.m.

❒ **Saturdays— Month of** _____
9:30 - 10:30 a.m.

Fee for three-class series for both child and adult is $24/Members and $30/non-Members. **Return to the Children's Museum, P.O. Box 201675, Houston, Texas 77216-1675.** To register by phone, call 713/522-8185.

(Please Print)

Parent's name _____

Child's name _____ Child's age _____

Address _____

City _____ State _____ Zip _____

Home phone ( ) _____ Work phone ( ) _____

_____ Membership expiration date (if applicable)

_____ Total amount enclosed

Method of payment: ❒ check ❒ MC ❒ Visa ❒ AMEX

Account # _____ Exp. date _____

Name on card _____

Signature _____

REGISTRATION FORM FOR SUMMER PROGRAMS

* Please use a separate registration form for each child.
* All grade levels indicate grade completed by time of camp.
* For more information about camp programs, contact the Education Secretary at 575-8684.

A. Child's Name_____ Nickname _____

    Grade Completed_____ Birth Date _____

    Address_____

B. Parent/Guardian _____

    Home Phone_____ Work Phone_____ Other_____

C. Emergency Contact_____Relationship_____

    Home Phone_____Work Phone_____Other_____

D. Physician_____Phone_____

    Explain <u>any</u> medical problems, allergies, handicaps, etc, that we should be aware of:_____

    _____

    Is your child on any medications? If so, please explain_____

    _____

E. During swimming activities children will be closely supervised at all times and will be required to stay with a "buddy". Rate your child's swimming ability. (Check one):
    Non-Swimmer_____ Beginner_____ Intermediate_____ Advanced_____

    List the programs you would like to register for in the space below. There is a $25 <u>non-refundable</u> registration deposit for each summer camp program that is subtracted from the total cost of that camp (Mountain Adventures requires a $50 <u>non-refundable</u> deposit). There is no charge to be kept on a waiting list. If you register for a class and then decide to cancel, PLEASE inform us so that others may take advantage of our programs. If you transfer a child from one camp to another, you will be charged a $5 transfer fee.

CAMP	TITLE	GRADES	DATES/TIMES

Send or bring completed forms & payment to:
    SUMMER PROGRAMS
    Tallahassee Museum
    3945 Museum Drive
    Tallahassee, FL 32310

TOTAL REGISTRATION $_____

DEPOSIT ($25 per camp) $_____

BALANCE DUE $_____

<u>IMPORTANT</u>! The following section must be filled out IN FULL for us to process your request.

    I,_____, hereby authorize my child_____ to participate in activities sponsored by thee Tallahassee Museum, which may include, but are not limited to, field trips, tours, swimming, and travel from the premises in Museum vehicles. In case of an accident requiring medical treatment, I authorize treatment for my child as the attending medical personnel deem appropriate. I also agree not to hold the Tallahassee Museum responsible for injuries suffered by my child during activities sponsored by it.

_____   _____
(Parent/Guardian Signature)   (Date)

REGISTRATION FORM FOR PRESCHOOL

*Please use a separate registration form for each child.
*This must accompany a registration fee whenever signing up for a class, or we cannot guarantee you a space in the class.

*For more information about the preschool, contact the Education Secretary at 575-8684.

CHILD'S NAME_____
　　　　　　　　(Last)　　　　　　　　　　　　(First or Preferred)

AGE_____　BIRTH DATE_____

PARENT/GUARDIAN_____

ADDRESS_____
　　　　　　STREET　　　　　　CITY　　　　STATE　ZIP

HOME PHONE_____　WORK PHONE_____

EMERGENCY CONTACT PERSON (not parent)_____

HOME PHONE_____　WORK PHONE_____

Physician_____　Phone_____
Explain any medical problems, allergies, handicaps, etc. that we should be aware of:_____
_____

List the programs you would like to register for in the spaces below. There is a non-refundable, non-applicable registration fee of $40 per child.

CLASS	DATES	TIMES
1._____		
2._____		

IMPORTANT! The following section must be filled out **IN FULL** for us to be able to process your request. I, _____, hereby authorize my child,_____, to participate in activities sponsored by the Tallahassee Museum which may include, but are not limited to, field trips, tours, and travel from the premises in Museum vehicles. In case of an accident requiring medical treatment, I authorize treatment for my child as the attending medical personnel deem appropriate. I also agree not to hold the Tallahassee Museum responsible for injuries suffered by my child during activities sponsored by it.

_____　　_____
Parent/Guardian Signature　　　　　　　　　Date

NEHRU SCIENCE CENTRE
(NATIONAL COUNCIL OF SCIENCE MUSEUMS)

DR. E. MOSES ROAD, WORLI, BOMBAY - 400 018.

Tel. : 493 26 67

No. NSCB/   Date :

From : The Director

To   : The Principal,

Dear Sir/Madam,

With reference to your letter / telephonic conversation with us, we hereby confirm your participation in the programme mentioned below.

1.	Programme	: ....
2.	Subject/topic	: ....
3.	Date	: ....
4.	Time	: ....
5	No. of Students	: ....

Please ask the **Group Leader** to carry this letter & be present at the Centre **FIFTEEN** minutes prior to the programme.

Thanking You,

Yours faithfully,

Curator/Education Officer

.... Cut from here ....

(For office use only)

.... students and ....Teachers/Staff members of ....

....

may please be permitted to visit the Centre & participate in the ....

Programme on ....

Authorised signatory

225

EXHIBITS

Loan checklist
Planning
Work order

Exhibition Title   INVENTORY OF INDIVIDUAL EXHIBIT COMPONENTS

All main components are labelled with the accession number, use the components labelled with the accession number for each exhibit only.

Acc No.	Exhibit Title	Components

Exhibits Department Work Sheet

no. _____

Site or department _____

Ordered by _____

Taken by _____

Date   ordered _____   due _____

Description

Work done by _____

First draft completed _____

Final work completed _____ Approved by _____

Final quantity_____ Estimated cost _____

To Be   ☐ Picked up   ☐ Hand delivered   ☐ Mailed or shipped

EXHIBITS DEPARTMENT ONLY remarks on completion

TECHNICAL WORKSHEET: SCIENCE INTERACTIVE EXHIBITS

TITLE		ACC NO. Sc / /
BASE EXHIBITION		LOC.

COMPONENTS	SUPPLIERS

REPAIRS / MAINTENANCE

DATE	REPAIRER	DETAILS

THE SCIENCE CENTRE & MANAWATU MUSEUM
Te Whare Pupuri Taonga o Manawatu

396 Main Street   Private Bag 11 055   Palmerston North   New Zealand   Phone +64 6 355 5000   Fax +64 6 358 3552

WORKSHEET: SCIENCE INTERACTIVE EXHIBITS

TITLE	ACC NO. Sc / /
BASE EXHIBITION	LOC.
INTENTION	DATE

SOURCE	TECHNICALS REQ'D
	power
DESCRIPTION	air
	light
	other
	SIZE maximum dimensions in mm
	h
	w
	d
	INS. VAL. $
	TOT. COST $
PARTS REQ'D TO OPERATE	LIFE SPAN

CONDITION

PACKING

RECORDED BY	DATE
DATA ENTRY ON COMPUTER: NAME	DATE

229

```
Black and white photocopy of exhibit photograph
```

NEG. NO

MOVEMENTS				
PURPOSE		DATE OUT	DATE IN	LOAN NO.
DEACCESSION DATE	REASON			
METHOD OF DISPOSAL				

NEVADA STATE MUSEUM
EXHIBIT DEPARTMENT

PLANNING & DESIGN WORKSHEET

Date Requested_____ Deadline_____

Requested By: _____

For: (Requestee's Dept. or Agency)_____

Date Completed: _____ Work By: _____

Amount of Time & Money_____

Title of Exhibit:_____

Theme Area: _____

Topic:_____

Main Message of This Topic: _____

_____

_____

What Important Points Need to be Addressed? _____

_____

_____

_____

Pictures *(list with approx. size)*   Describe exhibit technique:

_____   _____

_____   _____

_____   _____

_____   _____

_____   _____

Artifacts or specimens *(list)*:   _____

_____   _____

_____   _____

_____   _____

_____   _____

_____   _____

_____   _____

SHELDON MEMORIAL ART GALLERY
Exhibition Procedures List

Exhibition Title:_____

Gallery Space:_____ Curator:_____

Exhibition Dates:_____ Installation Dates:_____

Related Events:_____

Sponsorship/Support:_____

- -

CURATOR'S OFFICE

Pre-Exhibition Needs	Date/Initials	Printing/Publication	Date/Initials
Contract	_____	Announcement/	_____
Checklist	_____	Invitation	
Press Release	_____	Photography	_____
		Acknowledgments	_____
Press Photography	_____	Design	_____
Slides, Transparencies	_____	Printing	
Labels	_____	Brochure/Catalogue	
Didactic Panels	_____	Checklist	_____
		Essay	_____
Related Events	**Date/Initials**	Photography	_____
Reception	_____	Acknowledgments	_____
Symposium	_____	Design	_____
Gallery Talk	_____	Printing	_____
Lecture	_____		
Other	_____	**Post-Installation**	**Date/Initials**
Reservation Form	_____	Installation	_____
		Photography	_____

Security (Inform in Writing)

Special installation instructions_____

Related events_____

Special equipment_____

Photography Permitted   Yes _____   No_____

- -

PREPARATOR'S OFFICE

	Date/Initials		Date/Initials
Install Exhibition	_____	Matting/Framing	_____
Pedestals, Bases, Walls	_____	Lighting	_____
Labels & Didactic Panels	_____	Signage:	
		Indoor	_____
		Outdoor	_____
Special Equipment_____			

- -

REGISTRAR'S OFFICE

	Date/Initials		Date/Initials
Exhibition File	_____	Shipping:	
Checklist	_____	Arrival	_____
Condition Reports	_____	Departure	_____
Insurance	_____	Receipts:	
		Incoming	_____
		Outgoing	_____

3/16/93

MUSEUM OF ART
EXHIBITION PLANNING
PHASE 1: PROPOSAL

The exhibition proposal outlines in general narrative fashion the purpose, content, message, justification, timetable, and proposed gallery space of the proposed exhibition. The proposal will be evaluated according to its relation to the Museum's exhibition, acquisition, educational, and institutional, or other major goals; and its creativity, appropriateness, harmony with the established exhibition schedule, demands on Museum staff, and overall feasibility. Please confine your remarks to the spaces provided on this Proposal form.

TITLE: A working title will do. . . . .

ARTISTS: Name some or all of the artists represented. . . . .

. . . .

SOURCE: MOA permanent collection, on loan from another institution, or from any other source: . . . .

. . . .

LINEAR OR SQUARE FEET REQUIRED: . . . . **GALLERY:** . . . .

DURATION OF EXHIBITION: . . . .

PURPOSE: List the primary objectives of the exhibition. . . . .

. . . .

. . . .

MESSAGE: Summarize the proposed exhibition's interpretive focus and narrative content:

. . . .

. . . .

. . . .

CONTENT: Identify the types of art works or installation in this exhibition. Specify the approximate numbers of objects, their current location(s). Are permanent acquisitions expected from this exhibition?

. . . .

. . . .

. . . .

COST: Specify major expenses that are anticipated, e.g. conservation, exhibition fee, shipping, installation, travel, etc.

. . . .

REVENUE: Will this be a ticketed event? Indicate possible funding sources . . . .

. . . .

JUSTIFICATION:

1. Why is this a desirable exhibition for the MOA? . . . .
. . . .

2. Who are the intended audiences for this exhibition? . . . .
. . . .

3. How would this exhibition serve the Museum's audiences? . . . .
. . . .

4. How would this exhibition help fulfill the Museum's institutional goals? . . . .
. . . .

5. How would this exhibition relate to the Museum's present or future collections? . . . .
. . . .

6. How would this exhibition complement other exhibitions existing or being planned in the Museum?
. . . .
. . . .

OTHER VENUES: In the case of travelling exhibitions: . . . .
. . . .

PROPOSED BY: . . . . **DATE SUBMITTED.** . . . .

EXHIBITION PLANNING COMMITTEE RECOMMENDATION:

A. Accept _____   B. Reject _____   C. Defer _____

Comments: . . . .
. . . .

PROPOSED EXHIBITION PLANNING TEAM:

A. Curator _____

B. Designer _____

C. Educator _____

TIMETABLE: Preliminary development schedule: . . . .
. . . .

DATE FOR PHASE II REVIEW: _____   **APPROVED BY DIRECTOR:** _____

MUSEUM OF ART
EXHIBITION PLANNING
PHASE II: CONCEPT DEVELOPMENT

Exhibition Title: . . . .

Exhibition Team:

      Curator: . . . .

      Designer: . . . .

      Educator: . . . .

Gallery: . . . .

Opening Date: . . . .   **Closing Date:** . . . .

The following is a table of contents for this phase of the exhibition planning process. Responses to these issues should reflect a consensus of all team members and appear in a typewritten document appended to this form, and following its format. The completed document must be submitted to the Exhibition Planning Committee for review and approval.

I   **Preliminary Objects List** (include information about scale, media, present locations, ownership of works, and loan needs and conditions.)

II   **Conservation Needs** (Is conservation, matting, framing required ?- provide a schedule).

III   **Interpretive Framework:**

     A.   What sre the principle objectives for the exhibition as a whole and for each major section of the exhibition?

     B.   Explain the flow of ideas and information within the exhibition.

     C.   Identify interpretive techniques and media. List supporting photographs, graphics, objects, text panels, videos, audio tour, gallery guide, publications, electronic media, etc.

IV   **Educational Considerations:**

     A.   Identify target audiences

     B.   List and describe educational objectives (identify faculty and university courses that would benefit directly from the exhibition).

     C.   Identify potential for public programs and events (symposia, conferences, lectures, concerts, demonstrations, etc.)

     D.   Define needs for production of study guides, curricular material, docent training program, etc.

     E.   Travel and housing of invited speakers, curator, artist-in-residence, etc.

     F.   Formative (front end) evaluation

V   **Instalation and Fabrication:**

     A.   Gallery preparation (identify needs of exhibition design — remodeling, painting, lighting, etc)

    B.   Gallery furniture (identify needs for pedestals, vitrines, mounting systems, etc)

VI   Publicity, Advertising, and Visitor Services:

    A.   Invitations, brochures, posters, Museum Calendar, outdoor advertising, etc.

    B.   Press releases, interviews, editorials, paid advertising, radio, TV, etc.

    C.   Opening arrangements (gala, artists' reception, speakers, catering, etc.)

    D.   Member and donor events

    E.   Museum Store products, publications, promotions

    F.   Museum Cafe (menus, banquettes, promotions)

    G.   Speakers' Bureau

VII   Budget Impact:

    A.   Identify primary budgetary needs with reference to scale and special needs of project

    B   Identify revenue sources

EXHIBITION BUDGET WORKSHEET
Bjorn Evensen Sculpture and Painting
September 17, 1996 through January 15, 1997
1996/97 Fiscal Year

REGISTRATION			
	Travel		
	Insurance		
	Packing and Shipping		
	Other		
	Total Registration		$0
EXHIBIT DEVELOPMENT	Travel	$100	
	Graphic Design and Production	$1,600	
	Gallery Construction	$400	
	Gallery Painting	$2,500	
	Design Consulting		
	Cases, Platforms, and Panels	$1,500	
	Mount Production	$400	
	Interpretive Enhancement	$500	
	Lighting Equipment		
	Lighting Consulting		
	Deinstallation	$800	
	Documentation Photography	$150	
	Other	$600	
	Total Exhibit Development		$8,550
CURATORIAL	Travel		
	Exhibition Fee		
	Acquisitions		
	Curatorial Consulting		
	Other		
	Total Curatorial		$0
CONSERVATION	Frames and Matting		
	Materials		
	Outside Services		
	Other		
	Total Conservation		$0
ACADEMIC AND PUBLIC PROGRAMS	Audio Tour		
	Browsing Room Supplies		
	Education Consulting		
	Family/Gallery Guide		
	Lectures, Programs, and Symposiums	$100 a	
	Museum Teaching Supplies		
	School Curriculum and Services		
	Self-Guided and Disabled Tour Supplies		
	Study Gallery		
	Travel		

Bjorn Evensen Sculpture and Painting
1996/97 Fiscal Year

	Video, Film, Programs, and Multimedia		
	Docent Training	$100	b
	Speakers' Bureau/Outreach		
	Other		
	Total Academic and Public Programs		**$200**
PUBLIC RELATIONS AND MARKETING	Advertising		
	Press Releases	$100	
Museum Events	Invitations	$1,500	
	Mailing	$400	
	Refreshments	$300	
	Music	$300	
	Photography	$100	
Membership Events	Invitations		
	Mailing		
	Refreshments		
	Music		
	Other	$25	c
	Total Public Relations and Marketing		**$2,725**
PUBLICATIONS AND PRODUCTS	Catalog/Brochures		
(Marketing, Membership, Exhibition	Compact Disks		
Interpretation, Museum Store)	Post Cards		
	Posters		
	Other		
	Total Publications and Products		**$0**
SECURITY	Additional Security		
	Total Security		**$0**
TOTAL BUDGETED EXPENSES			**$11,475**
REVENUE SOURCES			
TOTAL BUDGETED REVENUES			**$0**
FOOTNOTES			
footnotes:			

Bjorn Evensen Sculpture and Painting
1996/97 Fiscal Year

SPENCER MUSEUM OF ART

EXHIBITION PLAN

Date Revised:_____

Title _____

_____

Dates _____

Galleries _____

Description _____

_____

Media/Numbers/Sizes _____

_____

_____

Staff Curator(s) _____

Guest Curator(s) _____

Organizing Institution _____

Address _____

Contact Person _____

Phone/Fax _____

Contractual Requirements:

Handling _____

_____

Environment _____

_____

Security _____

_____

Photography _____

_____

Publicity _____

_____

Credits _____

_____

Reports _____

_____

Funding

Grant from: _____ Written by: _____ Deadline:_____ Amount: $_____

Grant from: _____ Written by: _____ Deadline:_____ Amount: $_____

Other Funding: _____ $_____

$_____

$_____

$_____

Describe and estimate the following items, if applicable.

Rental Fee   Deposit $_____ due _____   Balance $_____ due _____   Total $___Loan Fees $

$_____

Conservation $_____

Packing/Crating $_____

Shipping $_____

$_____

$_____

Couriers $_____

Insurance $_____

Prep/Matting/Framing $_____

Installation $_____

Labels $_____

Other Logistics $_____

$_____

Catalogue: Cost $_____

   Publisher _____

   Author(s) _____

   Deadlines _____

Brochure: Cost $_____

   Author _____

   Deadlines _____

Poster Description, Cost: _____ $_____

Other Publications _____ $_____

$_____

Programs and Events: list dates, descriptions, and costs

_____ $_____

_____ $_____

_____ $_____

_____ $_____

_____ $_____

Other Venues for this Exhibition: list dates and locations

_____

_____

_____

Misc. Information, Deadlines, Etc.:

_____

_____

This form prepared by: _____

Oregon Historical SOCIETY

1200 S.W. PARK AVENUE, PORTLAND, OREGON 97205-2483

503/222-1741   TELEPHONE   FACSIMILE   503/221-2035

Exhibits Department

EXHIBITION PROPOSAL

Exhibition Title _____

Organized By: Organization _____

                            Name _____

                            Address _____

                            Phone _____

Exhibition Description _____

_____

_____

Gallery space(s) needed: _____

_____

Market/Audience (local, state, regional, national, international, specific interest):

_____

Collections resources

   OHS (specify: artifacts, archival material, photographs)

_____

_____

   Other collections (specify: artifacts, archival material, photographs)

_____

_____

Staff requirements

   Curator _____

   Guest Curator _____

   Designer _____

   Production Manager _____

   Other _____

Timing

   Estimated production time _____

   Opening date _____

   Closing date _____

(over)

Incorporating The Battleship Oregon Museum, Northwest Conservation Center, Oregon Geographic Names Board, Oregon Lewis & Clark Heritage Foundation

SERVING OREGON & ITS PEOPLE FOR MORE THAN A CENTURY

241

Travelling Exhibition Potential _____

_____

_____

Size of exhibition:

Square footage _____

Number of artifacts _____

_____

Interpretation:

Exhibit labels, text _____

Brochures, handouts, publications _____

_____

Programs, events _____

_____

Audiovisual material _____

_____

Educational material _____

_____

Approximate Cost: _____

Funding source(s): _____

_____

Justification (relevance to OHS mission, public value, contribution to field):

_____

_____

_____

_____

_____

Comments: _____

_____

_____

_____

Staff Contact/Coordinator _____

Date of Proposal _____

WORK ORDER

FORM 14B

Date Requested_____ Deadline_____

Requested By: _____

For: Requestee's Dept. or Agency) _____

Authorized By: (Exhibit Director) _____

Or: (NSM Director) _____

Date Completed: _____ Work By: _____

Amount of time: _____

Amount of Material: $$$_____

Cost Absorbed by the Exhibits Dept.: _____

Cost Billed to: _____

WORK REQUESTED: Attach additional pages and drawings if necessary.

(1)   PHOTO ORDERS: Use the reverse side and please be specific.

_____
_____
_____

(2)   ART & GRAPHIC ORDERS:

_____
_____
_____

(3)   FABRICATION/CONSTRUCTION ORDERS:

_____
_____
_____

(4)   DESIGN ORDERS:

_____
_____
_____

PHOTO ORDER CONTINUED

FIELD PHOTO WORK

DETAILS
_____
_____
_____
_____
_____

CONTENTS

QTY.

_____	Prints
_____	Stand. Size Neg.
_____	Non-Stand. Size
_____	Other

REQUESTS

QTY. m SURFACE

_____	Copy Negative
_____	Contact Print
_____	5 x 7 B/W
_____	8 x 10 B/W
_____	11 x 14 B/W
_____	Other

INTENDED USE

Publication _____
Display _____
Reseach _____
Other (Specify) _____
_____

SPECIAL INSTRUCTIONS

<u>ALL PRINTS WILL BE ON R.C. PAPER UNLESS SPECIFIED OTHERWISE.</u>

Person's Name: _____
$ Enclosed: _____
Negative (#'s) _____
_____
_____
_____

NEVADA STATE MUSEUM
EXHIBIT DEPT.

DESIGN & PRODUCTION WORKSHEET

Date Requested_____ Deadline_____

Requested By: _____

For: (Requestee's Dept. or Agency)_____

Date Completed: _____

Amount of Time: _____

DESIGN PHASE

Job	Assigned To	Due By	Completed
P & D Worksheet			
Research & Story Line			
Selection of Resources			
Floor Plan & Topic Flow			
Case & Panel Design			
Lighting Design			
Security Design			
Resources Delivered to Ex.			
Final Edit & Approval			

PRODUCTION PHASE

Job	Assigned To	Due By	Completed
Case & Panel Construction			
Gallery Carpentry			
Gallery Electrical Work			
Gallery Painting & Finishing			
Art Work & Graphics			
Typesetting & Graphics			
Photo Production I/H			
Photo Production O/H			
Full Graphic Installation			
Restoration & Preparation			
Special Effects			
Final Setup & Inventory			

Dallas Museum of Art

1717 N. Harwood, Dallas, Texas 75201

(214) 922-1267

PREPARATORS WORK REQUEST FORM

DATE:

FROM:

_____

Description of work needed (include special instructions):

_____
PLEASE SUBMIT COMPLETED FORM TO THE REGISTRAR'S OFFICE. THANK YOU.
_____

(Location change) New Location: _____ Date Moved: _____ by: _____

(Location change) Location updated in ARGUS: _____ by: _____

North Carolina Museum of History
DESIGN BRANCH WORK REQUEST

PROJECT NAME

ORIGINATOR USE		DESIGN BRANCH USE
Name	Date requested	Date received:
	Branch head approval	Branch head initials
Phone extension:		
Project Description		Project assigned to
		Project number
		Schedule for project
Date needed (Reason?)		

Notes

Materials and/or tools required

Budget line item/Amount(s)

Project completed by
Date completed

Purchase Order numbers

When project is complete, return form to Design branch head. Form to be filled in project book.

FUND RAISING

MUSEUM OF FINE ARTS, HOUSTON
INKIND GIFT ENTRY FORM

ID #:	INITIALS / DATE:

INDIVIDUAL/COMPANY MAKING INKIND GIFT:

NAME:

CORPORATE CONTACT/TITLE:

ADDRESS:

CITY:	STATE	ZIP
SPOUSE	DAY PHONE	NIGHT PHONE
FAX	E-MAIL	MISC.

CONSTITUENT TYPES:

☐ Trustee	☐ Individual	☐ Corporation	☐ Foundation	☐ Other

INKIND INFORMATION:

Donated Service Or Item(s):

Campaign Year	Campaign	Account Code

AMOUNT $	DEDUCTIBLE $

Value Of Gift Set According To:	☐ Donor	☐ Musuem Recipient

☐ Credit for	☐ In Honor of	☐ In Memory of	☐ MG to	ID #

☐ POP/	☐ **ANONYMOUS**	☐ Attributes

Comments:

INFORMATION SYSTEMS ACKNOWLEDGEMENT

Date Recieved:	Date Completed:	Completed By:

COPIES

☐ CORPORATION	☐ FOUNDATION	☐ INDIVIDUAL	☐GOVERNMENT	☐ CIVIC

INKFORM.DOC/Dec-97

248

OREGON HISTORICAL SOCIETY
Gift-In-Kind Record

Please complete sections A, B, and C, obtain necessary signatures, then forward to the Development Department.

A Donor Information

Name _____

Organization _____

Address _____

City, State, Zip _____

Phone _____

B Gift Information

Date of Gift _____   Rec'd by _____

Description of Gift _____

_____

_____

Restrictions _____

_____

Fair Market Value $_____

How was value determined? (e.g. by donor, appraisal, etc) _____

_____

Please attach copies of all relevant documents including correspondence, receipts, invoices, and/or appraisals which determine current fair market value.

C Booking Information

Program/Project Name _____

In-Kind Revenue Account _____ -41185 _____

Expense/Asset Account
and Object Code _____   Acct Name _____

D Approval

Program Director _____   Date _____

Deputy Director _____   Date _____

E For Development Department use only

PSI account number _____   Entry by _____

Drive _____

Usage Code _____ (_____ -41185) See In-Kind Revenue Account Code above.

Paymode IK   (45100-50635) In-Kind Clearing Account

Date recorded _____   To acctg _____

Date acknowledged _____

F For Accounting Department use only

Journal Entry Date _____   Entry by _____

Credit __45100-50635__ In-Kind Clearing Account

Debit _____ See Program/Project Expense Acct/Object codes above.

Put History In Your Future.

A Special Offer from the New Hampshire Historical Society

The New Hampshire Historical Society is offering you a special opportunity to become a member. Join now and save $10 on an annual membership.

The New Hampshire Historical Society is an independent nonprofit organization that relies on the support of people like you to preserve our state's history and provide educational programs for thousands of children and adults each year. As a member, you'll have the satisfaction of knowing that you are preserving New Hampshire's rich heritage for generations to come, and you'll receive many other benefits including:

- Free admission to the Museum of New Hampshire History, located at Eagle Square in downtown Concord.
- Free use of the Society's library, one of New England's outstanding research centers, located at 30 Park Street in Concord.
- A 10% discount on purchases in our unique Museum Store, specializing in New Hampshire books, gifts, and products.
- A quarterly newsletter, with up-to-date information on exhibitions, events, new publications, and programs.
- A subscription to *Historical New Hampshire*, an award-winning magazine of Granite State history.
- Reduced rates for lectures, tours, workshops, and other special programs.

Join the New Hampshire Historical Society today and save $10.

- ☐ Individual ~~$30~~ $20
- ☐ Couple ~~$40~~ $30
- ☐ Family ~~$50~~ $40

Name _____

Address _____

City/State/Zip _____

Telephone _____

Your full membership contribution will be tax-deductible if you elect not to receive a subscription to the Society's magazine, *Historical New Hampshire*, a $20 value. Otherwise, all but $20 of your membership is tax-deductible.

☐ Please do not send me *Historical New Hampshire*.

Please send your check, made payable to the **New Hampshire Historical Society**, and this form to:
New Hampshire Historical Society, 30 Park Street, Concord, NH 03301-6384

Special rates apply to new memberships only. For more information call (603) 225-3381.

Museums & Art Galleries of the Northern Territory Foundation Limited (A.C.N. 074 393 285)

Trustee of the Museums & Art Galleries of the Northern Territory Foundation Trust

DONATION & MEMBERSHIP APPLICATION FORM
Corporate Member

Company Details

Name and A.C.N.: _____

Address: _____

_____ | | | | |

Telephone No.: ( ) _____ Facsimile No.: ( ) _____

Contact Name: _____

Donation

Please accept the company's donation of $ _____ to the Museums & Art Galleries of the Northern Territory Foundation Trust to be paid a follows:

Single: 1 payment of $ _____ Annually: 5 payments of $ _____

Half yearly: 10 payments of $ _____ Quarterly: 20 payments of $ _____

Other: _____

To qualify for membership donations must be at least $5,000 over 5 years.

Donors of between $20,000 and $50,000 over 5 years qualify for membership as Fellows of the Foundation.

Donors of $50,000 or more qualify for membership as Foundation Benefactors.

Donations to the Museums & Art Galleries of the Northern Territory Foundation Trust are tax deductable.

Membership Application

Please accept the company's application for membership of the Foundation in the following category:

☐ Ordinary Member

☐ Fellow

☐ Foundation Benefactor

The company agrees to meet the payment undertaking set out above, and to comply with the rules of the Foundation.

_____ _____ _____

Signature   Print Name   Date

Other major activities include:

- since 1984, the National Aboriginal & Torres Strait Islander Art Award, now sponsored by Telstra Australia;

- since 1980, the National Craft Acquisition Award which, from 1996, will invite artists from Indonesia (the first craft award in Australia to include works from Southeast Asia);

- MAGNT travelling exhibitions in the Territory, nationally and internationally;

- the Regional Museums Program, providing advice and support to regional museums in the Northern Territory; and

- collaborative research with other national and international institutions.

Facilities in Darwin are:

- Museum & Art Gallery of the Northern Territory, Bullocky Point;

- Fannie Bay Gaol;

- Australian Pearling Exhibition, Darwin Wharf Precinct; and

- BAT House (Lyons Cottage).

Facilities in Alice Springs are:

- Central Australian Museum;

- The Residency; and

- Connellan Hangar.

Acknowledgement of Donors

The acknowledgement of support to the Foundation may include:

- acknowledgement on honour board;

- naming rights to an exhibition, acquisition or project;

- acknowledgement in publications such as annual reports, catalogues and scientific journals;

- invitations to special functions held at Museum & Art Gallery of the Northern Territory facilities.

Membership

The Foundation invites individuals and incorporated bodies to become members.

The qualification for membership is the making of a gift or gifts, whether in-kind or cash, of a value not less than $1 000 for individuals and not less than $5 000 for incorporated bodies in any five-year period.

There are three classes of membership:

- Ordinary members - individuals or incorporated bodies who contribute not less than $1 000 or $5 000 respectively in any given five-year period;

- Fellows - individuals who give through the Foundation $5 000 or more but less than $20 000 or incorporated bodies who give through the Foundation $20 000 or more but less than $50 000 in any five-year period; and

- Foundation Benefactors - individuals who give through the Foundation $20 000 or more, or corporate bodies who give through the Foundation $50 000 or more in any five-year period.

Taxation Advantages

The Foundation has established the Museums & Art Galleries of the Northern Territory Foundation Trust for the receipt of donations. Donations to the fund will be allowable deductions within the meaning of Section 78(5) of the Australian Income Tax Assessment Act.

Under the Taxation Incentives for the Arts Scheme, donations of cultural works of significance from private collections to the Museum & Art Gallery of the Northern Territory are encouraged. Donors are entitled to claim a tax deduction for the value of the donation and the cost of the valuations which are obtained specifically for the Taxation Advantages Scheme may be claimed as tax-related expenses.

Management of the Foundation

The Foundation is a company limited by guarantee incorporated under the Corporations Law. It is managed by a Council of (nine) Directors consisting of the following:

(a) President, who is appointed by the Museums & Art Galleries Board;

(b) Chair of the Museums & Art Galleries Board (ex officio);

(c) Director of the Museums & Art Galleries of the Northern Territory (ex officio);

(d) two (2) directors appointed by the Museums & Art Galleries Board, one of whom shall be the Secretary and Honourary Treasurer; and

(e) four (4) directors elected by the members of the Foundation.

NEHRU SCIENCE CENTRE

(National Council of Science Museums)
Dr. E. Moses Road, Worli, MUMBAI 400 018

APPLICATION FOR MEMBERSHIP OF THE CENTRE

Membership Category : 1. Student ☐   4. Family ☐

2. Teacher ☐   5. Institutional ☐ Educational/Research Org.

3. Individual Adult ☐   ☐ Corporate House

1. Name : _____

2. Age : _____ Male/Female _____

3. Address : _____

_____

Tel. No. (Office) _____ (Res) _____

Fax: _____ Email: _____

4. Profession : _____

5. Educational Qualification : _____

6. Particulars of family members (only in case of family membership)

1. _____ Age _____

2. _____ Age _____

3. _____ Age : _____

7. Particulars of Membership Fees (enclosed) : Rs. _____ Cheque / D.D. No. _____

8. Status of Membership : New / Old   Date of membership renewal _____
(In case of old Members)

Date :

Signature of the Applicant

Note : Membership is effective for one year (12 months) from the date of admitting the application. Membership fee is subject to change.

FOR OFFICE USE ONLY

Effective period of membership : from _____ to _____

Membership No. _____ Card No. _____ Amount _____ Receipt No. _____

Admit as : Student / Teacher / Individual (Adult) / Family / Institutional/ Corporate

253

Signature of Officer In-charge
Membership Services

GIFT MEMBERSHIP APPLICATION

Please print GIFT recipients name and address:

Mr./Mrs./Ms./Miss _____

Address _____

_____

City _____ State _____ Zip _____

Phone Number _____

Membership Category _____

❑ New Member   ❑ Renewal   ❑ Former Member

Donor

Mr./Mrs./Ms./Miss _____

Address _____

_____

City _____ State _____ Zip _____

Phone Number _____

Membership Category _____

❑ Member   ❑ Non-Member

Payment Method

❑ Check in the amount of $ _____ is enclosed.

❑ Charge my credit card:

❑ Visa   ❑ MasterCard   ❑ American Express

Credit Card # _____

Expires _____

Signature _____

Please make check payable to the Buffalo Bill Historical Center and mail in the attached envelope.

Membership cards will be sent directly to your gift recipient with a gift card in your name.

Please allow one - two weeks for receipt of membership cards.

BUFFALO BILL HISTORICAL CENTER

MEMBERSHIP APPLICATION

Please print name(s) exactly as you would like it to appear on your membership card.

Mr./Mrs./Ms./Miss _____

Address _____

_____

City _____ State _____ Zip _____

Phone Number _____

❑ New Member   ❑ Renewal   ❑ Former Member

Payment Method

❑ Check in the amount of $ _____ is enclosed.

❑ Charge my credit card:

❑ Visa   ❑ MasterCard   ❑ American Express

Credit Card # _____

Expires _____

Signature _____

Please make check payable to the Buffalo Bill Historical Center and mail in the attached envelope. Your benefits will start immediately.

I have selected the following membership category:

❑	Pahaska League	$2,000
❑	Benefactor	$1,000
❑	Sustainer	$500
❑	Sponsor	$250
❑	Centennial	$100
❑	Family/Household	$40
❑	Individual	$25
❑	Student	$15
❑	Corporate Founder	$10,000
❑	Corporate Contributor	$5,000
❑	Corporate Associate	$2,500
❑	Corporate Benefactor	$1,000
❑	Corporate Sustainer	$500
❑	Corporate Sponsor	$250
❑	Business Friend	$150
❑	One of One Thousand Society	$1,000
❑	CFM Sustainer	$500
❑	CFM Sponsor	$250
❑	CFM Friend	$150

❑	Yes, my employer has a matching fund program. I have requested the appropriate forms to be sent to the BBHC.
❑	Please send me information on planned giving.
❑	My additional contribution of $ _____ is enclosed.

Please allow one – two weeks for receipt of your membership cards. For gift membership see reverse.

SOUTH DAKOTA STATE HISTORICAL SOCIETY

MEMBERSHIP PROGRAM

YOUR MEMBERSHIP CARD

The enclosed membership card will allow you to get the most from membership in the South Dakota State Historical Society. Please read the following to get a better understanding of how you can make Society membership work for you!

THE MEMBERSHIP CARD

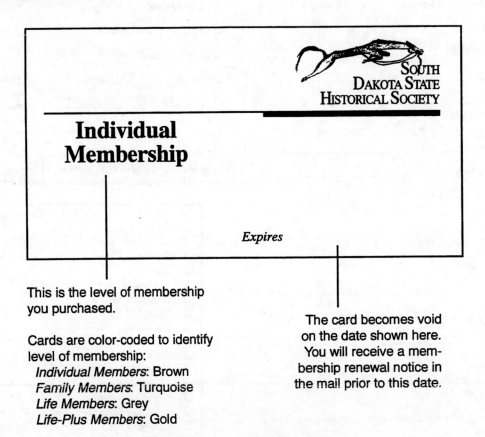

This is the level of membership you purchased.

Cards are color-coded to identify level of membership:
Individual Members: Brown
Family Members: Turquoise
Life Members: Grey
Life-Plus Members: Gold

The card becomes void on the date shown here. You will receive a membership renewal notice in the mail prior to this date.

IMPORTANT INFORMATION!

WHEN VISITING A MUSEUM OR MUSEUM STORE, PLEASE MAKE SURE YOU HAVE YOUR CARD TO GET FREE ADMISSION OR THE **10**-PERCENT STORE DISCOUNT. *YOU MUST HAVE YOUR CARD.*

MEMBERSHIP BENEFITS ARE ONLY EXTENDED TO THE PERSON WHOSE NAME APPEARS ON THE CARD. FAMILY MEMBERSHIP INCLUDES ADULT PARENTS/GUARDIANS AND MINOR CHILDREN. MEMBERSHIP IS NON-TRANSFERABLE.

MEMBERSHIP CARDS WITH EXPIRED DATES WILL NOT BE HONORED. PLEASE MAKE SURE YOUR MEMBERSHIP IS KEPT UP TO DATE. THANK YOU!

The Morton Arboretum

4100 Illinois Route 53
Lisle, IL 60532-1293

Gift/Pledge Form

I/We wish to support The Morton Arboretum with a tax-deductible gift of $_____
to the Volunteer Division of the 1997 Annual Giving Program.

_____ Enclosed is my/our contribution.

_____ Please bill me/us for the entire amount on _____, 1997.

_____ Please bill me/us in equal installments, beginning _____, 1997,

as follows: _____ Quarterly _____ Semi-Annually

_____ Please charge my credit card: ____ Visa ____ MasterCard or ____ Discover

Card number _____ Exp. Date _____

Signature _____

Name _____

Please <u>print</u> your name as you would like it to appear in donor recognition listings in our 1997 Annual Report. (You may remain anonymous; if so, please write Anonymous after your name above.)

Address _____

City, State, Zip _____

Phone _____ Date _____

Please return your completed Gift/Pledge Form to:
Development Office, The Morton Arboretum, 4100 Illinois Route 53, Lisle, Illinois 60532-1293

SPECIAL GIFT-GIVING CATEGORIES AND RECOGNITION

Thornhill Society (gifts of $1,000 or more)
Invitation to the annual Thornhill Society recognition event, special quarterly updates from the Executive Director of the Arboretum, a complimentary one-year membership to the Arboretum, plus the benefits listed below

Arbor Circle (gifts of $500-$999) and Contributor (gifts of $250-$499)
Invitation to the "Seasons" series of special programs, and listing in The Morton Arboretum Annual Report

Please note: If you have suggestions for worthy funding projects to consider for 1998, please write them on the back of this form and return it to the Development Office. You need not include your name if you wish your ideas to remain anonymous.

Celebrating
75
years

Chicagoland's
Garden of Trees

630-968-0074
Fax 630-719-2433
trees@mortonarb.org

256

ID# D FIELD(1)
FIELD(2)
FIELD(5)
FIELD(8), FIELD(9) FIELD(10)

Phone: FIELD(12)
Museum Member: YES
Past Giving: $ FIELD(13) in 19FIELD(11)

☐ Pledge $ _____
☐ No Pledge
☐ Think It Over
☐ Already Pledged/Mailed
☐ Incorrect Number

Caller	Date	Call Back	No Answer	Ans Machine

The Buffalo Museum of Science
1997 Annual Fund Drive

The Buffalo Museum of Science invites people of all ages and backgrounds to experience the excitement for scientific exploration and discovery through interactive exhibits and programs.

FIELD(2),

Thank You for your generous support
of the Museum with your pledge of:

☐ $500   ☐ $250   ☐ $100
☐ $75   ☐ $50   ☐ $25   ☐ Other $_____

ID# FIELD(1)

<u>Become a 'Dino Donor' Today:</u>

Psittacosaurus Society	$100 - $249
Allosaurus Associates	$250 - $499
Triceratops Troupe	$500 - $999
Tyrannosaurus Team	$1000 & Above

Method of Payment:

☐   Check made payable to the Buffalo Museum of Science is enclosed.
☐   Visa   ☐ MasterCard   ☐ American Express

Card# _____ Exp. _____ Signature_____
☐   Do you work for a MATCHING GIFT COMPANY? Over 1000 Companies nationwide will double, sometimes triple, the amount of your gift to the Museum. Contact your personnel department for your form today.

ID# D FIELD(1)

FIELD(2)
FIELD(5)
FIELD(8), FIELD(9) FIELD(10)

257
Please return these forms with your payment by December 31, 1997.

MUSEUM OF FINE ARTS, HOUSTON
PLEDGE ENTRY FORM

DATE OF PLEDGE:	PLEDGE NUMBER: **98-**

ID #:	INITIALS / DATE:

INDIVIDUAL/COMPANY MAKING PLEDGE:

NAME:

CORPORATE CONTACT/TITLE:

ADDRESS:

CITY:	STATE	ZIP
SPOUSE	HOME PHONE	WORK PHONE

GIFT/DONATION INFORMATION:

CAMPAIGN YEAR:	CAMPAIGN:	SOLICITATION:	ACCOUNT:

CONSTITUENT TYPES:

☐ Trustee	☐ Individual	☐ Corporation	☐ Foundation	☐ Other

PLEDGE INFORMATION:

AMOUNT PLEDGED: **$**	AMOUNT ENCLOSED: **$**

NO. OF PAYMENTS:	1	Amount:	Date:
	2	Amount:	Date:
	3	Amount:	Date:
	4	Amount:	Date:
	5	Amount:	Date:

ADDITIONAL GIFT/DONATION INFORMATION:

☐ Credit For	☐ In Honor Of	☐ In Memory Of	ID #:
☐ Anonymous		☐ Attributes:	

EXTENDED COMMENTS:

COPIES:

☐ Individual	☐ Corporation	☐ Foundation	☐ Government	☐ Civic

PLDGEFM.DOC/Dec-97

Witte Museum
Donor Profile
For Internal Use Only

Date:_____
Donor Name:_____
(Corporation/ Foundation/ Individual)
Donor ID #_____ Staff Contact: _____
Address_____
City, State, Zip_____
Phone _____

Corporation Contact Information (include direct phone numbers and correct titles)
Primary Contact:_____ phone_____
_____
President/Chairman of the Board_____phone_____
_____
Corporate Contributions Coordinator _____phone_____

Individual Donor Information
Individual donor's birth date Hers_____ His_____
Nickname(s)_____
Planned Giving Prospect ___Yes ___No

Current Donor Level $_____ As of _____
Lifetime Giving Amount $_____ As of _____
Donor Since _____ (year)

Known areas of interest in the Witte Museum
_____
_____
Known Special Donor Recognition:
_____
_____
_____

Other notes (relationship history, religious affiliations, private club memberships, board affiliations, family history etc.)
_____
_____
_____

Notes:

Witte Museum
Confidential Cultivation Plan
For Internal Use Only

Date:_____

Donor/Prospect:_____

Individual/ Corporation/ Foundation (Circle one)

Contact: _____

Donor ID #_____

Development Staff Assigned:_____

Natural Partner(s):_____

(Board Member, Staff, Volunteer, other donor,)

Immediate outcome goal(s) for the donor:

_____
_____
_____
_____

Long term goal(s) for the donor:

_____
_____
_____
_____

Last Contact:

Date_____

Method_____

_____
_____

By Whom_____

Next Contact: Date_____

Method_____

_____

By Whom_____

Attachments: __Witte Giving History__ Prospect Research __News clippings__ Donor Profile

Notes:

Kansas City Museum
Prospect Research Work Request Form

Time/Date requested:_____ Requested by: _____

Time/Date expected: _____ For what: _____

                                                     proposal, meeting, file, etc.

For whom:_____

                    Ucko, Esrey, Annie, volunteer, etc.

Prospect:_____

_____

_____

_____

_____

_____

(please provide as much information as you have on the prospect, e.g. address, name of company, title, affiliations and associations, where you saw the name, etc.)

Type of Request:

_____ new profile

_____ update to profile

_____ basic bio

_____ corporate info

_____ foundation info

_____ address, phone number and contact name

_____ giving history to Museum

_____ giving history to other organizations

_____ other (please specify) _____

Potential Grant Source

(Complete as much info as you have - use a form for EACH granting opportunity)

Funding Organization/Agency:_____

_____

Foundation Name: _____

Special Grant Program Name: _____

Full Address:_____

Contact Person:_____ Have you had Contact? ___yes ___no

Due Date: _____

Area of interest or brief summary of grant program: _____

_____

Can money be used for general operating funds? ___yes ___no

Must money be matched?___yes ___ no Percentage is ___% by us, ___% by them

Can match be in-kind service? ___ yes ___ no

Have we received money from them before? ___ yes ___ no ___don't know

They WILL NOT fund these areas: _____

_____

Is there a specific application form? ___yes ___no   Do we have it? ___*yes ___ no

Application procedures:_____

_____

_____

Your name: _____ Date: _____

Comments: _____

_____

_____

_____

*Attach Grant application/materials
Submit to Development Office - Thanks!

updated 4/17/97

1. Donor
2. Cataloguer/Cashier
3. Buyer

PENOBSCOT MARINE MUSEUM

Maine's Oldest Maritime Museum

SEARSPORT, MAINE 04974

207-548-2529

CATALOG #

Does donor wish invitation?

☐ yes   ☐ no

AUCTION

Donor's Name: (as it is to appear in the catalogue) or anonymous ☐

_____
(Please print **all** information clearly.)

Mailing Address: _____

_____

_____

Phone #: Days: _____   Evenings _____

Name of donor contact if not the same as above:

_____

Full description of donated item:

_____

_____

_____

_____

Fair market value for catalogue: $_____

Tax receipt requested?   ☐ yes   ☐ no

Restrictions/Comments: (e.g., dates, age, additional costs, etc.) _____

_____

_____

Advertising in catalogue: ☐ Requested   ☐ Not requested

This donation becomes the property of Penobscot Marine Museum and is to be offered for sale at an auction, the proceeds of which to go Penobscot Marine Museum.

_____
Donor signature

Donor contacted by: Name_____   Phone _____

Gift certificate required?   ☐ yes   ☐ no

Purchaser_____

(Last)   (First)   Paddle #

Address _____

Winning Bid $ _____   Paid by: ☐ Cash ☐ Check ☐ Visa ☐ Mastercard

10% buyers premium

~~Taxes~~ $ _____

Amount Due $ _____   263

The Children's **Museum** *of Houston*

Auction Donor Form

This is to verify that you have made a donation to the Children's Museum of Houston. We appreciate your generosity and cooperation. Please retain the pink copy of this form for your tax records. Fed. ID 74-2178563

(Please type or print)

Donor Information:

Donor name _____

Donor's address _____

City/State _____ Zip _____

Contact person _____ Daytime phone _____

Donation _____ Fair market value $ _____

Description of donation or comments _____

_____

_____

Do you wish to be acknowledged in the program? ❏ Yes ❏ No

If yes, donor listing should read _____

Item/Gift Information:

❏ Merchandise: Exchangeable ❏ Yes ❏ No

❏ Gift certificate: Expiration date _____

List any restrictions _____

_____

_____

❏ Attached ❏ Will be mailed ❏ Volunteer to collect

For Office Use Only:

Name of volunteer _____ Phone _____

Item received _____ Date _____

Catalog number _____ Response letter _____

1500 Binz • Houston, Texas 77004-7112 • 713/522-1138 ext. 233 • Fax: 713/522-5747

Museum/white copy
Chairman/yellow copy
Merchant/pink copy

Spencer Museum of Art   Event Booking

Date of Request: _____   Date(s) of Event: _____   Time: _____

Sponsor: _____   Contact Person: _____

Address: _____   Telephone: _____

Sponsor Type: _____   E-Mail Address: _____

KU Registered Organization? <u>YES</u>   FAX: _____

Description of Event: _____

Location(s): _____

Number of Performers: _____   Estimated Audience: _____

Type of Audience: ☐Public ☐Private ☐ KU Students Only ☐Other: _____

Admission Fee, if any: $_____   Estimated Total Receipts: $_____   Estimated Profit: $_____

Proposed Use of Profit: _____

Will Union provide food and beverages? <u>YES</u>   Other: _____   ☐ Catered OR ☐ Refreshment service

Will alcohol be served? <u>YES</u> Provider: _____

Entertainment: _____

Piano to be used? <u>YES</u>   Player: _____   Tuning Required? <u>YES</u>   Tuning Date: _____

Advertising/P.R.: _____

Enter Time each day for the following:	Date	Date	Date	Date	Date
Initial entry for delivery and setup:					
Open Entrance:					
Activity 1:					
Activity 2:					
Activity 3:					
Activity 4:					
Close Entrance:					
End Clean-up and Exit:					

Staff Hours Required: (number X hours)	Date	Date	Date	Date	Date	Total
Security Officers:						
Security Monitors:						
Event staff:						
Audio/Visual Assistants:						
Other:						

Event Booking   **Page 2**

Equipment	Provided by			Location
	SMA	**Sponsor**	**Other (specify)**	
Serving Tables (2)				
8' Round Dining Table				
5' Folding Tables (2)				
Butler Trays (4)				
Trash cans				
Chairs				
Camp Stools				
Portable Lectern				
Lavaliere Microphone				
Slide Projectors				
Film Projectors				
TV/VCR				
Video Projector				
Other A/V:				
Easel				
General Clean-up				

Fees:	Estimated	Adjustments after event	Final
Security Staffing	$		$
A/V Staffing:	$		$
Event Staffing:	$		$
A/V Equipment Fee	$		$
General Support Fee	$		$
Total	$		$

Funding Type: ☐ State (SOV) ☐ Endowment ☐ Other:_____

Approval/Disapproval: Y/N	Reasons/Conditions	Date
Events Committee: **YES**		
Director:		

Comments:

EB sent _____   EB received: _____   266 EB to WH: _____

LIBRARY - ARCHIVAL

General
Oral history
Material use

Oklahoma Historical Society

Founded May 27, 1893

2100 NORTH LINCOLN BLVD. • OKLAHOMA CITY. OKLAHOMA 73105 • (405) 521-2491

LOAN AGREEMENT

I, _____, the curator of the following described papers/manuscripts/artifacts and/or photographs and memorabilia do hereby loan said materials to _____, for the purpose of photocopying, displaying, microfilming and/or other duplication.

Description of item(s) or material:

I understand that the items listed above will be returned to the Archives and Manuscripts Division upon conclusion of said loan period.

(Signature)_____

(Date)_____

(Accepted by)_____

(Title)_____

Loaned for:

Display_____Copying_____Xerox_____Microfilming_____Duplication__

Loan Period:_____to:_____

Return materials to:_____Date:_____

Special Instructions:

Year of Acquisition: Accession Date:

Accessioned by: Accession Number:

Source:

Provenance:

Formal or distinguishing title:

Dates:

Brief description of contents (principal persons, subjects, locales):

Storage containers:
    The count of each type of contain and any notes should be sufficient to ensure that all the pieces of an accession have been located. Include additional description for any irregular material that must be stored "loose;" each loose item described is assumed to be single unless it includes a count.
___ (___ lf) folders
___ (___ lf) document boxes
___ (___ lf) record center boxes
___ (___ lf) flat boxes
__ loose items (unboxed items, describe below)

Storage location(s)

Collection Number(s)
    Assigned during processing.

Public Museum of Grand Rapids
ARCHIVAL FINDING AID

Archive Collection No._____

Accession Number_____

Source:_____

Date Acquired:_____/_____/_____

Span Dates:_____

Size:_____

Processor(s)_____

*Register of:*_____

(name of archive collection)

. . . .

ABSTRACT: (curator completes a brief (one paragraph) description of the collection and a summary of its contents)

HISTORY: (if known, & if relevant, curator provides a general introduction to the person or co. that generated the material)

SCOPE AND CONTENT: (curator gives an insight into the contents of the collection for research potential; for smaller collections this section may be exact duplication of "Abstract" section)

Archival Finding Aid - Part 2 of 3
Collection No._____
Register of_____

SERIES DESCRIPTIONS: (curator provides a synopsis of what is in each separate series, including span dates)

I. Series Name:_____
         Description:

II. Series Name:_____
         Description:

III. Series Name:_____
         Description:

IV. Series Name:_____
         Description:

V. Series Name:_____
         Description:

VI. Series Name:_____
         Description:

INDIVIDUAL PROFILE (ARCHIVE CREATOR)

title	first name	middle name/initials	last name

other name(s)

mailing address	city/province	postal code	phone	fax
			(h)	
			(b)	

place of residence	period of residence

date of birth	place of birth	citizenship	gender

father	mother

marital status	marital status date	marital status place	remarks

name of spouse	children

C

immigrated to	immigrated from	immigration date	remarks

occupation/profession	employer(s)	place of work	date(s) of work

remarks

C

military service	rank	date(s)

remarks

C

death date	place of death	place of burial	remarks

To: Profile Binder

associated with	nature of association	date

C

remarks

interests and activities

education

published references

C

interviewee	interviewer	interview date

C

interview remarks

associated batch number(s)	source name	other research sources

C

copyright on

CDM 22

ARCHIVAL MATERIAL CATALOGUE SHEET
FILE RECORD

Page

file number	title proper

forms part of (name of fonds)

batch number(s)

general material designation

dates of creation	1st date of content	last date of content

extent

other physical details

location

administration history / biographical sketch (see PROFILE)

custodial history

scope and content

variations in title proper

source of supplied title

physical condition

conservation

CDM 26

arrangement

language

location of originals

availability of other formats

restrictions

finding aids

associated material

accruals

related records

general note

BIOGRAPHICAL SURVEY

Museum of Western Colorado
and
Mesa County Oral History Project

Please fill out the following as completely as possible. Insert additional sheets as needed.

Full name _____ Nicknames _____

Address _____
(Street, apartment, box number, etc.)   City   State   Zip

_____ Date of Birth _____ Location _____

(Telephone Number)

Date of Current Marriage _____ Location of Wedding _____

Date of Death _____ Place of death _____

Father's name _____

Date of Birth _____ Place _____

Date of Death _____ Place _____

Mother's name (include maiden name) _____

Date of Birth _____ Place _____

Date of Death _____ Place _____

Spouse's name (include maiden name, previous marriages) _____

Date of Birth _____ Place _____

Date of Death _____ Place _____

Names and present addresses of children _____

_____

_____

Names and present address of grandchildren _____

_____

_____

Education (name of school, location, dates) _____

_____

_____

BIOGRAPHICAL SURVEY (page 2)

Awards (including college honors) _____

_____

Military service: **Branch** _____ **Dates** _____

                    Enlistment date _____ **Location** _____

                    Ranks _____ **Decorations** _____

                    Duty Stations _____

_____

Date of arrival & reason for coming to Western Colorado _____

Reason for leaving _____

Locations & dates of residency in W. Colorado _____

_____

Occupations (dates & locations) _____

_____

Spouse's occupations _____

Political offices (office, length of term, elected/appointed, location) _____

_____

Organizational affiliations (offices, honors, dates) _____

_____

Earliest memories, recollections of Western Colorado _____

_____

_____

_____

Your most memorable event _____

_____

Hobbies/Interests, etc. _____

_____

_____

Use back of page or add a page as needed for additional information.
3/1993

Public Museum of Grand Rapids
Established 1854

GIFT AGREEMENT / ORAL HISTORY RELEASE

Between The Public Museum of Grand Rapids, Grand Rapids, Michigan ("Museum") and,

Interviewee: _____
Address: _____
_____
Telephone: _____

Description of Gift:

Type of Recording: ( )audio ( )visual ( )audio-visual ( )other:

Subject of Recording/Interview: _____
_____

Date of Interview: _____

Conditions of Gift

I give permission to the Museum to use the above mentioned work for all standard museum purposes, including, exhibition, loans, reproduction and transmission.

I also give permission to the Museum that the above work and/or resulting reproductions or transmissions will become part of the collections of the Museum and will be made available for scholarly and educational uses under the direction of the Museum.

Limiting Conditions or Exclusions

I, the undersigned, do hereby grant permission and give to the Public Museum of Grand Rapids, as an unrestricted givet, legal title and all literary property rights including copyright in and to the recorded interview as described above.

Date:_____ Signed:_____
(Interviewee/Donor)

For the Public Museum of Grand Rapids:
*Date:*_____ *Signed:*_____

wp/oralhist022693MM

Van Andel Museum Center and Roger B. Chaffee Planetarium • 272 Pearl Street NW • Grand Rapids, MI 49504-5371
616-456-3977 • TDD/Text Telephone 616-456-3724 • FAX 616-456-3873
Blandford Nature Center • 1715 Hillburn Ave. NW • Grand Rapids, MI 49504-2452 • 616-453-6192
Voigt House Victorian Museum • 115 College Ave. SE • Grand Rapids, MI 49503-4403 • 616-456-4600

Museum of the Big Bend
Sul Ross State University

Accession Number: _____
Accession Date: _____

Military Service Profile: Veteran Oral History Project

1. Biographical information on: _____

2. Date of enlistment: _____

3. Date of separation: _____

4. Branch of service: _____

5. Basic training location and date:

6. Service in the Trans-Pecos area? ☐ Yes, or ☐ No (Check one)

7. Trans-Pecos duty stations, with dates:

8. Other permanent duty stations, with dates:

9. Military training specialization (s): _____

10. Units served in (List in chronological order):

11. Combat experience? ☐ Yes, or ☐ No

12. Campaigns served in (Areas and dates):

13. Highest rank achieved: _____

14. Decorations / Special honors:

15. Comments (Use back if necessary):

Rev. 8/98

INDIVIDUAL PROFILE

Page	title	first name		middle name/initials	last name
of					

other name(s)

mailing address	city/province	postal code	phone	fax
			(h)	
			(b)	

association with museum	mail	record restrictions	restriction detail
		YES / NO	

date of birth	place of birth	citizenship	gender

father	mother

marital status	marital status date	marital status place	remarks

C

name of spouse	children		

immigration to	immigration from	immigration date	remarks

occupation	employer(s)	place of work	date(s) of work

remarks

C

military service	rank	date(s)

remarks

C

death date	place of death	place of burial	remarks

CDM 08

associated with   nature of association   date

remarks

C

interviewee   interviewer   interview date

interview remarks

artist biography

school\style   flourished

C

published references

C

associated batch number   source name   other research sources

C

copyright on

CDM 06

The Sixth Floor Museum

411 Elm Street, Suite 120
Dallas, Texas 75202-3301
214/653-6659 Fax 214/653-6657
http:/www.jfk.org

❑Prearranged appointment
❑Walk-in

ARCHIVES ACCESS REQUEST FORM

Please note: The Museum makes no claim that it is the owner of any copyright in the materials contained in its archives. In providing access to such materials, the Museum does not assume any responsibility for obtaining or granting permission for publication or use. The responsibility for determining the nature and ownership of any rights and for obtaining the appropriate permissions to publish or use such materials rests entirely with the researcher.

REQUESTOR:

Name: Driver's License Number:
Organization:

Address:

   Phone: Fax:
   E-mail address:

What is the purpose of your visit/research?
Article:____   Book:____   Exhibit:____   Term paper/Thesis:____   Media project:____   Personal research:____
Other (please specify):____

Brief description of the above project/research:

Is study of material for publication or other commercial distribution? If so, please explain:

Describe the material you wish to see:

Do you wish to (check all that apply):
Consult accession files:____   View material in storage areas:____   Order copies of materials in storage:____
Other (please explain):____

Dates you wish to visit (Please note that the archives are only open to researchers by appointment or on Monday afternoons from 1 to 5 p.m.):

I understand that my access to the collection must be approved by the Museum staff, and that access may be limited regarding fragile or otherwise sensitive material. I agree to handle all items in the manner instructed and to observe all security regulations. I assume full responsibility for any damage, accidental or otherwise, I may inflict on any museum property. I agree to appropriately acknowledge, footnote, or credit The Sixth Floor Museum for any information derived from the collection.

Signature:_____   Date:_____

The Sixth Floor Museum is a non-profit organization, operated under the auspices of the Dallas County Historical Foundation.

Application for Research

The Homestead Museum permits use of its collections for scholarly research, interpretation, and exhibition and makes it available for study in accordance with its research polices and procedures (please read reverse side of application). Applications must be accompanied by a valid photo identification.

Permission is requested by:

Name (please print) _____

Company/Affiliation _____ [ ] non-profit corporation

Address _____

Daytime phone number _____

to use the collections of the Homestead for the purpose of (check any or all that apply):

☐ personal research, such as genealogy or history of your home.
☐ exhibition or display. Title & location: _____
☐ publication. Title & publisher: _____
☐ other: _____

on the subject(s) of: _____

_____ .

I have read and agreed to the policies and procedures for research.

X_____

    Signature of applicant   *Title (if applicable)*   *Date*

Approved by:

X_____

    Homestead representative   *Title*   *Date*

Identification: ☐ Driver's License #_____ ☐ Other: Type _____ #_____

Policies and Procedures for Research

The collections of the Homestead Museum preserve the history of southern California and the Workman and Temple families from 1830 to 1930. The collections are primarily for the use of museum staff for scholarly research, interpretation, and exhibition but are available to the public on a limited basis under the following policies and procedures:

Hours
Open to qualified researchers Monday through Friday, 10:00 a.m. - 4:00 p.m. by appointment only. Since staff is not always available, access is by appointment only.

Obtaining materials
1. Each researcher shall complete a research application and provide acceptable photo identification (e.g., driver's license).
2. Research materials may not be borrowed or removed from the museum. Researchers must request materials by filling out a call slip and a staff member will bring materials to the Reading Room. Materials may be used only in the Reading Room or other designated location. Researchers are not allowed in collection storage areas except when accompanied and supervised by staff.
3. The researcher is responsible for returning all material to a staff member. The museum reserves the right to inspect all bags, purses, briefcases, portfolios, etc.

Handling materials
1. Only pencils may be used. INK IS NOT ALLOWED
2. No smoking, eating (including gum or candy), and drinking is allowed.
3. All material must be handled with care. Paperclips or "post-it" notes may not be used; marks may neither be added nor erased; tracing and rubbing is prohibited. Loose sheets (such as photographs or manuscripts) should be handled by their edges. Some items require the use of gloves and staff supervision.
4. If material arrives in boxes or folders, remove only one folder or box at a time. Do not rearrange materials or remove documents from the folders. Please maintain the exact order of materials. If a mistake in arrangement is discovered, please call it to the attention of the staff; do not rearrange documents yourself.

Reproduction
1. Materials may be duplicated if it does not injure the materials and does not violate donor agreements or copyright restrictions. Please see staff regarding restrictions and fees.
2. All duplication of materials, whether by photocopying, photography, or other means, must be completed by museum staff. Researchers may not use their own cameras, scanners, or other duplicating equipment except by written permission.
3. It is assumed that all duplication is for personal use only. Any other use, such as exhibition, illustration, or commercial use, is not allowed except by written permission.

Restrictions on Use
The use of material may be restricted by law or by the donor. The Homestead may also to restrict access to materials which are not arranged, are being catalogued, or are exceptionally valuable and fragile. In some cases copies may be substituted for the originals.

APPLRESR.DOC 09/10/96

The Heard Museum

Rules for use of Materials

1. Briefcases, notebooks, purses, and other personal objects not essential to research are not allowed in the Reading Room. Items will be checked in by the Library and Archives staff.

2. Material must be used in the Reading Room only.

3. Eating, drinking, and smoking are not permitted in the Reading Room.

4. Material must be handled with great care. Leaning on, tracing over, or folding or handling material in any way which may cause damage is not allowed.

5. Pens may not be used in the Reading Room; the Museum staff will loan pencils and paper if needed. No marks may be made or post-it notes used on any material.

6. Photographs must be handled with cotton gloves.

7. Folders must be used one at a time.

8. The order of folders within archival containers must not be changed. The order of photographs within a folder or the contents of a folder must not be changed. Maintaining the original order of all material is mandatory.

9. All material must be returned neatly within a folder before returning it to the archival container. Papers and photographs must not extend beyond the folder edges.

10. Photocopying is not permitted for photographs.

11. Photocopying is not permitted for printed or archival material if it will cause injury to the original or if The Heard Museum does not own copyright. Request for photocopying must be made to the Librarian/Archivist. All photocopying is performed by the Library and Archives staff. The cost is $.20 a page; if photocopies are mailed, an additional $3.00 will be charged.

Registration form must be completed in order to use material from the following collections: Archives, Photographic Archives, Rare Books, Rare Pamphlets, and Manuscripts.

Library & Archives

The Heard Museum
22 East Monte Vista Road
Phoenix Arizona 850041480
Telephone: (602) 252-8840
Fax: 252-9757

REGISTRATION FORM

Name (please print) _____

Address (local) _____

City _____ State _____ Zip _____

Address (permanent, if different) _____

City _____ State _____ Zip _____

Institutional affiliation _____

Telephone _____

I have read and agree to abide by the Rules for Use of Materials, and wish to consult the following material:

Date _____ / _____
                 Time

Signature _____

_____

_____

_____

_____

_____

284

A/V Requisition Form

Title of Event:	
Date of Event:	
Contact Person:	
Telephone Number:	
Location of Event:	
Time of Event:	

EQUIPMENT NEEDS – Indicate your needs with 'X' or checkmark:

	Slide presentation – single
	Slide presentation – double
	Slide presentation – multiple
	Portable screen
	Lectern
	Microphone
	Public address system
	Audio Tape: cassette
	Tape duplication: cassette
	16mm film projection
	35 mm film projection
	Video presentation – 1/2" VHS
	Video presentation – 3/4 U-matic
	Video presentation – large screen projection
	Video documentation VHS
	Overhead projector
	Other – please specify below

Comments:

- Please make your request one week in advance. Requests that are not made at least 48 hours in advance cannot be guaranteed.
- Send request to MariAlice Grimes, A/V Manager, Museum Building [Phone 639-7329]

EDOUARD A. STACKPOLE LIBRARY AND RESEARCH CENTER

User Agreement Form

Name (please print)_____Date_____

Institutional Affiliation_____

Nantucket Address_____ Phone_____

Home Address_____

_____ Phone_____

Are you a member of the NHA?_____*If not, there is a $5.00 usage fee.*

Please describe the subject of your research_____

Do you plan to publish the results of your research?_____

*** I agree to abide by the regulations stated below.

*** If I should publish, I agree that, prior to publication, I will obtain the NHA's permission to quote from material I use in the library. I will also obtain the NHA's permission to reproduce photographs from the library's collections. Forms for obtaining permission to reproduce images are available in the library.

*** I understand permission to publish copyright material must be obtained from the appropriate holder of the copyright.

Signature_____

TO ASSURE PROPER PROTECTION OF THE RESEARCH COLLECTIONS THE FOLLOWING REGULATIONS HAVE BEEN ESTABLISHED:

All users shall sign the User Agreement Form.
Research materials shall be used only in the presence of the staff.
Whenever microfilm of records exist, they shall be used in place of the original documents.
No more than four folders or volumes shall be given to the researcher at a time.
*Pens shall **not** be used for note taking.*
Photocopying shall be done only by authorized personnel. There is a fee for this service.

NANTUCKET HISTORICAL ASSOCIATION
P.O. BOX 1016, NANTUCKET, MA 02554-1016 / 508-228-1894

Museum of the Big Bend Research Request

Name: _____ Date of request:_____

Address: _____ Received by:_____

City, State, Zip: _____ Phone:_____

Type of Request *(circle)*: Mail   Phone   Walk-in
Field trip required: *(circle)* Yes No   Assigned to: _____
Request:

Materials Searched *(use back if needed)*:
Artifacts (Accession No. & Nomenclature _____

_____

(circle)

Artifact Document File	Map(s)	Periodical(s)
Book(s)	Newspapers	Photograph(s)
Film/Video	Oral History Tapes	Reference Files
Mss. Collections	Oversize Materials	Other

Description of Materials Used *(details from above):*

Staff Action *(items mailed, special requests, photos copied, loans, etc.)*

Date Completed: _____ Time spent on request:_____
1. Upon completion, attach correspondence to this form and place in
Director's box. Director initial_____ Date _____.
2. When Director approves, this form is filed in the Collections drawer,
LF.02.F.

(2/95)

WELLINGTON COUNTY MUSEUM & ARCHIVES
R.R.#1, FERGUS, ONT.
N1M 2W3
(519) 846-0916

WELLINGTON PLACE
R.R. #1, FERGUS, ONT.
N1M 2W3
(519) 846-0916

SLIDE COLLECTION LOAN FORM

The Wellington County Museum and Archives hereby loans
the following slides to:

_____

Catalogue Numbers:

The Borrower agrees to the following conditions:
1. The borrower will return the slides in the same condition
   and the same order as received today.

2. The borrower agrees to cover any costs incurred in
   replacing lost or damaged slides.

3. The borrower agrees that he/she will not duplicate the
   slides.

Name of Borrower (please print) _____

Signature of Borrower _____

Address _____

_____

_____

Telephone Number _____

Date of Loan _____   Date to be returned _____

Staff _____

Date Returned _____

VIDEO TAPE DUBBING FORM
(Return to Peter Murphy, Media Specialist)

Date Needed: _____

Dept._____   WAC Staff Member _____   Ext._____

****

Master/Submaster Format:

        Hi 8_____   1/2" VHS_____   3/4" U-Matic_____   Other_____

Program Length: _____

****

Dub Format Requested:

        Hi 8_____   1/2" VHS_____   3/4" U-Matic_____   Other_____

Number of Dubs:_____

****

Compilation Tape (detailed explanation, attatch sheets):

****

Label Information:

Video Spine

Video Face

PHOTOGRAPHY - IMAGE

Copyright
Fees
General
Order
Rights and reproduction

RECEIPT FOR PURCHASE
WARRANTY AND INDEMNIFICATION
TRANSFER OF COPYRIGHT

245 West Olney Road • Norfolk, Virginia 23510-1587 • (757) 664-6200 • FAX (757) 664-6201

Received from _____
                                Name

_____
                                Address   Phone

the Work described below as a purchase, as approved by the Board of Trustees of The Chrysler Museum of Art (the "Museum") at its meeting on

_____.
Date

Number	Description	Purchase Price	Insurance Value

In consideration of the purchase by the Museum, from _____

("Vendor") of _____

("the Work"), Vendor, warrants that the Work listed above and described in detail as:

is authentic and complies with the stated description and is free and clear of all liens, claims and encumbrances, that its exportation from any foreign country has been in conformity with the laws of such country, that its importation to the United States is in conformity with laws of the United States, that Vendor is the legal owner of the Work or is the agent of the legal owner of the Work and authorized to sell the Work and execute this document on behalf of the legal owner, that the Vendor has the right to sell the work and that upon the Vendor's receipt from the Museum of _____ Dollars ($_____) as payment in full for the purchase of the Work, Vendor will transfer to the Museum full legal and equitable title to the work, together with all rights, title and interests pertaining to the Work. In addition, Vendor, upon receipt of the purchase price, transfers to the Museum any and all exclusive and non-exclusive copyright rights which may exist in the Work and transfers all photographic material including color negatives of the Work which are held by Vendor and by the legal owner of the Work and any and all copyrights in those materials with the exception of archival materials for the Vendor's gallery records. Vendor further states that the Work bears no copyright notation and that Vendor does not retain, claim or assert any copyright interests in the Work and that neither Vendor nor the legal owner has any knowledge nor information concerning copyright interests which have been retained, claimed or asserted by others in the Work. It is understood and agreed that this warranty and indemnification attaches to the purchase and sale noted herein and that the Museum shall receive from Vendor or its successor a full refund of the purchase price and related expenses paid for the Work if at any time any person, nation or entity successfully challenges the Museum's copyright rights and/or the Museum's free use and enjoyment of the Work. It is further understood and agreed that Vendor or its successor (the "Indemnifying Party") shall defend, indemnify and hold harmless the Museum, its Board of Trustees, its officers, employees and agents (the "Indemnified Parties") at the sole expense of the Indemnifying Party or its successor in regard to any claim or suit and for any damages and all other related expenses incurred by any of the Indemnified Parties which arise out of or result from a breach or alleged breach of the above warranties and representations in regard to the sale and purchase of this Work. It is further agreed that the law of Virginia governs this transaction.

Prepared: _____   _____
                    Registrar, The Chrysler Museum of Art   Date

AGREED TO BY:

BY:_____   DATE: _____

Please execute original and return to: Catherine Jordan, Registrar • The Chrysler Museum of Art

290

Please retain duplicate

**Mint
Museum
of Art**

NON-EXCLUSIVE PERPETUAL LICENSE

I, _____, the undersigned,
being the representative of the artist's copyright interests in the following work of art:

acquired by the Mint Museum of Art, hereby grant the Mint Museum of Art permission
to use the work for all museum purposes including, but not limited to, displaying the
work publicly, lending the work, or reproducing the work by methods involving a
photographic image. Reproductions and transmissions may be released through
media such as catalogues, books, film, television, slides, negatives, prints, videotapes,
and CD-ROM. It is understood, however, that the Mint Museum of Art will not
reproduce or distribute copies of this work, without my written permission. All
reproductions shall bear a copyright notice as follows (*please complete the blank*):

©_____
   (as you wish the work to be credited for publication purposes)

This non-exclusive license, which does not transfer ownership of the copyright to the
Mint Museum of Art, shall endure for the entire term of the copyright in and to said
work, and shall survive all assignments of copyright according to U.S. Title 17. Any
transfer or assignment of the copyright shall be reported to the Registrar, Mint Museum
of Art.

Date _____   _____
                                   Signature of artist's copyright representative

Celebrating Our 60th Year!

AMON CARTER MUSEUM

NONEXCLUSIVE LICENSE

I, _____, being the owncr and holder
of all copyright interests in the following work(s) of art:

COPY

give the Amon Carter Museum, and other parties duly authorized by the Amon Carter
Museum, the following nonexclusive license to reproduce the work(s) by methods
involving a photographic or digital image in its own catalogues, brochures, video
programs, publicity, educational materials, web site, commercial and trade publications
and broadcasts in conjunction with publicity for museum exhibitions, program
publications, to sell slides of the works for lectures and other scholarly purposes, and to
provide research (study) prints to researchers and scholars (specific written permission to
publish must be obtained in writing from the copyright holder). All reproductions shall
bear a copyright notice, as prescribed by the Copyright Law of the United States, which
shall read as follows (please complete blanks):

© _____   _____
   Date(s) of Copyright(s)   Name of Copyright Holder

This nonexclusive license, which does not transfer ownership of the copyright to the
Amon Carter Museum, shall survive all assignments of copyright.

_____   _____
Date   Signature of Copyright Holder

                              _____

                              _____
                              Printed Name and Address of Above

AMON CARTER MUSEUM
ATTN: Rights & Reproductions
3501 Camp Bowie Blvd.
Fort Worth, Texas 76107

TELEPHONE: (817) 738-1933
FAX: (817) 738-2034

ORDERING PHOTOGRAPHIC REPRODUCTIONS OF IMAGERY

PLEASE READ THE INFORMATION BELOW **BEFORE** SUBMITTING A WRITTEN REQUEST. Your letter should clearly identify the sculpture(s), painting(s), print(s), or photograph(s) you are interested in ordering. When possible, attach a photocopy of the item(s), made from an illustration in a book or other publication. Please note the credit lines in that publication and give the publication's title, author, and date of publication. Your letter should be mailed to the address at the top of this page. No request will be considered if material is needed less than four weeks from our receipt of your written request.

Upon receipt of your request we will mail you a form, which serves as both contract and invoice, and our list of conditions for reproduction of imagery. Sign the form (if you are requesting the image(s) for reproduction, the form must be signed by the person responsible for insuring that the reproduction conforms to the Museum's conditions) and return it with your payment. Allow 8-12 weeks for your request to be processed after we receive the signed form.

REQUESTS MUST BE FOR SPECIFIC ITEMS. A 1972 catalogue of paintings, prints, drawings, and sculpture, and a 1993 catalogue of the photography collection are available through our bookstore or public libraries. Eliot Porter's photographs are represented in numerous books, which may be obtained either through bookstores or libraries.

THE MUSEUM CANNOT PROVIDE REPRODUCTIONS OF WORK CONTROLLED BY THE ARTIST'S COPYRIGHT. In these instances, we will provide you with the appropriate address, if known, so that you can apply directly to the artist or the artist's estate.

Study prints or slides

The Museum can provide black and white photographic study prints or color slides of its holdings for the purpose of scholarly research. For prices, please see the Material Fees and Service Charge sections of the enclosed fee schedule. Items are not returnable for credit. Study photographs will not be retouched and will be embossed to prohibit duplication.

Reproductions of imagery

The Museum can provide black and white prints or color transparencies for reproduction in a publication, film, or other project. In addition to identifying the image(s) clearly, please note as much information about your publication or project as possible, including, when applicable:

1) title, **2)** author or editor, **3)** publisher or producer, **4)** projected date of publication or broadcast, **5)** press run size or number of broadcasts, **6)** whether you wish to reproduce the image on the cover of your project, **7)** language rights requested (English, all languages, or other), **8)** distribution requested (North American, world-wide, or other), **9)** whether the project is a 1st edition/broadcast, a reprint/re-broadcast, or a revised edition/production.

A fee schedule is enclosed.

MATERIAL FEES   *(6 month rental)*

8x10 in. black and white photograph $10.00
    If retouching is required .... add 15.00
    Failure to return photograph...10.00 or 25.00

4x5 in. color transparency 50.00
    Late return, per three months..25.00
    Lost or damaged charge 50.00

8x10 in. color transparency 75.00
    Late return, per three months..50.00
    Lost or damaged charge 75.00

35mm slide 5.00
    Failure to return slide 5.00

NEW PHOTOGRAPHY FEES

This fee may be charged if a work must be retrieved from storage or installation or if color materials are required for a black and white work of art or if a 3-dimensional object must be set up to provide a special angle shot. This fee is in addition to any material or use fees.

2-Dimensional objects 25.00-100.00
3-Dimensional objects 200.00

USE FEE*

The fee quoted is for one language. If "all languages" are required, multiply the fee by 10.

Inside Book, Journal, Magazine or Non-Broadcast Video or Film
    1-4,000 copies 50.00
    4,001-10,000 ....75.00
    10,001-20,000 ....100.00
    20,001-30,000 ....125.00
    30,001-40,000 ....150.00
    40,001+...quoted upon request

Inside Calendar or Brochure...500.00

Video or Film (Broadcast)
    One year (up to 3 times during year)....................................150.00
    In perpetuity 500.00

On Cover of any of above..500.00

SERVICE CHARGE PER ORDER

For study purposes...2.00
For reproduction of imagery 4.00

---

*Students and scholars publishing original research may apply for reduced Use Fees, which application should be made in writing. Material fees will not be reduced or waived.   (9/97)

FEE SCHEDULE-Electronic Use   **AMON CARTER MUSEUM**

MATERIAL FEES   *(6 month rental)*

8x10 in. black and white photograph $10.00
    If retouching is required .... add 15.00
    Failure to return photograph .... 10.00 or 25.00

4x5 in. color transparency...50.00
    Late return, per three months..25.00
    Lost or damaged charge 50.00

8x10 in. color transparency...75.00
    Late return, per three months..50.00
    Lost or damaged charge 75.00

NEW PHOTOGRAPHY FEES
This fee may be charged if a work must be retrieved from storage or installation or if color materials are required for a black and white work of art or if a 3-dimensional object must be set up to provide a special angle shot. This fee is in addition to any material or use fees.

2-Dimensional objects...25.00-100.00
3-Dimensional objects...200.00

ELECTRONIC MEDIA USE FEES

CD-ROM (commercial) $150.00
CD-ROM (educational) $75.00

Internet (commercial)..$200.00
Internet (educational) $75.00

SERVICE CHARGE PER ORDER
For commerical...4.00
For educational...2.00

Approved (9/97)

THE BROOKLYN MUSEUM
200 EASTERN PARKWAY
BROOKLYN N.Y. 11238-6052

CONTACT: KAREN TATES-DENTON
PHONE: (718) 638-5000 X202/X203
FAX: (718) 638-8116

RIGHTS & REPRODUCTIONS FEE SCHEDULE

BLACK & WHITE PHOTOGRAPHY

8x10 Glossy Print	$ 15.00
Permission to reproduce/Scholarly	$ 15.00
Permission to reproduce/Commercial	$ 25.00
Permission to reproduce/Cover for scholarly usage	$ 75.00
Permission to reproduce/Cover for commercial usage	$100.00

BLACK & WHITE NEW PHOTOGRAPHY

Two-dimensional/2D	$ 50.00
Three-dimensional/3D	$ 75.00

COLOR PHOTOGRAPHY

4X5 Color Transparency/3-month rental	$ 75.00
4x5 Color Transparency/dupe needed/3-month rental	$125.00
Permission to reproduce/Scholarly	$ 35.00
Permission to reproduce/Commercial	$ 60.00
Permission to reproduce/Cover for scholarly usage	$150.00
Permission to reproduce/Cover for commercial usage	$175.00

COLOR NEW PHOTOGRAPHY

Two-dimensional/2D	$125.00
Three-dimensional/3D	$150.00

35MM COLOR PHOTOGRAPHY

35mm color slide	$ 10.00
35mm color slide/dupe needed	$ 15.00

*****Permission to reproduce same as Color Photography

35MM NEW PHOTOGRAPHY

Two-dimensional/2D	$ 50.00
Three-dimensional/3D	$ 75.00

SPECIAL USES

Calendars, Posters, Notecards, and other commercial products...............................$350.00
Documentary/PBS...$175.00
Video...$250.00
Brochures/Scholarly...$150.00
Brochures/Commercial...$175.00

RUSH ORDERS

Scholarly...$ 35.00
Commercial..$ 75.00

PROCESSING/SHIPPING & HANDLING

Domestic...$ 5.00
Foreign..$ 10.00
Overseas collection charge for checks drawn on a foreign bank............................$ 50.00

NOTE: All 4x5 color transparencies remain the property of The Brooklyn Museum. Please note, 8x10 b&w prints from the Egyptian department also have a three-month rental period.

All rented material must be returned in good condition. If material is lost or damaged there will be a replacement cost of $150.00.

All fees must be prepaid including rental fees. If the decision is made at a later date not to reproduce the image there will be no refund of reproduction cost(s).

All requests for CD-ROM digital usage must be forwarded to Digital Collections Inc., 1301 Marina Village Parkway, Alameda, CA 94501, (510) 814-7200.

*****Please note, there is a 4-6 week processing period.

*New rates effective: 7/1/96

297

Guidelines for Digitally Reproducing Works of Art from the Museum of Fine Arts, Houston

The Museum of Fine Arts, Houston encourages the faithful reproduction of the works of art in its collections.

- Reproduction is permitted only from materials supplied by the Museum's Office of Rights and Reproductions. Reproduction from printed or other non-photographic materials or from photographic material not supplied by the Museum of Fine Arts, Houston is strictly prohibited.
- *NO* image may be in any way distorted, including but not limited to: rotation, inversion, change of proportion, color alteration, superimposition, animation, cartooning, removal of blemishes, and inscriptions.
- Use of a specific detail must be approved in advance by the museum and the caption must note that a detail has been used.

Photographs are <u>sold</u> outright and cannot be returned. Disks may be <u>rented</u> for publication purposes only. Disks remain the property of the Museum of Fine Arts, Houston and may not, under any circumstances, be duplicated.

If permission is granted, it is for one publication only. The museum defines "one publication" as a one language edition copyrighted and published under the imprint of one publisher.

Photographic material, including color separations, may not be reused either in a subsequent edition or in another publication or format in any medium, including media that may exist in the future, without the written permission of the museum. If such use is desired, a new application must be submitted.

Resource file must be hidden from view so that the file names and icons do not appear in windows or on the desktop.

Reproduction must be full-tone black and white or full color. Maximum resolution allowed is 72 DPI. Color must be displayed in a minimum of 8-bit color. Black and white must must be displayed in at least 8 bits of gray-scale information per pixel.

Full credit line as designated by the museum must appear exactly as specified by the museum and must be placed in the space surrounding the reproduction of the work on the same monitor screen.

Payments

To avoid delays in processing your order and / or improper crediting of payment, remittance should be mailed directly to :

The Office of Rights and Reproductions
The Museum of Fine Arts, Houston
P. O. Box 6826
Houston, Texas 77265

All photographic material charges and reproduction fees must be paid in advance and are non-refundable.

- Payments from outside the United States must be remitted in U. S. Dollars.
- Payment may be wired to Texas Commerce Bank, Houston 001 0026-5520 ABA113 000 609. ALL bank charges must be paid by the applicant.
- Payment may be made using an American Express, Visa, MasterCard, or Diner's Club charge card. Please supply number and expiration date. **3¼% WILL BE ADDED TO ALL AMERICAN EXPRESS CHARGES.**
- Additional fees incurred by the applicant are payable within 30 days of such billing.

Shipping

Standard shipping is by First Class Mail for domestic orders and Air Mail for international orders. **Any request requiring an urgent response must be accompanied by the applicant's Federal Express account number.**

IMPORTANT COPYRIGHT NOTIFICATION

The Museum of Fine Arts, Houston may grant the permission requested only to the extent of its ownership of the rights relating to the request. This permission does not purport to include any rights which persons other than The Museum of Fine Arts, Houston may have under the laws of various countries. Certain works of art, as well as photographs of those works of art, may be protected by copyright trademark, or related interests not owned by the museum. Works of art created after January 1, 1989 are not required to bear copyright notice. The responsibility and expense of ascertaining whether any such rights exist, and for obtaining all other necessary permissions, remains with the applicant.

---

rev. Feb, 1998

**PERMISSION TO REPRODUCE WALKER ART CENTER'S PHOTOGRAPHIC
IMAGE IS CONDITIONED UPON APPLICANT'S ACCEPTANCE OF AND
SATISFACTORY PERFORMANCE OF ALL OF THE TERMS AND CONDITIONS
OF THIS AGREEMENT. ANY BREACH OF ANY OF THESE TERMS AND
CONDITIONS WILL ENTITLE WALKER ART CENTER, AT ITS SOLE OPTION,
TO REVOKE THE PERMISSION GRANTED HEREIN AND SEEK ALL OTHER
APPROPRIATE REMEDIES, INCLUDING INJUNCTIVE RELIEF AND DAMAGES.**

1. **Scope of License.** Permission is given to reproduce the photographic image solely in the particular edition, language and medium specified. This permission is nonexclusive and nontransferable. The image for which permission is granted may appear only once and only as an editorial element within the edition; separate permission for the image to appear in any other position (e.g., cover; frontispiece; title page; end page; first screen display; chapter divider; non-editorial, decorative illustration; packaging), must be specified and accepted by the Walker separately in the space below. Permission to use the image in subsequent editions or revised editions or in different language versions or different media will be considered only upon separate application.

    ☐ No special permission granted   ☐ Special permission granted as follows:

    Approved by: _____   Approved by: _____
                   Publisher   Walker Art Center

    Position: _____   Position: _____

2. **Technical Requirements.** Reproductions must be made solely from the photographic image furnished to applicant by the Walker in the form of a color-corrected transparency or curatorially-approved black-and-white photograph. The reproduction must be full-color or full-tone black and white, as the case may be, and reproduced in its entirety in accordance with the image furnished. No cropping, bleeding, alteration, modification, inversion, rotation, superimposition or overprinting of the image may be made of any kind. For any digital reproductions of the photographic image, the resolution shall be a maximum of 72 dots per inch (DPI), and the image shall appear within a framed border, so that the image is not cropped by the edges of the display as it appears on a monitor or otherwise. Digital reproductions of color images shall be at a minimum of 8-bit color and a maximum of 24-bit color. For all digital reproductions of the image, the medium shall contain such encryption and other security features as are then standard in the industry for such medium for the prevention of unauthorized reproduction, distribution or use of the image.

3. **Identification and Credit.** Full identification of the work of art contained in the image (including the artist's name title of the work, date, medium and size) and the credit line must appear exactly as specified by the Walker, without editing, abbreviations, omissions or use of acronyms. Such identification information and credit line shall appear in the immediate proximity of the image wherever the image appears in the edition.

4. **Approval.** Applicant shall furnish to the Walker prior to publication of the edition a sample of the portion of the edition containing the image and the identification information and credit line as they will appear in the final version of the edition for review and approval by the Walker. Such approval shall not relieve applicant of any of its obligations under this agreement unless otherwise explicitly agreed to by the Walker in writing.

5. **Free Copy.** Applicant shall furnish to the Walker, without charge, one copy of the edition containing the image upon publication of such edition.

6. **Miscellaneous.** None of the rights under this agreement may be assigned and none of its terms or condition may be waived except by the written consent of the the Walker. This agreement shall be governed by the laws of the State of Minnesota and shall constitute the entire agreement between applicant and the Walker with respect to the subject matter hereof. This agreement may be modified only in a writing signed by both parties.

GLENBOW
MUSEUM • ART GALLERY • LIBRARY • ARCHIVES

PHOTOGRAPHIC REQUISITION

N⁰ 1254

TEL. (403) 268-4100
FAX (403) 265-9769

ORDER DATE _____ TEL. _____

BILL TO _____

_____

_____

_____ POSTAL CODE _____

TYPE OF WORK	TYPE OF PHOTOGRAPH		TYPE OF FINISH
☐ To Copy	☐ B & W	☐ Colour	☐ Glossy
☐ To Photograph	☐ Print	☐ Proof Sheet	☐ Non Gloss
☐ Printing	☐ Trans	☐ Slide	

GLENBOW USE

UNIT _____

DATE REQUIRED _____

ISSUED BY _____

PHOTO LAB USE

NEGATIVES _____

TRANSPARENCIES _____

PRINTS - FIBRE/RC _____

TIME _____

PHOTO NUMBER - IN NUMERICAL ORDER (or description)	SIZE	QUANTITY	PRICE	AMOUNT

PURPOSE

SPECIAL INSTRUCTIONS _____

_____

_____

SHIPPING ADDRESS
(if different than above) _____

_____

_____

METHOD OF PAYMENT

☐ Cash
☐ Cheque/Money Order
☐ Credit Card
  ☐ Visa
  ☐ Master Card
  ☐ American Express
☐ Invoice

PHOTOS	
RUSH FEE	
POSTAGE	
HANDLING	
SUB-TOTAL	
G.S.T.	
COMM. USE (0 Rated G.S.T.)	
TOTAL	

GST #107435695

CHEQUES PAYABLE TO: Glenbow Museum
130 - 9 Avenue S.E., Calgary, Alberta T2G 0P3

(Terms Net 30 Days)

I have read and agree to comply with the conditions stated on reverse.

Signature _____

INVOICE DATE

300

AMON CARTER MUSEUM
PHOTOGRAPHY WORK ORDER

Date issued _____   Date needed by _____

Account number 1 - _____ - 31.3 - _____ - _____

Requested by / for _____

Artist / Title / Accession No.(s) _____

Special Instructions _____

Return Object to _____

Location of Object _____

OBJECT TO BE PHOTOGRAPHED

Film size (circle)   No. of exposures

☐ B & W negative.   35mm   4x5   _____

☐ Color transparency.   4x5   8x10   _____

☐ 35mm slides.   No. of objects _____   No. of slides ea. _____

No. of negs. _____

PRINTS FROM NEGATIVES

Prints per neg. _____   Total _____

Print size (circle)   5x7   8x10   Other _____

lab use only: photographed   b/w _____   c/t _____
tests: 35   45   810   completed

Spencer Photo Order Form

Please refer all photo requests for use outside the SMA to the Rights and Reproductions staff. Photo requests for outside use must be in writing.

Your name _____

Date ordered _____   needed by _____

☐ **I. NEW ACQUISITION** standard: 1 8x10 b&w file copy for curatorial files, 3 b&w prints and slides for photography files, 1 color slide for slide library

☐ **II. OTHER**   **FOR**

  ☐ # ____ 35 mm color slide   ☐ Spencer publications/Calendar

  ☐ # ____ 4x5 color transparency   ☐ Curatorial files ☐ Sale or rental

  ☐ # ____ 8x10 b&w print   ☐ Slide library ☐ Staff project

☐ **OBJECT** Complete ALL information or put NK for not known.

Accession number _____

Artist, nationality, dates _____

Title, date _____

Medium, dimensions _____

Credit line _____

Location _____

  ☐ Include frame   ☐ Include base   ☐ Shoot details

☐ **EVENT** 5x7 black & white print, unless specified otherwise

Time, date, place _____

Person(s) to be photographed _____

☐ **PORTRAIT** 5x7 black & white print, unless specified otherwise

Name of person _____

Portrait session scheduled for _____

301

PHOTOGRAPHIC SERVICES DEPARTMENT
ORDER FOR NEW PHOTOGRAPHY - WORKS OF ART
(This form is also available on Quixis under "Query with Locations." Use the format command, "format reprod.format")

** Please allow a MINIMUM of three weeks for processing this order. *Please print clearly or type.***

Name _____ Ext. _____ Date _____

Purpose _____ Date Needed _____

I. Object Information

ACC # / TR # _____

LOCATION _____

ARTIST/CULTURE _____

PLACE/PROV. _____

TITLE _____
_____

OBJECT DATE _____

MEDIUM _____

DIMENSIONS _____

CREDIT LINE _____
_____

II. Detailed Photography Request Information

Standard policy is to take the 3 listed formats of photography while art work is available. If applicable, please indicate below which views should be taken. TO REQUEST THAT PHOTOGRAPHY BE SENT TO YOU WHICH YOU WILL NOT BE RETURNING, please place a "✓" in the lefthand column and provide account number to be charged.

☐ **ACCT #** _____ For PSD use only

☑	Format	Overall View(s)	Details	**# oa**	**# det.**	**TOTAL**
☐	Black & White			___	___	___
☐	Color transparency			___	___	___
☐	Color Slide			___	___	___

Other Instructions:

AREAS BELOW FOR PSD USE ONLY - Please attach a separate sheet if further instructions are needed.

Other Instructions for Photographer:

Information for Preparations :

Scheduled for photography : ___ / ___ / ___

Notify when photography complete :

Location : _____

	cc:
Completed : ____ / ____ / ____	TRD, photographer
Neg. : B/W 4 x 5 _____ 35 mm _____ other _____	KBC / RH, preparations
Color 4 x 5 _____ 35 mm _____ other _____	BMS, inventory control
Prints _____ Trans. _____ Slides _____ Contact Sheet _____	requester curator _____

rev. February, 1996

Brigham Young University

North Campus Drive

Provo, UT 84602-1400

T: 801-378-8256 F: 801-378-8222

RR # 1997 053

PHOTOGRAPHIC MATERIAL REQUESTED:
Print: B&W_____   Color_____

Color Transparency: 4x5 _____   35mm _____

Other: _____

_____

Date Required
$_____
Total Charges

M☉A
Museum
of Art

RIGHTS and
REPRODUCTION
AGREEMENT

Date_____
Please complete, sign and return to the attention of Imaging and Photographic Services. Type or print clearly.
Application for permission to reproduce works of art in the collection of the Museum of Art at Brigham Young University. This is an agreement (subject to the conditions listed on page two) between Brigham Young University and:

_____
Name/ Institution

CREDIT LINE:
The following credit line must be used in connection with this image:

_____
Title of Work Requested

_____
Artist
©Courtesy Museum of Art, Brigham Young University. All Rights reserved.

_____
Name of film/program/publication

_____
Publisher

_____
Author or Editor

_____
If non-profit, please give tax-exempt number.

One use, non-exclusive, one language only: Yes___No___ If no, please specify:

_____
Other use

_____
Projected date of publication

CONDITION OF SALE/RENTAL:

- Payment is required in UNITED STATES currency on all orders. Checks or money orders should be made to the **MUSEUM OF ART, BRIGHAM YOUNG UNIVERSITY**, and returned to the attention of the business office.
- All applications must be received in writing.
- Black & White photographs of works in the collection sold for purposes of reproduction cannot be returned.
- *Color transparencies are rented for a period of 3 months.* No transparencies will be sent for consideration, nor sold outright. For each additional month or fraction thereof, a $25.00 fee will be assessed even if no initial rental fee was charged.
- 35 mm slides may not be used for reproduction (in publications, films, filmstrips, videos, electronic media, etc.) or for duplication.

SCHEDULE OF SALE / RENTAL:

	Existing	New Work
Black and White Prints (8x10)		
Academic	❏ $10.00	❏ $50.00
Commercial	❏ $20.00	❏ $60.00
Rental of 4x5 Color Transparencies (one use)		
Academic	❏ $50.00	❏ $150.00
Commercial	❏ $100.00	❏ $200.00
Color Slides		
Academic	❏ $2.00	❏ $50.00
Commercial	❏ $4.00	❏ $52.00
Color Photocopy from 35mm Slide	❏ $5.00	❏ $50.00

Replacement fee for lost or damaged transparency: $200.00

❏ Rush Charge $_____
A rush charge will be applied to any order requiring delivery in less than normal processing time. Normal processing time is 15 working days.

❏ Shipping and Handling
A $5.00 shipping & handling charge will be added to each order. All orders will be sent First Class. Express mail will be charged to your account.

Address for Shipment: _____

_____

Address for Billing: _____

_____

Phone Number: _____

Fax Number: _____

303

CONDITIONS under which permission is granted to reproduce works of art in the collection of the Museum of Art at Brigham Young University (herein called MOA) appear on the back of this sheet.

Permission to reproduce is conditioned upon acceptance of these regulations. Any breach of these terms and conditions will automatically result, at the sole discretion of the MOA, in revocation of permission to reproduce.

1. All reproductions must be made from photographic materials supplied by the MOA. Reproduction from printed or other non-photographic materials is *strictly prohibited.*

2. Full documentation (as written on page 1) must accompany reproduction, either directly under it, on the page facing, on the reverse or elsewhere in the book, such as in the index or list of illustrations. In the case of filmstrips, the information must appear in an adjacent frame, or accompanying the manual. In the case of television, films or video, a general attribution must be included in the credits.

3. Permission is granted for only ONE usage in ONE publication, ONE edition, and ONE language. Any further reproduction shall require an additional fee and written permission from the MOA.

4. The reproduction must be printed in full-tone black and white or full color and may not be reproduced on colored stock. Nothing may be superimposed on the reproduction (i.e., lettering, or another image) without approval of the MOA. Permission here is limited to book and catalog covers of academic and museum publications where the image is reproduced in its entirety within.

5. The work must be reproduced in its entirety and must *not* be bled off the page or cropped in any way without permission of the MOA. Permission here is limited to book and catalogue covers of academic and museum publications where the image is reproduced in its entirety within.

   The reproduction of a specific detail must be approved in advance by the MOA and the fact that it is a detail noted in the documentation accompanying the reproduction. For use in video productions, panning and/or zooming in or out of the entire image is permitted provided the details thus produced are closely associated with the image in its entirety.

6. To ensure accuracy in COLOR reproduction, one (1) proof must be submitted to Photographic Services MOA for comparison with the original BEFORE publication. This department will advise the publisher of necessary color adjustment or grant approval of the proof.

7. The publisher must send one copy of the publication(s) in which the reproduction appears to Photographic Services of the MOA.

8. The MOA may order, at the time of printing, any overrun it may desire, to be paid for at cost or at a discount to be worked out between the MOA and the Publisher.

9. The MOA gives no exclusive rights to any Publisher, Author, or Photographer and makes no warranties or representations and assumes no responsibilities whatsoever for any claims against applicant or the MOA by an artist, his agent, estate or any other party in connection with the reproduction of the works of art in the collections of the MOA. Additionally , the applicant agrees to indemnify the MOA and hold it harmless against any and all such claims, including copyright infringement claims, royalty or fee demands and/or actions, including the costs thereof, arising as a

RR # <u>1997 053</u>

result of the applicant's reproduction of the works of art in the collections of the MOA.

The MOA will attempt to provide accurate and up-to-date information regarding the copyright status of the specific work requested. However, it is the responsibility of the Publisher to directly contact copyright owner. Reproductions of all copyrighted works must bear the copyright notice as perscribed by the Copyright Act of 1976 of the United States.

Copyright ownership and/or reproduction rights may be retained by the artist for works of art created after January 1, 1978. Any or all royalty payments or other requirements specified by the copyright owner of such a work must be adhered to by the Publisher or agent requesting reproduction permission.

10. Any unauthorized use of photographic materials supplied by the MOA by any person or entity, for any reason, will render applicant responsible and liable to the MOA for appropriate compensation and other costs, regardless of whether applicant has profited or is responsible for such unauthorized use.

11. The MOA reserves the right to limit the number of reproductions of works in its collections in any single publication if it appears that their number is disproportionate in relation to those from other sources.

12. The MOA reserves the right, at its sole discretion, to refuse permission for futher applications from a publisher or other applicant if, in its opinion, acceptable standards of reproduction of the MOA's objects have not been obtained or if adherence to the terms of previous contracts has not been upheld.

SPECIAL CIRCUMSTANCES:

(Please sign and return.)

I have read and understand these conditions and agree to abide by the terms therein,

_____

Applicant   (Signed) _____ **(Typed)**

Title or position _____ **Date**

_____

For and in behalf of: (Publisher)

_____

For and in behalf of the Museum of Art

Title or position _____ Date

page -2-

Dallas Museum of Art

Communications - Rights & Reproductions

1717 North Harwood, Dallas, Texas 75201

Publicity Print Media Reproduction Agreement

Name:_____

Company:_____Date_____

is granted permission to reproduce the following object. **This information must accompany the image:**

DMA Object #	**Maker/Culture**
Title	
Credit line	

☐ Slide ☐ B & W Photorgraph ☐ Transparency

for the following article / publication:

Title_____

Author_____

Publication Date_____

in accordance with the reproduction conditions specified below:

TERMS OF REPRODUCTION PERMISSION

1) Permission is granted for one-time, one-edition, one-language reproduction only, for the purposes expressly outlined in this agreement. Any subsequent re-use of the image(s) is forbidden without written permission from the Dallas Museum of Art. 2) Images must be reproduced in their entirety. Details are permitted with specific permission only. No guttering allowed without special permission. Cropping, bleeding or overprinting is not permitted. No reproduction on colored stock is allowed. 3) The complete caption, credit and copyright information, as provided by the Dallas Museum of Art must accompany the reproduction. The Dallas Museum of Art is the sole owner of the Copyrights to the photography of this object. No other agency or individual may attach their copyright notice to the reproduction. 4) The requestor agrees not to duplicate, transmit or distribute these photographic materials without specific permission from the Dallas Museum of art. The permission for use of this image(s) does not grant any digital rights.

I have read and agree to the terms and conditions set forth in this agreement.
I certify that I have full authority to enter into this agreement.

_____
Signature of Requestor / Requestor's Agent: Date:

Comments:

Unless otherwise specified, all photographic materials must be returned to:
Ellen Key
Communications Department
1717 North Harwood
Dallas, Texas 75201
214/922-1344
fax 214/954-0174

PLEASE FILL OUT, SIGN AND RETURN TO ELLEN KEY _PRIOR_ TO PUBLICATION

305

AMON CARTER MUSEUM
ATTN: Rights & Reproductions
3501 Camp Bowie Blvd.
Fort Worth, Texas 76107
Telephone: (817) 738-1933   FAX: (817) 738-2034

ELECTRONIC REPRODUCTION CONTRACT/INVOICE NO.:
DATE:

APPLICANT INFORMATION

NAME/TITLE:
AFFILIATION:
ADDRESS:

TELEPHONE: **FAX:**

I have read and understood the attached CONDITIONS which govern the reproduction of works of art in the Amon Carter Museum collections and agree to abide by each and every condition and to be legally bound in executing this contract. **(Please note: This contract should be signed by the person responsible for insuring that the reproduction described herein conforms to the Amon Carter Museum's conditions for reproduction of imagery.)**

_____
Applicant's signature   Date

PROJECT INFORMATION

PROJECT TITLE:

PUBLISHER/PRODUCER:

BIT DEPTH (number of colors):

IMAGE SIZE/DIMENSIONS (x pixels by y pixels):

HOW WILL CREDIT AND CAPTION INFORMATION BE PROVIDED ON SCREEN AND IN THE FILE ITSELF (if printed, downloaded, distributed):

CD-ROM REQUESTS
DOES THE PROGRAM ALLOW FOR DOWNLOADING OR PRINTING:

PROJECTED DATE OF PUBLICATION:

NUMBER OF COPIES PRODUCED:

LIST PRICE:

WWW (URL)/INTERNET REQUESTS
WWW/URL ADDRESS:

DATES IMAGE IS TO BE DISPLAYED:

FILE FORMAT:
____ GIF   ____ JPEG   ___ Other:

DISTRIBUTION CHANNEL:
____Consumer ___Educational ____Institutional   306

(CONTINUED ON NEXT PAGE)

IMAGES REQUESTED (6 month rental for materials)

MATERIAL FEE	USE FEE
1-00-4.1/.2-709-00	1-00-6.4/09-00
1-00-4.1/.2-022-00	1-00-6.4-022.00

SALES TAX   0.00
(1-00-73.5)
(If Texas non-profit, send tax exemption certificate)

SUBTOTAL   0.00

SERVICE CHARGE   0.00
(1-00-04.1/.2-022-00)
(1-00-04.1/.2-709-00)

TOTAL AMOUNT DUE   0.00
(PAYABLE IN ADVANCE)

CREDIT LINE MUST INCLUDE THE ARTIST, TITLE, DATE, MEDIUM, MUSEUM NUMBER LISTED ABOVE AND:
© Amon Carter Museum, Fort Worth, Texas

PLEASE RETURN THIS CONTRACT WITH YOUR PAYMENT. A COUNTERSIGNED COPY WILL BE RETURNED WITH YOUR ORDER.

Permission is granted to reproduce the works as described above:

For and on behalf of The Amon Carter Museum   Date

Name/Title

MATERIALS ARE DUE BACK ON OR BEFORE:

1) REQUESTS

All requests for permission to reproduce an electronic image must be made in writing, which must describe in detail the intended use, including publisher/producer, expected date of publication, and number of copies produced for CD-ROM requests, and WWW address and dates of use for WWW requests. Material and Use Fees are payable in advance. If the work is not used in the final product, the Use Fees may be refunded upon receipt of a written request. Material fees are not refundable.

2) PERMISSION

Permission for reproduction and fees paid cover only the specific use described on the Contract. Any use not specifically described requires a separate request and Contract and appropriate fees. Exclusive and serial rights are not granted.

3) REPRODUCTION

The work of art must be reproduced in its entirety. Nothing may be superimposed on the image (e.g. lettering, tone or another image) without special permission.

The reproductions may not be manipulated in any way that distorts the color or value of the transparencies or the photographs provided by the Museum.

4) RESOLUTION

The image must be reproduced at a resolution of 72 DPI, and a Bit Depth of no less than 8 BIT.

5) DETAILS

Applications to reproduce a detail of a work will be considered only upon receipt of a marked photograph or photocopy showing the exact area to be used. The word "detail" must appear in the caption with the complete credit line. Under most circumstances a request for detailing may be approved only if the work is shown in it's entirety elsewhere in the publication.

6) CREDIT LINE

The credit line must include artist, title, date, medium, accession number and : **Amon Carter Museum, Fort Worth, Texas** unless specifically stated otherwise on the contract. The credit line and/or copyright citation must appear with the image.

7) RETURN

All transparencies, photographs and slides remain the property of Amon Carter Museum and must be returned within six months. A replacement fee is charged if a transparency is returned in such a conditions that it cannot be reused.

8) GRATIS COPY (CD-ROM)

The publisher is to provide Amon Carter Museum with one complete gratis copy of the electronic publication in which the image is reproduced.

9) INDEPENDENT USE

Amon Carter Museum does not supply photographs, transparencies or slides to individuals or companies operating a rental and/or sales service.

10) DUPLICATION

Except for purposes of technical production of the contracted project, applicants may not duplicate in any way a color transparency or black and white print.

11) DISCLAIMER

Amon Carter Museum assumes no responsibility for any royalties claimed by the artist or on his/her behalf. In the case of works by living artists or other copyrighted material, the burden of obtaining all necessary reproduction permission rests with the requesting party.

12) IMAGE LIMIT
Amon Carter Museum reserves the right to limit
the number of reproductions of Museum-owned
works in any single publication, if it appears that
their number is disproportionate in relation to
those from other sources.

12) VIOLATION OF CONTRACT
If any condition noted in this contract is violated,
a minimum fee of at least $600.00 will be assessed
in addition to a requirement that the violation be
immediately corrected.

PLEASE NOTE: BY SIGNING THE AMON CARTER MUSEUM'S CONTRACT FOR
REPRODUCTION OF IMAGERY, YOU AGREE TO ABIDE BY ALL OF
THE CONDITIONS LISTED ABOVE.

PLEASE RETAIN THIS SHEET FOR YOUR REFERENCE.

Approved (09/97)

Museum of the Rockies, Montana State University, Bozeman, MT 59717

APPLICATION FOR PERMISSION TO REPRODUCE/PUBLISH

Please complete Sections A and B, and return to the Museum of the Rockies

==

Section A

Applicant's name_____   Publisher_____

Title_____   Contact person_____

Address_____   Address_____

City, State, Zip_____   City, State, Zip_____

Telephone_____   Telephone_____

Type of Publication_____ Title of Publication_____

Date of Publication_____ Edition /Issue_____ Language/Country_____

==

Section B

Permission is requested to use the following photographic materials from Section C:

Identification Code #

_____   _____   _____   _____

_____   _____   _____   _____

_____   _____   _____   _____

==

Section C (For Museum use)

The following photographs have been sent to the above:

Identification Code #   Image Description

_____

_____

_____

_____

_____

_____

_____

==

Section D (For Museum use)

Date of application_____Date of Approval_____Date sent_____How?_____

REQUIRED DATE OF RETURN_____Actual date of return_____

Approved Special Conditions_____

_____

_____

Department Signature   Photographic Services Signature

MUSEUM OF THE ROCKIES MONTANA STATE UNIVERSITY BOZEMAN, MONTANA 59717
406.994.5279   fax 406.994.2682
Photographic/Video Loan and Reproduction/Publication Application and Agreement

Photographs and video from the Museum of the Rockies' Archives and stock collections are available for loan and/or reproduction/publication, subject to the conditions set forth in this agreement.

All requests for use of Museum photographs/video must be accompanied by a Museum of the Rockies Application and Agreement. If there is an urgent need, the requested photographs/video will be sent with the Application and Agreement to expedite the request. However, the signed Application and Agreement must be returned to the Museum prior to reproduction/publication or within 15 days of receipt, whichever is earlier. Permission to use the Museum's photographs/video is not granted until the signed Application and Agreement is returned to the Museum.

The Museum prefers to send duplicate slides, but acknowledges original slides many be needed under some circumstances. Once photography is delivered to the applicant, the applicant is responsible for the photography. If an original slide is lost, damaged, or otherwise not returnable to the Museum a $500 minimum charge will be assessed to the applicant. For dupes a $100 charge will be assessed.

All photographs sent to the applicant for review are loaned on a temporary basis. There is no charge for the first 30 days, after which a rental fee of $20 per photograph per month, or partial month, will be charged for photographs that are not published. There will be no rental fee for those photographs that are subject to a reproduction/publication fee. Reproduction/publication fees shall be the applicant's page rate, subject to the Museum's minimum charge. All photographs are loaned for a maximum of 90 days, unless a longer period is approved in writing by the Museum prior to the expiration of the 90 day period.

If the applicant requests the Museum to send photographs for review, the applicant will be billed for appropriate services when it is known how many photographs will be reproduced. In addition to rental and reproduction/publication fees, there may be production charges which will be billed at the time of shipment.

All fees must be paid within 15 days of the billing date or reproduction/publication date, whichever is earlier. Payments must be made by check or money order payable in US currency through a US bank. A 10% late fee will be charged after the 15th day, and monthly thereafter.

Approved requests will usually be shipped within one week. However, special requests, such as specific photography or printing, may require up to three weeks. Production charges will be doubled for rush orders. Orders are shipped via US Mail. If a commercial courier service is preferred, the Museum will ship collect using the applicant's account number.

The following additional conditions apply to any reproduction/publication of Museum photographs/video where applicable:

1. Any reproduction/publication of Museum photographs/video must bear a copyright notice as prescribed by the Copyright Law of the United States.

2. If the copyright to the photographs/video is held outside of the Museum, the applicant must obtain the written permission of the copyright holder before reproducing or publishing.

3. If the copyright to the photographs/video is held by the Museum, permission to reproduce or publish is granted for one time use only and is subject to the payment of appropriate fees. Separate application must be made for use in additional languages, subsequent printings or revisions, and new editions, and will require an additional fee. The Museum reserves the right to refuse permission for further reproduction/publication if an applicant has not maintained acceptable standards of reproduction/publication, or has not observed the conditions set forth in this agreement.

4. Museum photographs/video shall not be used to show or imply Museum endorsements of any commercial product or enterprise, or to indicate that the Museum concurs with the opinions expressed in, or confirms the accuracy of any text used with the photographs/video. The Museum reserves the right to request a printers proof for approval prior to publication and reserves the right to revoke permission to use the photographs/video.

5. The credit line: MUSEUM OF THE ROCKIES/ (photographer's name on the slide when present) must appear in immediate proximity to the reproduction or in the section of the publication devoted to acknowledgements,

6. By the publishing date, two complete complimentary copies of the publication must be sent to the Museum's Photographic Services.

7. Any adjustment, such as cropping, overprinting, or bleeding of any photograph from the Museum's art collection must have prior written approval of the Museum. Details of the adjustment must be identified on the credit line.

8. Any manipulation of photographs or video MUST be requested in detail in advance and have written approval.

Failure to comply with the above conditions may result in the revocation of permission to use the photographs/video and the denial of application for future use. The application is on the reverse side. It is advisable to photocopy both sides of this agreement for your records.

I have read the above and agree to comply with the terms and conditions of this agreement.

Authorized signature	Company/Institution	Date

BUFFALO
MUSEUM
of SCIENCE

1020 Humboldt Parkway • Buffalo NY 14211-1293 • (716) 896-5200 • Fax (716) 897-6723

REPRODUCTION RIGHTS AGREEMENT

Name _____
PLEASE PRINT

Company _____

Address _____

_____

_____

_____

Telephone _____

applies for permission to reproduce the following work from the collections of the Buffalo Museum of Science:

_____

USE OF PHOTOGRAPHS

_____ Research or Personal (not to be transcribed or reproduced in any way)

_____ Public Display or Exhibition (specify) _____

_____ Publication (specify) _____

_____ Other (specify) _____

PUBLICATION DATA

Publication in which photograph will appear _____

Author _____

Publisher _____ Date of publication _____

I/We hereby agree to comply with the conditions on the reverse, to pay a reproduction fee of _____ , to credit the Museum with a line reading: "Buffalo Museum of Science", to include catalog numbers and photographer's credit if applicable and to send the Registrar a copy of the publication.

I have read and understand the conditions listed on the reverse of this form and agree to abide by the terms therein.

Applicant's signature _____ Date _____

Signature _____ Date _____
PRESIDENT & CEO – BUFFALO MUSEUM OF SCIENCE

WICHITA ART MUSEUM

619 STACKMAN DRIVE WICHITA KANSAS 67203-3296

| RIGHTS & REPRODUCTION ■ CONTRACT-INVOICE |
| Photographic Services Office |
| TEL(316)268-4921 ■ FAX(316)268-4980 |

Date: _____

Contract #_____

CONTRACT FOR PERMISSION TO REPRODUCE OBJECTS IN THE WICHITA ART MUSEUM COLLECTION

This contract is between the Wichita Art Museum (the 'Museum') and _____(the 'Applicant') in response of the Applicant's request for permission to reproduce from photographic materials obtained from the Museum's Photographic Services Office.

Applicant Information

Name/Title:
Institution:
Address:
Telephone: Fax:
Federal Exemption # (nonprofit status):

Image Information

Accession #   Artist   Title   Medium

CREDIT LINE MUST READ:

Project Information

Title/Type of publication: Inside or Cover use:
Author/Editor: B&W or Color use:
Name & Address of Publisher:
Expected Date of publication (volume, year):
Press run/copies distributed:
Distribution rights desired (one time use, one language):
    Single rights (one country, e.g. North America, Commonwealth):
    World rights (worldwide distribution):
    Language(s):
Commercial or Non-profit:

Payments

Material Fees:
Publication Permission Fees:
Postage & Handling:
Total Amount Due:

Signatures

Reproduction is limited to the above purpose for one time use only, unless otherwise agreed by the Wichita Art Museum in writing. This contract shall serve as an invoice. Materials will be sent on receipt of signed contract and payment of above charges. Please note contract number on any correspondence or payment.

The applicant agrees to abide by the terms and conditions herein, including on the reverse, and further agrees to **pre-pay** all applicable fees.

Please complete, sign and return contract with payment to: Photographic Services Office. A countersigned copy of the contract would be sent to the Applicant signifying official permission to reproduce.

Applicant: Agreed: Wichita Art Museum

By:_____ date:_____   By:_____date:_____
    (name and title)   (Dimitris Skliris, Photographic Services Office, 316-268-4921)

313

The Brooklyn Museum
Photographic Services
200 Eastern Parkway
Brooklyn
New York 11238

Application for permission to reproduce works of art in The Brooklyn Museum

Permission is hereby requested to reproduce the following work(s) from the collections of The Brooklyn Museum. The reproduction(s) will appear in a *☐ Book (in text)

☐ Newspaper/Periodical
(date and issue number . . . .)

*Check one or more boxes as applicable.

☐ Filmstrip

☐ Book cover/jacket

☐ Record album cover

☐ Advertising/promotional context

☐ Commercial product

Title (and author) of publication:

. . . .

. . . .

Anticipated date of publication . . . .

Reproduction will be in *☐ Color   *☐ Black and white.

Permission to reproduce, if granted, is condidioned upon unequivocal acceptance of the full regulations published by the Museum. Any breach of these terms and conditions will automatically result, in the sole discretion of the Museum, in revocation of permission to reproduce. Payment of appropriate compensation or damages to the Museum by the applicant may also be considered. **We have read and understand the regulations (1178) published by The Brooklyn Museum which govern the reproduction of works of art in its collections and we agree to abide by each and every term and condition detailed therein.**

Signed . . . .

Title or Position . . . .

for and on behalf of the Publishers

Company . . . .

Address . . . .

. . . .

. . . .

Date . . . .

✝ Applicant to complete, sign, and return the **two top copies** to: Coordinator of Photographic Services
The Brooklyn Museum
200 Eastern Parkway
Brooklyn
New York 11238
Telephone: (718) 638-5000, ext. 343 or 202
*PINK & GOLD COPY TO BE RETAINED BY APPLICANT.

Permission for the reproduction of the work(s) listed in this application is granted, for the purpose(s) specifically indicated only, premised and conditioned upon payment of the fees involved.

Signed . . . .

for and on behalf of The Brooklyn Museum

Date . . . .

Payment is due on receipt of the relevant invoice, which, when paid, together with this executed application, constitutes official permission for reproduction.

✝ Please submit color proofs.
✝ Please note, we require two complimentary copies due upon publication.

Reproduction of works of art in The Brooklyn Museum

Permission to reproduce is conditioned upon unequivocal acceptance of these regulations. Any breach of these terms and conditions will automatically result, in the sole discretion of the Museum, in revocation of permission to reproduce. Payment of appropriate compensation or damages to the Museum by the applicant may also be considered.

General conditions

1 Permission to reproduce and the fee payable cover **only the specific occasion and use detailed in the application.** Any and all reprints, further editions, re-employment of the printing plates or additional use of any kind must be preceded by a new application and is not covered by the original fee or permission to reproduce.

2 The paint area of a picture, or the area within the outline of a sculpture, may not be masked out, cut down, superimposed with type matter, or in any way defaced or altered. Reproductions which bleed are therefore permitted only in the case of "details."

3 Application to reproduce a detail from a work will be considered only upon receipt of a sketch or marked up photograph showing the area to be reproduced. The caption must include the word "detail."

4 Works to be reproduced in color require the submission of color proofs and the approval of the Museum before printing may proceed. Failure to comply with the corrections indicated by the Museum on submitted proofs may result in action as stated in paragraph 12.

5 Color slides, monochrome negatives, and photographic prints may not be made by outside companies or photographers for commercial purposes and without the prior written consent of the Museum.

6 Applications for permission to include works in filmstrips **must** be accompanied by a sample or samples of previous filmstrips produced by the applicant. The Museum reserves the right, in its sole discretion, to withhold permission, if, in its opinion, the standard of reproduction is not of acceptable quality.

7 **The Museum does not supply transparencies of works in its collections to companies or individuals operating a photograph rental and/or sales service.** Applicants will be required to represent as a pre-condition for permission to reproduce that no such use will be made of any material obtained from the Museum pursuant to any application hereunder.

8 Reproduction from printed or other non-photographic materials, or from photographic materials not supplied directly by the Museum, **is strictly prohibited.**

9 The minimum size of color transparency permitted for reproduction purposes is 4 x 5 inches.

10 All final reproductions, unless specifically excepted in writing by the Museum prior to the reproduction, must be smaller than the original work(s) of art, except sculpture.

11 Applicants will be responsible for the return to their safekeeping of all printing plates, transparencies, etc., upon completion of the publication(s) for which permission has been obtained. Any unauthorized use thereof, by any person or entity, for any reason, whether or not authorized by the applicant, will render applicant responsible and liable to the Museum for appropriate compensation and other costs, regardless of whether applicant has profited from or is responsible for such unauthorized use.

12 The Museum reserves the right, in its sole discretion, to refuse permission for further applications from a publisher or other applicant, if, in its opinion, the standard of reproduction has not been of acceptable quality.

13 The Museum will not grant an exclusive right to reproduce any work(s) of art in the Museum; nor will the Museum assume any responsiblity for duplication of subjects or reproduction of the same work(s) of art by other applicants or persons not authorized to reproduce said work(s). The Museum assumes no responsibility for claims against the applicant or the Museum by third parties, and applicants agree to indemnify the Museum and hold it harmless against any and all such claims and costs, including copyright infringement claims arising out of applicant's reproduction of the work(s) of art in question.

14 **On the publishing date a complete copy of each publication must be forwarded to the Coordinator of Photographic Services at the Museum for record purposes.**

Procedure

General

15 All communications connected with the reproduction of works of art in The Brooklyn Museum should be addressed to the Coordinator of Photographic Services, The Brooklyn Museum, 200 Eastern Parkway, Brooklyn, New York 11238; telephone (718) 638-5000, ext. 344.

16 Written permission to reproduce must be obtained **before** publication.

17 Requests for permission to reproduce works in the Museum will be considered only when application is made **by the publisher.**

Films

18 Applications for permission to film works of art require the same general procedure as with still reproductions, plus full details of the composition of the complete film. Principals will be bound by all regulations governing other forms of reproduction, particularly those relating to photography in the Museum as set forth in paragraphs 41 through 50. In addition, the applicant and the company carrying the filming will be required to accept full responsibility for any damage to life or property incurred while using the available facilities. Prior to any filming all electrical power requirements must be discussed with the museum staff (by appointment only).

Copyright

19 The Museum makes no warranties or representations and assumes no responsibility whatsoever for any claims, royalties or fees demanded by an artist, his agent, estate or by any other party in connection with the reproduction of works of art in the collections of the Museum. Additionally, the applicant agrees to indemnify the Museum and hold it harmless against any and all such claims, demands and/or actions, including the costs thereof, arising as a result of the applicant's reproduction of the works of art in the Museum.

Acknowledgement

20 With the exception of reproductions used in advertising *(see paragraph 22)* and in films *(see paragraph 21),* an acknowledgement, **as supplied by the Museum,** including, but not limited to, full ownership credit, the donor's name and the specific collection, **must appear** in immediate proximity to the reproduction or in the section within the publication devoted to acknowledgements, as specified by the Museum. Abbreviations are not permitted.

21 In case of television or films, full ownership credit and acknowledgement, as specified by the Museum, must be included in the credits.

22 When reproductions are used for advertising or promotional purposes, reference to The Brooklyn Museum is not permitted unless particularly applied for, and granted, in writing.

continued overleaf

Fees

23 Permission to reproduce is premised and conditioned upon payment of the fees involved prior to publication. Failure to pay the required fees means that permission has not been granted. Payment is due on receipt of the relevant invoice and may not be deferred until the date of publication. When paid, the receipted invoice, together with executed application, constitutes official permission for reproduction.

24 Reproduction fees, per subject, are as follows:
Color: $35.00 educational
                        $45.00 commercial
Color (including 3-month rental of transparency
  – *see paragraphs* $85.00 educational
  34–38): $95.00 commercial
Black-and-white: $10.00 educational
                        $15.00 commercial

Books, Newspapers, Periodicals, Television, Films, Filmstrips

25 Unless otherwise specified by the Museum, permission to reproduce covers world-wide distribution, in one language, in monochrome or in color *(see paragraph 1)*.

26 Students and scholars publishing original research may apply for remission of fees. Applications for such remission must be made in writing together with the application for permission to reproduce.

Advertising, or in a promotional context, or as an integral part of a commercial product

27 Application for permission to reproduce works of art in these categories must include a layout sketch and a full description of the proposed use of the reproduction and the context in which the reproduction will be used, together with details of intended distribution/circulation, etc. satisfactory to the Museum. The attention of applicants is particularly drawn to paragraphs 1, 2, 3 and 10.

28 Reproduction fees per subject, which may not be deferred with the date of publication and are due immediately upon receipt of the relevant invoice, are as follows:

Book covers / jackets / record album covers:
Color: $100.00
Color (including 3-month rental of
  transparency– *see paragraphs*
  34–38): $150.00
Black-and-white: $ 50.00

All other applications:
Where the proposed use of the reproduction is agreed to by the Museum, fees are formulated by the Museum, in its sole discretion. Fees cannot be apportioned until after formal application has been received. Applicants will be informed of the fees, and the Museum requires written confirmation of their acceptance before final permission is given. Fees so established apply solely to the specific application upon which they are based and will not serve as future precedent. Fees are not subject to negotiation.

29 In these categories, before the Museum issues final permission to reproduce works by living artists, the Publisher and the applicant must obtain written permission from the artist, or his authorized agent, to reproduce such works, and a copy of that permission must be delivered to the Coordinator of Photographic Services for the Museum.

Purchase of black-and-white photographs

30 The Museum maintains a library of negatives of works in its collections. Available photographic prints from this library can be supplied as follows:
8 x 10 single weight glossy print: $10.00
Sales tax additional, where applicable.

31 Where no negative exists, and the applicant is prepared to wait for the work to be photographed on the Museum's regular schedule, no extra charge will be made.

32 In more urgent cases, negatives may be made to order, subject to the Museum's prior work schedule and upon payment of an extra charge of $35.00 per photograph. Negatives remain the property of the Museum.

33 Black-and-white photographs are sold outright only, and cannot be returned.

Color transparency rental

34 Color transparencies (4 x 5) of a number of works in the collections of the Museum are available for rental. The charge per transparency for an initial period of three months is $50.00 *(see paragraphs 24 and 28)*.

35 Rental beyond three months is charged at $25.00 per calendar month. Retention of a transparency beyond the initial contracted period automatically incurs this charge, whether the transparency is used or unused.

36 Transparencies can be made to order, subject to the Museum's prior work schedule and upon payment of an extra charge of $75.00 per transparency. Transparencies remain in the property of the Museum.

37 Transparencies cannot be supplied on approval or sold outright.

38 Principals are liable for the full and complete costs of replacement should any transparency be lost or returned damaged in any way.

Postage and handling charges

39 The following charges will be applied, regardless of the size of order: Domestic: $2.50   Foreign: $6.00.

All domestic mailing is by First Class Mail.
All foreign mailing is by Air Mail.

Photography or Filming of works of art in The Brooklyn Museum

40 Permission is not given to private individuals to use, for publishing in any form, their own equipment for photography or filming within the Museum.

41 In special circumstances only, and subject to receipt by the applicant of prior written approval by the Museum, in the Museum's sole discretion, photography and/or filming in the Museum may be arranged. Applications must be fully detailed, and should particularly state the equipment, personnel, and facilities involved.

42 Photography and/or filming is permitted only under supervision by Museum staff. All costs for this supervision, and any other disturbance costs, are charged directly to the applicant in addition to any fees involved.

43 **Accredited professional photographers (only)** may be commissioned by the Publisher.

44 Principals and applicants will be required to indemnify the Museum against any damage to works, buildings, staff, visitors, equipment, or persons directly or indirectly caused by or attributable to the photography and/or filming undertaken.

45 No pictures or works of art can be unframed or unmounted for photographic purposes. Works may only be handled by Museum staff.

46 Works on exhibition must be photographed where they are displayed. All works, wherever located, may not be touched or moved and all persons involved in filming and/or photographing in the Museum are subject to the control and direction of the Museum staff at all times.

47 Works on loan to the Museum may not be included in any photograph and/or film, directly or indirectly.

48 The maximum lighting permitted is equal to a total of 4,000 watts at a distance of 8 feet, and a maximum duration of 2 minutes. Electronic flash is permitted.

49 No lamps are available at the Museum, and equipment using more than 15 amps may not be used without making special arrangements in advance and paying all additional charges for electrical and related services and costs.

REGISTRATION

Appraisal

Check list/Inventory

General

Gift

- Contract/Deed

- Declined

- Non-accessioned

Loan

- Agreement

- Extension

- General

- Incoming

- In-house

- Outgoing

- Specimen invoice

Purchase object

Receipt

Transfer/Exchange

Arizona State Museum
Tucson, Arizona 85721-0026
(520) 621-6281
FAX (520) 621-2976

THE UNIVERSITY OF

ARIZONA ®

TUCSON ARIZONA

LIST OF APPRAISERS
14 November, 1997

Museum policy - States that "staff members for the Arizona State Museum (ASM) may examine artifacts brought to the Museum by the public and give opinions on such matters as age, provenience and function. Under no circumstances will a staff member make an appraisal of artifact value for insurance, commercial or other purposes."

Choosing an appraiser - In cases involving potential gifts to the Museum, IRS regulations require that a third, disinterested party perform appraisals of tax-deductible gifts to non-profit institutions (ASM is a nonprofit institution). Currently, there is no legal certification of personal property appraisers and no government-required testing for the profession. There are, however, codified standards. For more information contact the Appraisal Foundation at 212/347-7727.

Items to consider and/or request - Credentials, written contract, signed statement of disinterest, appraisal documentation, type of value desired (fair market, replacement) and whether the appraiser has liability insurance. When contracting for appraisal services with a dealer, be aware that the dealer might be interested in purchasing the items at, or below, wholesale value.

Appraisal fee - Most appraisers charge rates based on hourly fees which can run up to $200 or more per hour. For federal tax purposes, it is illegal for the appraisal fee to be based on a percentage of the overall value of the item(s). A feasibility study may be requested of the appraiser to determine whether an appraisal is warranted. The cost of an appraisal might be tax-deductible in the case of charitable contributions. To find out specific requirements for claims, please contact the IRS or a tax accountant.

The following list - Includes the names, addresses and telephone numbers of individuals who identify themselves as personal property appraisers. This list might not be all-inclusive and **does not** indicate any preferences by the Museum. Where known, membership status in a professional appraisal association (ASA, ISA) is listed. Interested individuals are encouraged to contact listed appraisers or to seek additional listings in the Yellow Pages.

Tucson Area

AAA Appraisals, Inc. - **Silver, Indian Arts, Furniture** - Eleanor Smith (*ASA/ASA*), Marie Simonson (*ASA/ASA*)& Kathleen Sullivan (*ASA/ASA*) 7660 E. Broadway Blvd. Ste 203-2, Tucson AZ 85710, 520/296-3687, Fax # 520/296-9115

Absolute Estate & Auction Liquidators - **Furniture, Rugs, Paintings, Collectables** - Phil Fergione 2811 N. Country Club, Tucson AZ 85712, 520/326-0910

Adrian's of Budapest - **Silver, Oriental Art, Ceramics** - Cherie Van Dyke Adams (*ISA*) 2538 E. Elm St., Tucson AZ 85716-3417, 520/326-2682

Ambassador Diamond Jewelers - **Diamonds** - Stewart Kuper 4668 E. Speedway Blvd., Tucson AZ 85712, 520/327-8800, Fax # 520/795-5302

American Eagle Brokerage, Inc. - **Antiques & Decorative Arts** - Pauline E. Roed (*ASA/ASA*) 6738 East Opatas, Tucson AZ 85715-3337, 520/885-3635

Art Appraisers of Tucson - **Painting, Prints, Sculpture, Drawings & Watercolors** - Diane V. Kruse (*ISA/CM*) HCR #1 Box 627, Tucson AZ 85736, 520/822-1842, Fax # 520/822-1842

Artabella Jewelry Appraisals - **Gems & Jewelry** - Tracy Less Aros 7660 E. Broadway #203-2, Tucson AZ 85718, 520/751-7435, Fax # 520/296-9115

Asian Trade Oriental Rug Center - **Asian Rugs** - Kasra Massarat 3525 N. Campbell, Tucson AZ 85718, 520/326-7828, Fax # 520/326-1432

Continental Sutlers, Inc. (Orient East) - **Orientalia, Jade, Ivory** - Maurice J. Halper (*ISA*) PO Box 17066, Tucson AZ 85731-7066, 520/742-9809, Fax # 520/886-1083

Covington Fine Arts Gallery - **American & European Prints, Paintings** - Wayne Kielsmeier 6536 E. Tanque Verde Rd Suite 160, Tucson AZ 85749, 520/298-7878

Diana M. Warren (*ISA/AM*) - **Ceramics, Textiles, Silver** - 5555 N. Via Alcalde, Tucson AZ 85718-5107, 520/299-6645

Etherton Stern Gallery - **Fine Arts, Photographs** - Terry Etherton (*ASA/ASA*) 135 S. 6th Avenue, Tucson AZ 85701-2007, 520/624-7370, Fax # 520/792-4569

Glass Shop Coin - **Coins** - Hal Birt 4325 E. Broadway, Tucson AZ 85711, 520/323-8811

Green Valley Appraisal & Liquidation - **Collectables & Antiques** - Delia W. Sheldon (*ISP/AM*) PO Box 383, Green Valley AZ 85622-0383, 520/625-4751

Heerd's Antique West - **Antiques, Decorative Art** - Violet Heerd Ryan (*ASA/ASA*) 6881 East Nasumpta, Tucson AZ 85715, 520/885-3138

ASA-American Society of Appraisers (AM-Accredited Member,
ASA-Accredited Senior Member, FASA-Fellow)

ISA-International Society of Appraisers
(CP-Certified Member, AM-Accredited Member)

Tracking Number: _____

Collection/Object Name: _____

Accession Number: _____

Registrar's Checklist

Task	Date Completed	Name
TEMPORARY CUSTODY RECEIPT FORM		
generate Temporary Custody Receipt form		
museum signs form		
donor signs form		
make 1 copy of the form and give to donor		
make 1 copy of the signed form (for IA)		
file original in current year's Acquisitions File		
DEED OF GIFT FORM		
assign an accession number if it is a collection object		
generate deed of gift form		
museum signs		
make 1 copy (for donor)		
make a return envelope (if necessary)		
mail original form to donor with a note that asks for it to be signed and returned in the enclosed envelope. Also enclose the copy with a note that tells the donor to sign it and keep it		
signed form is returned to Museum		
make 2 copies of the signed form (source file and IA)		
file copy in the Donor's "Source" file		
record donation in source log (in Donor's "Source" file)		
file original in the current year's Acquisitions File		
SEND PACKET TO IA - contents:		
signed temporary custody receipt		
signed deed of gift		
memo to IA		
OBJECT PROCESSING		
label and tag		
fill out catalogue worksheet		
package and store object		
code and computerize (main frame)		Helen Pustmueller
produce Accession Register entry (main frame)	.	Helen Pustmueller
file catalogue worksheet in object file		

REGISTRATION CHECKLIST

☐ Deed of Gift   ☐ Purchase Letter

Date sent: _____

Date returned: _____

Accession #: _____ • _____

Temp. Custody #: _____

Source: _____

Item #	Description	Perm. Number	Cond. Report	Catalogued	Cat. Sheet	Review	Location Hist.	Photography	Comments

☐ continued on next page

Comments:

HOMESTEAD MUSEUM

City of Industry ▽ California

319

MUSEUM OF TEXAS TECH UNIVERSITY

Box 43191
4th and Indiana Avenue
Lubbock, Texas 79409-3191

Accession No. [   ]

(official use only)

Date: _____

Page: _____ of _____

ACCESSIONS CONTRACT FOR HELD IN TRUST OBJECTS/COLLECTIONS

The artifacts, specimens, objects, and documents described below and on all supplemental pages of this transaction have been deposited for care and managements with the Museum of Texas Tech University to be held in trust for the State and People of Texas or the Country and the People of the United States of America by the following state or federal agency:

_____   _____
Date   Signature of Authorized Agency Representative

_____
Agency

Telephone: _____   Fax: _____

_____   _____
Date   Signature of Museum Representative

No.   List Objects/Collections Held in Trust Below

Terms of Trust:

Length of Trust:

Distribution: ☐ Registrar   ☐ Collections   ☐ Agency

Contract for Scientific Collection Repository Services[1]

San Diego Natural History Museum (SDNHM)

and

_____

(ownership agency of record)

enter into this agreement for the professional identification, documentation, and care of scientific collections owned by **(agency)** and reposited at SDNHM for the duration of this contract.

Nature of the Material

This agreement attests to the transfer of _____ (number of ☐ specimens or ☐ lots) described as follows:

This material will be housed at SDNHM subject to the conditions set forth below.

Legal Restrictions on the Material

The material described above is legally restricted in its access and use because it is (please check one):

☐ Forensics material collected and retained as evidence in an ongoing civil or criminal case.
☐ Material from state or Federally protected species
☐ Voucher material from an ongoing scientific study

Ownership

This material is considered to be the legal property of **(agency)** for which SDNHM is acting as a repository. SDNHM agrees to provide professional collections care services in the form of expert and accurate taxonomic identification, curation, documentation, storage, and secure and restricted access. **(agency)** agrees to provide compensation for these ongoing services for the duration of this contract at the following rate (please check one):

☐ Single payment of $_____ for all services, plus an overage deposit of $_____ to cover the costs of unforeseeable expenses (conservation, rehousing, and treatment).
☐ Annual payment of $_____ for all services, to be paid on __/__/__ (date) annually for the duration of this contract, including an annual overage deposit of $_____ to cover the costs of unforeseeable expenses.

SDNHM agrees to notify **(agency)** immediately of the need to conserve, rehouse, and/or treat problematic material.

Access to Material

SDNHM agrees to house this material separately from the main collection in the **(agency)** department and to provide good security and restricted access. Access will be limited to a designated agency representative and to the SDNHM staff person in charge of this department, with emergency access limited to the SDNHM Biodiversity Research Center of the Californias director and the director of collections care and conservation.

---

[1] Repository Agreement Contract (draft for review)

Procedures for documenting every instance of access to this material will be presented to **(agency)** for approval.

Access by any other person must be approved by both SDNHM and **(agency)** and will not take place unless representatives of both SDNHM and **(agency)** are present.

Transfer of Ownership

For the duration of this contract, SDNHM agrees to protect the ownership rights of **(agency)** including the rights of access and publication. SDNHM may negotiate with **(agency)** for ownership of this material with no further compensation to either party under certain conditions.

SDNHM may negotiate for full legal ownership of this material under the following conditions:
1. This contract expires without renewal and **(agency)** prefers to transfer ownership to SDNHM in lieu of having the material returned to its custody
2. **(agency)** has ceased to exist as a legal entity at the time this contract expires, and there is no alternate agency of record with ownership rights (in which case the material will be treated as an abandoned loan).
3. **(agency)** at any time during this contract wishes ownership transferred to SDNHM

SDNHM does not accept permanent loans or other conditional donations. Transfer of ownership to SDNHM will give SDNHM the right to add this material to its records and collections, to deaccession material, to loan and exchange material, to allow research access to this material, and to publish on important specimens.

Review Procedures

Duly designated representatives of **(agency)** may schedule visits at any time to review the status and security of these holdings. SDNHM agrees to notify **(agency)** of any necessary changes in procedures, housing, or security, and to get the approval of **(agency)** before proceeding.

Damage Control and Disaster Response

SDNHM will document the condition of all entering material and notify **(agency)** of any problems noted. SDNHM will maintain the collection in good storage conditions and provide monitoring of temperature and humidity levels, light and UV levels, and pest presence. These records will be made available to **(agency)** at any time. SDNHM is liable for damage resulting from poor environmental control in storage systems and will not be entitled to compensation for treatment and conservation under these circumstances.

In the event of a building failure or natural disaster which cannot be foreseen or prevented, **(agency)** agrees to hold SDNHM harmless. SDNHM agrees to return the material to **(agency)** with no further compensation or obligation in the event that a disaster impairs SDNHM's ability to protect the material.

Repatriation Agreement

The Native American Graves Protection and Repatriation Act of 1990 (NAGPRA) provides definitions and procedures for the repatriation of certain Native American human remains and cultural items, as defined in 25 U.S.C. 3001-3013, in the possession of federal agencies and museums that receive federal funds to lineal descendants, Indian tribes, Native Hawaiian organizations, and Alaska Native villages and corporations; and

The representatives of the National Park Service _____[NPS unit] have engaged in consultation with representatives of _____[The TRIBE] to determine the applicability of these definitions and procedures to objects currently in the possession of the National Park Service _____[NPS unit].

The National Park Service _____ [NPS unit] and _____ [The TRIBE] do hereby agree to the following:

1. That _____ [The TRIBE] is recognized as eligible for the special programs and service provided by the United States to Indians because of their status as Indians, and thus has status to make a claim for repatriation under NAGPRA;

2. That all cultural items described on the attached list meet the criteria outlined in the Native American Graves Protection and Repatriation Act of 1990 (25 USC 3001-3013) and 43 CFR 10.2 (b), such that:

   a. all *human remains* are of Native American ancestry and do not include remains or portions of remains freely given by the individual from whose body they were obtained;

   b. all *funerary objects* are known or reasonably believed to have been placed intentionally at the time of death or later with or near individual human remains;

   c. all *sacred objects* are specific objects needed by traditional Native American religious leaders for the current practice of traditional Native American religions by their present-day adherents;

   d. all *objects of cultural patrimony* have ongoing historical, traditional, or cultural importance central to _____ [The TRIBE], rather than to an individual tribal member and, as such, may not be alienated, appropriated, or conveyed by an individual Tribal member; and such object shall have been considered inalienable at the time the object was separated from _____ [The TRIBE];

3. That all cultural items described on the attached inventory were produced or used by an identifiable earlier group;

4. That evidence exists of a shared group identity that can be reasonably traced between _____ [The TRIBE] and the earlier group;

5. That a Notice of Inventory Completion concerning the human remains or associated funerary objects, or a Notice of Intent to Repatriate concerning unidentified funerary objects, sacred objects or objects of cultural patrimony described on the attached list has been published in the *Federal Register*. In the time since that publication [at least thirty days] neither the National Park Service _____ [NPS unit] nor _____ [The TRIBE] has become aware of any competing claim;

6. That, effective on the date of execution of this Repatriation Agreement, the National Park Service _____ [NPS unit] transfers to _____ [The TRIBE] all responsibility associated with the items described on the attached inventory.

7. That this Repatriation Agreement releases the National Park Service from any future claims by _____ [The TRIBE] regarding the objects described on the attached inventory.

Repatriation Agreement (Continued)

Signatures

This agreement shall become binding upon its execution by the authorized representative of each party. Each party warrants that it has the requisite authority to execute, deliver, and consummate the transactions contemplated by this agreement.

For the NATIONAL PARK SERVICE:

Recommended:

Curator	Signature	Date
SO Curator [Please print]	Signature	Date
SO Archeologist [Please print]	Signature	Date
SO Ethnographer [Please print]	Signature	Date

Approved:

Superintendent [Please print]	Signature	Date

NPS Unit: _____

Address: _____

Telephone: _____ FAX: _____

For the TRIBE:

Approved:

Official Representative or Lineal Descendant [Please print]	Signature	Date
Title	Tribe/Organization	

Address: _____

_____

Telephone: _____ FAX: _____

Follow-up Contact: _____ Telephone: _____
                    Name [Please print]   FAX: _____

DEED OF GIFT

Strecker Museum Complex
Baylor University
P. O. Box 97154 • Waco, TX 76798
(817)755-1110

I/We＿＿＿＿＿＿＿＿＿＿＿＿＿＿＿＿＿＿＿＿ the undersigned, hereby unconditionally and irrevocably convey, donate, give, and deliver the item(s) listed and/or described below or on the attached pages to the Strecker Museum of Baylor University. I/we waive all present and future right, title, and interest in the listed item(s).

This gift also includes all present and future copyright, trademark, reproduction, and associated rights to the listed item(s).

I/We acknowledge that the Museum can and will use these in any manner that is deemed to be in the best interest of the Museum in accordance with the collections policy on the reverse of this agreement.

I/We have read and understand the conditions listed on the reverse of this agreement.

I/We also certify that I am/we are the only legal and lawful owner(s) of the item(s) listed below or on the attached pages, and have sole authority to make this gift.

I/We acknowledge actual delivery of the item(s) listed below to the Strecker Museum.

Donor(s): ＿＿＿＿＿＿＿＿＿＿＿＿＿＿＿＿＿＿＿

Address: ＿＿＿＿＿＿＿＿＿＿＿＿＿＿＿＿＿＿＿

＿＿＿＿＿＿＿＿＿＿＿＿＿＿＿＿＿＿＿

Phone: ＿＿＿＿＿＿＿＿＿＿＿＿＿＿＿＿ Date items received ＿＿＿＿＿＿＿＿

ITEM(S)/SPECIMEN(S): Accession Number: ＿＿＿＿＿＿＿＿

＿＿＿＿＿＿＿＿＿＿＿＿＿＿ ＿＿＿＿＿＿＿＿＿＿＿＿＿＿
Donor Donor

Date: ＿＿＿＿＿＿＿＿＿＿＿ (Please sign one copy and return it to the museum; retain the other copy.)

ACCEPTED BY and agreed to for Strecker Museum by:

＿＿＿＿＿＿＿＿＿＿＿＿＿＿ ＿＿＿＿＿＿＿＿＿＿＿＿＿＿
Name Title

Date: ＿＿＿＿＿＿＿＿＿＿＿

Tax receipt required: ＿＿＿＿＿ Detailed invoice requested: ＿＿＿ No. of Pages: ＿＿ Done: ＿＿ Date: ＿＿＿＿

325

9/92

COLLECTIONS POLICY OF THE STRECKER MUSEUM COMPLEX

GENERAL

- The Strecker Museum of Baylor University is organized and operated for educational purposes and is tax exempt as a 501(c)3 non-profit entity. Donations to Strecker Museum of Baylor University are tax deductible as charitable contributions to the extent allowed by law.
- The Museum does not appraise any donations. It is the responsibility of the donor to make arrangements for any appraisals. Should the donor wish an authorized representative of the Museum to sign the appropriate IRS documents regarding the gift, a copy of the appraisal with values must be filed with the Museum.
- Objects not on public display are generally available through responsible inquiry to scholars, researchers, and scientists for study.
- This acquisition and disposition policy has been established to provide guidance for potential donors, the Strecker Museum staff, or any others acting for the Museum to:
    1. Preclude conditional donations which inhibit development of the research/exhibit and study collections;
    2. Avoid excessive collecting with its attendant preservation and conservation responsibilities;
    3. Prevent misunderstanding among the donors and Baylor University and Strecker Museum.

COLLECTIONS

- The collections of the Strecker Museum consist of objects of natural and cultural origin and are owned outright and constitute an integral part of the Museum. Strecker Museum maintains three types of collections:
    1. Research/Exhibit Collections - These are items for exhibition and/or research which relate directly to the museum's purposes and are usually the best available.
    2. Study Collections - These are items related to the purposes of the Museum which are used for classroom study, demonstrations, and similar uses.
    3. Exchange Collections - These are items not normally needed or which are beyond the scope of the the Museum, but which can be used for exchange to acquire artifacts or other pertinent materials to complete the research/exhibit or study collections of the Museum.

ACQUISITIONS

- Objects are accepted or acquired for the Strecker Museum under the following conditions:
    1. The objects are relevant to and consistent with the purposes and activities of the Museum.
    2. The Museum can provide for the storage, protection, and preservation of the objects under conditions that ensure their continued availability for Museum purposes and in keeping with professionally accepted museum standards.
- The Strecker Museum will accept no restrictive or conditional donations for the collections. Title and applicable copyright to all objects acquired for the collections becomes the sole property of Baylor University and Strecker Museum, and is obtained free and clear for use or future disposition. In cases where the donor does not own the copyright, exceptions can be made providing the Museum is able to establish copyright ownership.
- All objects, donated or otherwise, obtained for the Museum are the property of Baylor University and Strecker Museum and not that of any individual paid or unpaid staff member of Baylor University or Strecker Museum.
- The Strecker Museum does not accept items from donors who do not have clear title nor does the Museum accept objects which have been illegally imported or exported as set forth in the 1970 UNESCO Convention on the Means of Prohibiting and Preventing the Illicit Import, Export, and Transfer of Ownership of Cultural Property, or subsequent agreements, or applicable state or federal statutes.
- The Strecker Museum cannot agree to place donated items on display, to keep donated items together as a unit, or to acknowledge publicly the donor's name with each item used in an exhibit or other use of the item.
- Decisions on the acquisition of objects for the collections will be the responsibility of the Museum Accessions Committee.
- The Strecker Museum will usually retain a maximum of two identical man-made objects, one designated for exhibit and the other for research/study. Other objects will be accessioned in quantities deemed appropriate by the Museum Accessions Committee.
- Records of accession will be made and maintained for all objects acquired for the collections.

DEACCESSIONING AND DISPOSING OF OBJECTS FROM THE COLLECTIONS

- Objects in the collections will be retained indefinitely if they continue to be relevant and useful to the purposes and activities of the Museum, and if they can be properly stored, preserved, and used. Deaccessioning of objects may be considered when these conditions no longer prevail or in the interest of improving the collections for the purposes and activities of the museum.
- Objects in the collections will be deaccessioned only upon recommendation of the Strecker Museum Accessions Committee and by approval of the President of Baylor University or a designated and approved representative of the University.
- In considering the various alternatives for the disposition of deaccessioned objects the Strecker Museum will be concerned that:
    1. The manner of disposition is in the best interest of the Strecker Museum and Baylor University, the scholarly or cultural communities that it represents, the public it serves, and the public trust it represents in owning the collections;
    2. Preference be given to placing in the state or county material that is part of its historical, cultural, or scientific heritage;
    3. Consideration be given to placing objects through gift, exchange, or sale in other tax-exempt, non-profit institutions where they may serve the purpose for which they were initially acquired by the Museum;
    4. If objects are offered for sale elsewhere, preference be given for sale at advertised public auction or to the public marketplace in a manner that will best protect the interests, objectives, and legal status of the Strecker Museum and Baylor University; and
    5. Objects not be given or sold privately to employees, officers, staff, or students of Baylor University, the Strecker Museum, or to their representatives.
- Before disposing of any objects from the collections, reasonable efforts will be made to ensure that the Museum is legally free to do so. For any objects under question, the advice of the Baylor University General Counsel will be sought.
- An adequate record of the conditions and circumstances under which objects are deaccessioned and disposed of will be made and maintained as part of the collection records of the Museum.

DEED OF GIFT

Accession No. _____

Division: _____

I (We), _____, hereby give to the
Peabody Museum of Natural History, Yale University, absolute and unconditional ownership of the
property described below. I (we) assign to the Peabody Museum of Natural History, Yale University
full powers of management, access, display, conservation and disposition at its sole discretion.

I (We) also give to the Peabody Museum of Natural History, Yale University, any copyright and
associated rights to the property that I (we) may have. (If there is a copyright to which you do not
own the rights please specify the owner:) _____.

Property description:

I (We) wish that the gift be identified to the public as: Gift of _____

I (We) own the property described above absolutely and without encumbrance and I (we) have the
right to convey it. To the best of my (our) knowledge, this property has not been imported or
exported into or out of any country contrary to its laws. The Museum is relying on these
representations in accepting this donation.

Donor: _____ Date: _____

Donor: _____ Date: _____

Accepted on behalf of the Peabody Museum of Natural History, Yale University, by:

_____ Date: _____
Signature of Curator

_____ Date: _____
Signature of Director

Approved, Board of Curators, November 7, 1994. **327**

DEED OF GIFT

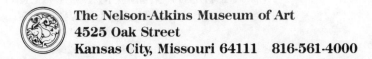

The Nelson-Atkins Museum of Art
4525 Oak Street
Kansas City, Missouri 64111   816-561-4000

I/We (the "Donor") have delivered, and hereby unconditionally and irrevocably give, the object(s) described below or on the attached pages, together with all copyright, trademark and associated rights of Donor therein, to the Trustees of The Nelson Gallery Foundation (the "Nelson"), operating The Nelson-Atkins Museum of Art, and acknowledge that the Nelson's acceptance of the gift is subject to the terms on the reverse.

Accession number	Object	Description

I/We wish the credit line to be listed as follows:

_____

_____

Signature of Donor(s): _____

Please type or print name(s): _____

Address: _____

Date: _____

Signature for the Trustees of the Nelson: _____

Please type or print name: _____

Title: _____

Date: _____

Please sign and date the completed Deed of Gift and return both copies to: Registrar, The Nelson-Atkins Museum of Art, 4525 Oak Street, Kansas City, Missouri 64111. The Registrar will sign and return your copy.

328

NAMA 8/87

Museum of Western Colorado

P.O. Box 20000-5020, Grand Junction, CO 81502-5020
Sites: History Museum, Cross Orchards Living History Farm, Dinosaur Valley

GIFT AGREEMENT

I (we) _____ hereby donate to the Museum of Western Colorado the articles that are described below. The Museum will consider the articles as unrestricted gifts which may be used in any manner that is deemed to be in the best interest of the Museum in accordance with the collections policy listed on the REVERSE of this agreement.

Accession Number: Description:

(Attach extra sheets as needed)

Having read and understood the CONDITIONS listed on this agreement and the collections policy listed on the REVERSE, and certifying that **I am (we are) the lawful owners** or have the authority to make this gift, I (we) donate the property herein listed to the Museum of Western Colorado.

_____   _____
(Donor)   (Title)

                                                          Grand Junction
_____   _____
(Address)   (City)

_____CO_____
(State)   (ZIP Code)   (Telephone Number)

Accepted for the Museum of Western Colorado by   _____

                                                          _____
                                                          Librarian/Archivist
                                                          (Title)

Dated this _____ day of _____ 19 __97____

                                                          No. of pages __1_____

(Please sign all copies, detach the second copy for your records, and **return the original**, and remaining copy to the Museum of Western Colorado. Thank you.)   329   6/1993

Building 322 • Fort Missoula, Montana 59801 • Phone 406-728-3476

DEED OF GIFT TO HISTORICAL MUSEUM AT FORT MISSOULA

By these presents I (we) irrevocably and unconditionally give, transfer, and assign to the *HISTORICAL MUSEUM AT FORT MISSOULA* by way of gift, all right, title, and interests (including all copyright, trademark and related interests*), in, to and associated with the object(s) described below. I (we) affirm that I (we) own said object(s) and that to the best of my (our) knowledge I (we) have good and complete right, title, and interests (including all transferred copyright, trademark and related interests) to give.

The donor understands that the *HISTORICAL MUSEUM AT FORT MISSOULA* will carefully and continually assess its collection. Items deemed surplus to the Museum's collection may be exchanged with another institution, returned to the donor, or otherwise disposed of in accordance with the Museum's Collection Management Policies and Procedures.

The Museum acknowledges receipt on this date of the physical delivery to the Museum of the gift as described above.

_____   Signature _____
Museum Representative (Please print)

Title _____   Date of Receipt of Gift and Deed: _____

_____
(Print Donor's Name)

Donor's Address _____

City _____ State _____

Phone _____ Zip _____   Donor _____
                                                                                          (Signature)

_____
(Print Donor's Name)

Donor's Address _____

City _____ State _____

Phone _____ Zip _____   Donor _____
                                                                                          (Signature)

*If less than all copyright, trademark and related interest are given, specify above or on reverse side of this Deed of Gift.
If pages are appended to this Deed, there are _____ pages total, including this page.

Live Animal Gift Agreement

Tallahassee Museum of History & Natural Science (Tallahassee Museum)

PLEASE complete, sign, and return the original of this form to the Tallahassee Museum. The copy is for the donor's records.

The Museum cannot accept responsibility for appraising gifts.

Type of Animal: _____

Animals Name (if applicable): _____

Distinguishing Characteristics (markings/coloration): _____
_____

Date of Birth:_____ OR, approximate age:_____

Sex ❑ M   ❑ F   ❑   Neutered   ❑ Unknown

Vaccinations (if any): _____   _____
                       _____   _____

Medical History (injuries, impairments, etc.):

Condition on arrival: ❑ good   ❑ poor

AGREEMENT I (we) as sole owner(s) unconditionally give the listed animal(s) to the Tallahassee Museum of History & Natural Science to use as the Museum determines best for its purposes.

DONOR SIGNATURE_____ DATE_____

    NAME (please print)_____

    ADDRESS_____ PHONE # (_____)_____

    _____

    _____

MUSEUM SIGNATURE_____ DATE_____

    TITLE_____

Tallahassee Museum of History & Natural Science   3945 Museum Dr.   (850) 575-8684
                                                        Tallahassee, FL 32310

University of Alberta
Edmonton

Canada T6G 2E1

We regret to inform you that the University of Alberta is unable to accept your offer to donate the Property described herein.

Please fill in as indicated and return to:

University of Alberta *(Authorized Officer)*

Name (please print)

Title

University Unit

Address

Phone

Date

Signature of Authorized Officer

Owner(s) *(to be completed by the Owner(s) of the Property)*

Name(s)

Address

Phone (residence/business)

Date

Signature

If the Property is in the custody of the University of Alberta, please indicate your preferred method of return below.

☐ I authorize the University of Alberta to dispose of the Property on my behalf.

☐ I will pick up the Property.

☐ I will notify the University of Alberta in writing about alternate pick-up/delivery arrangements.

Description of Property (the"Property")

☐ copies of Donation Offer attached to Owner's and University Unit's copies of this form

Receiver

The Receiver acknowledges the return of the Owner's property described below, in the same condition as on delivery to the University of Alberta.

Name (please print)

Title and Capacity (owner, executor, etc.)

Date of Receipt

Signature

*Distribution: **White** - Office of the Comptroller; **Green** - Donor(s);*
***Yellow** - Signing Authority, University Unit; **Pink** - Development Office;*
***Gold** - Museums and Collections Services, Library, or Archives. 1997*

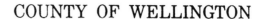

COUNTY OF WELLINGTON

WELLINGTON COUNTY MUSEUM & ARCHIVES
R.R.1, FERGUS, ONT.
N1M 2W3
TEL:(519) 846-0916
FAX: (519) 846-9630

WELLINGTON PLACE
R.R.1, FERGUS, ONT.
N1M 2W3
TEL: (519) 846-0916

RECEIPT FOR RETURN OF POSSIBLE DONATIONS

Thank you for your interest in and support of the Wellington County
Museum and Archives.

Received from _____

Address _____

_____ Phone _____

ITEMS RETURNED _____

_____

_____

_____

_____

_____

_____

_____

_____

Return authorized by _____ Date _____

Items returned to _____ Date _____

Staff signature _____ Date _____

Original copy - Museum and Archives
Photocopy - Owner

333

THE UNIVERSITY MUSEUM
UNIVERSITY OF ARKANSAS
FAYETTEVILLE, ARKANSAS 72701 USA

Gift of Non-Accessioned Materials

I (We) the Undersigned do hereby irrevocably and unconditionally give, transfer, and assign to The University Museum, University of Arkansas, by way of gift, all right, title, and interests (including all copyright, trademark, and related interests), in, to, and associated with the object(s) described below. I (We) affirm that I (we) own said object(s) and that to the best of my (our) knowledge I (we) have good and complete right, title, and interests to give. I (We) understand that the object(s) listed below may not be incorporated into the permanent collections of the Museum, and that the object(s) may be used for educational purposes.

Object	Description	Model/Serial #

Dated this _____ day of _____, 19_____.

_____   _____
Donor's Signature   Donor's Signature

_____   _____
Donor's Name   Donor's Name

_____   _____
Street Address

_____
City, State, Zip Code

The University Museum hereby expresses its gratitude for the generous gift of the object(s) described above, acceptance and receipt of which is hereby acknowledged. Gifts to The University Museum are deductible from taxable income in accordance with the provisions of the Federal Income Tax Law.

_____   _____
Museum Representative's Signature   Museum Representative's Name

_____   _____
Title   Date

Please sign both copies and return them to: Museum Registrar, The University Museum, University of Arkansas, Fayetteville, AR 72701. You will then receive your copy signed by a representative of the Museum.

334

(Jan. 1997)

SAN DIEGO NATURAL HISTORY MUSEUM
NON-CASH GIFT FORM

DONOR INFORMATION

Name_____

Address_____

City_____ State_____ Zip_____

Phone number   Home: (____)_____   Business: (____)_____

E-mail_____   FAX: (____)_____

GIFT INFORMATION

Date of gift____/____/_____   Received by_____
(department head or designate)

Description of item or service donated (include number of objects and age)
_____

_____

❐ Detailed donation list attached; original on file in department.

Condition: ❐ Excellent   ❐ Good   ❐ Fair   ❐ Poor

Problems noted:_____

Is there an assigned monetary value for this donation?   ❐ yes ❐ no   Amount:_____

How was this value determined?   ❐ Donor ❐ Appraiser   ❐ IRS   ❐ Other_____
(specify)

If independently appraised, who was the appraiser?_____

Date of appraisal: ____/____/_____ Phone number of appraiser:_____

Has a copy of the appraisal been provided? ❐ yes   ❐ no   (copy for permanent records required)

NOTE: If the donor has assigned the value, his/her signature is required.

_____   _____
    Signature   Date

FOR OBJECT OR SPECIMEN DONATIONS ONLY: PLEASE CHECK ONE

❐ This donation is assigned to ❐ a BRCC collection _____   ❐ Education   ❐ Other_____
               (specify)   (specify)

❐ This donation will be sold, in part or in whole, at the most appropriate time.

 Proceeds from sale are assigned to _____ department.

❐ Donor has been notified of museum's intentions.   ❐ Donor has signed a deed of gift (on file in department).

FOR INTERNAL USE ONLY

Donations of objects or services valued at more than $500, or otherwise historically or scientifically significant, should be acknowledged by both the Executive Director and the department head. All others may be acknowledged by the Department head only.

Donation acknowledged by ❐ Executive Director ❐ Department head ❐ Other_____

Date of acknowledgement: ____/____/_____   Copy provided to Institutional Development? ❐ yes   ❐ no

Gift should be mentioned on/in: ❐ Donor board   ❐ *Field Notes*   ❐ Annual report   ❐ Press release

Should donor receive a membership? ❐ Yes   ❐ No If so, at what level? _____

Special instructions:_____

Please send this to Institutional Development. Keep a copy for departmental files.

❐ Institutional Development: cc sent to Accounting Date ____/____/_____   Initials_____

Every non-cash gift which is accepted by the museum must be documented for reference. Here is a summary of the documents required:
❏ Original detailed donation list signed by donor: on file in department.
❏ Original deed of gift signed by donor: on file in department.
❏ Copies of letter(s) of acknowledgement: on file in department.
❏ Non-cash gift form: filled out in department.
   ❏ Original sent to Institutional Development (ID will send copy to Accounting as appropriate).
   ❏ Copy in departmental files.

The following documents may or may not be required, depending on circumstances:
❏ Original condition report prepared in-house: original on file in department, copy to Collections Care.
   Object/specimen donations only; usually requested if a problem needs documentation.
❏ Copy of independent appraisal: on file in department.
   Previously appraised materials only

It is the individual department's responsibility to notify the Executive Director if a donation is of sufficient historic or scientific significance (in lieu of assigned monetary value) to require a letter from the Executive Director as well as from the department head. Copies of all letters of acknowledgement should be kept in the departmental files. This will enable better tracking and reporting of all donations for donor recognition, grant applications and reports.

These files should be maintained by the museum in perpetuity.

If an object or specimen is dropped off at an admissions gate, it is the responsibility of the appropriate department to contact the donor, decide whether or not the gift will be accepted by the museum, and arrange appropriate disposition of the gift. A letter of acknowledgement is required for all items accepted into museum collections, no matter how minor. The receipt filled out by the donor at the gate should be kept on file in the appropriate department in lieu of a donation list and deed of gift. If the object is not accepted, it is the responsibility of the individual department to make arrangements to return the gift to the donor or to make alternative arrangements if th donor cannot be found.

Noncash Gift Policy (from the SDNHM collections policy, approved by the Board)
"Noncash gifts to SDNHM will be carefully reviewed prior to acceptance. The SDNHM does not make appraisals of cash value or recommend appraisers, though it may provide lists of appraisers for tax purposes. The SDNHM does not attempt to verify cash values placed on a noncash gift by the donor and maintains such cited values with donation records for audit references only."

Loan Number _____

OREGON HISTORICAL SOCIETY

1200 S.W. Park Avenue
(503) 222-1741

Portland, Oregon 97205
Fax: (503) 221-2035

LOAN AGREEMENT

Please complete and sign on reverse. Return original and retain copy for your records.

Incoming _____ Outgoing _____

Lender/Borrower _____ Tel. ( ) _____

Address _____

Place of Use _____

Responsible Person _____ Tel. ( ) _____

Purpose/Exhibit Title_____

Exhibit Dates: From: _____ To: _____

Loan Dates: From: _____ To: _____

Insurance Carrier _____ Total Value _____

Shipping Arrangement _____

DESCRIPTION   Total Number _____

Number	Description and Condition	Value
	Attach Additional Page and Condition Reports If Necessary	

Special Exhibit Instructions:

Credit Line _____

Office Use

RETURNED: _____
Signature   Date

337

Condition

AGREEMENT FOR LOAN

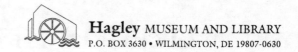

Hagley MUSEUM AND LIBRARY
P.O. BOX 3630 • WILMINGTON, DE 19807-0630

BORROWER:　NAME: _____

ADDRESS: _____

_____

TELEPHONE: _____　FAX: _____

LENDER:　NAME: _____

ADDRESS: _____

_____

TELEPHONE: _____　FAX: _____

IN ACCORDANCE WITH THE TERMS AND CONDITIONS PRINTED ON THE REVERSE, THE OBJECTS

LISTED BELOW ARE BORROWED FOR THE PERIOD　　FROM: _____

TO: _____

LOAN NUMBER: _____　FOR THE PURPOSE OF: _____

ACCESSION OR IDENTIFICATION NO.	OBJECT	CONDITION OF OBJECT	VALUE

**** S A M P L E　C O P Y ****

SHIPPING AND PACKING ARRANGEMENTS WILL BE AS FOLLOWS, UNLESS OTHERWISE AGREED TO IN WRITING:

_____

_____

_____

CREDIT LINE: _____

SIGNATURE OF LENDER	DATE	SIGNATURE OF BORROWER	DATE
TITLE		TITLE	

338

WHITE COPY - HAGLEY MUSEUM REGISTRAR　　　　　YELLOW COPY - LENDER / BORROWER

CONDITIONS

CARE AND EXHIBITION

THE BORROWER WILL EXERCISE THE SAME CARE FOR THE BORROWED OBJECT(S) (THE LOAN OR THE OBJECTS) AS IT DOES IN THE SAFEKEEPING OF COMPARABLE PROPERTY OF ITS OWN.

EVIDENCE OF DAMAGE OR LOSS TO THE OBJECTS WILL BE REPORTED IMMEDIATELY TO THE LENDER.

UNLESS AUTHORIZED IN WRITING BY THE LENDER, THE BORROWER WILL NOT ALTER, CLEAN, REPAIR, OR RESTORE THE OBJECTS.

THE LENDER RESERVES THE RIGHT TO INSPECT THE MOUNTING/INSTALLATION OF THE LOAN TO INSURE THAT STANDARD CONSERVATION PRACTICES ARE OBSERVED.

REPRODUCTION AND CREDIT

EXCEPT FOR LOAN-RELATED PUBLICITY AND CONDITION DOCUMENTATION PURPOSES, THE BORROWER MAY NOT PHOTOGRAPH OR OTHERWISE REPRODUCE THE OBJECTS WITHOUT WRITTEN PERMISSION FROM THE LENDER.

COPIES OF ANY CATALOG OR OTHER MATERIAL BEARING DESCRIPTION OR IMAGES OF THE OBJECTS WILL BE SENT TO THE LENDER AS A COURTESY.

UNLESS OTHERWISE INSTRUCTED IN WRITING, THE BORROWER WILL GIVE CREDIT TO THE LENDER AS SPECIFIED ON THE FACE OF THIS AGREEMENT IN ANY PUBLICATIONS OR EXHIBIT LABELS.

INSURANCE

UNLESS OTHERWISE AGREED TO IN WRITING, THE BORROWER WILL INSURE THE LOAN FROM THE TIME IT LEAVES THE LENDER UNTIL IT RETURNS TO THE SAME, IN THE AMOUNT DETERMINED BY THE LENDER.

PRIOR TO RELEASE OF THE LOAN, A BORROWER FROM HAGLEY MUSEUM (THE MUSEUM) MUST PROVIDE THE MUSEUM WITH A CERTIFICATE OF INSURANCE, DEMONSTRATING ALL-RISK, WALL-TO-WALL COVERAGE AND NAMING HAGLEY MUSEUM AND LIBRARY AS ADDITIONAL INSURED, OR PROVIDE OTHER ACCEPTABLE PROOF OF INSURANCE.

HAGLEY MUSEUM AND LIBRARY MAINTAINS AN ALL-RISK, WALL-TO-WALL INSURANCE POLICY SUBJECT TO STANDARD EXCLUSIONS AND, AS A BORROWER, WILL PROVIDE NECESSARY COVERAGE TO A LENDER THROUGH THIS POLICY. A LENDER TO HAGLEY MUSEUM WILL PROVIDE THE MUSEUM WITH A REASONABLE INSURANCE VALUE WHICH REFLECTS FAIR MARKET VALUE. IF NO AMOUNT IS SPECIFIED BY THE LENDER, THE MUSEUM WILL INSURE THE LOAN AT ITS OWN ESTIMATED VALUATION. SUCH VALUATIONS DO NOT CONSTITUTE AN APPRAISAL.

IT IS THE RESPONSIBILITY OF THE LENDER TO NOTIFY THE BORROWER OF NECESSARY ADJUSTMENTS IN INSURANCE VALUATIONS.

IF INSURANCE IS WAIVED BY THE LENDER, THIS WAIVER SHALL CONSTITUTE THE AGREEMENT OF THE LENDER TO RELEASE AND HOLD HARMLESS THE BORROWER FROM ANY LIABILITY FOR DAMAGES TO OR LOSS OF THE LOAN.

THE AMOUNT PAYABLE BY INSURANCE SECURED IN ACCORDANCE WITH THIS LOAN AGREEMENT IS THE SOLE RECOVERY AVAILABLE TO THE LENDER FROM THE BORROWER IN THE EVENT OF LOSS OR DAMAGE.

TRANSPORTATION AND PACKING

THE BORROWER WILL MAKE ARRIVAL AND DEPARTURE CONDITION RECORDS OF THE LOAN.

THE LENDER SHALL BE ENTITLED TO PRESCRIBE AND APPROVE METHODS OF PACKING AND SHIPPING, TO WHICH BOTH LENDER AND BORROWER MUST AGREE IN WRITING.

COSTS OF TRANSPORTATION AND PACKING WILL BE BORNE BY THE BORROWER UNLESS OTHERWISE AGREED TO IN WRITING.

BORROWER WILL RETURN THE LOAN IN THE ORIGINAL PACKING MATERIAL OR CRATE OR AN EQUIVALENT SUBSTITUTE.

CHANGE IN OWNERSHIP AND/OR ADDRESS

IT IS THE RESPONSIBILITY OF THE LENDER OR HIS/HER AGENT TO NOTIFY THE BORROWER PROMPTLY IN WRITING IF THERE IS ANY CHANGE IN OWNERSHIP OF THE OBJECTS (WHETHER THROUGH DEATH, SALE, GIFT, INSOLVENCY, OR OTHERWISE) OR IF THERE IS A CHANGE IN THE IDENTITY OR ADDRESS OF THE LENDER.

IF THE LEGAL OWNERSHIP OF THE OBJECTS CHANGES DURING THE PENDENCY OF THIS LOAN, THE NEW OWNER MAY, PRIOR TO ITS RETURN, BE REQUIRED TO ESTABLISH HIS/HER LEGAL RIGHT TO RECEIVE THE OBJECTS.

TERMINATION

UNLESS OTHERWISE AGREED TO IN WRITING, THE LOAN SHALL TERMINATE ON THE DATE GIVEN ON THE FACE OF THE AGREEMENT.

UPON TERMINATION OF THE LOAN, THE BORROWER WILL RETURN THE OBJECTS TO THE LENDER AT THE ADDRESS STATED ON THE FACE OF THE AGREEMENT OR TO A LOCATION MUTUALLY AGREED UPON IN WRITING BY THE BORROWER AND THE LENDER OF RECORD.

IF HAGLEY MUSEUM, AS THE BORROWER, DUE TO CIRCUMSTANCES CREATED BY THE LENDER, SHALL BE UNABLE TO RETURN THE LOAN TO THE LENDER WITHIN THIRTY (30) DAYS AFTER THE LOAN TERMINATION DATE, THE MUSEUM MAY PLACE THE OBJECTS IN STORAGE AT THE LENDER'S RISK AND EXPENSE. IF THE LENDER DOES NOT REMOVE THE LOAN WITHIN ONE (1) YEAR AFTER THE LOAN TERMINATION DATE, THE MUSEUM, FOLLOWING ESTABLISHED MUSEUM ACQUISITION OR DEACCESSION APPROVAL PROCEDURES, SHALL HAVE THE RIGHT TO CLAIM THE OBJECTS AS AN UNRESTRICTED GIFT OR TO DISPOSE OF THE OBJECTS IN ANY MANNER THE MUSEUM ELECTS.

WHEN THE LOAN IS RETURNED, A RECEIPT FORM WILL BE COMPLETED AND RETURNED PROMPTLY TO THE BORROWER. IF THE LENDER DOES NOT SIGN AND RETURN THE FORM WITHIN THIRTY (30) DAYS AFTER MAILING, THE BORROWER WILL NOT BE RESPONSIBLE FOR ANY DAMAGE OR LOSS.

ADDITIONAL CONDITIONS:

T H E
WITTE
MUSEUM

Attn: Registrar

LOAN CONTRACT

Lender(Institution) _____ (Contact person)

_____

Address _____ Telephone & Fax:

_____ _____

_____

Credit Line (exact form of lender's name for exhibition and publication credit)

_____

Dates of Loan: Exhibit_____Overall_____

Description of object(s) _____

   (Attach list if necessary) _____

Artist _____ Accession No._____

Title _____ Date _____

Medium _____ Size _____

Insurance (Insured Value in U.S. Dollars) _____

To be insured by _____

Effective Date of Coverage _____

Copyright: If the copyright was created after January 1, 1978, do you own the copyright

in the work?   Yes _____   No _____   If not, do

you know who does?_____ If not, who

was the previous owner? _____ Shipping

Instructions (including address if different from mailing)_____

_____

_____

LOAN GRANTED UNDER THE CONDITIONS ON THE BACK OF THIS FORM

The Witte Museum _____ Date_____

        Rebecca Huffstutler, Associate Curator of Archives

Lender_____ Title_____ Date_____

****

Returned to lender:

_____ Date_____The item(s) listed

above was(were) received in good condition.

3801 BROADWAY
SAN ANTONIO
TEXAS 78209-6396
210.3**340**1900
FAX 210.357.1882

WITTE
MUSEUM

Attn: Registrar

LOAN RENEWAL CONTRACT

Lender(Institution)   (Contact person)

_____   _____

 Address   Telephone & Fax:

_____   _____

_____   _____

Credit Line (exact form of lender's name for exhibition and publication credit)

_____

Dates of Loan: Exhibit_____Overall_____

Description of object(s) _____

 (Attach list if necessary) _____

Artist _____ Accession No._____

Title _____ Date _____

Medium _____ Size _____

Insurance (Insured Value in U.S. Dollars) _____

To be insured by _____

Effective Date of Coverage _____

Copyright: If the copyright was created after January 1, 1978, do you own the copyright
in the work?   Yes _____   No _____

If not, do you know who does? _____

If not, who was the previous owner? _____

Shipping Instructions (including address if different from mailing)_____

_____

LOAN RENEWAL GRANTED UNDER THE CONDITIONS ON THE BACK OF THIS
FORM

The Witte Museum _____ Date_____

           Rebecca Huffstutler, Associate Curator of Archives

Lender_____ Title_____ Date_____
****
Returned to lender:

_____ Date_____The item(s) listed
above was(were) received in good condition.

3801 BROADWAY
SAN ANTONIO
TEXAS 78209-6396
210.341.1900
FAX 210.357.1882

THE UNIVERSITY OF IOWA
HOSPITALS AND CLINICS
Iowa City, Iowa 52242

Medical Museum
319/356-7106

LOAN EXTENSION

The objects listed below, which are currently on loan to the University of Iowa Hospitals and Clinics Medical Museum, are approved for an extension to the original loan period.

Lender: _____

Address: _____

_____

_____

Original Loan Period: _____

Purpose of Original Loan: _____

Purpose of Extension: _____

Loan Extended to: _____

Objects on Loan

Accession Number	Object Name	Value

attach additional sheet if necessary

Authorizing Signatures:

Lender: _____ Date: _____

Borrower: _____ Date: _____

RETURN OF LOAN

MUSEUM OF ART
BRIGHAM YOUNG UNIVERSITY
North Campus Drive, Provo, Utah 84602
(801) 378-8256

The following objects have been returned from loan:

ACC.NO.	ARTIST	DESCRIPTION	CONDITION

Delivered by:_____
                    (Signature)

Borrowing Institution:_____

Date: _____

Received by:_____
                    (Signature and title)

Date:_____

OUTGOING LOAN/TOUR CHECK-OFF SHEET

EXHIBITION / LOAN: _____

DEPARTURE DATE: _____ OPENING DATE AT VENUE: _____

VENUE: _____

CLOSING DATE AT VENUE: _____ DATE RETURNED TO GMOA: _____

DOCUMENTS/MISCELLANEOUS ITEMS:

( ) Contract/loan agreement sent to borrower. Date: _____.
( ) Signed contract/loan agreement returned from borrower. Date: _____.
( ) Certificate of Insurance received. Date: _____.   ( ) Not applicable.
( ) Labels and text panels ready.   ( ) Not applicable.
   ( ) Actual labels. Number of text panels:_____. Date sent: _____ by_____.
   ( ) Hard copy/checklist ( ) Disk Date sent: _____ by: _____.
( ) Condition Report Book completed or condition report on file (individual objects).
( ) Hanging apparatus affixed (D-rings, wires, etc.).   ( ) Not applicable.
( ) Outgoing release prepared.   ( ) Signed.
( ) Additional items: _____.
(state items and amounts)

CATALOGUES/BROCHURES: (Number to be sent: _____.)

( ) Shipped/delivered with exhibition.
( ) Sent previously by _____. Date: _____.
( ) Not applicable.

CURATOR'S APPROVAL:

Name of exhibition curator: _____.
( ) Checklist approved. Date on checklist: _____.
( ) Packing method approved.

**CURATOR'S SIGNATURE: _____ Date: _____.

REGISTRAR'S APPROVAL:

Packing Method
( ) Crates   ( ) Soft-pack   ( ) No wrap
Total number of crates/objects/packs: _____.
Total number of miscellaneous items: _____.
( ) Address labels on crates/objects/miscellaneous items.

Shipping Method
( ) GMOA van/staff   ( ) Rental truck/GMOA staff
Drivers: _____.
Departure date: _____.
( ) Borrower's van/staff. Pickup date: _____.
( ) Commercial carrier
Company: _____. Pickup date: _____.
( ) Hand carry   ( ) GMOA staff   ( ) Other: _____.

**REGISTRAR'S SIGNATURE: _____ Date: _____.
(Signature required before objects leave GMOA)

San Diego Museum of Art

LOAN AGREEMENT

Shipping Address:
Balboa Park
San Diego, CA 92101-1697

Mailing Address
Post Office Box 2107
San Diego, CA 92112-2107

1583

Telephone 619•232-7931

Telex 883594

Agreement The undersigned ("Lender") hereby lends to the San Diego Museum of Art ("SDMA") the object(s) described herein for the purposes, and subject to the terms and conditions set forth.

EXHIBITION
Dates and Locations: _____

Term of Loan: _____

LENDER Institution or Individual: _____
Address: _____
<small>(Unless otherwise instructed below, work will be shipped from and returned to this address)</small>

Telephone: *(business)* _____ *(home)* _____ Contact Person: _____
Credit: _____
<small>(Exact form of lender's name for catalogue, labels and publicity)</small>

WORK OF ART Artist: _____
Nationality: _____ Life Dates: Born _____ Died _____
Exact title of work: _____
Medium or Materials and Support: _____ I.D. No.: _____
Signed or inscribed as follows: _____
Date of work: _____ Dated or inscribed as follows: _____

DIMENSIONS
☐ centimeters
☐ inches

Painting, drawing, etc. (excl. frame or mat): H _____ W _____
(If print indicate ☐ plate, ☐ image, or ☐ sheet):
Outer dimensions of frame: H _____ W _____
Sculpture (excl. pedestal) or relief: H _____ W _____ D _____ Approx. Wt. _____
Pedestal: H _____ W _____ D _____ Approx. Wt. _____ Detachable? _____

If necessary for the safety of the work, may we reframe, remat, or back it? ☐ Yes ☐ No   Substitute Plexiglas for glass? ☐ Yes ☐ No

INSURANCE
Value *(estimated fair market value in U.S. $)*: _____ *SDMA will insure unless otherwise advised.*
Do you prefer to maintain your own insurance? ☐ Yes ☐ No   If so, estimated premium _____
Do you prefer to waive insurance? ☐ Yes ☐ No   If so, initial ˣ .... (Lender)

PHOTOGRAPHY If black & white photographs and/or color transparencies suitable for reproduction are available, please state type and where they may be obtained: _____

SHIPPING ARRANGEMENTS
Case already available _____ case needs to be built _____ case unnecessary _____
To be packed/crated by: _____
<small>(Unless notified to the contrary, the loan will be returned to the address listed under "Lender")</small>

Date required for receiving loan: _____

COMMENTS (Provenance, Special Handling Requirements)

The lender acknowledges that he has full authority and power to make this loan, that he has read the conditions above and on the back of this form, and that he agrees to be bound by them:

Signed: _____
<small>Lender</small>   Title   Date

By: _____
<small>Registrar, San Diego Museum of Art, a California Public Benefit Corporation</small>   Date

LENDER: Two part form. Please sign and return original. Retain copy.

**EXHIBITION
LOAN AGREEMENT**

SHIPPING ADDRESS:
501 HEMPSTEAD PLACE
CHARLOTTE, N.C. 28207
REGISTRAR: (704) 337-2005

MINT
MUSEUM OF ART
2730 RANDOLPH RD.
CHARLOTTE, N.C.
28207
704 · 337 · 2000

EXHIBITION:

DATES: LOAN PERIOD:

SUBSEQUENT TOUR?   *See attached itinerary of venues and dates*

LENDER: TELEPHONE: H ( )

ADDRESS: W ( )

Return shipment will be made to this address unless otherwise instructed.

CREDIT LINE.

Lender's name exactly as it should appear in catalogue and on gallery label.

TITLE:

ARTIST/MAKER:

NATIONALITY / LIFE DATES / ADDRESS OF ARTIST:

MEDIUM:

DATE OF WORK:

SIZE (INCHES):				
PAINTING, DRAWING, PRINT, ETC.	H:	W:		
If print, please include sheet size				
OUTER DIMENSIONS OF FRAME	H:	W:		
SCULPTURE, DECORATIVE ARTS	H:	W:	D:	APPROXIMATE WEIGHT:
PEDESTAL	H:	W:	D:	IS PEDESTAL DETACHABLE?
TEXTILE	H:	W:		
COSTUME OR RELATED MATERIAL				

CONDITION   *IS THE WORK IN STABLE CONDITION FOR TRAVEL?*

SPECIAL HANDLING REQUIREMENTS, IF ANY:

FRAMING   *MAY WE REFRAME OR REMAT?*   *MAY WE SUBSTITUTE PLEXIGLAS FOR GLASS?*

MAY WE ALTER HANGING DEVICE?

PHOTOGRAPHY AND REPRODUCTION   *WHICH OF THE FOLLOWING ARE AVAILABLE FOR CATALOGUE REPRODUCTION?*

B/W (8 x 10):	TRANSPARENCY:	35MM SLIDE:
TO ORDER, CONTACT:		CHARGES:

COPYRIGHT RESTRICTIONS, IF ANY:

LOAN FEE   *DO YOU HAVE A LOAN FEE?*   AMOUNT:

INSURANCE   *DO YOU WISH THE MINT MUSEUM OF ART TO INSURE? See conditions on reverse.*

IF YOU PREFER TO MAINTAIN YOUR OWN INSURANCE, ESTIMATE PREMIUM: $

VALUE   *ESTIMATED FAIR MARKET VALUE IN U.S. CURRENCY:* $ SELLING PRICE (IF WORK IS FOR SALE): $

SHIPPING CARRIER: TO ARRIVE BEFORE:

SPECIAL INSTRUCTIONS:

The Mint Museum of Art will not accept C.O.D. shipments.

COMMENTS:

THIS LOAN IS SUBJECT TO THE CONDITIONS STATED ABOVE AND ON THE REVERSE OF THIS FORM. PLEASE COMPLETE, SIGN ON REVERSE AND RETURN ORIGINAL TO REGISTRAR, MINT MUSEUM OF ART.

REGISTRAR'S COPY

346

CONDITIONS GOVERNING LOANS

GENERAL

In general, when the Mint Museum of Art (the Museum) borrows property (the Property), it intends to arrange for its transportation, to provide for insurance coverage during the loan period, and to extend the same level of care and protection it would for its own collections. The specific conditions of this loan are listed below. These conditions, plus any special conditions which may appear on the reverse of this form, constitute the terms of this agreement. It is assumed that the signer(s) agrees to all conditions and cannot change them without written consent.

TRANSPORTATION AND PACKING

The Museum coordinates transportation, and bears the cost of packing and shipping except for circumstances governed by other arrangements. The method of shipment must be agreed upon by both parties.
1. Property will be returned packed in the same or similar materials as received unless otherwise authorized by the lender.
2. Customs regulations will be adhered to in international shipments.

INSURANCE

The Museum arranges insurance for Property so that, should damage or loss occur, the lender will be fairly compensated. When borrowed property is part of an exhibition which travels to other museums or institutions, The Museum will either provide insurance or insist that participating organizations take over the insurance coverage with their own policies, and at the same level of protection afforded by the Museum. However, the lender may elect to carry his/her own insurance instead. In any case, it is the Museum's clear intention to contain all liabilities to the recompense afforded by insurance coverage alone, and the lender agrees to this condition. Therefore, the lender should be certain that proper values are assigned to his/her Property. In signing, the lender agrees to this general position, and to the following specifics:
1. Unless the lender chooses to maintain his/her own insurance, the Museum will insure the Property under its fine arts policy for the amount specified by the lender, on the reverse, against all risks of physical loss or damage from any external cause while in transit and on location during the period of the loan; provided, however, if the work has been industrially fabricated and can be replaced to the artist's specifications, the amount of such insurance shall be limited to the cost of such replacement.
2. If no amount has been specified by the lender, the Museum shall insure the Property at its own estimated valuation; provided, however, that such estimated valuation shall not be construed to be an appraisal of the Property by the Museum for any purpose other than insurance.
3. The Museum's fine arts policy contains the usual exclusions for loss or damage due to invasion, government confiscation, nuclear damage, war, gradual deterioration, moths, vermin or inherent vice.
4. The lender agrees that, in the event of loss or damage, recovery shall be limited to such amount, if any, as may be paid by the insurer, hereby releasing the Museum, each of the participating museums, and the Trustees, officers, agents and employees of the Museum and each of the participating museums from liability for any and all claims arising out of such loss or damage.
5. If the lender elects to maintain his/her own insurance, the Museum must be supplied with a certificate of insurance from the lender's insurance company, naming the Mint Museum of Art and each of the participating museums as an additional insured, or waiving subrogation against the Museum and each of the participating museums. Otherwise, the loan agreement shall constitute a release of the Museum and each of the participating museums from any liability in connection with loaned Property. The Museum can accept no responsibility for any error or deficiency in information furnished to the lender's insurers or for lapses in coverage.

CONSERVATION

The lender provides his/her property in good condition, and the Museum may inspect and photograph it. The Museum agrees not to alter the Property, and to report any damage or other findings to the lender.
1. It is understood that the Museum will not clean, restore, reframe or otherwise alter Property covered by this receipt without the written consent of the owner(s) and agreement as to costs and responsibilities for payment of same.
2. If damage or deterioration is noted, the lender will be notified at once. Should damage occur in transit, the carrier will also be notified and all packing materials saved for inspection.
3. The Museum assumes the right, unless specifically denied by the lender, to examine the Property according to standard curatorial practices. Information thus gathered will remain confidential unless released by specific consent of the lender.
4. The lender certifies that the Property lent is in good condition and will withstand ordinary strains of packing, transportation and exhibition.
5. Unless the Museum is notified in writing to the contrary, it is understood that the Property lent may be photographed for the catalogue and for educational, publicity, and archival purposes connected with the exhibition, and that slides of the Property may be made for educational use. The work will not be unframed for photography without the consent of the lender.

SALE

If the Property listed on the face of this receipt is for sale, it is understood that the selling price shall include a Museum handling charge of 30%.

RETURN OF PROPERTY

The Museum and lender agree as to when the Property will be returned, to whom, and where. The lender may not withdraw the Property from loan until the end of the loan period. Also, the Museum establishes its right to return the Property at the end of the loan period without undue difficulty, prolonged delay or extraordinary expense; and to limit its liabilites with regard to these factors.
1. The Property will be returned only to the owner, or lender, or his duly authorized agent at the address stated on the reverse unless the Museum is otherwise instructed.
2. If the legal ownership of the property shall change during the period of this loan, whether by reason of death, sale, insolvency, gift or otherwise, the new owner will, prior to its return, be required to establish his legal right to receive the Property by proof satisfactory to the Museum.
3. If the location of the new owner shall be of much greater distance than the point from which the loan was borrowed, the new owner will be required to pay any difference in the charges for the delivery of the Property.
4. The Property shall remain in the possession of the Museum and/or the other organizations participating in the exhibition for which it has been borrowed for the time specified on the reverse, but may be withdrawn from exhibition by the Museum or any of the participating organizations with the authorization of the Museum.
5. The Museum's right to return the Property shall accrue absolutely at the termination of the loan period.
6. If the Museum, after making all reasonable efforts and through no fault of its own, shall be unable to return the Property within sixty days of the termination of the loan period, then, the Museum shall have the absolute right to place the Property in storage, to charge regular storage fees and the cost of insurance therefore, and to have and enforce a lien for such fees and cost. If, after four years, the Property shall not have been reclaimed, then, and in consideration for its storage, insurance and safeguarding during such period, the ownership of the Property shall be automatically transferred, entirely and without restriction, further claim or interest, to the Museum.

SIGNATURE

_____   _____
Lender or authorized agent Title   Date

SIGNATURE

_____   _____
For the Mint Museum of Art Title   Date

AUCKLAND MUSEUM
REQUEST FOR INCOMING LOAN/EXHIBITION

DEPARTMENT_____DATE_____
Please forward this form, completed, to the Registrar

LENDER: CONTACT:

ADDRESS: PHONE: (H)
                                                  (B)
                                           FAX:

_____

LOAN PURPOSE:_____
NAME OF EXHIBITION, if applicable_____
EXHIBITION DATES FROM:_____TO:_____

Is the material already on-site?_____, if no, note desired
Arrival date_____Return Date _____

Are other department requesting material from this lender for this loan/exhibition?
_____Department(s)

INCOMING MATERIAL
Attach a list providing: object number if applicable, name of object, medium,
material, period and individual value. Include support material and value.

TOTAL VALUE OF LOAN MATERIAL $_____

ATTACHMENTS:
☐ Temporary Receipt; if previously sent #_____   ☐ Correspondence   ☐ Other
Note any specific instructions, requirements or transportation arrangements made
for the loan. _____
_____
_____

RECOMMENDATIONS: (signatures)
Section Head - Collection Management_____Date_____

Conservation, if applicable_____Date_____

     WHEN THE ABOVE IS COMPLETE, PLEASE FORWARD TO REGISTRATION

Registrar   _____Date_____

APPROVALS:
Director Professional Services_____Date_____

Director   _____Date_____

Museum Board_____Date_____

....
Registration use:

Dept. notified of decision............Loan form to ADC............Loan form to Borrower..........Returned.......

Shipping arrang..............Conserv. Notified...............Receipt prep...........Objects returned.............

Museum & Art Gallery
of the Northern Territory

GPO Box 4646 Darwin NT 0801
Conacher Street Bullocky Point Darwin NT 0820 AUSTRALIA
Telephone: (08) 8999 8201 Facsimile: (08) 8999 8289 ISD: 61-8-8999 8201

LOAN AGREEMENT - INCOMING

Loan No: **Date:**

Lender: **Contact:**

Address:
                                                               Telephone:

                                                               Fax:

Purpose:

Venue/s:

Period of Loan From: **To:**

The Lender agrees to loan the following material to the Museum and Art Gallery of the Northern Territory under the conditions set out overleaf:

Description: **Value**

                                                      Total Valuation

Credit line:

         (Please state if you wish to be listed as 'Private Collection')

Copyright owner:

Address:

Pickup address:

Telephone:

Address for return of loan (if same as 'pickup', write 'as above'):

Telephone:

Please read the Conditions of Loan, and sign and date the relevant section on the following page of this Agreement

349

FROM / TO:

VIRGINIA MUSEUM OF NATURAL HISTORY
1001 Douglas Avenue, Martinsville VA 24112
(703) 666-8600

DIVISION:

FROM / TO:

ATTENTION: _____

INVOICE NUMBER _____
DATE _____

SHIPPING INFORMATION

Date _____
Insured For _____
Packed by _____
No. packages _____
Type of container(s)_____
_____
Other _____

Method:
___ UPS
___ Postal - priority / airmail
___ Postal - library rate
___ Truck freight
___ Overnight service
___ Hand-carried by:
_____

PURPOSE
___ loan at your request
___ loan for examination at our request
___ exchange
___ gift
___ return of material

APPROVED BY: _____

DATE DUE: _____

SPECIES DESIGNATION	CATALOG NUMBER(S) or NUMBERS OF SPECIMENS	DESCRIPTION OF CONDITION

MATERIAL RECEIVED BY _____   DATE RECEIVED _____
(condition noted above)

○ Please sign and return one copy. When returning specimens, please pack and ship as received. If specimens are needed for a longer period, a written request for renewal of loans should be made .

○ Please advise us of taxonomic changes when materials are returned. The acronym "VMNH" should be used for citations in publications.

350

8/22/90

VIRGINIA MUSEUM OF NATURAL HISTORY
LOAN GUIDELINES

All specimens loaned from the Virginia Museum of Natural History (VMNH) are subject to the following guidelines. All exceptions must be requested and granted in writing. Failure to follow the Museum's guidelines may jeopardize future borrowing privileges.

LENGTH OF LOANS

The length for each loan will be negotiated at the time of the loan, generally not to exceed six months. Requests for extensions should be made in writing to the Collections Manager.

Specimens may not be forwarded to another institution without written permission from VMNH.

SPECIMEN CARE

Specimens should be stored according to professional standards in cases and/or facilities that are free from hazards (insects, rodents, fire, vandalism, theft, water damage, etc.). VMNH will recommend storage and handling guidelines for unusual or sensitive materials.

Specimens should not be sampled, dissected, remounted or in anyway altered without written permission. Special permission is required for destructive testing of any kind.

All original documentation accompanying the specimens must never be discarded or covered over (examples include original locality labels, previous identification labels, etc.).

TYPE SPECIMENS

Type specimens are loaned only from certain divisions and are subject to restrictions. All types must be returned within 30 days of receipt by registered priority mail.

Invertebrates: Types for species originating from VMNH must be returned to the Museum for deposit, even if specimens of the taxon(taxa) were previously ceded to specialists as desiderata. By prior written agreement, a portion of the type series may be retained by the specialist.

TAXONOMIC CHANGES

All material sent out on loan must be returned by the specified due date even if incorrectly identified. We would appreciate notification of taxonomic changes when the material is returned.

Invertebrates: Unidentified invertebrate specimens identified by the specialist may be retained in part, as agreed to in correspondence (desiderata); major geographical localities, stages, and both sexes should be represented in series of specimens returned to VMNH.

SHIPPING INSTRUCTIONS

The specimens are the responsibility of the borrower until received by VMNH. Therefore, they should be packed and shipped according to national and international laws governing transportation, and in a manner similar to or better than as received. Wooden shipping containers must be returned to VMNH.

Types must be returned by registered priority mail.

Specimens must be insured for the value indicated on the original shipping invoice.

Copies of documentation verifying legal collecting and transportation activities should be included both inside the shipping container and in an envelope on the outside of the container (examples: USFWS importation & exportation forms, collecting permits from country of origin; CITES permits, etc.).

PUBLICATIONS

Authors are requested to send 2 reprints of any publication based in whole or in part upon material loaned from the Museum. Please mark these to the attention of the Collections Manager.

The acronym "VMNH" should be used for citing the Museum's specimens.

22 Aug 1990

SONOMA COUNTY MUSEUM
425 Seventh Street
Santa Rosa, CA 95401
(707) 579-1500

SONOMA
COUNTY
MUSEUM

INCOMING LOAN AGREEMENT

The Sonoma County Museum agrees, subject to the terms and conditions printed on the reverse of this agreement, to borrow the objects described below from:

Name of Lender:_____

Institution:_____

Address:_____

_____
City   State

Zip:_____ Phone:_____

Dates of Loan:_____

Insured by:_____

Credit Line:_____

Purpose of Loan:_____

_____

ACCESSION NO.	TITLE/DESCRIPTION	CONDITION	VALUE

☐ Extra sheets attached. Sign and date all copies.

Special Conditions:_____

I hereby acknowledge that I am authorized to lend the objects listed above to the Sonoma County Museum and that I have read and agree to abide by the terms and conditions printed on the reverse governing this loan:

Signature of Lender:_____ Date:_____

The Sonoma County Museum gratefully acknowledges receipt of object(s) herein described:

Received by:_____ Date:_____
(Signature of Authorized Museum Representative)

Name & Title:_____

RETURN OF ABOVE LOANED OBJECTS IS HEREBY ACKNOWLEDGED:

Signature of Lender:_____ Date:_____

White - Museum office ~ Yellow - Donor ~ Pink - Collections
PLEASE PRESS FIRMLY
352

THE FRICK COLLECTION
1 EAST 70TH STREET
NEW YORK, NEW YORK 10021

Telephone: (212) 288-0700

LOAN AGREEMENT FORM: EXHIBITIONS

EXHIBITION TITLE: _____

DATES OF EXHIBITION: _____

DATE WORK DUE AT THE FRICK COLLECTION: _____

LENDER: _____

Address: _____

Telephone: _____

Exact form of lender's name for exhibition label and catalogue:

_____

OBJECT LENT:

    Name of artist: _____

    Title of work: _____

    Accession number: _____

    Medium or materials: _____

    Signature form and location: _____

SIZE:

    Height: _____ Width: _____ Depth: _____

    Dimensions of frame: _____ Dimensions of base: _____

CONDITION REPORT: _____

_____

Please send photographs available: Black & white _____ Color transparencies _____ Color slides _____

If not available, how can The Frick Collection obtain photographs of this work?

_____

Does The Frick Collection have permission to reproduce photographs for the catalogue? _____

May The Frick Collection give permission to reproduce photographs for publicity? _____

INSURANCE:

    Insurance value of work: _____

    Do you wish The Frick Collection to insure the work "wall to wall"? _____

    Do you wish to maintain your own insurance and bill the Collection? _____

        If so, what is estimated cost of premium? _____

    If the lender elects to maintain his own insurance, The Frick Collection must be supplied with a certificate of insurance naming The Frick Collection as additional assured or waiving subrogation against The Frick Collection. Otherwise, this loan agreement shall constitute a release of The Frick Collection from any liability in connection with the loaned property. The Frick Collection will accept no responsibility for any error or deficiency in information furnished to the lender's insurers or for lapses in coverage.

SHIPPING: Estimated date of shipping: _____ mo. _____ day _____ year

            Point of departure: _____

            Type of carrier: _____

            Size of shipping case: _____

RETURN OF WORK: Unless the Collection is notified to the contrary in writing before the close of the exhibition, the work will be returned to the lender's address given above.

ANY SPECIAL REQUIREMENTS? _____

_____

_____

Signed: _____

Title: _____ Date: _____

MUSEUM OF TEXAS TECH UNIVERSITY
HISTORY DIVISION IN-HOUSE COLLECTION LOAN FORM
(Not to be used for external loans)

Borrower's name (regular Museum staff only) _____

Division using objects _____

Date borrowed _____ Date to be returned _____

Place used _____

Purpose _____

Transportation method _____

Secure storage location (before and after use) _____

_____

*REGISTRAR AND COLLECTION MGR. WILL NOTE LOCATION CHANGES ON ACC'N RECORDS

Objects/Specimens	I. D. Number	Storage Location

NO ALTERATIONS, FREEZING, OR TREATMENT WITHOUT WRITTEN APPROVAL OF LENDING DIV.

I accept full responsibility for these objects/specimens _____

signature

Divisional approval _____ Date _____

Returned by _____ Date _____

Received by _____ Date _____

Distribution:

[   ] Original/Registrar [   ] Lending Division [   ] Borrowing Division

UNIVERSITY of DENVER(Colorado Seminary)
MUSEUM OF ANTHROPOLOGY
FACULTY, STAFF, STUDENT OUTGOING LOAN AGREEMENT

2130 South Race Street • Denver, Colorado 80208 • (303) 871-2688 • FAX (303) 871-2736

The object(s) described below is (are) lent by the Denver University Museum of Anthropology (DUMA) to the borrower identified below. Loans are subject to conditions printed on the reverse.

BORROWER INFORMATION

NAME: _____ TITLE: _____

CAMPUS ADDRESS: _____ CAMPUS TELEPHONE: _____

HOME ADDRESS: _____ HOME TELEPHONE: _____

Borrower Type:	FACULTY:	STAFF:	STUDENT:	OTHER:

BORROWED OBJECT(S)

    CATALOGUE #   DESCRIPTION

1.
2.
3.
4.
5.
6.
7.
8.
9.
10.

LOAN PURPOSE (*The object(s) above is (are) borrowed for the following purposes only*)		
	DISPLAY OR EXHIBITION,	TITLE: _____
	RESEARCH/STUDY,	DESCRIBE: _____
	INSTRUCTION,	TITLE/ CLASS NUMBER: _____
	OTHER,	DESCRIBE:

LOAN PERIOD
FROM: TO:

PACKING & TRANSPORT
(All packing and transporting shall be done by the Museum Collections Staff unless otherwise noted in this agreement)
OTHER ARRANGEMENTS:

STORAGE & DISPLAY
WHERE WILL THE LOAN OBJECT(S) BE STORED OR DISPLAYED?
DESCRIBE: _____
APPROVED BY MUSEUM COLLECTIONS STAFF: INITIALS:

EXHIBIT MOUNTS

PLAN SUBMITTED: _____	INITIALS/DATE: _____
MOUNTS APPROVED	INITIALS/DATE:

TRAINING *(The loan will not be made until the Borrower is trained in object handling by the DUMA Collections Staff.)*
Has the Borrower been trained in object handling?   INITIALS/DATE:

SPECIAL REQUIREMENTS

formdulo.dot 6/13/97

UNIVERSITY OF DENVER MUSEUM OF ANTHROPOLOGY
FACULTY, STAFF, STUDENT
OUTGOING LOAN AGREEMENT

Conditions of Loan

1. Objects covered by this agreement shall remain in the condition in which they are received. Artifacts shall not be cleaned, repaired, retouched, or altered in any way except with the written permission of the Museum.

2. All transportation shall be arranged by the Museum Collections Staff and all costs shall be borne by the Borrower.

3. Damages are to be reported to the Museum in writing immediately.

4. The Borrower will be trained in object handling by the Museum Collections Staff before the loan is approved.

5. Storage facilities and exhibit cases shall be inspected by the Museum Collections Staff before the loan is approved. Loan material shall not be removed from the University Park Campus without prior written permission.

6. The Borrower shall submit exhibit mount and installation plans to the Museum Collections Staff for approval prior to mounting and installation.

7. On return, the loan shall be packed and transported by the Museum Collections Staff unless otherwise noted in this agreement. If the Borrower is given written permission to repack the loan, the loan material shall be packed in the same manner as received and with the same cases, pads, and packing materials. If the packing materials are damage, the Borrower must contact the DUMA Collections Staff for instructions before packing.

8. Any changes in the condition of the loan object(s), variation from the stated guidelines in this agreement, loss, theft, or damage to the loan, in transit, during storage, use, or exhibit must be reported immediately to the Museum Collections Staff and a full written condition report will be sent to the Staff within 48 hours of the incident.

9. The Borrower must undertake to maintain constant and adequate protection of the loan object(s) to minimize the risk of theft or damage.

10. The Borrower must undertake to maintain constant and adequate protection of the loan object(s) from hazards of fire and flood, exposure to harmful light levels, extremes of temperature and relative humidity, insect attack, and pollution.

11. In the event of damage to the loan object(s) while in the custody of the Borrower, the Borrower will be responsible for all conservation costs necessary to return the loan object(s) to the same or better condition.

12. The Borrower may photograph the objects covered in this agreement only for a record or for publicity. The Borrower may not reproduce objects in any media for sale other than in the above mentioned instance.

13. If DUMA agrees to photographic reproduction of the loan object(s) for publication or creation of a saleable object, the Borrower will ensure that the ownership of the loan object(s) is indicated as: **University of Denver Museum of Anthropology**, and each object shall also be identified by its catalogue number.

14. The credit line for all loan objects used on exhibit shall be: **University of Denver Museum of Anthropology** (DUMA if an acronym is appropriate). Each object shall also be identified with its catalogue number.

I have read and agree to the above conditions:

_____, _____ Date: _____
(Borrower)   (Title)

Approved for the University of Denver Museum of Anthropology

_____, _____ Date: _____
(Museum's Authorized Agent)   (Title)

(Please sign and return Registrar's Copy)

RETURN OF LOAN   Date: _____   Received by: _____, Title: _____
Condition upon return:

Outgoing Loan Agreement

Outgoing Loan No.

NPS UNIT (Lender):

(Street/Box)   Telephone:

(City, State, Zip)   FAX Number:

Superintendent (please print):

Shipping Address (if different):

BORROWING INSTITUTION (Borrower):

(Department)

(Street/Box)   Telephone:

(City, State, Zip, Country)   FAX Number:

Responsible Official (Borrower):   Title:

Shipping Address (if different):

Check one: ☐ non-NPS   ☐ NPS

PURPOSE OF LOAN:

☐ Exhibit   ☐ Study   ☐ Conservation   ☐ Exhibit Preparation   ☐ Storage

☐ Collections Management (including cataloging and storage)   ☐ Other (describe):

Credit Line:

OBJECTS IN LOAN: ☐ List Attached

INITIATION DATE: TERMINATION DATE:

INSURANCE AND SHIPPING/PACKING:

☐ Insurance to be waived   ☐ To be carried by Borrower

Insurance company: Policy No:

Outgoing packing by: ☐ Lender   ☐ Other:

Return packing by: ☐ Borrower   ☐ Other:

Method of shipping: Outgoing: Return:

Charges to Borrower: ☐ yes   ☐ no   Describe:

NPS Form 10-127 Rev.
July 1995

Outgoing Loan Agreement (Continued)

LOAN CONDITIONS:

Outgoing loans are subject to the terms and conditions noted on the attached Conditions for Outgoing Loans.

Facilities form required: ☐ yes   ☐ no

Additional Loan Conditions:

SIGNATURES:

ON INITIATION OF THIS AGREEMENT: The undersigned borrower is an authorized agent of the borrowing institution. Signature indicates agreement to terms specified in this loan agreement and attached conditions.

PLEASE SIGN BOTH COPIES AND RETURN THE ORIGINAL TO THE NPS.

Name of Responsible Official (Borrowing Institution), Title (Please print)

Signature   Date

Name of Superintendent (Lending NPS Unit), (Please print)

Signature   Date

RETURN STATUS:

☐ Complete   ☐ Partial (list catalog numbers and date of return):

Extension Termination Date:

RETURN OF LOAN:

The undersigned is an authorized agent of the lender. Signature acknowledges receipt of all material in good condition or in condition as noted on this agreement or in attached object condition report(s). A signed copy is sent to the borrower to acknowledge the return of the loan.

Name of Superintendent (Lending NPS Unit) (Please print)

Signature   Date

NPS Form 10-127 Rev.
July 1995

US Department of the Interior
National Park Service

Conditions For Outgoing Loans

GENERAL

1. It is the Borrower's responsibility to become familiar with stipulations covering this transaction. Responsibility for meeting the terms agreed to in this loan agreement remains with the borrowing institution and authorized agent.

2. No loans will be made until all necessary documentation has been received by the lending park, and the Outgoing Loan Agreement has been signed by both parties.

3. The borrowing institution is not permitted to make third party loans. Such loan requests shall be treated as an independent outgoing loan and negotiated between the lending park and the second borrowing institution, unless specifically agreed to in writing on the attached loan agreement.

4. Borrower agrees to incur all expenses relating to this loan unless otherwise noted.

5. Borrower agrees not to use the museum property in the loan for commercial gain.

6. If loaned material is to be displayed, the NPS shall be credited for all materials furnished as part of this loan. The credit line should read as noted on the loan agreement. The NPS is not responsible for the quality of the display or final interpretation placed on objects.

7. The Borrower shall provide to Lender a copy, at no cost, of any publication or report for which NPS objects have been lent.

8. The Borrower, in the event of a change of address, shall provide the NPS with written notification thereof within 15 days of such change.

9. Museum collections loaned to a repository for the purposes of collections management and/or storage will be cataloged according to the NPS *Museum Handbook*, Part II, and in accordance with requirements established by the lending park unless otherwise agreed to. Copies of all catalog records and electronic data will be sent to the lending park by the borrowing repository.

10. Federal policies and mandates governing NPS museum collections take precedence over state and local laws, regulations and/or statutes.

COPYRIGHT AND PHOTOGRAPHY RESTRICTIONS

1. Loaned materials are subject to restrictions outlined in the copyright law of the United States (Title 17, U.S. Code). Borrower will honor copyright restrictions as they apply to the collections and will ensure that the appropriate copyright releases are obtained.

2. Unless otherwise agreed to in writing, no reproductions are permitted by the Borrower except photographic copies for condition reports, documentation, damage, educational, and publicity purposes related to the stated purpose of this loan.

INSURANCE

1. All material shall be continuously and fully insured at the Borrower's expense for the amount specified on the loan agreement, unless waived and so noted on the agreement. Insurance shall be wall-to-wall, and provide coverage against all risks of physical loss or damage from any external causes while in transit and on location for the entire duration of the loan. Borrower shall provide proof of insurance to the lending park. The NPS must be notified in writing at least 20 days prior to any cancellation or meaningful change in the Borrower's insurance policy. If additional coverage is taken by the Borrower, the lending park must receive from the Borrower a copy of the certificate of insurance naming the lending park as an additional insured.

2. Any lapses in coverage or any failure to secure insurance and/or any inactions by the Lender regarding notice will not release the Borrower from liability for loss or damage.

3. Dollar values provided are confidential and are for insurance purposes only. The NPS reserves the right to increase the amount of insurance coverage required on the loaned objects, if reasonably justified.

4. If insurance is waived, the Borrower agrees to indemnify any and all loss or damage to the museum collections occurring during the course of the loan, except for loss or damage resulting from inherent vice, war, and nuclear incident.

5. Borrower agrees to waive all claims and recourse against the NPS for loss or damage to persons or collections arising from this agreement. Borrower agrees to defend, indemnify, and save harmless the NPS from all liability, loss, cost, or obligation on account or arising out of any injury to any person or property of any kind, from any cause whatsoever, in any way connected with Borrower's use of said property, including acceptance and redelivery thereof.

CONDITION, ALTERATION, AND CONSERVATION

1. Each object is considered to be in good condition unless otherwise noted.

2. Objects may not be cleaned, repaired, retouched or altered in any way without the express permission of the Lender.

3. Loss, damage or deterioration must be reported to the lending park. If damage occurs, it is understood that any necessary conservation treatment will be arranged for or handled by NPS staff, and that the Borrower or its insurance company is liable for all costs resulting from damage, including the cost of conservation, for any reduction in value or replacement.

359

Conditions For Outgoing Loans (Continued)

HANDLING AND CARE

1. All physical care (e.g., handling, storage, exhibition) should meet or exceed the standards set down in the NPS *Museum Handbook*, Part I and NPS Special Directive 80-1.

2. Loss or damage, whether in transit or on the borrower's premises, and regardless of who may be responsible, must be reported immediately. Photographs and documents of the damage (e.g., condition report) with dates, names, and other details of the occurrence (e.g., damage reports) must be sent to the lending park within 5 working days of the loss or damage.

SECURITY AND ENVIRONMENTAL CONTROLS

1. Borrower must provide at all times, adequate security in order to protect objects against risk of damage, loss or deterioration due to theft, vandalism, fire, smoke, and water. Adequate protection against insects, vermin, fungi, mold and pollutants must be provided. Conditions should comply with museum standards and the NPS *Museum Handbook*, Part I.

2. Museum collections must be protected at all times against damage caused by exposure to direct sunlight, ultraviolet light, excessive humidity, or proximity to heating or cooling sources. Temperature and relative humidity levels should be monitored on a daily basis. Levels are controlled to minimize short-term fluctuations and to avoid harmful extremes. Conditions should comply with museum standards and the NPS *Museum Handbook*, Part I.

3. If these conditions cannot be met, the lending park must be advised in writing. The amended conditions should be attached to the loan agreement and noted in the additional conditions on the face of the attached agreement prior to the completion of the agreement.

PACKING AND SHIPPING

1. Packing and transportation must be by safe methods designated and approved in advance by the Lender and noted on the attached agreement. Borrower must comply with shipping and packing instructions provided by the Lender.

2. Lender will pack the collection item(s) and will provide packing materials for the loan. If required by the terms of the agreement, packing materials will be paid for by the Borrower.

3. Unpacking and repacking must be done by experienced personnel under competent supervision. The loan must be repacked in the same manner as received and with the same packing materials if possible, unless otherwise mutually agreed upon by Lender and Borrower. All packing materials should be stored, if possible, during the loan period in a place fully conditioned to the same temperature and relative humidity as those under which the loan itself 's stored or displayed. All packing materials that are to be reused must be protected from contamination by insects, mold, dust, and airborne pollutants.

ACCESS

1. Access to loaned objects by individuals for purposes other than those identified on the attached agreement must receive prior approval by the Lender and must be supervised by the Borrower. Use of loaned material must be restricted to a supervised area. Researchers will be subject to the Lender's current user rules and restrictions. Borrower will be responsible for any misconduct by persons "using" materials.

2. Borrower must provide access to Lender's staff or representatives during regular hours of operations for the purposes of inspections, inventory, repacking, research and condition reporting.

3. Borrower agrees to provide access to original material only when all other options, such as photographs or reproductions, have been exhausted.

4. Borrower is subject to NPS annual inventory procedures as noted in the NPS *Museum Handbook*, Part II. Either the Borrower will confirm Lender's inventory or will provide access to the Lender to conduct inventory, as noted in the special conditions on the agreement.

EXTENSION AND RECALL

1. Any extensions of the loan period must be requested by the Borrower. The Lender will prepare extension documents to be completed and signed by the Borrower and received by the Lender at least 30 calendar days prior to the original loan expiration date shown on the attached agreement. All additional insurance will be extended by the Borrower and proof of insurance will be provided to the Lender by a copy of the certificate of insurance naming the NPS Lender as an additional insured and dated with the new termination date of the loan.

2. The Lender reserves the right to inspect or audit the objects on loan at any time. Should the Lender desire to recall any of the loan material for its own purposes, it may do so by giving at least 30 days notice to the Borrower. Loaned objects may be withdrawn by the Lender without prior written notice to the Borrower if it is determined that they are receiving improper care.

3. Borrower agrees to give at least 30 days written notice to the Lender if electing to cancel this loan prior to the term of this loan agreement.

4. Repository loans must remain at the designated repository until such time as they are requested by the lending park or until such time as the repository is unable to care for the loan in accordance with the loan stipulations. The loan may be terminated by either party, given 3 months notice, or within 30 days if the lending park determines the loan stipulations are not being met. Should the Borrower be unable to continue care for the collection it must be returned to the lending NPS park or another designated repository.

NPS Form 10-127a
July 1995

Outgoing Loan Number:

Termination Date:

OUTGOING LOAN FOLDER COVER SHEET

INSTRUCTIONS: This Outgoing Loan Folder Cover Sheet may be used whenever a park lends museum collections to other parks, repositories, or non-NPS institutions. Insert this in the outgoing loan folder.

A. TYPE OF LOAN

☐ NPS   ☐ non-NPS

B. BORROWER

C. PURPOSE

☐ Exhibit   ☐ Collections Management
☐ Study   ☐ Storage
☐ Conservation   ☐ Other (describe):
☐ Exhibit Preparation

Initiation Date _____
Termination Date _____
Extension Date   _____

C. OUTGOING LOAN AGREEMENT DOCUMENTATION IN THIS FOLDER

☐ Outgoing Loan Agreement and List of Objects
☐ Correspondence relating to outgoing loan
☐ Insurance documents
☐ Shipping documents
☐ Packing documents
☐ Conservation records
☐ Restriction records relating to outgoing loan
☐ Photographs
☐ Facility Report
☐ Other(Specify):
☐ Loan extension request and documents

D. RETURN OF OUTGOING LOAN

☐ Loan Returned

Partial (date):

Complete (date):

☐ Comments

AUCKLAND MUSEUM
REQUEST FOR OUTGOING LOAN

DEPARTMENT_____DATE_____
Please forward this form, completed, to the Registrar
_____

BORROWER: CONTACT:

ADDRESS: PHONE:
                                             FAX:

_____

LOAN PURPOSE:_____

NAME OF EXHIBITION, if applicable_____

EXHIBITION DATES FROM:_____TO:_____
Approximate   Approximate
Shipping Date_____Return Date_____

Is any other department contributing to this loan?
_____Department(s)
LOAN MATERIAL
Attach a list providing: Accession/registration number, name of object, medium,
material, period and individual value. Note if any of this material is on loan to
Auckland Museum and any other specific instructions or requirements of the loan.

TOTAL VALUE OF LOAN MATERIAL $_____
CREDIT LINE_____
_____
_____

BORROWER QUESTIONAIRE REQUIRED?   YES / NO

RECOMMENDATIONS:
Curator   _____Date_____

Conservation_____Date_____

Section Head - Collection Management_____Date_____

Registrar   _____Date_____

APPROVALS:
Director Professional Services_____Date_____

Director   _____Date_____

Museum Board_____Date_____
....

Registration use:

Dept. notifie of decision............Loan form to ADC............Loan form to Borrower.........Returned.......

Shipping arrang..............Conserv. Notified..............Receipt prep............Objects returned.............

362

VALENTINE MUSEUM
1015 East Clay Street, Richmond, VA 23219

OUTGOING LOAN AGREEMENT

This agreement is between the Valentine Museum (herein called the "Museum"), a Virginia corporation, and the borrower whose name appears below (herein called the "borrower"), and provides for the loaning to the borrower of the object(s) described below, for the purpose of exhibition or study and subject to all the terms and conditions of this agreement, including those set forth on the reverse of this sheet.

BORROWER *(full legal name, address, telephone):*

LOAN PERIOD:

TITLE OF EXHIBITION:

Accession Number	Description	Value

INSURANCE: Subject to the conditions on the reverse side, borrower's mark in one of the blanks below signifies selection of the insurance arrangement marked:

_____ Borrower will insure loaned object(s) under own policy and forward certificate of such insurance, showing the Museum as an additional insured, for receipt by the Museum prior to shipping date.

_____ Borrower will insure loan under Museum's policy and will pay pro-rata cost in the amount of $_____.

_____ Borrower agrees to assume liability for loss or damage in lieu of insurance (option available only when total value of all objects loaned for a specific exhibit is less than $1,000).

SHIPPING INSTRUCTIONS:

Date materials should be shipped:

Method of shipment preferred (subject to approval by the Museum):

SIGNATURE BELOW SIGNIFIES ACCEPTANCE OF ALL TERMS AND CONDITIONS OF THIS AGREEMENT, INCLUDING THOSE SET FORTH ON THE REVERSE SIDE

_____

_____   VALENTINE MUSEUM
(Full legal name of borrowers, typed or printed)

By: _____   By: _____
        (signature)   *(signature)*

Title: _____   Title: _____

Date: _____   Date: _____

Please sign and return both copies. After the loan has been approved we will return your copy.

Objects sent _____ by _____   Objects returned _____ by _____

KALAMAZOO VALLEY MUSEUM
A Participatory Museum Of History, Science And Technology

OGL# _____

OUTGOING LOAN AGREEMENT
[Long-term]

BORROWER _____   DATE _____

(name)

_____

(address)   TELEPHONE _____

_____

In accordance with the conditions printed on the reverse, the following objects are loaned to the Borrower from the Kalamazoo Valley Museum for the following purpose:

_____

for the period _____ to _____

CAT/ACCN # _____   OBJECT DESCRIPTION   CONDITION   INSURANCE VALUE

CREDIT LINE   See Reproduction and Credit instructions on reverse of agreement _____

INSURANCE (see conditions on reverse)
_____ to be carried by Borrower; name of Insurer _____
_____ to be carried by the Kalamazoo Valley Museum
_____ to be waived

SPECIAL CONDITIONS _____

I have read and agree to the conditions printed on the reverse and certify that I am authorized to agree thereto:

_____   _____
(signature of Borrower)   (signature of authorized KVM official)

_____   _____
(title)   (title)

_____   _____
(date)   (date)

RETURN OF LOANED OBJECTS IS HEREBY ACKNOWLEDGED:

_____   DATE _____
(signature of museum official)

revised 5/96

INVOICE OF SPECIMENS

STRECKER MUSEUM COMPLEX
Baylor University
P.O. Box 97154
Waco, TX 76798

A letter has, has not
been written.

TO: _____

_____

_____

Attention: _____

Loan _____ Exchange _____

Gift _____ Transfer _____

For: _____

LOANS ARE ORDINARILY MADE FOR A PERIOD OF SIX MONTHS OR LESS.
A WRITTEN REQUEST FOR RENEWAL SHOULD BE MADE IF IT IS NECESSARY TO KEEP SPECIMENS FOR A LONGER PERIOD.

NO.	NAME	DATA

Date of shipment _____

Method of shipment _____

Prepaid _____ Collect _____

Sent by _____

ONE COPY IS TO BE RETAINED BY THE RECIPIENT; THE OTHER COPY IS TO BE SIGNED TAND RETURNED ON RECEIPT OF THE MATERIAL

Received in good order on _____ Signed _____

365

4/97

POLICIES AND PROCEDURES FOR OUTGOING LOANS
STRECKER MUSEUM COMPLEX

CONDITIONS
1. Loans of research materials are generally made to institutions only. They will be made in care of affiliates or employees of such institutions. Loans to legitimate students will be made in care of the student's advisor or another institutional supervisor or major professor.
2. Loans of research materials to unaffiliated individuals will be made only on a case by case basis.
3. Loans of student study materials may be made to unaffiliated individuals.
4. Loans of specimens or artifacts may not be made to a third party without prior written permission from Strecker Museum.

CARE OF OBJECTS
1. Loaned material will be cared for properly and protected at all times.
2. Fluid preserved specimens will be kept in the fluid they are received in and will not be transferred into any other fluid.
3. Specimens or artifacts may not be analyzed using destructive sampling or invasive techniques without additional prior written permission.
4. Additional prior written permission is required for restoration, conservation, or cleaning of objects, pest treatment, or further preparation of specimens. If permission is granted for any of the above, a complete written and photographic record of materials and techniques used must be supplied.
5. Changes may not be made to the specimen or artifact record or label. Labels may not be removed or altered. Any suggested changes must be made on a separate comment card.

COPYRIGHT
1. Additional written permission must be granted for specimens or artifacts to be photographed, cast, or otherwise reproduced.
2. Strecker Museum retains the copyright to any photograph, cast, or other reproduction of any specimen or artifact unless other written arrangements are made.

DURATION
1. All loans are made for specified periods of time, generally negotiated for the borrower's projected use of the material.
2. Loans are usually made for no more than a six-month period. They are renewable, in writing, for additional time, if necessary.
3. Strecker Museum does not make permanent loans.
4. The Museum retains the right to recall loans at any time.

SHIPPING
1. The borrower must return the loan in the same or comparable packaging in which it was shipped.
2. Loans must be shipped with extra address labels inside, carry proper insurance, and be properly labeled on the outside of the package.
3. All costs of returning borrowed material are the responsibility of the borrower.

INSURANCE
1. Insurance coverage will be the responsibility of the borrower.
2. Insurance for archaeological or ethnographic material with significant monetary value will be wall-to-wall all-risk, with standard exclusions.
3. The borrower will provide the Museum with a copy of the insurance certificate upon request.
4. The amount of insurance coverage will be set by the Strecker Museum as lender.

PUBLICATIONS
1. Credit will be given to the Strecker Museum Complex for loan of all material. The standard acronym for Strecker Museum is SM.
2. The borrower will request a catalog number from the Strecker Museum before using references to loaned materials in any publication and will not assign any other numbers or letters.
2. A copy of any publications resulting from the loan of specimens or artifacts will be deposited at no cost in the Strecker Museum library.

4/93

SPECIMEN LOAN REMINDER

TO:_____

_____

_____

_____

Sent by: _____

Registered/Insured_____

Date sent_____

Date of Return_____

Our records indicate that the specimens listed below are out on loan in your name. Please return the specimens or notify us should you wish to apply for an extension of the loan.

DM Acc No	FAMILY	SPECIES	REMARKS

_____

Curator : Entomology

_____

Date

Purchase Agreement

Eiteljorg Museum
of American Indian and Western Art
500 West Washington Street
Indianapolis, IN 46204-2707
(317) 264-1715

Vendor Information

Name: _____

Address: _____

City, State, Zip: _____

Telephone: _____

Taxpayer ID/Social Security No: _____

Date Received: _____ _____

Page _____ of _____

Accession Number: _____

Accession Number	Object	Purchase Price

The objects described above have been received by the Eiteljorg Museum as a purchase, and the vendor desires to absolutely transfer full title by signing below. Except as otherwise described by the vendor in writing attached to this Purchase Agreement, the vendor represents and warrants to the Eiteljorg Museum and its successors and assigns (i) that the vendor owns all right, title and interest in the property described above, (ii) that no other person has any right, title or interest in the ownership, use, or possession of such property, and (iii) that such property is given, assigned and conveyed to the Eiteljorg Museum free and clear of any lien, security agreement or encumbrance whatsoever. The vendor further represents and acknowledges that the Eiteljorg Museum has paid to the vendor full price. The vendor hereby gives, assigns and conveys, finally and completely, without any limitation, condition or reservation, all right, title and interest in the property described above to the Eiteljorg Museum, including (without limitation) all copyrights therein, and the right to copyright the same.

Vendor _____   **Date** _____

Museum Director _____   **Date** _____

Museum Curator _____   **Date** _____

368

Auckland Museum
Te Papa Whakahiku

COLLECTIONS PURCHASE AGREEMENT

Auckland Institute
and Museum

Private Bag 92018
Auckland
New Zealand

Telephone
09 - 309 0443

Facsimile
09 - 379 9956

This form records the details of a purchase by the Auckland Museum from the Vendor as set out below.

DATE: 3 September 1997

DEPARTMENT: «Department»

VENDOR: «Source»
ADDRESS: «Address»
                  «City»

PHONE: «Phone»   FAX: «Fax»

The Vendor agrees to sell to Auckland Museum the Objects at the Purchase Price.

Object(s)   **Purchase Price**: «Price»

«Objects»

PURCHASE CONDITIONS

The Vendor agrees to sell to Auckland Museum the Object(s) at the Purchase Price, on the basis that:

-The Vendor transfers to the Museum clear title to the Object(s).

-The Vendor confirms that the Object(s) is/are not the subject of any trust, mortgage, or other third party interest, and that there is no restriction on the Vendor's right to make this sale.

-The Museum may use and dispose of the Object(s) in any way appropriate to the fulfilment of the Museum's objectives.

-In the case of Objects originating outside New Zealand, the Vendor is not aware of any breach of the laws of any country relating to the collection or export of the Object(s).

-In the case of Object(s) taken from land not owned by the Vendor, all necessary consents and permits have, as far as the Vendor is aware, been obtained from the landowner and from any relevant authority.

_____   _____

Signature of Vendor   **Date**

_____   _____

Signature of Authorised   **Date**
Representative of Auckland Museum

<u>**PLEASE SIGN BOTH COPIES AND RETURN THE WHITE ONE TO THE MUSEUM**</u>

Office Use Only
«Department»   Accession Number:

369

ROYAL ONTARIO MUSEUM
REQUEST FOR PURCHASE APPROVAL

DEPARTMENT: _____   DATE: _____

Vendor: _____   Currently on Loan: [ ] No
Contact/Auction House: _____   [ ] Yes (Loan No.) _____
Auction date: _____
Address: _____   Requires   [ ] No
                                         copyright license: [ ] Yes

Telephone: _____   FAX: _____

CREDIT LINE: _____   Copyright holder   [ ] Donor
                                                            [ ] Other _____

ITEM(S): If more than one, provide list in duplicate.

_____

CURATOR'S DECLARATION: In accordance with ROM Policy 4.3.4, I have inquired as to the provenance of this material and am satisfied that the vendor can transfer legal title to the ROM, and where applicable, material has been exported and imported in full compliance with applicable legislation. Adequate storage/gallery space is available for the material listed above, and I therefore recommend that these items be accepted as a purchase by the ROM.

Curator: _____   Date: _____

FUNDING SOURCE:

(A)   Internal Source $
       Account Number and Name:

(B)   External Source $
       Donor Name(s): $

Estimated Associated Costs $
(Conservation, shipping, etc.)

Total: _____ $ _____

APPROVALS: (Per ROM Policy 4.3.5)

Curatorial Department
Head   _____   Date_____

VP, Collections & Research_____ Date_____

Director   _____   Date_____

Planning & Research Committee_____ Date_____

Board of Trustees _____   Date_____

                                         Reg.11.97

OREGON HISTORICAL SOCIETY
AT THE *oregon history center*

1200 S.W. PARK AVENUE   PORTLAND, OREGON 97205-2483
503/306-5200 TELEPHONE   503/221-2035 FACSIMILE   503/306-5194 TDD

TEMPORARY RECEIPT
(to be completed in duplicate)

Date Received _____   Date to be Returned _____

(Not to exceed 90 days from date of receipt)

Source _____   Telephone _____

Address _____

City _____   State _____   Zip _____

<table>
<tr><td colspan="3" align="center">PURPOSE</td></tr>
<tr><td>Examination for Possible:</td><td>_____ Loan</td><td>_____ Gift   _____ Purchase</td></tr>
<tr><td>Duplication:</td><td>_____ Photograph</td><td>_____ Photocopy</td></tr>
<tr><td>Identification _____</td><td colspan="2">Other _____</td></tr>
</table>

Please note: loans, gift and purchases require curatorial approval

DESCRIPTION OF ITEMS RECEIVED

_____
_____
_____
_____
_____
_____
_____
_____

    The Oregon Historical Society agrees to notify the owner of the above described property of the Society's decision concerning the item(s) within 60 days of the above date.
    Place initials here if you do not wish to have item(s) returned: _____
    If the Society decides not to accept the item(s), the owner has 30 days from the date of notification to reclaim the item(s). If the item(s) is not reclaimed in that time, the item(s) become(s) the property of the Oregon Historical Society, and the Society may govern its disposition.

_____   _____
(Owner)   (Accepted By)

The above has been returned to me, thereby rescinding the above Temporary Receipt.

_____   _____
(Owner)   (Date)

THE STATE HISTORY MUSEUM, LIBRARY & PRESS

Incorporating The Battleship Oregon Museum, the Museum Store, Oregon Folk Arts Program, Oregon Geographic Names Board, Oregon Heritage Tourism Resource Center,
Oregon Historical Society Affiliates Program, Oregon Lewis & Clark Heritage Foundation, Oregon Lewis & Clark Trail Committee   1/97/BJS

Cooper-Hewitt
National **Design** Museum
Smithsonian Institution

Cooper-Hewitt
National Design Museum
Smithsonian Institution
2 East 91 Street
New York, New York 10128-9990
TEL 212 860 6868 FAX 212 860 6109

5116

Receipt for Object(s) Temporarily Left in the Custody of Cooper-Hewitt Museum

The object(s) listed below has been received by the Cooper-Hewitt Museum (CHM) and is subject to the terms and conditions set forth.

Received from: _____

Name of owner ☐   agent ☐

_____
If agent, name of owner

_____
Address of owner

_____
City   State   Zip Code

(_____) _____   (_____) _____
Telephone: business   home

Date Received: _____

Via : _____
hand, mail, other

For the Following Purpose: Consideration for Gift ☐   or Purchase ☐   or Loan ☐   or Study ☐

Scheduled Date of Removal of Object(s) is: _____(unless otherwise mutually agreed upon and stated here, the object(s) shall remain in CHM's custody for a limited period, not to exceed 90 days. Please note section #6 on reverse side.)

Description of Object(s)
(title, maker, materials, date)

Owner's Valuation
(US $ amount)

Received by: _____

Signature for CHM   Date   Department

When Completed Sign & Date: I have read and agree to the conditions above and on the reverse side of this receipt. I certify that I have full authority to agree thereto.

_____   _____
Signature of depositor   Date
owner ☐   agent ☐

Registrar

Date Received _____	**Schenectady Museum Association**
Received by _____	Nott Terrace Heights
Date Returned _____	Schenectady, NY 12308
Received By _____	(518) 382-7890 • FAX (518) 382-7893

TEMPORARY CUSTODY RECEIPT

Deposited for: ☐ DONATION TO COLLECTION ☐ SALE TO COLLECTION ☐ UNRESTRICTED DONATION
☐ RESEARCH or ☐ EXHIBIT (a loan form must be filed with the Registrar) ☐ BEQUEST ☐ OTHER _____

All proposed additions to the permanent collection are subject to a monthly review by the Collections Committee.
If item is not accepted for the permanent collection (please initial one):

_____ PLEASE RETURN _____ MAY BE DISPOSED OF AT THE DISCRETION OF THE MUSEUM

Received From: _____

Address: _____

Phone: _____ FAX _____

I accept the conditions listed on the back of this receipt (sign here) _____

ITEM DESCRIPTION (color, material, associated papers?)_____

_____

_____

_____

_____

Office use only

CONDITION _____

MEASUREMENTS _____

MAKER'S MARKS/ LOCATION _____

_____

COUNTRY OF ORIGIN _____ DATE / ERA _____ ASSOCIATED PAPERS?_____

1ˢᵗ CLASSIFICATION _____ 2ⁿᵈ CLASSIFICATION _____

DONOR RELEASE: TYPED _____ SENT _____ RETURNED _____ FILED _____

CATALOGUED BY _____ DONOR CARD TYPED AND FILED _____ PHOTOGRAPH MADE _____

NUMBERED BY _____ ARTIST'S CARD TYPED & FILED _____ REFERENCE FILE MADE _____

INITIAL VALUE _____ LOCATION _____ ACCESSION #_____

One copy to bailor, one copy to registrar, one copy with item.

CONDITIONS FOR TEMPORARY CUSTODY

- By signing this receipt, the bailor certifies that he/she has the legal authority to deposit the item listed on reverse and knows of no restrictions either physical or of copyright to the listed item.

- Loans to the Museum are insured by a fine arts policy subject to standard exclusions.

- If the item listed on reverse is offered exclusively as a donation to the collections of the Museum and is not accepted by the Museum for donation, the bailor must claim the item within 60 days of notification. After 60 days, the Museum will assume the item to be an unrestricted donation and will dispose of the item in a manner consistent with the goals of the Museum. The bailor must notify the Museum in cases of change of address, telephone number or ownership. New owners must submit proof of ownership that is acceptable to the Museum before an item will be released. In the event of the demise of the bailor within the holding period, it is the responsibility of the bailor's heirs or estate to notify the Museum.

- The item listed on the reverse of this form may be photographed by the museum and used for educational or documentation purposes.

extra description space

_____
_____
_____
_____
_____
_____
_____
_____
_____
_____
_____

Collections Committee Criteria Checklist	YES	NO	NOTES
1. Legal & ethical to acquire?	☐	☐	_____
2. Physical or literary restrictions?	☐	☐	_____
3. Item's history well-documented?	☐	☐	_____
4. One-time opportunity to collect?	☐	☐	_____
5. Storage conditions adequate?	☐	☐	_____
6. Item better suited to other institution?	☐	☐	_____
7. Item a hazard to people or collections?	☐	☐	_____
8. Undue burden on museum resources?	☐	☐	_____
9. Item for sale which can be donated?	☐	☐	_____
10. Better condition than access. item?	☐	☐	_____
11. Unmanageable time constraint?	☐	☐	_____
12. Item conform to mission statement?	☐	☐	_____
13. Is there a regional relationship?	☐	☐	_____
14. Is the item unique/significant?	☐	☐	_____
15. Represent new field of collecting?	☐	☐	_____
16. Fit scope/depth of current collection?	☐	☐	_____
17. A good use of the collecting budget?	☐	☐	_____

OUTGOING RECEIPT

The Nelson-Atkins Museum of Art
4525 Oak Street
Kansas City, Missouri 64111   816-561-4000

The object(s) described below, or on the attached pages, have been released by The Nelson-Atkins Museum of Art, subject to the conditions listed on the reverse.

Shipped to

Name	Owner's name (if different)
Street address	Street address
City, state, zip code	City, state, zip code
Business telephone	Business telephone
Home telephone	Home telephone

Purpose _____

Date shipped _____ Insured by _____

Transport via _____

Packing _____

Condition _____

Released by _____

Signature for the Trustees of The William Rockhill Nelson Trust and The Nelson Gallery Foundation

_____
Name and title

Museum Reference Number	**Description**	**Insurance value**

Receipt of the object(s) described above, in good condition unless otherwise noted, is hereby acknowledged, subject to the conditions on the reverse.

_____   _____
Signature of Recipient   Title

_____   _____
Please type or print name   Date object(s) received

Please sign and complete the bottom section of this receipt, and return the white copy to: Registrar, The Nelson-Atkins Museum of Art, 4525 Oak Street, Kansas City, Missouri 64111. The yellow copy is for your records.

375

NAMA 8/87

SHIPPING INVOICE

BISHOP MUSEUM
1525 Bernice Street
Honolulu, HI 96817-0916 USA
Phone (808) 847-3511

BP — 19114

SHIPPED TO
Responsible Person:
For use by:
Institution:
Mailing address:

|_____|
|_____|
|_____|

office use

SHIPPING INFORMATION
Shipped via _____
Contained in _____
Permit controlled _____
  (BPBM CITES No. US 24)

Date shipped _____
Loan due date _____

SHIPPED AS
Return of your material _____
  (BPBM In-Loan No. _____
  Owner's Invoice No. _____)

Loan at your request _____
Loan at our request _____

Exchange for _____
Other _____

Open Exchange _____
Gift _____

Authorized by _____ Registrar _____

QUANTITY	SPECIMEN NAME	LOCALITY	COLLECTOR/SOURCE	ID. NO.

/ / continued on additional sheet(s)

LOANS: Extension of the loan period should be requested through the Registrar's Office. All specimens and parts thereof must be returned except those that Bishop Museum authorizes you to keep. All primary type material designated from specimens on loan to you must be deposited at Bishop Museum. No destructive procedure, conservation, or photography may be conducted without specific permission. Any damage or loss must be reported immediately. Additional conditions may be specified on an attached sheet. Primary types must be returned by registered air mail. Please return material to Department of _____, attn: _____.
Other instructions:

Please **SIGN** and **RETURN** this sheet promptly to

1

REGISTRAR'S OFFICE
Bishop Museum
1525 Bernice Street
Honolulu, HI 96817-0916 USA

376

Accepted in good condition (exceptions should be noted above):

SIGNATURE _____

DATE _____

Reg. Form 101A Effective Nov. 1996

THE UNIVERSITY OF IOWA
HOSPITALS AND CLINICS
Iowa City, Iowa 52242

Medical Museum
319/356-7106

Incoming Loan/Gift Receipt

The materials listed below have been received by the University of Iowa Hospitals and Clinics Medical Museum in good condition unless noted, on this date: _____.

Lender/Donor _____
_____
_____
_____

Shipped Via _____
_____

Objects Received

Lender's Accession Number	Medical Museum Temp. No.	Description	Condition	Value

A condition report has been completed and filed for each item listed upon receipt by the UIHC Medical Museum. Copies are available to lenders upon request.

Registrar's Signature _____

THE UNIVERSITY OF IOWA
HOSPITALS AND CLINICS
Iowa City, Iowa 52242

Medical Museum
319/356-7106

Receipt of Delivery

The object(s) described below has (have) been released by the UIHC Medical Museum
on this _____ day of_____, 19_____.

Purpose of loan: _____
Date Received by Medical Museum: _____

To:

Via:

Registrar's signature_____Date_____

Medical Museum Temp. Number	Lender's Accession Number	Description	Insurance Value

Please sign and return the original of this form to confirm that you have received the
above mentioned items and have found them to be in satisfactory condition. Notify the
UIHC Medical Museum and the carrier immediately of any damages.

Received by_____Date_____

Delivered by_____Date_____

By signing this receipt the lender indicates agreement with the conditions as stated on the
loan agreement form.

378

THE LOCAL HISTORY MUSEUMS
IZINQOLOBANE ZEZOMLANDO WESIFUNDA

RECEIPT OF OBJECT(S)

Receipt No:........ 1000 ....

Date:.............

Receipt of undermentioned objects is hereby acknowledged

Presented by: .... Tel: (W)............. (H).................

Address:...

....

.... Code: ....

Capacity:................Tel: (W) ....(H).................
(e.g. authorised representative/owner)

Donors Name and Address (if different from above):..........

....   Gift ☐   Loan ☐

.... Code: ....   Purchase ☐   Assesment ☐

OBJECT/ DESCRIPTION	ACCEPTED/ REJECTED	ACC NO.
WAITING NO.:	RETURN DATE:	

Copyright Holder:...........................

Address and Telephone No.:.......................

Remarks:

I confirm that I have read/have been read to, understood and accepted the conditions stated on the reverse side hereof, these being the condition under which the Local History Museums accepts the item(s). I certify that I in the above mentioned capacity have the absolute authority to dispose thereof.

Signed by presenter: ....

ID No.:................................

Signed by official:..........................

Contact No.:............. Witnessed by:..............

MM. 47

GLENBOW
MUSEUM • ART GALLERY • LIBRARY • ARCHIVES
130–9th Avenue S.E., Calgary, Alberta, Canada T2G 0P3

RECEIPT

INWARD READ TERMS AND CONDITIONS ON BACK OF FORM ☐   OUTWARD ☐

INSTRUCTIONS:
- **If completing as a *Receipt Inward*, make certain that *terms and conditions* on back of form are read and agreed to before signing.**
- Please complete entire form, typing or printing clearly with ball point pen using block letters.
- Once form has been fully completed and terms and conditions on back of form have been read and understood (if applicable), obtain signatures of both parties at the bottom of form.
- **Distribute** copies as indicated on bottom of form.

NAME _____

ADDRESS _____

PHONE: RES. _____ BUS. _____

DELIVERED ☐   PICKED UP ☐   BY: _____

SUBMITTED FOR: GIFT ☐   PURCHASE ☐   EXAMINATION ☐   LOAN ☐   OTHER ☐ _____

INSURED BY: GLENBOW ☐   DEPOSITOR/RECEIVER ☐

THIS IS TO ACKNOWLEDGE _____'s RECEIPT OF THE FOLLOWING

NUMBER	DESCRIPTION	OWNER'S ESTIMATED VALUE

DEPOSITOR / RECEIVER:

SIGNATURE _____

NAME (PLEASE PRINT) _____

TITLE _____ DATE | YR. | MO. | DA. |

GLENBOW – ALBERTA INSTITUTE:

SIGNATURE _____

NAME (PLEASE PRINT) _____

380 TITLE _____ DATE | YR. | MO. | DA. |

DISTRIBUTION: WHITE AND CANARY – REGISTRAR   PINK – CURATORIAL   GOLDENROD – DEPOSITOR/RECEIVER

Exchange Agreement

In accordance with the authority granted to the Secretary of the Interior by the Museum Act of 1955 (16 USC, Sect. 18 [f]), and in consideration of the mutual promises set forth in this Agreement, the National Park Service and _____ (other party) enter into this agreement for the exchange of museum objects.

1. _____ (NPS Unit) hereby becomes the owner of the objects listed on the first attached inventory (Attachment 1 of this Agreement). _____ (other party) hereby becomes the owner of the objects listed on the second attached inventory (Attachment 2 of this Agreement).

2. _____ (other party) represents and warrants that he/she/they will possess clear title, free of all liens, claims, and encumbrances of any kind, to the objects listed in Attachment 1 at the time the exchange takes place. If at the time the exchange is to occur _____ (other party) is unable to present the objects listed on Attachment 1 and proof of ownership for the said objects he/she/they is/are exchanging, the National Park Service is under no obligation to complete the exchange.

3. _____ (other party) represents and warrants that the objects listed on Attachment 1 were secured in compliance with all applicable International, Federal and State laws. Documentation evidencing the source of acquisition of the objects listed on Attachment 1 will be attached to this Agreement at the time the exchange takes place (Attachment 3).

4. _____ (other party) represents and warrants that the objects listed in Attachment 1 have been authenticated and appraised in writing, at market value, by at least one objective appraiser within six months previous to the date of this agreement. Copies of the appraisals for the NPS and non-NPS items are attached to this Agreement (Attachment 4).

5. _____ (other party) represents and warrants that he/she/they is/are the sole owner(s) of all rights in the objects listed on Attachment 1. _____ (other party) hereby assigns in _____ (NPS unit) all of _____ (other party's) common law and statutory copyrights to the objects listed in Attachment 1. _____ (other party) agrees to indemnify _____ (NPS unit) against any claims, damages, losses, or expenses of any kind that _____ (NPS unit) may suffer as a result of any infringement or alleged infringement of the copyrights to _____ (NPS unit).

6. Title to the objects exchanged under this agreement shall pass when the objects have been delivered pursuant to the terms of this Agreement and the parties have inspected the objects and found them to be in a satisfactory condition and are as represented in this Agreement. Inspections of the objects shall occur on the date of delivery.

7. As provided by 41 U.S.C. §§ 22, no member of or delegate to Congress, or Resident Commissioner shall be admitted to any share or part of this Agreement or to any benefit that might arise therefrom; but this provision shall not be construed to extend this Agreement if made with a corporation for its general benefit.

8. No NPS employee or members of a NPS employee's immediate family shall be admitted to any share or part of this Agreement or to any benefits that may arise therefrom.

9. The exchange of all firearms must be in compliance with all state and local law enforcement regulations related to the acquisition of firearms. Upon consummation of this Agreement, the National Park Service shall not be liable for any action related to the use of firearms described within the Agreement.

10. The National Park Service will pay all costs of transporting and insuring the objects listed on Attachment 2 to _____.

Exchange Agreement (Continued)

11. The parties agree that the physical transfer of all objects covered by this Agreement will occur on or before _____ (date) and that time is of the essence to this Agreement. If _____ (other party) fails to deliver the objects listed on Attachment 1 to the agreed-upon place of delivery by the date given in this paragraph, the National Park Service may, at its option, terminate this Agreement, recover any objects which it may have delivered pursuant to this Agreement and sue for damages for undue delay of the performance of this Agreement or for specific performance of this Agreement. _____ (NPS unit) remedies hereunder are not exclusive and _____ (NPS unit) retains the right to pursue any and all legal remedies available to it for the breach of this Agreement.

12. Catalog information on all NPS objects incorporated under this Agreement is included by reference to the NPS catalog number listed on Attachment 2.

For the NATIONAL PARK SERVICE (Receiving):

Recommended: _____
              (Park Curator)   (Date)

Approved: _____
          (Superintendent)   (Date)

For the other PARTY

Name: _____

   Approved: _____
                                                                (Date)

   Approved: _____
                                                                (Date)

   Address: _____

            _____

            _____

   Telephone: _____   FAX: _____

PANHANDLE - PLAINS HISTORICAL MUSEUM

EXCHANGE/TRANSFER AGREEMENT

The material listed below, property of Panhandle-Plains Historical Museum, is hereby (circle one):   transfer   exchange   sale

_____

Receiving Entity   Circle: Institution   Individual

Accession Number: _____
Description:

Exchanged for:
PPHM Accession Number: _____
Description:

Attach Transfer of Title from exchanging institution or Gift Agreement from individual.

If sold, sale price: $ _____

    Method of sale: _____

    Disposition of funds: _____

Attach sales documentation to this form.

It is understood that once this document is executed, the recipient gains full ownership of the material received from Panhandle-Plains Historical Museum.

_____   _____
Authorized PPH Museum Representative   Date

_____
Title

_____   _____
Accepted by   Date

_____
Title

2401 Fourth Avenue
Canyon TX 79015

806-656-2244 •,FAX 806-656-2250
On the Campus of West Texas A&M University, a Member of The Texas A&M University System

WTAMU Box 967
Canyon TX 79016

SECURITY - FACILITIES

ACCESS AND KEY ISSUANCE AUTHORIZATION FORM

1 **ADMINISTRATIVE** (For Administration use only.)

Approval _____ _____
date

Type of access granted and/or key issuance designated. Applicant is _____
status

- [ ] Limited (check-out)
- [ ] Student (by semester)
- [ ] Supervised (volunteer)
- [ ] StaffT (defined period)
- [ ] StaffP (indefinite period)

2 **APPLICANT** (Please print legibly.)

Name _____ Assigned Division _____
Last   First   MI

Home Address _____ Tel: Home _____
Street/PO

_____ Business _____
city   state   zip

Permanent Address if different from _____ Tel # (___)
above or if Student not from Lubbock _____

SSN [ ][ ][ ] - [ ][ ] - [ ][ ][ ][ ]   Date of Birth _____/_____/_____
M / D / Y

DL# _____
state/country

3 **REQUESTER/AUTHORIZER**

Name _____ Title _____

Division _____ Tel # _____

Duration of authorization:
Begin _____ End _____
date   time   date   time

Signature _____ _____
date

4 **AREA/BUILDING** (of Access)

Key (leave blank)	Area/Building	Key (leave blank)	Area/Building

5 I, the Applicant, by my signature below indicate that I have read and understood the conditions and policies (reverse side) that apply to my being issued keys to the Museum and the responsibilities inherent in the privilege of being granted this permit, and that I will in good faith abide by said conditions and policies.

_____ _____
signature   date

384

Museum Form: OPS 1

INSTRUCTIONS

This form must be completed by the Requester/Authorizer (area supervisor, manager, or curator) and the Applicant in accordance with Museum policies governing access and key issuance. The form must then be submitted to the Associate Director for Museum Operations and Programs (Associate Director) for processing and approval prior to access or key issue. The Applicant must read the policies below.

Complete the following blocks: Applicant #2. Requester/Authorizer -# 3 & Area/Building portions of #4. <u>Leave blocks #1 & #5 blank.</u>

ACCESS AND KEY ISSUANCE POLICIES - The following policies are to insure the safety of the personnel and collections housed in the buildings and on the grounds of the Museum of Texas Tech University. Granting of access (authorization to enter a restricted area), and key issuance (control method for authorized access), is the sole prerogative and authority of the Executive Director of the Museum, in keeping with the policies of Texas Tech University, as prescribed in TTU OP 76.26. All keys to campus buildings are the property of the State of Texas, are subject to State Law and enforcement, and may not be duplicated.

I. The access and key needs of each staff, association, or faculty member, student, associate, or volunteer will be assessed by the Executive Director prior to access being granted and/or keys issued. Normally, access and/or key permits will be only for those areas to which the person is assigned during regular working hours, and will not include after-hour access. After-hour security access may only be granted by the Executive Director, and only in exceptional circumstances. Types of access/issue are: Limited, Student, Supervised, StaffT, and StaffP.

II. The supervisor, manager, or curator of a storage area, collection area, laboratory, shop, exhibit area, or office may request access and/or key permits for persons under their supervision, and they are responsible for any access granted and/or keys issued at their request. Allowing access automatically places responsibility on the requesting area supervisor, manager, or curator for any actions of the person(s) granted access and/or keys.

III. Key requests, issuance, turn-in, and safe storage are the delegated responsibility of the Associate Director. Requests by staff, association, or faculty members for access and/or key issuance, key turn-in, and access approval/disapproval will be processed through that office, where a permanent record will be maintained.

IV. <u>Transferring or loaning of keys is prohibited.</u> Persons who transfer or loan keys are responsible for the actions of the borrower and may forfeit all subsequent access and/or key permits, be charged for re-keying costs, face immediate termination of access and/or key permits, and, <u>in the case of students and former students, have transcripts withheld and/or be denied future registration applications.</u>

V. Volunteers and nonemployed students will not normally be issued keys. Limited access of a specified duration may be granted at the written request of a staff, association, or faculty member, and only if deemed in the best interests of the institution.

VI. Staff, association, or faculty members, students, research associates, or volunteers may not allow access to any area of the Museum other than that to which they are assigned. Anyone allowing access automatically assumes liability for any actions of the person or persons granted entry.

VII. Upon specific instructions from the Executive Director or the Associate Director, Security personnel may allow access to a Museum area. Sign-in and -out procedures will be observed.

VIII. Campus maintenance or contracted personnel must sign-in and -out with Security at the front desk of the building accessed.

IX. All Supervised access permits will be on file with the Security Division prior to admittance to a specified area. Sign-in and -out will be observed by those persons granted supervised access to an area of the Museum.

X. Any unidentified person or person(s) known to be without permission to enter a restricted area of the Museum, should immediately be reported to the Security Division. Determination of authorization, or the need for removal of persons from restricted areas, is a function of the Security Division. Difficulty in removing a person, clearly without authorization, from a restricted area may require the presence of the University Police Department.

XI. Other than public access doors, all unattended doors of ingress/egress/passage to any Museum area will remain locked and be key-accessed only. <u>Doors may not be blocked open</u> or left unlocked unless someone, normally a staff member, is in attendance.

XII. All keys must be returned to the Associate Director's office or be returned in a manner specified by that office, if the following conditions exist: 1) Upon the order of the Executive Director; 2) termination of employment; 3) completion of course work; or 4) termination of temporary access. Extensions of access and key permits may be granted if justified in writing by a Requester/Authorizer. It is their responsibility to aid in insuring the timely return of keys.

XIII. Keys should be deposited with the Associate Director for holding if a leave of absence is planned. If appropriate, those keys will be returned to the depositor upon return to duties.

XIV. <u>Failure to return keys may result in actions being taken by University or State Police for recovery,</u> in accordance with University and State regulations.

XV. Failure of a Requester/Authorizer to aid in the timely return of keys may result in the Executive Director's disapproval of subsequent requests for access and/or key permits. Difficulties involving key returns may result in the assessing of a deposit for the issuing of subsequent keys, as deemed appropriate by the Director. Students who fail to return keys may have their transcripts withheld and/or subsequent registration denied.

XVI. Loss or theft of keys should be reported immediately to the Administration office. Re-keying and issuing of new keys will be through the Associate Director's office. Loss due to negligence may result in the assessment of re-keying costs and/or a deposit for replacement keys, as deemed appropriate by the Executive Director.

XVII. The making or issuing of copies of keys to any portion of the Museum is solely by authority of the Executive Director. Copying and issuing of keys is through the Office of the Associate Director. <u>The making or issuing of keys outside proper channels may result in disapproval of subsequent requests, and/or the immediate termination of access and/or key issue permits.</u>

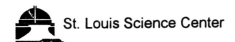 St. Louis Science Center

PROPERTY REMOVAL PASS

NAME_____ DEPT/EXT. _____ DATE/TIME _____

QUANTITY   ITEM   LOCATION (Removed From)

_____ _____   _____

_____ _____   _____

_____ _____   _____

Total number of items removed_____ [ ] Permanent   [ ] Temporary   Date to be returned by_____

_____

Leadership Approval (signature)   Date

- -

Protection Services Department Use

Removal Checked By _____ Date _____ Time _____

Return Checked By _____ Date _____ Time _____

Follow-Up needed _____

_____

Supervisor _____ Date _____

Distribution: White-Protection Services, Yellow-Department, Pink-Employee

rev. 1/95, S. Miskel   c:\pm5\othrdept\baremove.pm5

Property Removal Pass

Pass to be completed in two copies and presented to Security whenever an employee, visitor or contractor removes personal, company or other property that is not itemized on authorized documents.

TO BE FILLED OUT BY SECURITY PERSONNEL

_____   _____
DATE OUT   DATE RETURNED

NAME   DEPARTMENT   DATE

DESCRIPTION OF PROPERTY _____

_____

_____

_____

SIGNATURE OF DEPARTMENT HEAD   SIGNATURE OF SECURITY GUARD AT EXIT

_____ PERSONAL PROPERTY   _____ OTHER (EXPLAIN)
_____ COMPANY PROPERTY   _____
_____ COMPANY PROPERTY ON LOAN

All Material Subject to Inspection by Security Personnel

BUFFALO MUSEUM of SCIENCE

LAFAYETTE NATURAL HISTORY MUSEUM

COLLECTION STORAGE FACILITY ACCESS RECORD • Postal Square Primary (Large)Room

DAY & DATE	TIME IN	LNHM PERSONNEL	OTHER ENTRANT(S)	SPECIFIC REASON(S) FOR ENTRY	TIME OUT

WITTE MUSEUM DELIVERY/ACCEPTANCE LOG

DATE	TIME	TO	FROM	REC'D BY	TYPE*	NOTIFICATION Date	Time	By	Date	Time	By	PICKED UP BY (Signature)	DATE	TIME

*TYPE: L = LETTER   E = LG ENVELOPE   P = PACKAGE   FX/L = FEDERAL EXPRESS LETTER   FX/P = FEDERAL EXPRESS PACKAGE

(FX = REFERS TO ALL OVERNIGHT SERVICES/AIRBORNE ETC.)

388

BOMB THREAT CARD

WHERE IS THE BOMB?_____

_____

WHEN WILL IT GO OFF?_____

_____

HOW MUCH TIME IS LEFT?_____

_____

WHAT KIND OF BOMB IS IT?_____

_____

_____

WHAT DOES THE BOMB LOOK LIKE?_____

_____

If the building is occupied, inform the caller that the explosion will cause death and injury.

WHY IS THE BUILDING BEING BOMBED?_____

_____

HOW DO YOU KNOW ABOUT THE BOMB?_____

_____

_____

WHY ARE YOU CALLING?_____

_____

WHAT IS YOUR NAME?_____

ADDRESS?_____

VOICE CHARACTERISTICS

VOICE CHARACTERISTICS		SPEECH	
LOUD	RASPY	FAST	SLOW
SOFT	PLEASANT	STUTTER	DISTINCT
DEEP	NASAL	SLURRED	DISTORTED
HIGH	INTOXICATED		

LANGUAGE		ACCENT	
POOR	OBSCENE	LOCAL_____	
FAIR	PROFANE	FOREIGN_____	
GOOD	ABUSIVE	RACIAL_____	

(Back of Form)

MANNER

CALM	RATIONAL	IRRATIONAL
COHERENT	DELIBERATE	INCOHERENT
LAUGHING	ANGRY	EMOTIONAL
SERIOUS		

BACKGROUND NOISES

OFFICE MACHINES	FACTORY MACHINES
TRAINS	PLANES
ANIMALS	VOICES
QUIET	UNDETERMINED
MUSIC	PARTY NOISES
TRAFFIC	

☞ Non-University Police employees: Write out the caller's message in its entirety as accurately as possible; then contact the University Police immediately at extension 8-2222.

☞ University Police employees: Write out the message in its entirety and contact the Watch Commander or the ranking University Police officer.

☞ All University employees: Talk to no one concerning the incident other than your supervisors and the University Police.

* *

NAME_____

DEPARTMENT_____ PHONE_____

DATE_____ TIME_____

SIGNATURE_____

ADDITIONAL DETAILS: _____

_____

_____

_____

_____

_____

_____

_____

_____

_____

ANNISTON MUSEUM OF NATURAL HISTORY

Bomb Threat Report

Date of Call: _____ Time: _____

Exact words of caller: _____

_____

_____

_____

_____

Do not interrupt the caller except to ask the following questions:

When is the bomb going to explode? _____

Where is the bomb right now? _____

What kind of bomb is it? _____

What does it look like? _____

Where are you calling from? _____

Why did you place the bomb? _____

As soon as the caller hangs up, report immediately to the Building & Grounds Supervisor or Director. Police will be notified. Following notification, fill in the following information and file this report report with the Business Manager:

1. Did caller appear to be familiar with building?

_____ Yes   _____ No   _____ Could not tell

2. Voice characteristics of caller:

_____ Male _____ High Pitch _____ Soft _____ Old _____ Familiar

_____ Female _____ Raspy _____ Deep _____ Young _____ Loud

_____ Intoxicated _____ Pleasant _____ Middle Age

3. Speech:

_____ Fast _____ Stutter _____ Slow _____ Nasal _____ Distinct

_____ Slurred _____ Distorted _____ Other

4. Language:

_____ Excellent _____ Foul _____ Poor _____ Good _____ Other

5. Accent:

_____ Local   _____ Foreign   _____ Other

(Report continued on other side)

Bomb Threat Report (continued)

6.   **Manner:**

_____ Calm _____ Rational _____ Coherent _____ Deliberate

_____ Laughing _____ Righteous _____ Angry _____ Irrational

_____ Incoherent _____ Emotional

7.   **Background Noises:**

_____ Office Machines _____ Factory Machines _____ Bedlam

_____ Animals _____ Quiet _____ Mixed _____ Street Traffic

_____ Airplanes _____ Trains _____ Voices _____ Music

_____ Party Atmosphere

8.   **Any other information that you feel might be helpful to the Police:**

_____

_____

_____

_____

Name of Person Receiving Call   **Date**

TECHNICAL
information
SERVICE

Revised

Standard Facility Report

1998

American Association of Museums
Registrars Committee of the American
Association of Museums
Professional Practice Series

The Standard Facility Report – Revised Edition

What is a Standard Facility Report and how is it used?

A facility report is a document which provides detailed information about an institution's physical plant and its policies and procedures related to areas such as security, handling and environmental controls. Facility reports are generally used by lenders and insurance personnel to determine if an institution has the ability to safely borrow, ship, handle, secure and install objects requested for loan.

Although it is unknown when or by whom facility reports first came into use, as professional standards were refined in the 1980s, their use gained momentum. Many museums devised their own forms, frequently patching together information from other institutions. As a result, content varied widely and it was difficult to retrieve consistent information. Early versions were time-consuming to complete and each variant required additional research. In 1988, the Registrars Committee adopted a standard facility report to provide a uniform format for collecting and assessing information. This unprecedented document was widely adopted and today the review of a borrowing institution's *Standard Facility Report* (SFR) is considered a basic requirement in evaluating loan requests.

As its use spread, additional ways of using the *Report* were discovered. Its comprehensive nature makes it a useful self-assessment tool and it has proved to be helpful in determining priorities for capital improvements. Engineers and architects use the form to understand some of the physical requirements of museum buildings. Some institutions use it in training new staff members because it so effectively conveys the complexity of conditions related to lending and gives an overview of museums' standards of care.

Why were revisions needed and how were they undertaken?

After six years of use, countless photocopied versions and a number of innovations in the field, it was evident that the document needed to be produced on disk. In 1994, RC-AAM initiated a review process of the *Report*. Suggestions for improvement were solicited nationally through professional newsletters and at the annual meeting of the American Association of Museums. The recommendations were tabulated and forwarded to readers from museums of various sizes and disciplines, and to representatives of the loss-prevention industry. This revision also contains a glossary of technical terms used in the document. It will benefit experienced and new users alike and will further simplify assessing the report's contents.

How to use the SFR

Successful use of facility reports relies on the integrity of the party supplying the information and the common sense of the party reviewing the information. If a borrowing institution provides inaccurate information, a loan could be inappropriately approved, possibly jeopardizing the condition of a collection item. Conversely, if data provided in a facility report are too narrowly interpreted, the approval of an important loan to an exhibition could be compromised. Ideally, members of various departments (e.g., registration, security, curatorial, facility management) should collaborate to complete the *Report*. It is important to note that not all questions in the *SFR* will be relevant to every institution or to each type of loan.

More to be done

Many colleagues have inquired about the development of a shortened version of the *SFR* which they believe would be better suited for small institutions or as a preliminary overview of an institution's strengths and weaknesses. While this idea has merit, it must be noted that the shortened version provided in the original Report was not widely used. Also, since our profession and the standards of care we provide to our collections have become more sophisticated, it is unlikely that an abbreviated version would meet the majority's needs.

Other colleagues have acknowledged the need for a document specifically for evaluating foreign loan venues. The problems identified by the sub-committee that produced the original document – inconsistent terminology and different standards of museum care in other countries – still exist and are not addressed in the scope of this revision. Work has begun on a French version of the SFR and I am confident that it will be produced in the next several years. Although not specifically designed for this purpose, this revised edition can be adapted for assessing foreign institutions.

Revised Standard Facility Report
Table of Contents

STANDARD FACILITY REPORT -- UNITED STATES
Registrars Committee of the American Association of Museums
Adopted 1998

Borrowing Institution Profile

Name of Borrowing Institution/Loan Venue	
Contact Person	
Title	
Mailing Address	
Street Address	
Shipping Address	
Telephone Number	
Fax Number	
E-mail Address	
World Wide Web URL	
Purpose of Loan/ Exhibition Title	
Dates at Loan Venue	

1

HOW TO ORDER

AAM accepts purchase orders from **U.S. institutions only.** A signed letter on official institutional stationery also serves as a purchase order. Institutional orders must include a current institutional AAM membership number to obtain member discounts. Individual membership numbers will not be billed. Institutional orders are billed net 30 days.

All other orders MUST be prepaid. AAM accepts checks payable in U.S. dollars, MasterCard, and VISA. Orders should include the following: AAM membership number, shipping address, order number, title, quantity, price, shipping method, shipping and handling charge, and payment. Please include current membership number on all orders to receive member prices. Individual membership is nontransferable.

By Mail: Please use the order form provided and mail with payment or institutional purchase order to American Association of Museums, Department 4002, Washington, DC 20042-4002.

By Phone: Call 202/289-9127 to place credit card orders only. Please complete the order form provided to organize your order before you call. Collect calls cannot be accepted.

By Fax Machine: Dial 202/289-6578 to place an order with a credit card or institutional purchase order.

Via the Internet: You can visit AAM's Web site and on-line bookstore at http://www.aam-us.org. Fill in the order form, print it, and fax or mail it to AAM as listed above.

Via E-mail: Send your name, telephone number, a list of titles and quantities desired, shipping address, and Visa/Mastercard or institutional purchase order number to: bookstore@aam-us.org, and we will process your order.

International Orders (including Canada and Mexico)

Payment MUST accompany all international orders. Payments can be made by MasterCard, VISA, or by a check in U.S. dollars drawn on a U.S. bank. This check must include the printed A.B.A. bank code on the bottom of the check. A wire transfer may be made directly to AAM's bank:

> Crestar Bank, N.A..
> 1445 New York Ave. N.W.
> Washington, DC 20005
> Bank Code: 05440005222
> AAM Account #206-554-761

Please send a copy of the wire transfer receipt, date of the wire, and the order form provided listing the titles ordered. If payment is not made by any of these methods, include a $25 bank handling and processing fee. Orders not following these guidelines will be returned.

Shipping and Handling

Allow 21 business days for U.S. delivery. Orders delivered in the U.S. are shipped by UPS or first class mail. Please supply a street address for UPS delivery. Rural routes and P.O. boxes will be shipped via first class mail. When requesting UPS delivery, Alaska, Hawaii, and Puerto Rico residents must use UPS 2nd Day delivery. International orders, including Canada and Mexico, will be sent via international surface or air mail.

Note: Order from this catalogue through March 1999. Prices, policies, and availability subject to change without notice.

Please include appropriate shipping and handling charges from the chart below:

Orders	United States		International	
	UPS or 1st class mail	2nd day UPS*	Surface	Air Mail
Up to $10	$4	$12	$8	$20
$10.01–$49.99	$6	$16	$10	$25
$50–$99.99	$8	$20	$12	$30
Over $100	10% (of total order)	20%	15% (of total order)	30%

*When requesting UPS, Alaska, Hawaii, and Puerto Rico residents must use UPS 2nd day delivery.

Quantity Discount

Specially marked titles are available at the following discount schedule:

10–24 copies	15%
25–49 copies	20%
50–99 copies	25%
100 or more copies	30%

Titles cannot be mixed for discount. Volume discounts apply to member prices for AAM members and regular prices for non-members.

Sales Tax

All orders delivered within the District of Columbia are subject to 5.75% sales tax on books and shipping. Institutions exempt from District of Columbia sales tax must provide a copy of their D.C. sales tax exempt certificate with their order.

Claims and Returns

Claims for shorts, misshipments, or damaged books must be made to the bookstore manager within 30 days of receipt of shipment. Damaged books will be replaced, and discrepancies will be corrected. **Not responsible for replacement of any orders shipped surface mail.**

Authorized returns must be accompanied by a copy of our invoice. **Bookstores please note:** Authorization for return will not be given for overstocks. Books returned without prior authorization or without our invoice will be mailed back to the customer at the customer's expense. No credit or refunds. Audio and video tapes cannot be returned.

Back Orders

Orders for titles not yet published or temporarily out of stock will be automatically placed on back order. Written requests to cancel back orders may be sent to:

> American Association of Museums
> Attn: Back Order Department
> 1575 Eye St. N.W., Suite 400
> Washington, DC 20005

Cancellations will be refunded the price of the publication only.

Museum & Art Gallery
of the Northern Territory

GPO Box 4646 Darwin NT 0801
Conacher Street Bullocky Point Darwin NT 0820 AUSTRALIA
Telephone: (08) 8999 8201   Facsimile: (08) 8999 8289   ISD: 61-8-8999 8201

FACILITIES REPORT FOR BORROWING INSTITUTIONS

To assist us in assessing your request to borrow material from our Collections or to give us information about your display facilities for travelling exhibitions, please complete the following and forward to the Registrar, Museum and Art Gallery of the Northern Territory.

Name of Borrower: ....
(Please Note: this organisation or individual must be able and willing to assume LEGAL RESPONSIBILITY for the loan material).

Postal Address: ....

....

Street Address: ....

....

Telephone: ....   Facsimile: ....

If legal responsibility is to be vested in an organisation, please provide the full name and position of the EXECUTIVE OFFICER who is empowered by that organisation to commit it to such legal responsibility for material on loan.

Name: ....

Position: ....

Telephone: ....   Facsimile: ....

Contact for this application: ....

Telephone: ....   Facsimile: ....

Alternative Contact: ....

Telephone: ....   Facsimile: ....

397

General Access

Do you have a loading dock? YES / NO

If yes, is it undercover? YES / NO

What is the maximum height of vehicle that can be accommodated? ....

Is there a raised dock? YES / NO   Height of dock: ....

What is the maximum size of delivery access door? .... h. x .... w. mm.

If there is no loading dock, where and how are exhibition crates, etc., unloaded?

....

....

What loading equipment do you have?
- ☐ Gantry
- ☐ Fork Lift
- ☐ Dollies
- ☐ Trollies
- ☐ Other (please specify): ....

....

How many staff are available to unload travelling exhibitions? ....

Access to Display Area

If your building has a goods lift to access exhibition space or storage, what are the maximum dimensions it will take?
....

What is the maximum size of an artefact/packing crate that can be brought into your exhibition space by normal means?
....

Display Area

Please attach a floor plan of your display area.

What is the floor space in square meters? ....

What is the approximate weight bearing limit of floor? ....

What is the total wall length in running metres? ....

How long is the largest uninterrupted area of wall space in running metres? ....

What is the height of the highest wall? ....

What is the height of lowest wall? ....

If factors such as false ceilings, hanging systems or architectural features affect the hanging height, please provide the hanging height:

of the highest wall: ....

of the lowest wall: ....

Can works be suspended from the ceiling?   YES / NO

Display Furniture and Fittings

Do you have additional display screens or panels?   YES / NO
How are they installed?   ☐Standing   ☐Hanging

Please list the height and total running length of any additional screens or partitions:

....

....

How many lockable display cases are available for travelling exhibitions? ....

What is the maximum size of artefact that could be accommodated in your largest display case?

....

How many plinths/stands are available for travelling exhibitions? ....

Environmental Control

Is the display area airconditioned?   YES / NO
Continuous 24 hours per day?   YES / NO

If no, between what hours does it operate? ....

What is the temperature range? ....

What is the relative humidity range? ....

Are temperature and relative humidity monitored on a regular basis?   YES / NO
Please give details:

....

....

Do you have dust filters on your intake? YES / NO

State particle size: ....

Do you have activated carbon filters on your air intake? YES / NO

Lighting

What type of lighting does your display area have? ....

....

....

Does any natural daylight enter your display area? YES / NO

If your display area has natural daylight, how do you control the light falling on objects within the area?

....

....

Do you have ultraviolet filters? YES / NO

Do you have a light meter? YES / NO   Do you have a U.V. meter? YES / NO

What levels of visible and U.V. light are maintained in your display area?

....

Are these adjustable? YES / NO

Fire Protection

Please give details of your fire detection system: ....

....

....

Do you have a sprinkler system? YES / NO

What other fire protection equipment do you have? ....

....

....

Do you have an alarm system connected to the Fire Department? YES / NO

Does your organisation have a disaster plan that incorporates loan or temporary exhibition material?   YES / NO

Security

Do you have security staff on duty during opening hours?   YES / NO
Do you have security staff on duty after hours?   YES / NO

Are security staffing levels sufficient to keep the display area and all exits from this area under constant visual surveillance?   YES / NO

Are all external doors fitted with alarms?   YES / NO

Do you have any other electronic security devices?   YES / NO

Please give details: ....

....

....

Is the building patrolled externally after hours?   YES / NO

Pest Control

Is your display area monitored on a regular basis for pest activity?   YES / NO

Is the display or storage area subject to any fumigation?   YES / NO

If yes, please give details: ....

....

....

Insurance

The Museum and Art Gallery of the Northern Territory may require a summary of your insurance policy .
Do you have an all-risk museum coverage on a wall to wall basis for material owned or borrowed?   YES / NO

What is your limit of liability for property of others in you care, custody or control? ....

Have you had damages or losses of property on loan from others in the past three years?   YES / NO

If yes, please give details: ....

....

Artefact Care and Handling

Do you have specially trained staff to pack and handle artefacts?   YES / NO

If no, who undertakes the packing, installation or handling of this material? ....

....

Do you have a trained conservator on staff?   YES / NO

If no, who usually undertakes condition reporting of incoming objects and exhibitions?

....

Do you have access to professional conservation services?   YES / NO

Do you have a room specifically for unpacking/repacking?   YES / NO

If yes, does this room have the same environmental conditions as your display area?
                                                                                                        YES / NO
If no, please give details: ....

....

Storage

Do you have a room or area specifically for storing packing crates and materials?
                                                                                                        YES / NO
If yes, does this room or area have the same environmental conditions as your display area?
                                                                                                        YES / NO

If no, please give details: ....

....

Do you have locked and alarmed facilities for the storage of objects?   YES / NO

Is access to storage areas controlled?   YES / NO

Does your object store have the same environmental conditions as your display area?
                                                                                                        YES / NO
If no, please give details: ....

....

Does your object store have the same fire protection facilities as your display area?
                                                                                                        YES / NO
If no, please give details: ....

....
Please forward the completed form to the Registrar, MAGNT. Thankyou for your assistance.

SECURITY DEPARTMENT / CONTROL CENTER REPORT

NAMES:_____ _____	DAY / DATE: _____/_____	SHIFT: _____

CHECK OFF ITEM(S)	( ) YES / ( ) NO	COMMENTS
1. Are all cameras and monitors operational?	1. ( ) YES / ( ) NO	
2. Are both Honeywell systems operational?	2. ( ) YES / ( ) NO	
3. Are all printers operational?	3. ( ) YES / ( ) NO	
4. Are the following items present: a. Control Center Manual b. Fire & Emergency Manual c. Pass-On Book d. Memo Book e. Absentee Book	4. ( ) YES / ( ) NO a. ( ) YES / ( ) NO b. ( ) YES / ( ) NO c. ( ) YES / ( ) NO d. ( ) YES / ( ) NO e. ( ) YES / ( ) NO	
5. Is the Scantrack present?	5. ( ) YES / ( ) NO	
6. Is the Paging system on?	6. ( ) YES / ( ) NO	
7. Is the Engineer's radio present and turned on?	7. ( ) YES / ( ) NO	
8. Are all Security radios accountable for?	8. ( ) YES / ( ) NO	
9. Review the Pass-On & Memo Books for new information.	9. ( ) YES / ( ) NO	
10. Is the VCR operational and recording?	10. ( ) YES / ( ) NO	
11. Is the Ademco Security system operational?	11. ( ) YES / ( ) NO	
12. Are both Fire Alarm systems operational?	12. ( ) YES / ( ) NO	
13. Is the emergency Key Box sealed and secured?	13. ( ) YES / ( ) NO	
14. Is the HIRSH panel box secured?	14. ( ) YES / ( ) NO	
15. Is the External Intercom system operational?	15. ( ) YES / ( ) NO	
16. Are the phones operational?	16. ( ) YES / ( ) NO	
17. Is the Master Key cabinet secured?	17. ( ) YES / ( ) NO	

FIRE		DESCRIBE PROBLEM & LOCATION
	FIRE ALARM	
	SMOKE	
	ACTUAL FIRE	
SAFETY HAZARDS		**DESCRIBE PROBLEM & LOCATION**
	WATER	
	ELECTRICAL	
	TRIPPING HAZARD	
	EQUIPMENT HAZARD	
SECURITY ALARMS		**DESCRIBE PROBLEM & LOCATION**
	ALARM DEVICE MALFUNCTION	
	ALARM PANEL MALFUNCTION	
	HONEYWELL	
	ACTUAL UNAUTHORIZED ENTRY OR ATTEMPTED ENTRY	
	OUTSIDE BUILDING SECURITY PROBLEM	
	OTHER SECURITY EQUIPMENT PROBLEM	
PROBLEMS WITH EQUIPMENT		**DESCRIBE PROBLEM & LOCATION**
	ELECTRICAL PROBLEM	
	POWER FAILURE	
	NATURAL GAS LEAK	
	WATER FLOW OR LEAK	

UNIVERSITY OF KANSAS ALCOHOLIC BEVERAGE REQUEST

TO: David E. Shulenburger   Date:_____
        Provost

FROM:_____   Phone #:_____

_____   Signature:_____

1. Sponsoring organization:_____

2. Date of event: _____   Day of week: _____

    Time of event: _____   Time of beverage service: _____

3. Purpose of event (include specific information about how the event relates to official business and/or fund raising):

_____

4. Location, including room #: _____

5. Expected attendance: _____

6. Alcoholic beverage(s) to be served: _____

7. Other beverage(s) to be served: _____

8. Should the University police be notified of this event?   No _____   Yes _____

    If yes, please give reason: _____

9. Person responsible for enforcing these requirements:

    a. That no alcoholic beverages <u>other than those served by the staff of the Kansas Union will enter</u> the designated area.
    b. That no alcoholic beverages are carried outside the area designated for beverage service.

Signature:_____Title:_____

Acknowledged:_____
Name and title of person responsible for approving location named above   Date

Acknowledged:_____
James A. Long, Director, Kansas and Burge Unions   Date

Recommended/
Not Recommended:_____
David E. Shulenburger, Provost   Date

Approved/
Disapproved:_____
Robert E. Hemenway, Chancellor   Date   (Rev. 9/97)

9/3/97

REGULATIONS FOR THE USE OF ALCOHOLIC LIQUOR AT UNIVERSITY EVENTS

Liquor may be served only at events related to legitimate University functions held in Allen Field House, Anschutz Sports Pavilion, the Art and Design Gallery, Hall Center for the Humanities (Watkins Home), James Naismith Society Room (Athletic Complex Expansion), the Kansas and Burge Unions, Lied Center, Lippincott Hall, Murphy Hall, the Museum of Natural History, Regents Center (designated areas), Spencer Museum of Art, Spooner Hall, or Summerfield Hall (School of Business Placement Center). Observe these guidelines.

A. No liquor sale is permitted.

B. All service will comply with the Kansas Liquor Control Act. Alcoholic liquor includes all alcohol-containing beverages except those defined as "cereal malt beverages."

C. The Chancellor must approve all liquor services. The Provost will recommend to the Chancellor whether approval is warranted. Those wishing to serve liquor must submit to the Provost a plan before making any announcement, in no case less than two weeks before the event.

D. The group hosting the event must provide the liquor, unused portions of which belong to the group and must be removed from University property after the event.

E. Whenever liquor is served, nonalcoholic beverages and food must also be provided.

F. The Kansas and Burge Unions exclusively will cater liquor on campus and control its dispensing, providing all necessary qualified personnel. The Union may furnish, for a fee, any setups or other services. As caterer, the Union will follow these definitions and regulations:

 1. Events mean prearranged functions not advertised to the public and limited to members of the sponsoring group and guests. Members are the basic makeup of the sponsor; guests are members' spouses and invited personal friends.

 2. The sponsor and the Union will determine the length of pre-dinner liquor service. One to one and a half hours are advised.

 3. The Union will designate those areas in approved buildings where liquor can be served and patrons controlled.

 4. No liquor other than that served by Union staff will be dispensed.

 5. Members and guests may not carry alcoholic beverages outside the area where they are being served.

 6. Union staff will refuse liquor service to anyone under the age of 21 or appearing to be intoxicated.

G. Alcoholic liquor service shall be available from 10:30 a.m. until midnight daily.

(This is a condensed version of the University's policy on serving liquor on campus. The full policy is available from the offices of the Provost or the University General Counsel.)

9/3/97

NELSON-ATKINS MUSEUM OF ART
SECURITY DEPARTMENT

GENERAL INCIDENT REPORT   PAGE___OF___PAGES

TYPE OF INCIDENT	INCIDENT REPORT NUMBER
( )DISTURBANCE ( )FIRE/SMOKE ( )INJURY ( )GENERAL INFO. ( )HAZARDOUS ( )ILLNESS ( )ART DAMAGE ( )PROPERTY DAMAGE ( )CRIMINAL OFFENSE	

DATE OF INCIDENT	TIME OF OCCURRENCE	DATE REPORTED	TIME REPORTED

LOCATION OF INCIDENT:

WITNESS	DEPT. / POST # / ADDRESS	PHONE #
1.		( )
2.		( )
3.		( )

SUBJECT INFORMATION:	N.A.M.A. INFORMATION:

HOME ADDRESS:	HOME PHONE #:
_____ STREET / CITY / STATE / ZIP CODE	( )_____

WORK / SCHOOL ADDRESS:	2nd. PHONE #:
_____ STREET / CITY / STATE / ZIP CODE	( )_____

RACE	SEX	DATE OF BIRTH	Height	Weight	Hair Color	Eye Color
	( )MALE ( )FEMALE					

CLOTHING DESCRIPTION	DETAILS
( ) High Heels	( )Eye Glasses ( )Dark Glasses / Shades ( )Bald ( )Short Hair ( )Long Hair ( )Facial Hair:_____ ( )Scar(s) ( )Other:_____

407

GENERAL INCIDENT REPORT   PAGE___OF___PAGES

DESCRIPTION OF DAMAGED OR MISSING PROPERTY:

KCPD CALLED	KCFD CALLED	AMBULANCE CALLED
( ) YES / ( ) NO	( ) YES / ( ) NO	( ) YES / ( ) NO
OFFICER'S NAME / BADGE NUMBER		AGENCY'S REPORT NUMBER
/		( ) K.C.P.D. #:_____ ( ) K.C.F.D. #:_____ ( ) AMBULANCE #:

FACTS AND DETAILS:

REPORTING PERSON'S SIGNATURE	SECURITY SUPERVISOR'S SIGNATURE
ASST. SECURITY MANAGER'S SIGNATURE	SECURITY MANAGER'S SIGNATURE

COPIES SENT TO
( ) DIRECTOR   ( ) DIR. OF FINANCE & OPERATIONS   ( ) DEPARTMENT:
( ) CURATOR: ( ) CONSERVATION ( ) REGISTRAR ( ) PUBLIC RELATIONS
( ) ADMIN. COLLECTIONS MGM'T. & SPEC. EXH.   ( ) BUILDING SUPERINTENDENT
( ) HUMAN RESOURCES   ( ) INSURANCE COMPANY   ( ) EDUCATION

St. Louis Science Center
The Playground For Your Head

Security Department
Daily Activity Report

This report reflects the key actions performed by this department daily. A day, for the purpose of this report, is between 0600 the first day and 0559 the following day. This report is to be completed by Post 1 officer prior to the end of each day.

The information is transferred by supervisors to the Monthly Activity Report which is submitted to Facility Operations Director at the conclusion of each calendar month.

Vehicle Control

Tags issued _____   Tickets issued _____
Vehicle accidents _____   Vehicle towed _____

Building Passes

Visitor _____   Visitor w/Escort _____
Contractor _____   Temporary Staff _____

Accidents and Incidents

Visitor accident/illness _____   Employee accident/illness _____
Incident _____   Persons detained _____
Persons ejected _____   Disturbance _____
Unruly groups _____   Bomb threats _____
Power failure _____   Water leaks _____
Unsecured - area _____   Security Violation _____
Safety Violation _____

Alarms (Response Required)

Motion Detector _____   Doors _____
Send help _____   Glass break _____
After hrs. Response _____   Fire alarm actual _____
Fire alarm false _____   Evacuation drill F.P. _____
Evacuation drill 5050 _____   Fire alarmTest _____
Fire alarm Training _____

Services Provided

Keys issued (Daily) _____   Keys issued (Permanent) _____
Access card (Daily) _____   Access card (Permanent) _____
Property Passes _____   Lost & Found (+$5.00) _____
Lost children _____   Cash escort _____
Escorts _____   Vehicle lockouts _____
Vehicle jump-starts _____   Other Vehicle Assist. _____
 Lock/unlock doors _____   Safety/Energy Notices _____

Attendance & Revenue

Days Attendance _____   Revenue _____

FORT WORTH MUSEUM OF SCIENCE AND HISTORY

SECURITY DEPARTMENT REPORT FORMS

date [Wednesday, February 25, 1998]

hour [ ]

name [ ]

street # [ ]

city [ ]

state [ ]

phone [ ]

male ☐   staff ☐

female ☐   visitor ☐

       other ☐

approximate age [ ]

INJURY ☐

ILLNESS ☐

medical assistance requested ☐

requested by [ ]

provided by [ ]

location where injury occurred

[ ]

transported to medical facility ☐

museum nurse notified ☐

INCIDENT/
COMPLAINT ☐

ALARM ☐

fire/smoke ☐

intrusion ☐

holdup ☐

means of notification

[ ]

FWPD respond ☐

FWFD respond ☐

FWMSH notified ☐

VEHICLE ☐

staff member(s) responding [ ]

situation narrative

[ ]

Signature [ ]   cc: [ ]

410

Homestead Museum

Incident Report for Theft, Loss, or Damage

Use this form to report any property theft, loss, or damage exceeding $25.00. Reports should be made within 24 hours of knowledge. Report significant personal injury or illness separately.

Type: ☐ Theft/Loss   ☐ Damage   ☐ Other:_____

Description of theft, loss, or damage

Date and time of incident:	☐ estimate ☐ unknown
Specific object, building, or site affected *(e.g., window on northeast side of Workman House)*:	
Value of lost or damaged object(s): $	☐ estimate ☐ unknown
Location where incident occurred or began:	
Activity being performed, if applicable *(e.g., painting ceiling, guiding tours, listening to concert)*:	
Equipment, materials and chemicals in use *(e.g., ladder, paint can, brush, drop cloths)*:	

How theft, loss, or damage occurred, if known. Describe sequence of events, specifying object or activity which directly produced the theft, loss, or damage. Use separate sheet if necessary.

☐ unknown

Resulting health and safety hazards:	☐ serious	☐ minor	☐ none	☐ unknown
Resulting security concerns:	☐ serious	☐ minor	☐ none	☐ unknown

Suspect or Person Responsible   ☐ none   ☐ unknown

Name:	Phone number:
Home address:	
Description:	

Victim or Owner   ☐ none   ☐ unknown

Name:	Phone number:
Home address:	

Witness   ☐ none   ☐ unknown

Name:	Phone number:
Home address:	

Staff response

Action taken:	
Name:	Date:

Supervisor's or Director's Review

Signature:	Date:

Homestead Museum

Incident Report for Injury or Illness

Use this form to report all personal injuries requiring medical treatment beyond minor first aid or illnesses that result in recuperation beyond the date of the incident. Reports should be made within 24 hours of knowledge. Report significant property theft, loss, or damage separately.

Type: ☐ Injury ☐ Illness ☐ Other:_____

Injured or ill person ☐ unknown

Name:	Phone number:
Home address:	
Gender: ☐ male ☐ female	Date of birth:

Description of injury or illness

Date and time of injury/illness:	a.m. / p.m.

Specific injury/illness and part of body affected *(e.g., second degree burns on right arm)*:

Location where incident occurred or began:

Specific activity being performed *(e.g., painting ceiling, guiding tours, listening to concert)*:

Equipment, materials, and chemicals in use when event occurred *(e.g., ladder, paint can, brush, drop cloths)*:

How injury/illness occurred. Describe sequence of events, specifying object or activity which directly produced the injury/illness. Use separate sheet if necessary.

Witness ☐ none ☐ unknown

Name:	Phone number:
Home address:	

Staff response

Action taken:	
Name:	Date:

Supervisor's or Director's Review

Signature:	Date:

INCDREPT.DOC 3/8/96

EMPLOYEE COUNSELING AND CRITICAL INCIDENT REPORT

EMPLOYEE'S NAME:_____

SUPERVISOR'S COMMENTS: Describe the problem; include dates and times. State the policy or procedure that has been violated. Describe the disciplinary action (warning, probation, suspension). Describe the consequences that could occur if the problem is not corrected.

The above named security officer is being counseled for excessive tardiness during the preceding thirty (30) day period from (date)_____ to (date)_____. The security officer was tardy a total of _____ times (dates and amounts of tardiness are listed below) during this period. This conduct cannot be tolerated since there is so little time after employee clocks in to assign posts, conduct inventory of works of arts, and to get security officers to their assigned post by the time the museum opens. This activity is in direct violation of the security department's policy on tardiness. This behavior reflects a lack of commitment to your job and the inability to follow orders. This is your _____ counseling for excessive tardiness. If this pattern of behavior continues, you should expect the following consequences to occur in the order stated: _____ more written counseling(s) followed by a two-day suspension without pay, followed by termination.

DATES	TIME
_____	_____
_____	_____
_____	_____
_____	_____
_____	_____

EMPLOYEE'S COMMENTS: The employee may enter comments here or use additional paper, if necessary. The employee must sign the form to acknowledge receipt of this information; the signature does not necessarily indicate agreement.

_____   _____
SUPERVISOR'S SIGNATURE   **DATE**

_____   _____
EMPLOYEE'S SIGNATURE   **DATE**

Weddings
At The
Village

Reservation Form

Black Creek Pioneer Village
1000 Murray Ross Parkway
Downsview, (Toronto), Ontario
M3J 2P3

Bride's Name _____   Groom's Name _____

Bride's Address _____   Groom's Address _____

City/Town _____   City/Town _____

Province _____ Postal Code _____   Province _____ Postal Code _____

Tel: Home _____ Office _____   Tel: Home _____ Office _____

The following facilities have been requested: (Consult Price Schedule for Rental Costs)

_____ Fisherville Church   _____ Horse & Carriage/Large Vehicle   _____ Canada West Dining Room

_____ Mennonite Meeting House   _____ Horse & Carriage/Small Vehicle   _____ Half Way House Dining Room

_____ Town Hall

Wedding Date _____   Time _____

Rehearsal Date _____   Time _____

A $100.00 deposit is required to confirm a booking (cheque payable to Black Creek Village). Of this deposit, $50.00 is non-refundable; $50.00 is refundable only if written notification is received by this office more than 60 days prior to the booked wedding date.

The balance owing is required no less than 30 days prior to the wedding date. In the event of non-payment by that time the deposit will be forfeit and the "Village" will be free to take a new reservation.

Note: The cost of catering is NOT included in this agreement. To reserve the Half Way House Dining Room or the Canada West Room at Black Creek please contact the Dining Rooms Manager directly at 736-1740. To avoid disappointment call as soon as possible.

I agree to the listed costs and conditions

Name _____   Date _____

_____

Receipt of $ _____ is hereby acknowledged.   Date _____

_____

Black Creek Pioneer Village

BOOKING SHEET
for Auckland Museum Function Rooms

Name of Organiser :

Function :

Date :

Day : ☐ Mon ☐ Tues ☐ Wed ☐ Thurs ☐ Fri ☐ Sat ☐ Sun.

Booking for : ☐ Board Room   ☐ Foyer   ☐ Education Room

☐ Staff Room   ☐ Exhibition Room 1   ☐ Other _____

☐ Weird & Wonderful   ☐ Exhibition Room 2

1.   Details:

No. expected	Door	Open	Mtg. starts	Finishes
Seating : ☐ Normal ☐ Other				

2.   Security:

Underpass	Unlocked from	until
Alarm	Off from	until

3.   Special Requirements:

☐ Slide projector & remote   ☐ Pointer for slides   ☐ Overhead projector

☐ Lectern/Sound System   ☐ TV/Video   ☐ Portable screen

☐ Wall screen   ☐ Electronic whiteboard   ☐ Radio cassette

☐ Video projector   ☐ Jug of water & glasses   ☐ Photo CD player

☐ AV Projector   ☐ Flipchart   ☐ Other

4.   Catering:

None	Boiling water	Tea, instant coffee,	Coffee Urn	Other arrangements

BB's Cafe Catering :   YES/NO
(Please give details of requirements and attach your coded invoice to this booking sheet)

_____

_____

_____

Outside Caterer :   YES/NO
(Please state name, address, telephone or fax no of company)

_____

_____

5.   Charging: YES/NO
(if applicable)

Name :   Tel:

Address :   Fax:

_____

_____

☐ **File Copy**   ☐ **Althea Sargent**   ☐ **Darcy Solomon**   ☐ **BB's Cafe**

ART MUSEUM
OF SOUTHEAST TEXAS

ART MUSEUM OF SOUTHEAST TEXAS
FACILITY USE
LEASE AGREEMENT

This Lease Agreement (the "Lease") is made and entered into on this _____ day of _____, 19__, by and between the Art Museum of Southeast Texas (the "Owner"), whose mailing address is c/o Wallace Olmedo, 500 Main Street, P.O. Box 3703, Beaumont, Texas 77704 and _____ (the "Tenant"), whose mailing address is _____

_____.

For the term and upon the consideration and covenants hereinafter set forth, Owner hereby leases, lets and demises to Tenant, and Tenant hereby leases and lets from Owner: The Art Museum of Southeast
500 Main Street
Beaumont, Tx. 77704

Use of the Art Museum of Southeast Texas will take place on _____ from_____.

                                                   Date   Time of Event

Tenant shall not commit or permit to be committed any activity in or about the Leased Premises, nor use or permit the use of the Leased Premises for any purpose, which shall be detrimental or damaging to the appearance, condition or structural soundness of the Leased Premises, or which shall result in the cancellation (or threatened cancellation) of any policy of insurance upon the Leased Premises.

Tenant agrees to indemnify and hold Owner (and Owner's officers, directors and employees) harmless against any and all claims, demands, damages, costs and expenses (including attorney's fees for the defense thereof) made against, suffered or incurred by Owner (or Owner's officers, directors or employees) arising from or out of the conduct or management of Tenant's (or any sublessee's) business in or on the Leased Premises or from any breach on the part of Tenant in any condition or covenant of this Lease, or from any act or negligence of Tenant, its agents, contractors, employees, customers, clients, invitees, assignees, sublessees and subtenants in or about the Leased Premises. In case of any action or proceeding brought against Owner (or Owner's officers, directors or employees) by reason of any such claim, Tenant, upon notice from Owner, covenants to defend any such action or proceeding by counsel acceptable to Owner.

Tenant has read and agrees to comply with the policies and procedures as detailed in the Facility Use Packet. Rentee also agrees to pay the Museum additional hourly rental rates if the event exceeds specified times. Rentee also agrees to pay additional rental fees in the amount of $100.00 extra dollars per hour in addition to the regular fees for events running after 11:30 p.m.

One-half of Tenant's Rental Fee of $ _____ is enclosed, said payment will hold Tenant's Event Date.
Tenant will remit the balance of $ _____ **on or before** the last week prior to the event.

Tenant's Security/Damage Deposit ($500 minimum) $_____ will be paid at the time of tenent's acceptance of rental agreement. **Said Security/Damage Deposit will be held and returned to Tenant unless damage occurs or our event goes beyond the pre-scheduled time.**

Tenant has enclosed Facility Use Worksheet.

_____   _____

Rentee's Name   Date

_____

Rentee's Address

                11/95 Facility Use Lease Agreement

Art Museum of Southeast Texas • 500 Main Street • P.O. Box 3703 • Beaumont, TX 77704 • (409) 832-3432 • Fax (409) 832-8508

GUIDELINES FOR CATERERS AND AGREEMENT FORM

The Art Museum of Southeast Texas is pleased that you will be catering an event in our facility. Below are required guidelines to insure you, your client, and the Museum's safety.

DUE TO THE FACT THAT THE MUSEUM LEASES THE CAFE' AND KITCHEN AREAS AS A PUBLIC RESTAURANT, THERE IS A REQUIRED FEE OF $100.00 TO BE PAID BY THE CLIENT FOR KITCHEN USAGE / CAFE' BREAKDOWN, THIS PAYMENT IS DUE IMMEDIATELY UPON CLIENT'S BOOKING THEIR DATE.

Access to the kitchen and café area will begin at 5:00 p.m. (weekdays) for both set-up and food preparation unless special arrangements have been made with the Museum and Public Affairs Manager.

All deliveries must come through the kitchen side door or loading dock.

All food items or rentals must be taken out of the Museum the same day that they are brought in. Any storage of these items overnight must be approved by the Museum and Public Affairs Manager.

It is Museum policy that you take **ALL** trash to the Museum dumpsite.

Due to our new Café in the Art Museum, there is no longer storage / refrigeration space available.

To be provided by the caterer: trash bags
dish towels
serving carts
ice chests
dishes, glassware, service ware, etc.
janitorial supplies (this includes brooms and mops)
and other supplies that you feel you may need

To be provided by the Art Museum (after 5:00 p.m. Mon. - Fri., after 9:00 on weekends):

stove
microwave
coffee / tea brewer, (caterer will need to provide their own pots and filters)
adequate amounts of paper towels
hand soap

417

CLEAN - UP IS THE RESPONSIBILITY OF THE CATERER

It is very important that the caterer clean anywhere that food was served during the function. This includes the foyer, tea room, kitchen and courtyard if food is served outside. These areas must be swept and mopped. Many times you may be finished before the client is ready to leave, in this case you will need to leave someone behind so that they can clean these areas after everyone has left. Failure to adhere to this policy will result in the client losing their $500.00 deposit.

ALL decorations must be approved by the Museum and Public Affairs Manager.
ALL deliveries must come through the side kitchen door.

Use of the Museum equipment, (other than previously listed), such as maintenance and janitorial equipment is strictly prohibited.

The Museum / Museum staff is not liable for any equipment, glassware, or personal items left after an event.

Museum space will be available for caterer for set-up at 5:00 p.m. or two hours prior to your event. **Under no circumstances will any set-up be allowed prior to this time.**

BARTENDING RULES AND REGULATIONS

- Client or caterer must provide their own bar supplies such as straws, napkins, garnish, water, (the bar does not have running water), pitchers, ice chests, bottle openers, corkscrews, mixers, etc.
- No tip jars are allowed.
- Bar set-up time is two hours prior to the event. Tear down can last for up to one hour after the event.
- After the event, you are to clean the bar area completely. These duties include;
  remove all ice from bar area
  remove all glassware and bar supplies from area
  wipe down bar and countertops
  sweep and mop bar area floor
  take all trash to Museum dumpsite
  any alcohol to be stored must be locked in the service hall

The Museum is not liable for any alcohol, mixers, or bar supplies that are left to be stored.

Museum staff, because of insurance regulations are not allowed to help move any equipment or other supplies that are not supplied by the Museum.

NON-COMPLIANCE WITH MUSEUM POLICIES WILL RESULT IN YOUR SERVICES BEING DISALLOWED FROM THE MUSEUM AND YOUR CUSTOMER LOSING THEIR DEPOSIT.

OLD CAPITOL MUSEUM
Mississippi Department of Archives and History
P.O. Box 571
Telephone 601-359-6920   **Jackson, MS 39205-0571**   **Facsimile 601-359-6981**

FACILITY USE CONTRACT

<u>Please review this contract carefully; sign and return it with the appropriate fee to the Facility Use Coordinator.</u>

By this agreement, User does contract with the Old Capitol Museum, hereafter referred to as the Museum, to use Museum facilities/services on the above date.

Name of Organization/User: _____

Name of Co-Sponsor, if applicable: _____

Authorized Contact Person: _____

     Address: _____ Business Telephone: _____ Facsimile: _____

     _____ Home Telephone: _____

Name of Event: _____

Date of Event: _____ Time Event is to Begin: _____ Time Event is to End: _____

Access to area needed for set-up/rehearsal: Date: _____ From (time): _____ To (time): _____

Cleanup to be completed by (time): _____

The User agrees to abide by the Operating Policies and Facility Use Conditions, which are attached hereto and made part of this contract, and to inform its members/guests of said Policies and Conditions. The User assumes responsibility for the behavior of its members and for the consequences of that behavior while on Museum premises.

The User agrees to designate one person to be in charge while at the Museum. The person in charge must be present while the event is being set up and must remain with the group until all its members and others connected to the event have left the Museum. This person should also be responsible for cleanup. If different from Authorized Contact Person completing this form, include name of:

Person Responsible for Cleanup: _____

     Address: _____ Business Telephone: _____ Facsimile: _____

     _____ Home Telephone: _____

The User assumes liability for loss or damage to Museum property that results from its use of the facility, and agrees to hold the Museum harmless for loss or damage to the persons or property of its members or guests while at the Museum. The User assumes responsibility and liability for illness resulting from the serving of food and drink at the Museum, and agrees to hold the Museum harmless.

The User agrees to pay the total use fee of $_____ upon the signing of this contract. Checks should be made payable to the Old Capitol Museum. If the event must be postponed, the payment will apply to the later date. If the event is canceled, written notification must be received by the Museum <u>at least 10 working days</u> prior to the scheduled date in order for the User to receive a refund of 80% of the total payment. If the event is canceled <u>less than 10 working days</u> prior to the scheduled date, the User forfeits all payment. Postponement and/or cancellation must be in writing and signed by the Authorized Contact Person for the User.

I certify that I have read, understand, and <u>accept the conditions</u> set forth in the Operating Policies and Facility Use Conditions, and that I agree to the stipulations listed above.

_____   _____
Authorized Contact Person for the User   Date

_____   _____
Authorized Representative for the Museum   Date

usecon1.doc 7-1-97

The area(s) and equipment checked below were requested in the Facility Use Application you submitted and resulted in the Total Use Fee indicated in this contract. Please review carefully, since additional equipment cannot be provided the date of your event.

☐ **House of Representatives Chamber**

Basic Use Fee	**$25.00**	**Special Use Fee**	$_____
Overtime	$_____	Overtime	$_____

Optional Equipment Available
☐ Floor lectern $5.00
☐ Table-top podium $5.00
☐ Public address system $10.00
☐ Table(s), 8' long; _____ (quantity) @$5 $_____
☐ Table(s), 6' long; _____ (quantity) @$5 $_____
☐ Chairs; _____ (quantity) @50¢ $_____
☐ Projection screen $10.00
☐ Piano (cannot be moved) N.C. (user responsible for tuning)
☐ Table (located outside Chamber) N.C.

Subtotal Use Fees $_____

☐ **Senate Chamber**

Basic Use Fee	**$25.00**	**Special Use Fee**	$_____
Overtime	$_____	Overtime	$_____

Optional Equipment Available
☐ Portable public address system $10.00
☐ Table(s), 8' long; _____ (quantity) @$5 $_____
☐ Table(s), 6' long; _____ (quantity) @$5 $_____
☐ Chairs; _____ (quantity) @50¢ $_____

Subtotal Use Fees $_____

☐ **High Court**

Basic Use Fee	**$25.00**	**Special Use Fee**	$_____
Overtime	$_____	Overtime	$_____

Optional Equipment Available
☐ Table(s), 8' long; _____ (quantity) @$5 $_____
☐ Table(s), 6' long; _____ (quantity) @$5 $_____
☐ Chairs; _____ (quantity) @50¢ $_____

Subtotal Use Fees $_____

☐ **Other** (as specified on attachment to this contract)   **Special Use Fee** $_____

Total Use Fee $_____

Additional equipment approved, if applicable:

Equipment _____

Supplier _____ Telephone _____

Delivery _____ Pickup _____
    (day)   (time)   (day)   (time)

Other proposed plans discussed with and approved by the Museum include the following, checked, if applicable:
☐ Any video taping or audio taping of approved events
☐ Any lights brought on site for video taping, filming, or photography of any kind
☐ Any decorations, banners, signage, etc., supplied by the user
☐ Any use of the building, such as rehearsals or set-up prior to the designated meeting time
☐ Any special parking needs
☐ Any additional security needs
☐ Special access to building, use of a back door entrance

For OCM Use Only
Amount of fees outstanding _____
Facility Use Contract mailed _____ Contract and fee received from User _____
Fee forwarded to MDAH Finance Office _____ Executed copy of contract mailed to User _____

usecon2.doc 7-1-97

WORK ORDER

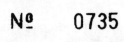

N⁰ 0735

Requested on_____   .

To Be Done By: (check one only)

( ) President   ( ) Maintenance   ( ) Exhibits   ( ) Security

( ) Business   ( ) Collections   ( ) Development   ( ) _____

( ) Gift Shop   ( ) Education   ( ) Public Relations   ( ) _____

TO BE DONE NO LATER THAN: _____
date / time

TO DO: _____

_____

_____

_____

_____

_____

_____

_____

Est. Cost. _____   Charged To _____

As Part Of _____   By _____

                project title   initiator

                                            initials   date

APPROVAL: Project Director   _____   _____

                         Director or Department Head   _____   _____

                         Operations V.P.   _____   _____

* * * * * * * * * * * * * * * * * **DEPARTMENT USE ONLY** * * * * * * * * * * * * * * * * *

Assigned to: _____   Date: _____

* *

AND Copies to:

( ) President   ( ) Maintenance   ( ) Exhibits   ( ) Security

( ) Business   ( ) Collections   ( ) Development   ( ) _____

( ) Gift Shop   ( ) Education   ( ) Public Relations   ( ) _____

Original (white):   to department assigned / returned to initiator   _____

1st Copy (yellow):   to department assigned file   **LOGGED IN**

2nd copy (pink):   retained by Operations Department   **421**   _____

Attachment #2

Walker Art Center
Technical Request Form

Date of Event_____
Start Time_____

EVENT_____

Artist and/or Technical Contact (For Groups Please Attach A List of Participants)_____

_____

Walker Staff in Charge_____Ext._____Dept. & Budget Code_____

Location(s) of Event_____

Date/Time of Rehearsal (if more than 1 day attach schedule)_____

Running Time of Event (For Film Events Please Attach List With Titles & Length_____

Requirements for Technical Staff (please check): ❑Set-up and strike only ❑Run Event

# of Technical Staff Required and Responsibilities_____

_____

GENERAL SET-UP REQUIREMENTS:

❑podium & mic: location_____   ❑piano Auditorium Only)

❑music stands(# needed)_____   ❑carpets (Auditorium Only)

Traveler: ❑open   ❑ closed (Auditorium Only)

*Request from John Lindell :   ❑chairs(# needed)____   ❑tables(# needed)____

SOUND REQUIREMENTS: (attach diagram/stage plot if applicable)

❑vocal mics (#needed)____   ❑instr. mics(#needed) ____   ❑direct box (#needed) ____

❑Cassette playback   ❑CD playback   ❑DAT deck   ❑reel to reel: ❑1/2   ❑1/4 trac

❑portable cassette deck: ❑boom box   ❑marantz recorder   ❑monitors (#needed____

other sound requests:

LIGHTING REQUIREMENTS:

❑ general stage lighting   ❑ specialized lighting

describe specialized lighting _____

_____

other lighting requirements:

AUDIO VISUAL REQUIREMENTS:

❑slide projectors (#needed)_____ controlled from: ❑booth ❑podium ❑stage

❑video: ❑1/2" ❑3/4" ❑beta sp ❑s-vhs ❑pal ❑video monitor (#needed)_____

❑16mm film ❑35mm film ❑8mm film ❑overhead projector ❑video projector

❑projection screen: size of screen:_____

other audio visual needs:

DOCUMENTATION REQUIREMENTS:

❑ audio recording Walker staff: ❑ cassette ❑ DAT

❑ audio recording by non-Walker staff _____arrival time for set-up

contact name and # for recording engineer_____

❑ video recording Walker staff : ❑ documentation ❑ to be edited

❑ video recording by non-Walker staff _____arrival time for set-up

contact name and # for videographer_____

other documentation needs:

HOSPITALITY REQUIREMENTS:

*Request from Tracy Reuter for Auditorium Events : ❑water ❑coffee ❑tea
Hospitality (please describe)_____
_____

*Request from John Lindell for Other Events (circle): ❑water ❑coffee ❑tea
Hospitality (please describe)_____
_____

RENTAL EQUIPMENT REQUIREMENTS: (list venders, delivery times, and contact #)

Restroom Log

____ / ____ / ____

List the date, time, initials, and tasks performed for each condition check of the restrooms.

Date/Time	Initials	Circle Tasks Completed								
		PT	DP	SF	M	SC	S	T	CT	UT
		PT	DP	SF	M	SC	S	T	CT	UT
		PT	DP	SF	M	SC	S	T	CT	UT
		PT	DP	SF	M	SC	S	T	CT	UT
		PT	DP	SF	M	SC	S	T	CT	UT
		PT	DP	SF	M	SC	S	T	CT	UT
		PT	DP	SF	M	SC	S	T	CT	UT
		PT	DP	SF	M	SC	S	T	CT	UT
		PT	DP	SF	M	SC	S	T	CT	UT
		PT	DP	SF	M	SC	S	T	CT	UT
		PT	DP	SF	M	SC	S	T	CT	UT
		PT	DP	SF	M	SC	S	T	CT	UT
		PT	DP	SF	M	SC	S	T	CT	UT
		PT	DP	SF	M	SC	S	T	CT	UT
		PT	DP	SF	M	SC	S	T	CT	UT
		PT	DP	SF	M	SC	S	T	CT	UT
		PT	DP	SF	M	SC	S	T	CT	UT
		PT	DP	SF	M	SC	S	T	CT	UT
		PT	DP	SF	M	SC	S	T	CT	UT
		PT	DP	SF	M	SC	S	T	CT	UT
		PT	DP	SF	M	SC	S	T	CT	UT
		PT	DP	SF	M	SC	S	T	CT	UT

Task Legend:

PT-Restocked Paper towels; **DP**-Emptied Diaper Pail; **SF**-Swept Floor; **M**- Mopped Floor; **SC**-Cleaned Sinks and Counters; **RS**-Refilled Soap; **T**-Emptied Trash Bin; **CT** Cleaned Toilets; **UT**-Unclogged Toilets

If this restroom needs attention, please inform the Admissions Staff. Thank You

VISITOR

Attendance
Survey

NATIONAL
MUSEUM
of
AMERICAN JEWISH HISTORY

ATTENDANCE STATISTICS
FACILITY RENTALS

MONTH _____   YEAR _____

DATE	ORGANIZED BY	NAME OF GROUP	# ATTENDING	TOTAL
TOTALS				

5 5   N O R T H   5 t h   S T R E E T
I N D E P E N D E N C E   M A L L   E A S T
P H I L A D E L P H I A ,   P A   1 9 1 0 6 • 2 1 9 7
(2 1 5) 9 2 3 • 3 8 1 1   F A X :   (2 1 5) 9 2 3 • 0 7 6 3

425

Admissions Entry Form
Please return to Cyndi by 1st Friday of the month, with info from prior month

Month _____ year _____

Day	Date	OUTREACH Name	OUTREACH Attendance	Group Name	GROUP TOUR ATTENDANCE JChild	NChild	POP	JSenr	NSenr	JAdult	NAdult	DAY'S TOTAL

NEVADA STATE MUSEUM

MONTHLY ATTENDANCE REPORT

Month of: _____

    Meter Reading Present Month: _____

    Meter Reading Previous Month   _____

    Total Attendance   _____

MONTHLY TOURS REPORT

GUIDED:

No. of School Groups	_____	No. Students Guided	_____
No. Non-School	_____	No. Persons Guided	_____
Total	_____	Total	_____

UNGUIDED:

No. School Groups	_____	No. Students Guided	_____
No. Non-School	_____	No. Persons Guided	_____
Total	_____	Total	_____

GRAND TOTAL ALL TOURS   _____   GRAND TOTAL PERSONS   _____

CAPITOL BUILDING TOURS

No. of Tours   _____   No. of Persons   _____

VISITOR SURVEY

Our museum with the support of the Lila Wallace - Reader's Digest Fund is undertaking a long-term study of museum audiences across the country. We would like to know more about our audiences to better serve our community and we appreciate your assistance in this survey. **YOUR ANSWERS ARE ANONYMOUS AND WILL BE KEPT COMPLETELY CONFIDENTIAL.** Thank you in advance for your cooperation.

1. **Is this your first visit to The Museum of Fine Arts, Houston?** ____ Yes ____ No
   (If you answered YES, please skip to question #5)

2. **If no, how many times do you usually visit each year?**
   ____ Less than once a year ____ 2 or 3 times ____ 4 or 5 times ____ More than 5 times

3. **Are you a museum member?** ____ Yes ____ No ____ In the past, but not now

4. **Have you ever visited this museum for any of the following activities?** (Check all that apply)
   ___ A special exhibition or program ___ A concert ___ A guided tour
   ___ A family program ___ A lecture ___ A studio class
   ___ The museum shop ___ A film ___ Restaurant or cafe
   Other (specify)_____

5. **What motivated you to visit the museum today?** (Please select three choices in rank order. A ranking of "1" indicates your first choice, "2" your second choice, and "3" your third choice.)

   ___ a. See a particular exhibition. Which one (specify) _____
   ___ b. Attend a particular program. Which one (specify) _____
   ___ c. Visit the entire museum
   ___ d. Visit the museum shop ___ i. Spend time with friends
   ___ e. Visit the cafe/restaurant ___ j. Spend time with family
   ___ f. Take advantage of a free admission day ___ k. Entertain out-of-town visitors
   ___ g. Enjoy a spiritual experience ___ l. Enjoyed a past visit
   ___ h. Conduct research/do a school assignment ___ m. Other (specify) _____

6. **As a child, did you ever visit a museum with:**
   your family? ___ Yes ___ No **If yes, how often?** ___ Frequently ___ Seldom ___ Rarely
   your school? ___ Yes ___ No **If yes, how often?** ___ Frequently ___ Seldom ___ Rarely

7. **What did you do while you were at the museum today?** (Check all that apply)

   ___ a. Saw a particular exhibition. Which one (specify) _____
   ___ b. Attended a particular program. Which one (specify) _____
   ___ c. Visited the entire museum
   ___ d. Visited the cafe or restaurant ___ f. Visited the museum shop
   ___ e. Conducted research/did a school assignment ___ g. Other (specify) _____

8. Which of the following interpretive aids did you use during your visit today? For each interpretive aid that you used, please indicate (by circling a number) how helpful you found these aids in increasing your understanding of the exhibition.

	Used	Didn't Use	Not helpful at all				Very helpful
Object label/interpretive text	___	___	1	2	3	4	5
Printed handouts	___	___	1	2	3	4	5
Tour guide	___	___	1	2	3	4	5

9. If you did not use any interpretive aids today, why not?
    ___ Didn't know they existed
    ___ Not comfortable using technology
    ___ Rental cost was too high
    ___ Audiotapes required a specific route
    ___ Other (specify)_____

10. Did you have contact with any of the following museum staff during your visit? If yes, how welcome did they make you feel? (Circle a number)

	Yes	No	Not welcome				Very welcome
Ticket seller	___	___	1	2	3	4	5
Security guards	___	___	1	2	3	4	5
Tour guide	___	___	1	2	3	4	5
Cafe/restaurant staff	___	___	1	2	3	4	5
Museum store staff	___	___	1	2	3	4	5
Other (specify) _____			1	2	3	4	5

11. What three words would you use to describe this museum to a friend?
    _____, _____, _____

Please answer the following questions by circling a number on the scale from 1 to 5, with "5" indicating the most positive response.

		Not at all				Very much
12.	To what extent did today's visit meet your expectations?	1	2	3	4	5
13.	How much did you enjoy this visit?	1	2	3	4	5

		Not at all likely				Highly likely
14.	How likely are you to come back for other visits within the next twelve months?	1	2	3	4	5

15. What would encourage you to come back to this museum? (For example, a family day, extended museum hours, etc.) _____

16. Did anything interfere with your ability to enjoy your visit today?   ___ Yes   ___ No
    If YES, please specify _____

17. During your visit, approximately how many visitors did you encounter from your racial or ethnic group? _____

18. Is there any kind of art that has a particular personal significance for you? ___ Yes ___ No
    If YES, what kind? _____

19. How do you feel about The Museum of Fine Arts, Houston? Please respond to each statement by circling the appropriate number on the scale.

	Strongly Disagree				Strongly Agree
I feel comfortable coming to the museum	1	2	3	4	5
I will recommend it to a friend	1	2	3	4	5
The museum has welcomed people from my community	1	2	3	4	5
The museum exhibits the type of art/objects that are interesting to me	1	2	3	4	5

Other (specify) _____

20. How did you get to the museum today?
    ___ Automobile ___ Tour bus ___ Public transit ___ Walked/biked/etc.

21. Is there a convenient way for you to get here using public transportation:
    On weekdays? ___ Yes ___ No   On weekends? ___ Yes ___ No
    In the evenings? ___ Yes ___ No   Don't Know ___ Yes ___ No

22. How did you hear about the museum?
    ___ Newspaper   ___ Bus advertisement
    ___ TV   ___ Billboard
    ___ Radio   ___ Flyer
    ___ Magazine   ___ Word-of-mouth
    ___ In the mail   ___ Other (specify) _____

23. What is your zip code? ___ ___ ___ ___ ___. In what town do you live? (optional) _____
    If you don't live in the USA, in what country do you live? _____

24. How long have you lived in the city/town mentioned in question #23?
    ___ Less than 5 years ___ 5-10 years ___ 10-20 years ___ More than 20 years

25. How far do you live from The Museum of Fine Arts, Houston? (For students, use your school address)
    ___ Less than 1 mile ___ 1-5 miles ___ 6-10 miles ___ 10-30 miles ___ More than 30 miles

26. Is anyone visiting the museum with you today? ___ No ___ Yes
    If you answered YES, please specify who is visiting the museum with you:
    ___ Spouse/partner/significant other   ___ Friend (s)
    ___ Relative (s)   ___ Child (ren) under age 18
    ___ Tour group   ___ Other (specify) _____

*Museum Management Consultants Inc./Polaris Research & Development
San Francisco, California*

27. Do you ever bring children under 18 years of age with you when you visit this museum?
___ Yes ___ No

28. Are you ___ Male? ___ Female?

29. How many people live in your household?
___ Total people ___ Children under age 18 ___ Adults age 65+

30. What is your age? ___ 18-24 ___ 25-34 ___ 35-44 ___ 45-54 ___ 55-64 ___ Over 65

31. What is your highest level of education?
___ Less than High School   ___ Some College
___ High School Graduate (or GED) ___ College Graduate (Bachelor's Degree)
___ Vocational School after High School ___ Post Graduate

32. What is your approximate annual household income?
___ Less than $15,000   ___ Between $50,000 and $74,999
___ Between $15,000 and $24,999   ___ Between $75,000 and $99,999
___ Between $25,000 and $34,999   ___ $100,000 or more
___ Between $35,000 and $49,999

33. What is your racial or ethnic identity? _____

34. What is your religious affiliation? _____

35. What is the primary language spoken in your home? _____

Thank you for your help.

For Office Use Only	
Self-administered by visitor	Date of administration ___ / ___ / ___
The Museum of Fine Arts, Houston	Time of administration _____

Museum Management Consultants Inc./Polaris Research & Development
San Francisco, California

B.C. MUSEUM OF MINING

NATIONAL HISTORIC SITE

B.C. MUSEUM OF MINING
1997 VISITOR QUESTIONNAIRE

1. **Are you a local (Greater Vancouver, Squamish, Whistler) resident? Yes____No____**
   If other than above, where are you from_____
   and where did you stay last night?_____

2. **Are you traveling with children? Yes____ No____**
   If yes, how many?_____ Ages of children?_____

3. **Is the B.C. Museum of Mining your only tourist destination today? Yes____No____**
   If no, name others_____

4. **Is this your first visit to the B.C. Museum of Mining? Yes____No____**
   Would you recommend it to a friend or relative? Yes____No____

5. **Do you regularly visit museums, galleries, etc. when traveling? Yes____No____**

6. **How did you hear about the Museum?**
   Drive By/Signs_____Friends/Family_____School_____Tour Agency/Guides_____
   Newspaper/Magazines_____Internet_____Brochures/Pamphlets_____
   Other (explain)_____

7. **When you entered the Museum site from Highway 99, were you traveling**
   North (toward Squamish)_____ or South (toward Vancouver)_____
   When you leave, will you travel North_____ or South_____?

8. **What did you like best about the Museum?_____**
   _____
   _____

9. **Are there any comments you would like to make that would help us to improve the**
   Museum?_____
   _____
   _____

Guest Name:_____ Guide Name:_____
Address:_____
_____
_____ Date:_____

British Columbia Historic Landmark
P.O. Box 188, Britannia Beach, B.C. V0N 1J0
Toll Free from Vancouver Area (604) 688-8735 • Britannia (604) 896-2233 • Fax (604) 896-2260
Governed by Britannia Beach Historical Society (1971)

432

H-E-B Science Treehouse of The Witte Museum
Science Comes Alive! Questionnaire

Name of Presentation: _____

Date: _____   Time: _____

Type of Presentation:
　　　( ) gallery theater play　　　( ) demonstration　　( ) storytelling

How did you find out about the presentation?
　　　( ) saw a sign or notice in the museum　　　　( ) from a handout
　　　( ) heard a spoken announcement　　　　　　 ( ) other
　　　( ) followed other people to the presentation
　　　( ) happened upon the presentation in progress

Could you see, hear, and understand the presenter?　( ) yes　( ) no
　　　If "no," why?

What do you think was the purpose of this presentation?
　　　To show...

What was your **favorite aspect** of the presentation?

Was there **anything you disliked** about the presentation?

What was your overall response to the presentation (circle the appropriate number)
　　　1　　　　　　2　　　　　　3　　　　　4　　　　　5
　　 (poor)　　　　　　　　　 (average)　　　　　 (excellent)

Your age: ( ) 0-24　　( ) 25-45　　( ) 46+
You consider yourself:　　　( ) Asian American　　( ) African American　( ) Caucasian
　　　　　　　　　　　　　( ) Latino/a　　　　　( ) Native American　( ) Other

THANK YOU FOR YOUR TIME! PLEASE RETURN TO A MUSEUM STAFF MEMBER OR
THE FRONT DESK.
Your answers help us plan better programs for our guests!

NationsBank Gallery Theater at The Witte

Visitor Questionnaire   Date_____   Time_____

Name of Play_____

Did you plan to watch the performance when you came into the exhibit today?
( ) yes   ( ) no

How did you find out about the performance?
( )   **read about it in the newspaper**
( )   **saw a sign or notice in the museum**
( )   **heard a spoken announcement**
( )   **followed other people to the performance**
( )   **happened upon the performance in progress**

Did you watch all of today's performance?   ( ) yes   ( ) no
If "no," why?

Could you see, hear and understand the performer?   ( ) **yes**   ( ) **no**

Were you comfortable while watching the performance?   ( ) **yes**   ( ) **no**

Was there anything that kept you from paying attention to the performance?

What was your **favorite aspect** of the performance?

Was there **anything you disliked** about the performance?

Did you learn anything about the exhibit from the performance?
( ) **yes**   ( ) **no**

What was your **overall response** to the performance? (circle appropriate number)

1   2   3   4   5
(poor)   (average)   (excellent)

I am: ( ) female   ( ) male
( ) 0-24   ( ) 25-45   ( ) 46+

My **zip code** is_____

I consider myself: ( ) **Asian**   ( ) **Black**   ( ) **Caucasian**
( ) **Latino**   ( ) **Native American**   ( ) **Other**

THANK YOU FOR YOUR TIME!
Your answers help us plan future performances.
PLEASE RETURN TO THE FRONT DESK

434

VOLUNTEER

Applications
General

She Is Looking For Volunteers

For The Huntington Museum of Art

Yes,

I am interested in becoming a volunteer at the Huntington Museum of Art!

Name: _____

Address: _____

City/State: _____

Zip: _____

Telephone: (_____)_____

I would like to volunteer my services in the following area(s): (You may select more than one.)

- ☐ Administrative
- ☐ Development
- ☐ Curatorial
- ☐ Education
- ☐ Library
- ☐ Conservatory
- ☐ Museum Store
- ☐ Hospitality

I would prefer assignments on the following day(s): (You may select more than one.)

- ☐ Monday
- ☐ Tuesday
- ☐ Wednesday
- ☐ Thursday
- ☐ Friday
- ☐ Saturday
- ☐ Sunday

I would prefer assignments during the following time period(s): (You may select more than one.)

- ☐ 9 a.m. - 11 a.m.
- ☐ 11 a.m. - 1 p.m.
- ☐ Other (specify): _____
- ☐ 1 p.m. - 3 p.m.
- ☐ 3 p.m. - 5 p.m.

Comments: _____

_____

_____

Please detach and leave at Reception Desk or stamp and drop into U.S. Mail.

Houston Museum of Natural Science
VOLUNTEER APPLICATION

Date: _____

PERSONAL:

Last Name: _____

First Name: _____ Initial: _____

Address: _____

City: _____ State: _____ Zip: _____

Home Phone: _____ Business Phone: _____

OFFICE USE ONLY: Type: _____

DEMOGRAPHICS:

Personal ID Number (choose a number between 4 and 10 digits in length): _____

Contact in Emergency: _____

Phone: _____ Relationship _____

Do you have any medical condition that you feel we should know about? ❏ Yes ❏ No

If yes, please explain: _____

_____

Date of Birth: Month _____ Day _____ Year _____

Foreign Language (specify only if fluent) _____

EMPLOYMENT BACKGROUND:

❏ Current ❏ Former Job Title_____

Employer _____

EDUCATIONAL BACKGROUND:

❏ High School   ❏ College   ❏ Graduate School

Other _____ Degree(s) _____

Area of Study _____

MUSEUM MEMBER: ❏ Yes ❏ No Membership Number _____

How did you find out about volunteer work at the Museum? _____

VOLUNTEER EXPERIENCE: _____

_____

_____

AVAILABILITY: At what times can you commit to volunteering?

WEEKDAYS: ❏ Morning ❏ Afternoon ❏ Evening ❏ Am Flexible

WEEKENDS: ❏ Morning ❏ Afternoon ❏ Evening ❏ Am Flexible

INTERESTS:

❏ Anthropology ❏ Archeology ❏ Astronomy ❏ Butterflies

❏ Chemistry ❏ Education ❏ Environment ❏ Gift Shop

❏ Geology ❏ Live Animals ❏ Museum Theatre ❏ Outreach

❏ Paleontology ❏ Plants ❏ Public Relations ❏ Teen Program

❏ Zoology

❏ Other _____

SKILLS:

❏ Art ❏ Computer ❏ Graphics ❏ Mechanical

❏ Photography ❏ Public Speaking ❏ Research ❏ Secretarial

❏ Sign Language ❏ Teaching ❏ Typing ❏ Writing

❏ Other _____

How would you describe your ideal volunteer position? _____

_____

Which of your skills do you feel will contribute most to the Museum? _____

_____

VOLUNTEER OPPORTUNITIES: Please indicate any that are of interest.

DOCENTS work directly with the public as an interpreter or guide to the Museum's many exhibits. Weekday and weekend placements available. Docents may assist with:

❏ School Tours ❏ George Observatory ❏ Butterfly Center ❏ Outreach

❏ Exhibits _____

VISITOR SERVICES VOLUNTEERS assist Museum visitors in many capacities, including:

❏ Information Desk ❏ Ticket Takers ❏ School Greeters ❏ Security

STAFF VOLUTEERS work where helping hands are needed in the Museum's offices. Can you help with:

❏ Answering phones ❏ Raise butterflies ❏ Prepare mailings

❏ Other _____

FUNDRAISING VOLUNTEERS organize the ❏ Museum's annual Gala.

SPECIAL EVENTS VOLUNTEERS are short term placements, generally helping the Museum for special events such as the:

❏ Annual Dinosaur Dash ❏ Members' Christmas Party.

VOLUNTEER AGREEMENT:

As a member of the professional unpaid staff at the museum, I agree to:

- Commit to one year service at the Museum, a minimum of 2 hours per month (or equivalent)
- Attend a 3 hour Museum Orientation within my first three months of service, to become familiar with the Museum's goal and mission and layout
- Become familiar with and abide by the policies and procedures as outlined in the Volunteer Handbook or explained by staff
- Represent the Museum at all times in an appropriate and responsible manner
- Be prompt and reliable in reporting for assignment, tours, meetings, and training sessions
- If unable to report, check substitute list and find a replacement
- Keep reliable record of hours
- Inform the Volunteer Office in writing at least 3 weeks in advance of resignation or leave of absense
- Understand that irregular attendance, poor performance, or failure to cooperate with HMNS policies may be interpreted as a volunteer's desire to resign

Volunteer Signature: _____ Date:_____

SO WHAT'S NEXT?

After your application has been received, the Volunteer Office will contact you to arrange for an initial interview. During this brief visit, lasting for about 30 to 60 minutes, we will help you select a volunteer placement that is appropriate, based on your time commitment, interests, and talents. If you have any questions, please contact the Volunteer Office at 639-4643. Thank you for your interest in volunteering!

STAFF USE ONLY:

Date of interview: _____

Placement Counselor: _____

Available schedule: _____

Comments: _____

_____

_____

_____

Applicant's job choices:

1. _____ Dept._____ Job _____
2. _____ Dept._____ Job _____
3. _____ Dept._____ Job _____
4. _____ Dept._____ Job _____

Volunteer Application

ANNISTON MUSEUM OF NATURAL HISTORY

Date: _____

Name: _____
First   Middle   Last

Address: _____

_____

Home Phone: _____ Business Phone: _____

Age: Under 21 ☐   21-59 ☐   60+ ☐

Special Interests/Obligations (Including hobbies, current employment, volunteer activities or other)

_____

_____

Would you prefer to work with the public? Yes _____ No _____

Check the volunteer position (s) in which you are interested: (See reverse for descriptions of positions listed)

_____ Live Animal Care   _____ Membership Assistant
_____ Collections   _____ Museum Store Assistant
_____ Docent (Tour Guide)   _____ Special Events Assistant
_____ NatureSpace Facilitator _____ Other (Please specify) _____

Please check the days you are available to volunteer:

	Mon	Tues	Wed	Thurs	Fri	Sat	Sun
Morning							
Afternoon							

Hours per week you could be available to work: _____

Please list any physical limitations that should be considered in volunteer assignments:

_____

Approximate length of time you can commit to volunteering at the Museum:
_____ 1-6 months   _____ 6-12 months   _____ 1 year +   _____ Indefinite

Personal references
    Name   Address   Phone
1. _____

2. _____

I agree to volunteer my services for the Anniston Museum of Natural History and understand that I am not an employee. I understand that I will receive training and supervision from the Museum and must abide by standards and policies of the Anniston Museum of Natural History as described in the Volunteer Manual.

Signed _____ Date _____
                Volunteer

In case of emergency, notify _____
           Phone _____ Relationship _____

WHAT VOLUNTEERING CAN DO FOR YOU:

Thank you for your interest in becoming a Volunteer with the Anniston Museum of Natural History. As you contribute your time and skills, we hope you will also recognize the many benefits available to you. Through volunteering, you can:

-- Gain valuable work experience
-- Make use of your talents and skills
-- Achieve new skills
-- Secure job references
-- Explore career possibilities
-- Improve communication skills
-- Stimulate new friendships
-- Receive personal satisfaction
-- Expand your horizons!

(Spring 1985 Voluntary Action Leadership, reprinted from VIC newsletter)

Several volunteer opportunities are listed below. Please select the areas in which you are most interested.

Live Animal Care - Working in the Museum's Live Animal Building in basic animal care. Unique opportunity to work with a variety of species in general maintenance, exercising, and helping staff in public programs involving live animals.

Collections - Working in the Museum's Collection Management Area with the Museum Registrar. Duties include cataloging, research, geology, biology, Museum scrapbook, etc.

Docent (Tour Guide) - Derived from Latin "docere" (meaning "to teach"), these volunteers are Museum teachers who guide student and/or adult groups through the Museum exhibits.

NatureSpace Facilitator - Working in the new hands-on discovery room *NatureSpace: Beyond My Backyard* with diverse groups of various ages. Involves instructing visitors on how to use the hands-on exhibits and basic security in this hall.

Membership Assistant - Assist Membership Coordinator with clerical work. Includes cross-referencing lists, filing, addressing and stuffing envelopes, working with member files, etc.

Museum Store Assistant - Assist Store personnel with display and merchandising, inventory control, product research, and assist customers with purchase decisions.

Other - Many other opportunities for volunteers arise throughout the year. For example:

Office Assistant	Class Instructor
Public Speaking	Brochure Distribution
Cooking for special events	Decorating for special events
Assisting staff at special events	Carpentry
Photography	Grounds Maintenance
Gardening	Nature Trail Work

Please choose from as many categories as you like and return the information to me as soon as possible. I look forward to hearing from you!

Thank you,
Daphne Rogers
Community Services Coordinator

Oregon Historical Society
Application for Volunteer Work

Date of Interview _____

Name _____

　　　　　　Last Name　　　　　　　　　　　　　　　　　First Name

Address _____

　　　　　　Street　　　　　　　City　　　　　　　State　　　　Zip Code

Telephone Number _____ Bus. Tel. _____

Business Address _____

Name of Partner _____

Whom to call in an emergency _____ Telephone _____

EDUCATION

High School _____

College _____ Degree _____

Other _____

VOLUNTEER EXPERIENCE

_____

_____

_____

_____

PROFESSIONAL EXPERIENCE

_____

_____

_____

441

INTERESTS, HOBBIES, SKILLS

_____

_____

Computer skills _____

Please check the skills you're interested in using as a volunteer:

__ Calligraphy	__ Cataloging	__ Clerical	__ Compiling
__ Computer	__ Conservation	__ Data Entry	__ Documentation
__ Editing	__ Filing	__ Gardening	__ Greeting
__ Identifying	__ Interpreting	__ Interviewing	__ Indexing
__ Labeling	__ Lifting/Moving	__ Mailing	__ Organizing
__ Presentation	__ Proofreading	__ Planning	__ Record Research
__ Restoring	__ Selling	__ Summary	__ Sewing
__ Sorting	__ Survey	__ Transcription	__ Translation
__ Typing	__ Word Processing	__ Writing	__ Welcoming
__ Other (describe)			

Please check your areas of interest:

__ Administration	__ Bookstore	__ Docent Program	__ Information Desks
__ Library	__ Newspaper Clipping	__ Maps	__ Photographs
__ Film	__ Oral History	__ Manuscripts	__ Museum
__ Exhibitions	__ Bybee/Howell House	__ Publications	__ Special Events
__ Other (describe)			

TIME BOX
Please let us know the best days and hours of the week for you to work.

	Mon.	Tue.	Wed.	Thurs.	Fri.	Sat.	Sun.
a.m.							
p.m.							

Number of hours per week you wish to volunteer _____

What interested you about volunteering for the Oregon Historical Society? _____

_____

_____

Source of referral _____

Signed _____

• •

Placement _____

BUFFALO MUSEUM of SCIENCE

1020 HumboldtParkway • Buffalo NY 14211-1293 • (716) 896-5200 • Fax (716) 897-6723

APPLICATION FOR VOLUNTEER SERVICE

Name _____

Address _____

_____

Telephone _____

Occupation _____

Employer _____

Address _____

_____

Telephone _____

Please indicate the shifts for which you are definitely available to volunteer (**V**) and also when you might be available to be called in as an emergency substitute (**S**).

	a.m.	p.m.
SUNDAY		
MONDAY		
TUESDAY		
WEDNESDAY		
THURSDAY		
FRIDAY		
SATURDAY		

I am also interested in volunteering for special events:

☐ Weekday evenings ☐ Weekend days ☐ Weekend evenings

Please print your name in the box below as you would like it to appear on your identification badge.

_____

• Please indicate educational background:

High School _____ Degree _____

College _____ Degree _____

Graduate Study _____ Degree _____

• Please list previous work experience (place, dates of service, position held): _____

_____

_____

• Are you a Member of the Museum? _____

443

• How did you learn about the volunteer opportunities at the Museum?_____

• Please note the type of volunteer position you are seeking (clerical, working with visitors, exhibit preparation, library, etc.):

_____

• Please describe any previous volunteer experience: _____

_____

_____

• We often receive unexpected requests for volunteer service throughout the Museum. To help us answer these needs, please list any skills, hobbies, special training, or interest that you may have. (Ex. CPR certification, photography, calligraphy, data entry, drawing, etc.):

_____

_____

• Are you proficient in a foreign language? _____If yes, please explain:_____

_____

• Do you have any experience or interest in working with special needs groups? _____If yes, please explain: _____

_____

• Please list any medical restrictions, requirements, allergies:

_____

_____

_____

• In case of an emergency, notify:

Name_____ Relationship_____

Address _____ Telephone _____

Work Address _____ Telephone _____

• Please indicate the names, addresses and telephone numbers of two people we may contact as references for you:

_____

_____

_____   _____   _____
APPLICANT'S SIGNATURE   DATE   INTERVIEWED BY

VOLUNTEER PROGRAM--PERSONAL PROFILE

Name:_____ Date:_____

Address:_____ City:_____ Zip:_____

Daytime Phone:_____ Best time to call:_____

How did you hear about the program and why do you wish to volunteer at the Homestead Museum?

_____

_____

What is your educational background? Include schools, dates, majors, and degrees.

_____

_____

What is your recent work experience? Provide company name, dates, and responsibilities.

_____

_____

What clubs, societies, and organizations are you involved in; what volunteer experience do you have? What are your skills, interests, or hobbies?

_____

_____

What other languages do you speak fluently?

_____

Are there any medical conditions that may affect working at the museum?

_____

What days and hours are you available?_____

Please return this profile to the Volunteer Coordinator at the address below.

15415 East Don Julian Road ♀ City of Industry, California 91745-1029 ♀ Telephone (818) 968-8492 Fax (818) 968-2048

5/97

GLENBOW

MUSEUM • ART GALLERY • LIBRARY • ARCHIVES

STAFF ASSESMENT SURVEY ON
VOLUNTEER INVOLVEMENT

As part of our organizational plan to utilize volunteer resources, we would like you to complete the following questionaire. This survey is designed to assess our readiness to use volunteers and to determine what we need to do to ensure continued delivery of high quality services to our visitors/clientele. All of the informantion collected will be kept confidential.

I. EXPERIENCE WITH VOLUNTEERS

1. Have you previosly worked in an organization which used volunteers?

Yes   No   Don't Know

2. Have you previously supervised any volunteers?

Yes   No   Don't Know

3. Do you do volunteer work yourself?

Yes   No   Once did, but not anymore.

II. ASSESMENT OF VOLUNTEER INVOLVEMENT

1. What is your overall assesment of the desirability of utilizing volunteers in our organization at this time?

Very desirable   Somewhat desirable   Would never be appropriate

Uncertian   Not desirable at this time

2. What is your overall assesment of our current readiness to utilize volunteers?

Very ready   Somewhat ready   Uncertian   Not ready

3. Are there any areas or types of work for which you think that volunteers are particulary needed and suited?

_____

4. Are there any areas or types of work which you think volunteers should not do in our organization?

_____

5. What issues or concerns would you like to see addressed before we utilize volunteers?

_____

6. What type of training as assistance would you like to receive before you are asked to work with volunteers?

_____

7. Are there any other comments, concerns, questions that you would like to express about the involvment of volunteers in our organization?

_____
_____
_____

Please return this Questionaire to Volunteer Resources by _____.

ref:surv.frm

VOLUNTEER CONTRACT

As a volunteer, you are an important member of the museum staff and act as a representative of the Museum to the community at large. For a better understanding of what you can expect as a volunteer and what is expected of you by the Museum, we ask you to read and sign the following Volunteer Contract.

The Museum will provide for you:

- Beneficial and life-enriching experiences.

- Comprehensive orientation and general training sessions plus any specialized training for specific jobs, such as docents and interpreters.

- Opportunities for professional development and social interaction with other volunteers.

- An opportunity to learn about History, Anthropology, Paleontology, and many other fields as well as a chance to learn how museums operate behind the scenes.

- To provide a specific job description detailing duties and responsibilities.

The Museum asks that you:

- Work an agreed number of hours on a scheduled basis that is acceptable to both you and the Museum.

- Choose an assignment within your abilities, interests, and time.

- Attend a scheduled orientation, training classes, and tour of the Museum.

- Notify the Museum beforehand if you will be absent or if you have arranged a substitute.

- Conduct yourself in an appropriate and ethical manner at all times when dealing with visitors, staff, and collections.

- Have fun and agree to ask questions if needed. Remember we are here for you!

_____

By my signature I declare that I have read, understand, and agree with all parts of the Volunteer Contract and will strive to fulfill all parts therein.

_____   _____
Volunteer Signature   Date

YOUTH VOLUNTEER PARENTAL APPROVAL FORM

YOUR SON/DAUGHTER IS EXPECTED TO:

- Attend orientation and training sessions as scheduled and undertake continuing education when provided to maintain and enhance competence in assigned tasks.

- Consider volunteer work as a serious commitment and view the position as valid and important.

- Represent Glenbow, at all times, in an appropriate and responsible manner.

- Be aware of and abide by the policies and procedures of Glenbow.

- Follow the volunteer position description and accept supervision.

- Act as a member of the Glenbow team when working with other volunteers and staff.

- Be prompt and reliable for work and follow through on any commitments.

- Provide reasonable notice to the appropriate supervising staff member if unable to fulfil responsibilities due to exams, vacation, or change in personal schedule.

- Accurately record volunteer hours served.

- Wear the volunteer name tag and security pass when volunteering at Glenbow.

- Provide supervising staff member and the Manager of Volunteer Resources with adequate notice before terminating position.

- Dress in an appropriate manner for the position assigned.

I PERMIT MY SON/DAUGHTER _____ *TO VOLUNTEER IN*

THE _____ *PROGRAM AT GLENBOW.*

I UNDERSTAND THE RESPONSIBILITIES AND COMMITMENT REQUIRED.

_____

Signature of Parent/Guardian   **Date**

Please sign and return this page to:

Glenbow Museum Volunteer Resources
130 - 9 Avenue SE
Calgary, AB T2G 0P3
(Fax: 262-4045)

APPENDIX

APPENDIX

This is an alphabetical listing of the institutions whose forms are reproduced in this volume. Page numbers follow each entry to designate where the institutions's forms may be found. Because a museum can be known by various names, try alternate listings if you do not find the entry under the name printed on the form.

American Association of Museums
1575 Eye Street Northwest, Suite 400
Washington, DC   20005

392,393,394,395,396

American Quarter Horse
Heritage Center & Museum
2601 I-40 East
Amarillo, Texas   79104

221

Amon Carter Museum
3501 Camp Bowie Blvd.
Fort Worth, Texas   76133

292,293,294,295,301,306,307,308,309

Anniston Museum of Natural History
Box 1578
Anniston, AL   36202-1578

4,34,34,171,172,195,262,390,391,439,440

Arizona State Museum
Box 210026
Tucson, AZ   85721-0026

102,181,317

Arkansas State University Museum
Box 490
Jonesboro, AR   72467-0490

10

Art Care, Inc.
17 Windy Meadow Lane
Canyon, Texas   79015

114,115,116,117

Art Museum of Southeast Texas
500 Main Street
Beaumont, Texas   77704

3, 181,4116,417,418

Auckland War Memorial Museum
Private Bag 92018
Auckland, New Zealand

348,362,369, 415

Beaumont Heritage Society
2985 French Road
Beaumont, Texas   77706   214

Biggar Museum & Gallery
Box 1598
Biggar, Saskatchewan S4P 2N4
Canada   138,139

Bishop Museum
1525 Bernice Street
Honolulu, HI   96817   50,51,52,53,54,376

Black Creek Pioneer Village
1000 Murray Ross Parkway
Toronto, Ontario   M3J2P3
Canada   208,209,414

Bombay Natural History Society
Hornbill House Shaheed Bhagat Singh Road
Bombay, Mambau   400 023
India   141

Boot Hill Museum
Front Street
Dodge City, KS   67801   79,80

British Columbia Museum of Mining
Box 188
Britannia Beach, British Columbia VON IJO
Canada   432

Brooklyn Museum of Art
200 Eastern Parkway
Brooklyn, NY   11238   296,297,314,315,316

Buffalo Bill Historical Center
720 Sheridan Avenue
Cody, WY   82414   19,72,113,175,176,177,204,254

Buffalo Museum of Science
1020 Humboldt Parkway
Buffalo, NY   14211-1293   55,56,191,192,217, 257,312,286,443,444

Canadian Museum of Nature
Box 3443 Station D
Ottawa, Ontario KIP 6P4
Canada   81

Caroline Davies Posynick
933 Colusa Avenue
Berkeley, CA   94707   12, 13

Children's Museum
300 Congress Street
Boston, MA   02210   23, 25,60

Children's Museum of Houston
1500 Binz
Houston, Texas   77004   222,264,424

Chrysler Museum of Art
245 West Olney Road
Norfolk, VA   23510-1578   290

Cooper-Hewitt, National Design Museum
2 E 91st Street
New York, NY   10128   91,372

Dallas Museum of Art
1717 North Harwood
Dallas, Texas   75201   246,305

Denver Museum of Natural History
2001 Colorado Blvd.
Denver, CO   80205-5798   141

Durban Natural Science Museum
Box 4085
Durban   4000 , South Africa   367

**Eiteljorg Museum of American Indians
& Western Art**
500 West Washington Street
Indianapolis, IN   46204   368

Frick Collection
1 East 70th Street
New York, NY   10021   353

Fort Worth Museum of Science & History
1501 Montgomery Street
Fort Worth, Texas   76107   410

Georgia Museum of Art
University of Georgia, 90 Carlton Street
Athens, GA   30602-1719   118,344

Glenbow Museum
130 9th Avenue SE
Calgary, Alberta T2GOP3
Canada   29,58,185,215,300,380,446,448

Government Museum and Art Gallery
Sector 10 -C
Chandigarh 160 011, India   145

Hagley Museum & Library
Box 3630
Wilmington, DE   19807   338,339

Health Museum of Cleveland
8911 Euclid Avenue
Cleveland, OH   44106-2039   31

Heard Museum
22 E. Monte Vista Road
Phoenix, AZ   85004   268,284

Historical Museum at Fort Missoula
Building 322, Fort Missoula
Missoula, MT   59803   330

Historic Deerfield, Inc.
PO Box 321
Deerfield, MA   01342   126,127,180

History Trust of South Australia
59 King William Street
Adelaide, South Australia   5001   150,151,152,153

Homestead Museum
15415 E. Don Julian Road
City of Industry, CA   91745-1029   63,88,89,213,218,282,283,319,411,412,445

Honolulu Academy of Arts
900 S. Beretania Street
Honolulu, HI   96814   112

Houston Museum of Natural Science
1 Hermann Circle Drive
Houston, Texas   77030-1799   436,437,438

Idaho State Historical Museum
610 N. Julia Davis Drive
Boise , ID   83702   97,98

Jack S. Blanton Museum of Art
23rd & San Jacinto, University of Texas
Austin, Texas   78712-1205   435

Kalamazoo Valley Museum
Box 4070
Kalamazoo, MI   49003-4070   87,364

Kansas City Museum
3218 Gladstone
Kansas City, MO   64111   36,37,38,39,40,41,59,261

Lafayette Natural History Museum
637 Girard Park Drive
Lafayette. LA   70503   20,387

Louisiana State Museum
Box 2448
New Orleans, LA   70176-2448   180

Lyman House Memorial Museum
276 Haili Street
Hilo, HI   96720   16

McAllen International Museum
1009 Nolana
McAllen, Texas   147,148

McNay Art Museum
6000 N. New Braunfels Ave
San Antonio, Texas   78209   183

Mint Museum of Art
2730 Randolph Road
Charlotte, NC   28207-2031   11,146,291,346,347

Mississippi Museum of Natural Science
111 North Jefferson Street
Jackson, MS   39201   76,77

Missouri State Museum
RM B-2 Capitol
Jefferson City, MO   65101   173

Morton Arboretum
4100 Illinois Route 53
Lisle, IL   60532-1293   166,167,168,169,256

Museum & Art Gallery of the Northern Territory
GPO Box 4646
Darwin, NT 820
Australia   101,122,251,252,349,397,398,399,400,401,
                                               402

Museum of Art, Brigham Young University
North Campus Drive
Provo, UT   84602   94,95,174,233,234,235,236,237,238,303,
                                               304,343,389

Museum of Fine Arts, Houston
PO Box 6826
Houston, Texas   77265-6826   42,43,44,45,46,47,48,49,70,71,189,197,198,
                                               205,210,211,212,219,248,258,285,298,302,
                                               413,428,429,430,431

Museum of New Mexico
Box 2087
Santa Fe, NM   87504   135,136,155,156

Museum of Texas Tech University
PO Box 43191
Lubbock, Texas   79409-3191   28,99,100,131,320,354,384,385,447

Museum of the Big Bend
Box C-210
Alpine, Texas   79832   32,278,287

Museum of the Confederacy
1201 East Clay Street
Richmond, VA   23219   220

Museum of International Folk Art
PO Box 2087
Santa Fe, NM   87504   193,194

Museum of the Rockies
Montana State University Bozeman
Bozeman, MT   59717-0272   310, 311

Museum of Western Colorado
Box 20000-5020
Grand Junction, CO   81502-5020   133,134,160,161,162,163,164,184,199,202,
                                  203,275,276,329

Museums Association of Saskatchewan
1808 Smith St.
Regina, Saskatchewan S4P 2N4
Canada   143,144,271,272,273,274,279,280

Nantucket Historical Association
Box 1016
Nantucket, MA 02554   286

National Museum of American Jewish History
55 N. 5th Street
Philadelphia, PA 19106   9,425,426

North Carolina Museum of History
5 East Edenton St.
Raleigh, NC   27601-1011   30,247

Nehru Science Center
Dr. E. Moses Road
Worli, Mumbai 400018
India   225,253

Nelson-Atkins Museum of Art
4525 Oak Street
Kansas City, MO   64111-1873   119,120,132,178,179,190,328,375,403,404,
                               407,408

Nevada State Museum
600 N. Carson Street
Carson City, NV 89701 · · · · · · · · · · · · · · 231,243,244,245,427

New Hampshire Historical Society
30 Park Street
Concord, NH 03301 · · · · · · · · · · · · · · · 250

Oklahoma Historical Society
2100 North Lincoln Blvd.
Oklahoma City, OK 79832 · · · · · · · · · · · · 227,267

Old Capitol Museum of Mississippi History
Box 571
Jackson, MS 39205-0571 · · · · · · · · · · · · 419,420

Old Court House Museum
Aliwal Street
Durban 4001 South Africa · · · · · · · · · · · 379

Oregon Historical Society
1200 SW Park Avenue
Portland, OR 97205 · · · · · · 64,65,66,241,242,249,337,371,441,442

Panhandle-Plains Historical Museum
WTAMU Box 60967
Canyon, Texas 79016 · · · · · · · · · · · · · 82,83,84,85,92,149

Peabody Museum of Natural History
Box 208118
New Haven, CT 06520-8118 · · · · · · · · · · 157,158,159,327

Penobscot Marine Museum
Box 498
Seaport, ME 04974 · · · · · · · · · · · · · · 125,263

Public Museum of Grand Rapids
272 Pearl Street NW
Grand Rapids, MI 49504 · · · · · · 2,96,129,182,269,270,277

Richard Nixon Library & Birthplace
18001 Yorba Linda Blvd.
Yorba Linda, CA 92886 · · · · · · · · · · · · 128

Royal Ontario Museum
100 Queen's Park
Toronto, Ontario M5S 2C6
Canada   123,370

San Antonio Museum of Art
200 West Jones Avenue
San Antonio, Texas   78215   57

San Diego Museum of Art
Box 2107
San Diego, CA   92112-2107   345

San Diego Natural History Museum
Box 1390
San Diego, CA   92116   321,322,335,336

Schenectady Museum Association, Inc.
Nott Terrace Heights
Schenectady, NY   12308   373,374

Science Centre & Manawatu Museum
Private Bag 11055
Palmerston North, New Zealand   109,226,228,229,230

Sheldon Memorial Art Gallery & Sculpture Garden
University Nebraska, 12th & R Street
Lincoln, NE   68588-0300   232

Sixth Floor Museum
411 Elm Street, Suite 120
Dallas, Texas   75202   1,78,281

Sonoma County Museum
425 7th Street
Santa Rosa, CA   95401   352

South Dakota State Historical Society
900 Governors Drive
Pierre, SD   57501-2217   14,21,74,90,206,207,216,255

Southern Illinois University Museum
Mailcode 4508
Carbondale, IL   62901-4508   110,111

Spencer Museum of Art
University of Kansas
Lawrence, KS 66045

26,27,73,186,187,188,239,240,265,266,301,
405,406

Saint Louis Science Center
5050 Oakland Avenue
St. Louis, MO 63110

142,386,409

Strecker Museum of Art
Box 97154
Waco, Texas 76798-7154

17,18,325,326,365,366

**Tallahassee Museum of History and
Natural Science**
3945 Museum Drive
Tallahassee, FL 32310

200,201,223,224,331

United States Department of the Interior
Box 1456
Fort Davis, Texas 79734

86,93,124,165,323,324,357,358,359,360,
361,381,382,383

University of Alberta
Edmonton, Alberta T6G 2E2
Canada

332

University of Arkansas Museum
Museum Building 202
Fayetteville, AR 72701

22,334

University of Colorado Museum
Box 218
Boulder, CO 80309

170

**University of Denver, Museum of
Anthropology**
2130 S. Race Street
Denver, CO 80208

104,105,106,107,108,137,154,318,355,356

**University of Iowa Hospitals &
Clinics Medical Museum**
8014 RCP/200 Hawkins Drive
Iowa City, IA 52242

7,8,103,342,377,378

University of Nebraska State Museum
W436 NH
Lincoln, NE   68588-0514   130

Valentine Museum
10115 E. Clay Street
Richmond, VA   23219   363

Vesterheim Norwegian American Museum
502 West Water Street
Decorah, IA   52101   5,6

Virginia Museum of Natural History
1001 Douglas Avenue
Martinsville, VA   24112   15,121,140,350,351

Walker Art Center
Vineland Place
Minneapolis, MN   55403   24,67,68,69,289,299,422,423

Wellington County Museum & Archives
RR1
Fergus, Ontario N1H 6J2
Canada   288,333

Wichita Art Museum
619 Stackman Drive
Wichita, KS   67203   196,313

Witte Museum
3801 Broadway
San Antonio, Texas   78209   33,51,62,75,259,260,340,341,388,421,433,
                                             434